THE TRAVEL AGENT

DEALER IN DREAMS

Fourth Edition

DISCARD

ARYEAR GREGORY, **CTC**

Regents/Prentice Hall, Englewood Cliffs, N.J. 07632

Library of Congress Cataloging-in-Publication Data

Gregory, Aryear.
  The travel agent : dealer in dreams / Aryear Gregory. — 4th ed.
    p. cm.
  Includes index.
  ISBN 0-13-948340-3
  1. Travel agents.   I. Title.
  G154.G74 1993
  338.4′791023—dc20

92-24747
CIP

Editorial/production supervision and
    interior design: *Eileen M. O'Sullivan*
Cover design: *Ray Lundgren Graphics Ltd.*
Manufacturing buyer: *Ed O'Dougherty*
Prepress buyer: *Ilene Levy*
Acquisitions Editor: *Robin Baliszewski*
Editorial Assistant: *Rose Mary Florio*

© 1993, 1989, 1985, 1975, by REGENTS/PRENTICE HALL
A Division of Simon & Schuster
Englewood Cliffs, New Jersey 07632

Printed in the United States of America

10 9 8 7 6 5 4 3 2 1

ISBN   0-13-948340-3

PRENTICE-HALL INTERNATIONAL (UK) LIMITED, *London*
PRENTICE-HALL OF AUSTRALIA PTY. LIMITED, *Sydney*
PRENTICE-HALL CANADA INC., *Toronto*
PRENTICE-HALL HISPANOAMERICANA, S.A., *Mexico*
PRENTICE-HALL OF INDIA PRIVATE LIMITED, *New Delhi*
PRENTICE-HALL OF JAPAN, INC., *Tokyo*
SIMON & SCHUSTER ASIA PTE. LTD., *Singapore*
EDITORA PRENTICE-HALL DO BRASIL, LTDA., *Rio de Janeiro*

Contents

CHAPTER 3 **RULES/REGULATIONS GOVERNING TRAVEL AGENCIES** **25**

CHAPTER 7   **AIRLINE SALES AND RESERVATIONS**   **114**

CHAPTER 8   **AIRLINE TICKETING**   **134**

Preface

This book deals with the travel industry—specifically the Travel Agency—its creation, problems, techniques, and the promotion of travel. It is written for the reader who, at one time or another, may have thought of opening his own agency; for readers interested in employment in the travel industry; for travel secretaries; and for those already in the industry who would like to learn more about the travel agent.

The primary aims of this book are to provide training material for new employees and to furnish owners and managers a source of reference material. It is not intended to encourage inexperienced people to open new agencies. In fact, I intend to discourage new owners unless, or until, they have the necessary qualifications and finances.

This book also is written in the hope that it will explain to so many job applicants who "just know they would be a good travel agent because they love to travel" why the agent shudders and tells them he doesn't have any openings.

My introduction to the travel industry came in 1956 while I was employed by a national car-rental company which had just started business. Among my responsibilities was the authorization of the payment of commissions to travel agents and others and auditing and processing for payment the airline invoices for tickets issued on the Universal Air Travel Plan for the company's executives. I enjoyed a very hectic and exciting three years of opening car-rental stations all over the U.S.A. and Europe.

During that period, I observed all levels of management in planning and organization. It was a valuable experience to watch the effects of management decisions on the profitability of the company.

From there, I went into the travel agency business and since then have been involved with change-of-ownerships, opening branch offices and starting new agencies. My experiences with the car-rental company and the various travel agencies have convinced me that there is a definite need for improvement of professionalism within the industry and a need for educating not only the members of the travel industry—but also the general public—with the Travel Agent.

The travel industry is very young compared to other industries. It didn't really start to grow until after World War II. It has changed drastically in just the past fifteen years and there are many drastic changes in the making. The pessimists fear that the travel agent is doomed for extinction (they have been expressing these fears during the past 25 years), but I firmly believe that the travel agent's role will increase in importance as the traveling public will need more and more the unbiased, dependable, personalized services of a professional travel counselor when faced with decisions on the many new and varied possibilities in travel.

I feel fortunate that I started in a travel agency as a bookkeeper. The bookkeeper in any business works closely with owners and managers and not only learns more about the actual operations of a business but is in the position to audit and evaluate the salespeople in the business and thus learn the right and wrong ways to service a customer.

After being pressed into service as a travel consultant during the busy seasons, I discovered that I enjoyed selling travel more than recording it and eventually became a manager. I then went on to all the trials and tribulations of starting a new agency right from 'scratch' as an owner.

During all those years of establishing bookkeeping systems, opening branch offices and new agencies, I had accumulated a volume of notes on office procedures and training methods. I put all of those notes into a travel course which I taught in Cleveland, Ohio during 1968. I started the Travel Agents Training School in Parma, Ohio in 1972 (which is still in operation) and have been using this book for the class since the First Edition was published in 1975.

Many of the revisions in this new edition are a result of classroom experiences, questions and comments from the students and others in the travel industry.

The two prime requisites for a good travel agent are: 1—first-hand experience and, 2—knowing where to go for the factual information needed to service the customers' needs. The first-hand experience can be gained only by the individual, but I hope this book will be of some value in learning what a travel agent does and how he does it.

Aryear Gregory, CTC
(Certified Travel Counselor)

Acknowledgments

A very special acknowledgment to the seven travel industry publications for their accurate coverage of news items and the many surveys, interviews, editorials, and case histories of how other travel agents solve their problems—without which a large portion of this textbook could not have been written:

THE TRAVEL AGENT
THE TRAVEL TRADE
THE TRAVEL WEEKLY
TRAVELAGE MIDAMERICA
ASTA NEWS AND BULLETINS
BUSINESS TRAVEL NEWS
TOUR AND TRAVEL NEWS

I would also like to acknowledge with many thanks the following organizations who generously provided material and/or photographs for this book. In order to be fair to all, they are listed alphabetically:

Air Canada
American Airlines
American Hawaii Cruises
Argonne National Laboratory
California Parlor Car Tours
Carnival Cruises
Celebrity Cruises
Commodore Cruise Line
Cleveland Plain Dealer, Travel Advertising Department
Cunard Line
Greek National Tourist Board
Greyhound Corporation
The Hertz Corporation
International Air Transport Association (IATA)
International Airlines Travel Agent Network (IATAN)
International Association for Medical Assistance (IAMA)
Leading Hotels of the World
Mines Press Inc.
National Tour Association, Inc. (NTA)

Official Airline Guides
Princess Cruises
Princess Vacations International
Rail Europe
Renaissance Cruises
Royal Cruise Lines
Seabourn Cruise Line
Tauck Tours
United Airlines
Travel and Tourism Research Association
U.S. Tour Operators Association (USTOA)
Zeus Tours & Yacht Cruises

Although I have singled out the companies/associations which gave me direct support with this book project, I would like to commend *all* of this industry's sales offices and sales representatives—most notably the airlines and cruiselines. During the past 32 years that I have been a travel agent I cannot ever recall receiving a refusal on information or assistance when needed. As I explained to my editor, who was amazed at the cooperation I received, we are all selling travel. Each and every travel agent who is sincerely promoting travel will receive all the assistance needed from all facets of the industry.

Thank you all for your cooperation.

PHOTO CREDITS:

The publisher and the author gratefully acknowledge the following for the chapter opening photographs reproduced in this text:

Chapter 1   SAMOS—Port Vathy Waterfront. Page 1

Chapter 2   Reprinted by special permission from California Parlor Car Tours. All rights reserved. Page 12

Chapter 3   Middleton Place Gardens and Plantation Stableyards, Charleston. Courtesy of the South Carolina Department of Parks, Recreation & Tourism. Page 25.

Chapter 4   Lindos, Rhodes. Reprinted by permission from the Greek National Tourist Board. All rights reserved. Page 56.

Chapter 5   American Airlines—Ticketing Counters (Courtesy of American Airlines, Inc.) Page 70

Chapter 6   The Tropical Princess Country Club Pool. Contact: Cindy J. Weir, Princess Vacations International, 1031 Ives Dairy Road, Miami, Florida 33179. Page 92

Chapter 7   Reprinted by special permission from United Airlines Boeing 747-400. All rights reserved. Page 114

Chapter 8   American Airlines, Inc. 747-SP Luxury Liner. Courtesy of American Airlines, Inc. Page 134

Chapter 9   Tauck Tours, 11 Wilton Road, Westport, Ct. 06881 (203) 226-6911. Page 148

Chapter 10   Reprinted by special permission from California Parlor Car Tours. All rights reserved. Page 162

Chapter 11   Courtesy of the Netherlands Board of Tourism. Page 176

## chapter 1

What Is a Travel Agent?

OBJECTIVES

When you have finished this chapter you should be able to:

1. Define a *travel agent*.
2. Describe the services offered by a travel agent and who the travel agent represents.
3. List the statistics regarding agency locations.
4. Identify the average travel agent's customer (client).
5. Discuss the difference between service charges and commissions.
6. Determine the importance of cost studies.
7. Evaluate the relationships between carriers and travel agents.

INTRODUCTION

"Your Travel Agent Is . . . ," "See Your Travel Agent," "Consult Your Travel Agent—He's an Expert." Remarks such as these are found in most travel brochures and many ads placed by airlines and other carriers, hotels, and tour operators. However, the general public is still amazingly unaware of what a travel agent is, what he or she can do for them, and what is charged for these services.

This lack of knowledge of what a travel agent is extends throughout the travel industry itself and in today's business, social, and legal world: "Everyone thinks he knows what a travel agent is and what a travel agent does, but not many really know for sure." Joel M. Abels, editor and publisher of *Travel Trade*, in an editorial series, posed the question: "What is a travel agent?" A poll of travel agency industry leaders responded with definitions ranging from the simple to the complex. In essence, each described the travel agent as a person who is either qualified or authorized, or both, to sell travel.

Mr. Abel's concern, shared by most travel agents, is for a definition of the phrase *travel agent* that would be descriptively accurate and legally supportable in terms of any future legislation or regulation. His definition is as follows: "A travel agent is an individual who, based on recognized industry standards of expertise and experience, is deemed qualified by travel agent peers and by travel principals to offer and sell travel arrangements and services to the general public."

The ASTA (American Society of Travel Agents) gives this definition of a travel agent in their December 1990 *ASTA Travel Agent Manual*:

> An agent is a person who undertakes a job for another person, who is the "principal." The principal in such a relationship not only sets the goals of the job, such as selling tickets, but also may control the means and manner in which the job is done.
>
> The relationship between travel agents and all of their suppliers is usually that of "agency." This has many important implications. One of the most important is the rule of law that a person who discloses that he is acting as agent for an identified principal is not liable for the failure of the principal to perform.

At this time there are no formal industry standards of expertise and experience. However, this is a matter that is being discussed by all facets of the travel industry and, hopefully, will be settled in the near future.

NEW FEDERAL CODING

The federal government has officially given the travel industry its own separate classification codes, making analysis of industry data easier. The codes are used to analyze business receipts, employment, wages, tax receipts, and other data. Effective January 1, 1987, the Office of Management and Budget (OMB) began to distinguish between travel agencies and tour operators, which formerly were lumped together.

Other changes included a new code for car rental companies, to distinguish them from auto-leasing firms and separate categories for scheduled and nonscheduled air transportation. Cruise lines are now separated from freight transportation by water and a category was created for passenger travel on lakes and rivers.

The U.S. Travel and Tourism Administration (USTTA), the U.S. Travel Data Center, and other industry associations and firms had pushed for this and other changes to the coding system. The changes will increase recognition of the economic impact of the travel and tourism industry.

In 1964, the Better Business Bureau of Metropolitan New York, with the cooperation of ASTA (American Society of Travel Agents), published a pamphlet "The Travel Agent and You" which did an excellent job of describing the services offered by a travel agent; and a revised edition, "What Is a Travel Agent?" is still being distributed to the public by ASTA. The following paragraphs are quoted from the original booklet.

> Travel is more and more becoming a popular activity for the average budget-conscious American family. Each year millions of Americans travel in this country and abroad, spending billions of dollars. Many make their own travel arrangements, with varying degrees of success. But a good proportion find that the expert services of a travel agent can save them considerable time, money and legwork, while also avoiding disappointments and vexation while on their trip.
>
> The overwhelming majority of travel agents take pride in the services they render and deal with the public fairly and honestly. Their knowledge of the complexities of transportation, accommodations, sightseeing, and many related services can help to assure a trouble-free trip.
>
> A competent travel agent *is not merely a ticket seller* [italics added]. He is a specialist whose experience and know-how enable him to counsel you on how to travel wisely and within the confines of your budget. Here are some of the ways in which the travel agent serves his clients:
>
> 1. Arranges transportation—air, steamship, cruises, bus, rail, car rentals in the U.S. and abroad, and car purchases abroad.
> 2. Prepares individual itineraries, personally-escorted tours and group tours and sells prepared package tours.
> 3. Arranges for hotels, motels, resort accommodations, meals, sightseeing, transfers of passengers and luggage between terminals and hotels, and special features such as music festivals and theatre tickets.
> 4. Handles and advises on the many details involved in modern day travel and baggage insurance, language study material, travelers' checks, auto garaging, foreign currency exchange, documentary requirements (immunizations and other inoculations).
> 5. Uses professional know-how and experience, e.g., has schedules of air, train, and bus connections; rates of hotels and their quality; whether rooms have baths; and whether their rates include local taxes and gratuities. All of this is information on which the traveler can spend days or weeks of endless phone calls, letters, and visits to secure—and still may not get it right.
> 6. Arranges reservations for special-interest activities such as religious pilgrimages, conventions and business travel, gourmet tours, sporting trips, etc.*

Twenty-five years later this description still holds true, but agents now have the added responsibility of interpreting and advising clients of the many complex excursion, discounted, and charter fares now offered by the airlines; they are also required to warn clients of "overbooking" and their legal rights when that should occur. Airline and tour operator bankruptcies in recent years require more careful monitoring of the travel agents' suppliers and the obligation to advise clients of a supplier's shaky financial position, especially if it is a matter of public record.

*ASTA, "The Travel Agent and You," 1964. ASTA revised this booklet in June 1991. It is now entitled "ASTA Travel Agents—'Your Ticket to the World'" and can be ordered directly from ASTA.

Acts of terrorism around the world, political upheavals, and actual outbreaks of war have placed serious responsibilities on the travel agent to observe and advise their customers of "travel advisories" issued by their own governments or received through a subscription service that specializes in travel alerts around the world.

WHO THE TRAVEL AGENT REPRESENTS

In other words, a travel agency is a department store of travel. Even if the customer is only "dreaming" of taking a trip, the experienced travel agent can help make that dream a reality. He represents *all* airlines, *all* bus lines, *all* steamship lines, sightseeing companies, car rental companies (his suppliers), and *all* hotels, resorts, and tour operators (his wholesalers) all over the world. He is a packager and retailer of travel components. Although he is in the unique position of competing with his own suppliers and wholesalers in the travel market, it is only in the travel agency that *all* components of *all* travel products are available to the consumer. It is only in the travel agency that the consumer can receive answers to all of his travel questions and the special guidance and direction that he needs.

The term *agent* is used throughout the travel industry when referring to the travel agency itself or to the owner/manager of the agency. According to the dictionary: "agent—1. a person acting on behalf of another, called his principal. 2. Colloq.—a representative of a business firm, especially a salesman; a canvasser; solicitor." The travel agent is all of this and much more. He is the middleman between the customer and the principals, who will actually provide the services requested for the customer.

This fact must be clearly emphasized to the agent's clients. The travel agent is the "retailer"—not the "supplier." Unless the travel agent is also a "wholesaler" or "supplier," the average agency does not have an inventory of airline seats, hotel rooms, or other services to be sold to the public. The agent's responsibility ends when the client picks up her tickets and vouchers, provided, of course, that the reservations are confirmed and the tickets have been properly written. The responsibility for providing services to the client now falls on the carriers, tour operators, hotels, and so on. However, if the client returns and has a legitimate complaint that she did not receive the services expected, it becomes the agent's duty to contact the principal (preferably in writing) to try and get an explanation, refund, or at least a written statement or apology for the mishaps that may have occurred.

Most travelers are unaware that the travel agent acts for a third party. Except for a few agents who also are wholesalers, the agent does not actually arrange or operate the tours or "packages" which include the hotel, transfers, car rentals, and/or the sightseeing tours but simply sells and promotes them on behalf of the airlines and tour operators (wholesalers). However, according to recent court rulings, the agent can be held responsible for *selection* of the carrier or tour operator. As a "professional" the agent is expected to select the tours that are put together and operated by reliable wholesalers with a good reputation for providing all the services mentioned in the brochures. She can also be held responsible if she does not advise her clients (in writing) that she is acting as an agent for a third party.

Although most travelers know that the travel agent does not own the airline or hotel that overbooked and caused him the aggravation and expense that he experienced during his travels, the clients and courts know that it is easier to find the local agent than to try and get satisfaction from a foreign hotel or tour operator. Rulings in most cases against travel agents have agreed that agents should know what they are selling. The courts have concluded that the *seller* of travel services, not the buyer, is in the best position to know the nature and potential shortcomings of such services. Travel agent attorneys have recommended a simply written "disclaimer" stamped or printed on the face of the bill to the client advising the client that the agent is not responsible for any negligent act by a carrier, tour operator, or hotel but is responsible only for his own negligence. This is, of course, not foolproof. It will not prevent all lawsuits, nor will it prevent the agent from being held liable to his client, but it would tend to reduce the exposure to litigation and reduce the risk of loss on the part of the agent.

NUMBER OF TRAVEL AGENCIES

The Airlines Reporting Corporation (ARC) and the International Airlines Travel Agent Network (IATAN) are appointing new agencies in the United States and Canada at the rate of about 1000 per year, an increase of 2 to 3 percent each year. At the end of 1969, there were 7119 U.S. and Canadian agencies; today, this number has increased to over 38,000 [15 percent of these were satellite ticket printers (STPs), whose growth has been explosive during the past few years], and predictions are that this will increase to more than 58,000 by the end of the decade.

Contrary to the fears often expressed that the proliferation of new locations would dilute the market for existing agencies, the figures show exactly the opposite. Twenty-five years ago, the air volume per agency was an average of $127,000 per year; January 1991 sales reached $3.2 billion and that reflected a 9 percent decrease in domestic airline bookings and a 22 percent decrease in international airline bookings, due to the Persian Gulf War. Statistics also show that 82 percent of domestic travel and 85 percent of international air travel is booked through the travel agent.

The travel agency share of the market has grown steadily in business travel as well as in recreational travel. Travel agents' sales through the area settlement plan are predicted to be over $80 billion by the end of the decade. It has been my experience that new agencies will bring in new business—business from the traveling public and the business community that had never used a travel agency in the past.

Studies and surveys of the travel market sponsored by travel publications and the U.S. Travel Data Center in Washington, D.C. have established the growing importance of the retail travel agent in the increase of travel and tourism as an industry. Statistics are available from many sources; however, it is important that we not get bogged down by statistics and forget the basics of travel. People travel for change—to get away from the stress that they encounter on all sides, for relaxation, to see new sights, and to visit friends and relatives. Travel is no longer simply an annual vacation but a necessary part of life. Travel, in general, may suffer somewhat during a downturn in the economy, but it continues to have a high priority for affluent, middle-aged Americans. During a recession or periods of concern over global wars and terrorist activities abroad, many foreign pleasure trips are converted into domestic journeys rather than dropped altogether.

Considering that 84 percent of the traveling public still uses the family car for their vacations and only 5 percent of the public has taken a cruise, there is a vast market for potential travelers to be tapped by the sales-aggressive travel agent.

CUSTOMERS' PROFILE

Travelers today are more knowledgeable about travel than they were 25 years ago. This knowledge is not restricted to veteran travelers—first-timers are also well informed. Books, newspapers, movies, television, and videotapes bring faraway places into their homes and stimulate their desire to see the world for themselves. Many travelers walk into a travel office with definite ideas as to where they want to go and will even tell the agent in what hotel they wish to stay and on what flights they want to go. They go to the agent because they depend on the agent's "know-how" to assure them of the type of vacation experience they want. But they are open to suggestions and the agent can bring them up to date on changes or new services available and can recommend the service best suited to the client. No matter how sophisticated the traveler might be, he expects and prefers professional direction. However, travelers are looking at value, price, and security measures more closely than at any time in recent years. Service expectations are higher.

First-time travelers have more fears and worries; they are suspicious and mistrustful of airlines and hotels because of the unfortunate experiences of friends or relatives who were refused space due to overbookings. They need facts to overcome their fears: They need to be reassured that they will not be left stranded at the airport or the hotel lobby—that the airlines and hotels will provide alternative facilities. They worry about all sorts of imagined complications. The agent must have the patience and honesty to admit that these things do happen and then advise them how to cope with emergencies.

Figure 1-2 Athens: Southwest view of the Theseion (Hephaesteion), the most perfectly preserved classical temple in Greece. (Greek National Tourist Office photo.)

Although the cost of travel is often given as the reason why personal trips are put off, it is the first-timers' fears of the unknown that deters many of them from experiencing the pleasures of travel. It is the agent's responsibility to answer both spoken and unspoken questions as completely and thoroughly as possible. Procedures that experienced travelers take for granted can seem insurmountable to first-timers. Simple directions or maps of airports and instructions on how to check in when departing and how to claim baggage upon arrival can do wonders in allaying apprehensions and qualms about air travel. General information literature (obtained from tourist offices) will also ease clients' minds about what to expect when they arrive at their destinations. There is no denying that the main reason that anyone goes to a travel agent is for the convenience of having someone take care of all the details involved in travel, whether for business or pleasure.

THE "EXPERT" IN A CHANGING BUSINESS

The travel agent is called an "expert"—but in the words of a person who has been in the business for 30 years: "No one can be called an expert in such a rapidly changing and expanding business." Fifty-six years ago, the travel agent had it made. The competition was limited, the clientele were wealthy, and the commissions earned from high-priced steamship, rail, and tour arrangements also made many a travel agent wealthy.

True—this is a rapidly expanding business. True—a computer in the office will compute fares and routes and issue tickets more quickly and perhaps better than the agent could do it. But computers have not yet been programmed to give customers the *personalized service* they expect and receive from a professional travel agent. Automation only provides an agent with more efficient selling tools that will enable her to give even better service to clients.

As an expert, the agent cannot be expected to know every little detail about every corner of the globe. It is certainly not physically possible, or even necessary, for an agent to have been everywhere and seen everything before he can advise a customer, but as an expert who makes travel his business, he should *know where to go for the right answers*. An experienced travel agent can sell an area he has never visited simply because he can relate his experiences in similar areas and situations. Through these experiences and the study of reference books, brochures, promotional material, trade seminars, and current information picked up from others, he can do a good job of advising and selling his customers.

Most of the agent's work is done in connection with travel to be made one month, six months, or even a year from the date the agent first talks to her customer. Her real work begins after she hangs up the phone or the customer has left the office. Most travel agents are dedicated to their work. They feel that it is their personal responsibility to make their customer's trip run as smoothly and as enjoyable as possible. This is not as altruistic as it sounds; repeat business is the foundation of a successful travel agency. Satisfied customers will come back and will bring other business in. They provide free advertising by recommending your agency to their friends, business associates, customers, relatives, and so on.

However, there is no denying that most agents are in the travel business purely because they love it. The work can be exasperating, frustrating, irritating, and low paying (in comparison to other industries), but there is a great deal of personal gratification when a customer calls or comes in to tell the agent how much he enjoyed the trip that was arranged for him. The agent is a "dealer in dreams"; she sells experiences and memories that the customer will never forget.

THE QUESTION OF SERVICE CHARGES

When it comes to making the travel arrangements, a good agent knows where to look, how much it costs, and (very important) whether or not he will make a commission on it. The travel agent's payment for services rendered comes from commissions that he receives from carriers, hotels and resorts, tour operators, and other principals that he will contact on behalf of clients. (To paraphrase the airline definition that a "customer becomes a passenger when he buys a ticket," the travel agent's customer becomes his client when he requests more than straight transportation.) Customers have the convenience of getting their transportation, hotel or resort room, or tour reservations made for him at the same price that he would pay if he went directly to the airline, hotel, or tour operator. Only when more complicated services are required, such as independent itineraries, making reservations at international hotels or pensions that do not pay commission, or making last-minute phone calls or cables on the client's behalf, will the agent charge for his services.

This is one of the little-known facts that has kept part of the public from coming in to the travel agent's office. Ironically, this same "No charge for our services" policy has kept others away because they feel that there is something suspicious about professional people who don't charge for their services. They suspect that the prices are marked up to allow for the agent's commissions.

This "no service charge" policy may change in the future, as there is a growing trend in the travel agency business in favor of service charges, or at least, imposing cancellation fees. Many feel that the time has come for the agent to stop being so generous with her time and services. It is time for her to become more of a professional and more businesslike. When she sets a value on her services and insists on receiving it, she will gain the respect that she deserves from both the general public and her principals.

Many of the services that agents perform for their customers are done with the full knowledge that they will not earn a commission. Booking "convention" hotels or making reservations at a hotel where the businessperson receives a corporate discount is a good example of this. Exchanging or reissuing tickets at a lower fare can also take up a lot of nonproductive time. These services are performed strictly for building goodwill with customers in the hopes that a future sale will make up for the present loss. Many agents hesitate to charge for their services because they are afraid that the customer will object and will go on to someone else just as knowledgeable who does not charge for his services. This fear is unwarranted as long as the client *knows in advance* exactly what he is going to get for his money. I firmly believe that the public would take the service charge in their stride; they would feel more comfortable dealing with professionals who charge for their services.

Many agents are now using a *nonrefundable deposit* policy in lieu of a service charge, especially for vacation travelers. This policy would weed out "shoppers"— travelers who cannot make up their minds and will visit several agents and make duplicate, even triplicate, reservations until they can decide where they would like to go. This policy would also eliminate the nonproductive time spent with customers who have no intention of going anywhere but simply want to come in and talk about travel. Remember, an agent does not earn any money until a ticket has been issued or money has been received for a tour, cruise, hotel, or car rental.

With the proliferation of discounted fares offered by competing airlines, some fares dropping as low as $29 a ticket, the debate on service charges by travel agents has increased.

It has been estimated that it costs an agency $25 (average overhead plus salaries) to issue an airline ticket; therefore, many agents are introducing service fees to compensate for the reduced income. More and more agencies are also imposing penalty charges, such as cancellation fees, reissue charges, and change fees. Airlines keep 90 percent of their cancellation/change fees; hotels, cruise lines, and tour operators keep 100 percent of their fees. The agency loses their commissions with no compensation unless they notify clients that there will be an additional fee for cancellations and/or changes to be paid to the agency.

Agents must be realistic in their approach to service charges. A repeat customer who only occasionally books a low-priced ticket should not be charged a fee. Nor should the customer who also books hotels and car rentals with the ticket, but the walk-in customer who comes in only for a cheap air ticket should be advised of the charges (preferably in writing). A list of fees should be posted in the agency, and customers should be advised of the fees before the agent starts work.

However, charging a service fee may also change the liability status of the travel agency. By asking for a fee for services rendered the agent can be held responsible as an agent for the customer, as well as an agent for the supplier. An errors-and-omissions insurance policy wold protect the agency from any problems that may develop from charging a service fee.

COMMISSION STRUCTURE

Since deregulation in 1978, the airlines are free to set their own levels of commission; for competitive reasons, most domestic (U.S. and Canadian) airlines are paying 10 percent on all tickets issued in the agent's office. The international airlines vary between 8 and 9 percent for straight transportation and add an *override* of 3 percent additional commission on the ticket if it is issued in conjunction with an advertised tour package. Additional bonus commissions can be earned from the various airlines according to production levels. Also, as a result of deregulation, there is no official published list of commission scales. The agent must keep track of these from bulletins sent out by the individual airlines or call the airlines' sales offices for current rates. Charter airlines pay between 10 and 12 percent.

Most tour operators pay a standard rate of 10 percent. A few pay up to 15 percent for specific destinations. Many of the larger tour operators will set a quota of sales for agents and will increase the commission as the quotas are met. For example, sales from $1 to $4999 receive 10 percent, sales between $5000 and $6999 receive 12 percent, and so on.

Hotels and resorts in the United States and Canada pay 10 percent, a few pay 15 percent, and some do not pay any commission at all. International hotels vary from zero to 5, 7, 8, or 10 percent.

Car rental companies fluctuate also; although the majority pay 10 percent, new companies may pay 20 or 25 percent to encourage travel agents to send them business. Reservations made for businesspeople who are receiving corporate discounts will still earn 5 percent commission for the travel agent.

Amtrak (U.S. passenger trains) pays agents 10 percent and in recent years have added bonus plans based on productivity. Foreign railroads pay between 7 and 8 percent commission on rail tickets and 10 percent on Eurailpass orders.

Steamship lines pay 10 percent on cruises and 7 percent on transportation only (there is very little of that being sold now).

Bus lines pay 10 percent on tickets or tours. Sightseeing bus companies pay 10 percent.

Travelers' insurance companies pay 35 percent of the premiums collected.

Commissions can also be earned when ordering bon voyage gifts for clients. Ethnic agents can also earn commissions on orders sent from the United States to purchase goods for relatives in Europe.

In all areas of the industry, additional commissions are earned by booking groups (a group usually consists of 15 or more paid passengers). Not only is the commission increased, but free passage for the tour escort or manager is also given. Everyone welcomes groups and will also provide promotional material to help sell the group.

COST STUDIES

Several cost studies have been made to define the role of the travel agent and of the airlines in the marketing of air transportation and to recommend ways in which these roles might be improved. The first study conducted by the Systems Analysis Research Corporation (SARC), jointly financed by travel agents and airlines, was completed in 1967. The second was a cost study by a well-known accounting firm, Touche, Ross, Baily & Smart, and was completed in 1969.

Both studies revealed that travel agents were losing money every time they wrote an airline ticket at the 5 percent commission that was in effect at that time since it cost the agents 8.14 percent to write a ticket. The studies also revealed that 44 percent of all travel agencies ran their business at an overall loss.

Ten years later a follow-up economic study took place, again jointly financed by the travel agents and the airlines and again conducted by Touche, Ross. Despite the increase in commission levels to 7 percent after 1969, the study reported that 43 percent of the agencies were losing money. In matching the findings of its latest agency cost study with the 1968 survey, Touche, Ross & Co. found that all the retail industry figures are spiraling upward except one: profitability. Industry costs on a point-to-point domestic fare were placed at 9.1 percent.

Other major findings of the 1978 report was that travel agents and airlines essentially serve two different segments of the air travel community. Travel agents tend to handle trips involving greater complexity, while airlines deal primarily with travelers who want fewer services. Travel agents have a greater degree of influence on the travelers' final travel plans than do the airlines.

The commission from domestic carriers increased to 10 percent in 1980; however, the costs involved in selling and servicing air travel have also increased. The cost of automation and the increase in the cost of living—higher rents, salaries, and other overhead expenses—have cut down on the agent's profitability.

There is still a need to define the agent's cost of doing business and to provide facts and figures to answer the question of what would be reasonable compensation to travel agents. Numerous airline marketing executives have stated that agencies have proven to be the most efficient distribution outlet, but the losses sustained by the airlines during the past 14 years of deregulation have caused some of them to wonder if there isn't a cheaper way of selling tickets.

The American Society of Travel Agents (ASTA) has initiated a continuing study of the economics of the travel agency business. *ASTA Stat*, a statistical newsletter, is published monthly and sent to ASTA members. It is a compilation of statistics from the U.S. Travel Data Center, the Airlines Reporting Corporation, the Immigration and Naturalization Service, various magazine surveys, and other industry sources. Although this newsletter is very helpful to agents, it should be followed by another cooperatively financed Touche, Ross type of inquiry, and it should be done every two or three years to stay current. Historically, the airlines have refused to accept figures from the agency side alone. They prefer to rely on neutral research.

Eric Friedham, editor of *Travel Agent*, in an address to the New York chapter of ASTA, stated: "We speak constantly about the agency/airline relationship. Often we call it a partnership. But a salesman who gets paid only when he makes a sale can't be considered a partner. Partners share in carrying the load of the entire business: overhead, hiring and firing, administration, recordkeeping, rent, and taxes. The agent must bear these burdens alone out of his commissions." He concluded by saying that agents can avoid the disastrous results of having commissions cut "by continually proving your case through the efficiencies and fine service you've given the public, especially since deregulation. You can also do it through continuous vigilance in making your operations more cost-efficient, but without sacrificing expertise at the counter or counseling desk. You can also do it by supporting ASTA's efforts to keep up a steady stream of facts and figures which prove there is no viable substitute for the agency system as it now exists."

SALESPERSON FOR THE CARRIERS

An important fact often overlooked by travel agency owners is that when an agent applies for an appointment as an "approved travel agent" for the airlines, he is, in reality, applying for a job as their salesperson. As his employers, who will be paying him a commission on the tickets he will sell, an airline naturally has the right to investigate the agency's owner and his employees, and to examine his premises to determine if he is trustworthy and dependable and to make sure that the customers will be serviced properly and that their tickets will be written accurately. As his employers, they will expect him to observe their rules and regulations just as the agent expects his employees to follow his orders. Also, as his employers, the carriers have the right to set productivity quotas and the right to drop the agent from their lists if he cannot maintain that quota.

However, an equally important fact overlooked by the airlines is that just as a good employee expects to be rewarded financially by her employer, the good travel agent should also receive her financial reward. The airlines freely admit that the good, responsible travel agent is a valuable salesperson for the airlines as well as an important developer of travel. Virtually all statisticians agree that the number of travelers will double or even triple within the next 10 to 15 years despite the economy, currency fluctuations, fuel costs, or whatever. In fact, if the four-day workweek becomes a reality, this would open up a new market in three-day vacation packages. This would make it vital that agents and principals improve their efforts in better communication and cooperation among themselves to better serve the growing traveling public as well as to improve their own financial positions.

The well-informed, highly skilled, and competent travel agent will always survive despite deregulation, automation, licensing, or whatever may come up in the future. The professional travel agent is needed now more than ever. Today's travelers need expert and unbiased advice when trying to determine the best values as they seek to fulfill their dreams through the exciting medium of travel.

QUESTIONS AND PROBLEMS

1. Give a brief description of the travel agent and the services he offers to the public.
2. Would you agree that a travel agent is a "dealer in dreams"?
3. How does the travel agent assist the veteran traveler? The first-time traveler?
4. What criteria would you use in deciding on a service charge?
5. How can you increase an agency's income?
6. As the "salesperson" for the travel industry, what selling aids would help the travel agent do a better job for the industry as well as for herself?
7. How would you rate a good travel agent? What qualities would impress you most?

chapter 2

The Travel Consultant

OBJECTIVES

When you complete this chapter you should be able to:

1. Describe the travel consultant's duties in an average travel agency.
2. List the requirements/qualifications for a travel consultant.
3. Discuss the importance of good sales abilities.
4. Suggest methods to improve geography awareness.
5. Report on training methods and travel/tourism courses.
6. Name the programs that have developed to improve the professional standing of the travel agent.

The terms *travel agent*, *travel consultant*, and *travel counselor* are used interchangeably throughout the industry to designate the employee in the travel agency who has the actual contact with the client and initiates the procedures needed to book the travel arrangements.

Misconceptions about the travel consultant's duties are amazing. An ad in the help-wanted column for a part-time experienced travel consultant brought in at least 100 replies in the two-week period in which it appeared. A good 95 percent of the replies were from applicants who had no experience but who wanted very much to learn the travel agency business. When asked if they had any previous airline or travel agency experience, the answers were both amusing and exasperating. The public thinks that the travel consultant's job consists of sitting at a desk and talking to people about travel. When the conversation is finished, the consultant pushes a button in the inner office and the search for the most convenient flight, the best tour available, the type of hotel or resort the client prefers, the telephone calls to check for availability, the correspondence involved with the reservations, the ticket issuing and assembling all the confirmations, general information, visas, or tourist cards (when required) are performed automatically and the consultant hands the client the package with wishes for a bon voyage.

The public does not realize that the consultant's work begins after the client has left the office. He will spend more than an hour on a simple round-trip ticket to a nearby city, from the original request to the bookkeeping entry. An independent itinerary will take at least two hours of research and about 12 hours just to prepare the first draft.

When a client asks for a reservation or a travel plan, she does not stop to think that there is a lot of time and work involved in getting that reservation and making the travel plans. Travel agents are hardworking businesspeople. They are not dilettantes, as some people think. Together with their technical knowledge and experience, they need a willingness to work 12 hours a day when necessary—and during the busy seasons it may be necessary to work seven days a week. A psychologist said that most agents are gluttons for punishment. They endure more stress in the job than do workers in the majority of occupations, but they seem to like it that way.

This is also a low-paying job. Even managers in most agencies do not earn the equivalent salary they would earn as office managers in other industries. It is true that after one year, or on some occassions, six months, of employment in an approved travel agency, the consultant is eligible for discounted tickets from the airlines, steamship lines, and railroads, reduced rates or complimentary rooms from the hotels and tour operators, and there are occasional free *familiarization* (fam) trips offered by the airlines and tour operators and the government tourist boards. However, a travel agent's employees' travels are limited to the off-seasons and then only if the office can spare them at the time they want to travel. The number of discounted tickets per employee have also been cut down. Consultants cannot take their immediate family with them on most trips, which often creates dissension and resentment with spouses. Since the airlines allow pooling the discounted passes in an agency, an employee may not travel at all if the owner or manager decides that his or her trip is more important than the employee's.

According to the U.S. Travel Data Center's 1989–1990 Economic Review of Travel in America, the travel industry continues to be one of the fastest-growing industries in the United States and offers significant opportunities for women and minorities. It is the third largest U.S. retail industry and the second largest in terms of employment. Sales receipts for the travel industry have doubled since 1980. Travel agent salary levels are on the rise, and benefits such as medical insurance are becoming increasingly common.

Travel agent salary levels vary according to the geographical location of the travel agency. The 1989 survey by ASTA (American Society of Travel Agents) and a 1990 survey compiled by DCA Stanton Group, Inc. in Minneapolis for a group of agencies that included Carlson Retail Travel Network, American Express, and IVI Travel, among others, agree that agent salaries are lower in the midwest and mid-America regions. The ASTA survey showed that salaries in the five biggest respondent states revealed that agents with three to five years' experience earn an average salary of $17,065 in California, $16,018 in Illinois, $18,674 in New York, and $15,898 in Florida.

Cross-tabulations of survey data show that agency size has a strong influence on the average salary paid to sales agents. Agents entering the field at larger agencies usually start at higher salaries and the increases are larger. Business travel agencies with an annual sales volume of $5 million or more employ 10 or more full-time workers. The majority of agencies (51.9 percent) employ from three to five full-time workers and have an annual sales volume of less than $1 million. Salaries for leisure travel agents lag behind corporate travel even though it takes a lot more expertise to service the vacation/leisure traveler.

Forty-six percent of the ASTA agents say that finding new employees is the most serious problem facing their company. There are not enough qualified applicants to fill the available positions. Recruitment problems are caused by opening new agencies, expanding offices, and competition from the airlines and hotels, which are aggressively seeking travel school graduates to work at reservation centers. Competition from suppliers has left many agencies with only a few sources of new employees. The one most often used is personal recommendations from present employees. Other sources are newspaper ads, travel schools, and employment agencies.

Although starting salaries are higher in the larger, business-oriented agencies, an entry-level employee will learn more about the overall travel industry in a smaller agency.

REQUIREMENTS/QUALIFICATIONS

More than one job applicant has taken it as a personal insult when told that her college education, extensive travel, past experience as teacher, lawyer, in public relations and customer surveys, or as a secretary or stewardess did not qualify her as a travel consultant. A college diploma or one or two years of a liberal arts program can be most helpful to travel consultants but is not really essential if they are alert individuals, great readers, and keep up to date on world affairs as well as the local news. An uprising in the Middle East, terrorists' activities in Europe, a revolution in one of the South American countries, or a hurricane in Florida can greatly affect the agent's business. The travel business is a luxury business. A drop in the stock market or a strike in a large industry will immediately reflect the agent's bookings, as the nonessential business trip or vacation trip will be the first to be dropped from the average person's budget.

Contrary to what most people consider as good qualifications for a travel consultant's job, the applicant who has traveled extensively or has lived in foreign countries is not as well qualified as the applicant who has had business school training or actual experience in typing, filing, accounting, journalism, advertising, and sales. The ability to get along with people and the ability to use plain, good common sense when an emergency occurs is more valuable than having taken a trip around the world.

Most agency owners prefer to start inexperienced personnel as secretaries or file clerks for at least one year, until they learn the terminology, office procedures, and how to use the many reference books and official guides that the consultant has to work with. Quite often new employees are not allowed even to discuss travel with a customer until they have mastered the technicalities needed to make a reservation and issue a ticket. An overeager but inexperienced travel consultant can lose a valuable client by incorrectly quoting fares or flight schedules or other travel information.

The most powerful tool for the travel consultant is words. He must be capable of expressing himself orally and in writing. The customer comes to him not only to get reservation problems solved, but also to get the benefit of the consultant's knowledge and experience. Knowledge is still transmitted primarily by words. Even if the agency is large enough to afford secretaries, the consultant must know the fundamentals of English composition and business letter writing. He must also know how to type—even if it is the hunt-and-peck method. No matter what his duties are, the ability to type will serve him well. Typing speed is not important, and lengthy descriptions are not important—except in promotional letters or advertisements. A clear, concise letter that has been double-checked for accuracy is important. (A "little book," as it has come to be called, *The Elements of Style* by William Strunk, Jr. and E. B. White, is highly recommended to help you communicate more effectively.)

A basic knowledge of bookkeeping and accounting will keep the consultant aware that the office must make a profit on each sale or there will soon be no office and no job. The need for properly invoicing the customer for all services rendered and making sure that all monies collected are forwarded to the principals involved in the transaction is often neglected by the consultant. A delay in forwarding deposits and/or full payments can cause embarrassing situations for the customer and the agency. A delay in making up airline sales reports can cause an agency serious problems.

It goes without saying that a good travel consultant has a keen interest in travel, a fascination for geography, and a big bump of curiosity for places and people everywhere. Travel consultants must get along well with all types of people and have the patience of Job. They will often have to listen to a customer's life history while waiting for him to decide whether he wants a morning flight or an afternoon flight. Consultants need endless patience to concentrate on the many details involved in even a simple reservation. They must be very flexible and, like a juggler, be able to keep many files going at the same time while giving each customer the feeling that his or her trip is the most important trip in their files.

The competent travel consultant is modest and unpretentious, but at the same time must convey to the customer the confidence that he is dealing with a knowledgeable and experienced agent. No matter how much or how little agents know, they must not waver or show uncertainty before the customer. They must always present a personable, yet professional image to their clients. They must sell themselves before they can sell their services. They must inspire the faith in the customer that the agent can provide the personal services that the customer cannot find anywhere else. But they must not go to extremes and become overly impressed with the customer's dependence on their knowledge and advice. This sort of behavior might make them forget that they are there to serve the public's needs. If the customer insists on her own selections and refuses the consultant's suggestions, consultants should not take it as a personal affront. They must not forget that satisfied customers mean repeat business, which is vital to a travel agency.

Overawing the first-time traveler with a big display of your travel experiences can be just as dangerous as trying to bluff the experienced traveler. The first-timer does not like to be made to appear stupid or a fool because she has not traveled before; and at the other extreme, the travel consultant should not hesitate to say, "I don't know, but I will be glad to look it up for you" when a customer asks a question that cannot be answered immediately. Most experienced travelers are aware of the complexity of fares and the many changes that occur in this business.

They will be patient and tolerant with the consultant who is honest with them and has shown that the customer's interests always comes first.

GENERAL DUTIES

In most travel agencies, everyone employed in the office can double as a consultant. This is especially true in the small agency (two to five employees). As the agency becomes larger, it becomes more departmentalized. The onwer and/or the manager is then more concerned with supervision and acts as an advisor and troubleshooter for the consultants. It is up to the owner or manager to make the decisions on office procedures, personnel policies, and office maintenance; to order supplies and equipment; to set up advertising and promotional campaigns, group tour arrangements, and co-op ventures with tour operators and other travel agents; to install bookkeeping and accounting procedures; and to interpret (or seek an interpretation of) the many rules and regulations with which an agent must abide.

In a large agency, consultants may specialize in certain areas or destinations, such as commercial accounts, Europe, Florida and the Caribbean, cruises, Las Vegas, ski tours, and so on. The large agency will also have bookkeepers, secretaries, file clerks, and ticket writers, whereas the small agency owner will, out of necessity, expect his consultants to be capable of performing all of these chores as well as to sell travel. Routine duties such as opening the daily mail, routing it throughout the office, posting current bulletins on the board, stamping and filing brochures, mailing brochures to telephone and mail inquiries, and even stuffing envelopes for a mailing are all important to the success of the business, and all employees should be willing to share these duties. Sales have been lost because a brochure was not immediately available or the files were not up to date and the consultant quoted an incorrect fare or was unaware of important changes in regulations regarding validity periods on special fares or on tour offers. In a computerized office, the *queues* must be checked and worked each morning.

The travel consultant basically is the salesperson for the travel agency and for the entire travel industry. The consultant is engaged entirely in servicing the client's needs, and the success or failure to satisfy the client reflects on all travel agents as well as on the individual office.

SALESMANSHIP

A good salesperson knows his product. In many other enterprises, the salesperson and the technician are two different types of people. The builder does not have to be a salesperson, but the travel agent has to *know* as well as *sell*. Firsthand experience is useful in selling travel; however, being well-traveled is not as important as knowing where to go to get the travel information needed. In this business, the picture changes so fast that last year's "best" hotel may be this year's second or third choice; or last year's popular tour is refused by this year's traveler.

The ability to communicate, to understand others, and to make himself understood are the most important requirements for a good travel consultant. Clear and effective communication is absolutely essential to the success of the travel agency. Correspondence and business reports constitute an important segment of the work of the office, and accuracy is vital. A 10-minute error in a flight itinerary could cause a hurried businessperson to miss a flight; the wrong date on a hotel reservation request will put clients through hours of aggravation to find a room for the night; an incorrect fare code on a ticket or tour voucher can create problems that the client will always hold against travel agents, especially if it means cutting into personal spending money to cover additional unexpected expenses.

To quote Joel M. Abels, editor of *Travel Trade*: "Turning travel dreams into realities, and preventing them from turning into travel nightmares, is unquestionably the single most important reason why most experienced travelers, of both the pleasure and the business travel variety, prefer to use the services of a travel agent."

Travel agents wear two hats. They are the consultants to their clients, and they are the customers to their principals, who will actually provide the services they are requesting. To do this most efficiently, they must be good listeners. An attentive, understanding, sympathetic listener will be better able to give clients what they want. Consultants must catch the signals the client is sending and tailor the arrangement to suit the client's expressed and *unexpressed* needs. They must then translate and forward the requirements to the principal that can best supply the desired services. They must try to keep an impartial view in respect to the carriers, hotels, and other services they contact for their customers. They must use whatever is best for their customers—not necessarily what is best for them or their agency, or their principal.

From the customer's viewpoint, only minor differences may separate one travel agency from another. Most people know that an advertised tour can be sold by all travel agents. So why should they buy from you? How can you make your company stand out from all others? The answer, in a word, is *service*. You must supply a high-quality product and then be willing to go to any lengths to ensure customer satisfaction.

It is not just the customer always being right—it is knowing and observing the basics of salesmanship:

1. Be on time for every appointment.
2. Greet customers with a smile and do not forget to introduce yourself.
3. Make only promises you can keep; never break a promise.
4. Talk about the customers needs, wishes, and objectives for travel, not your own.
5. Thank her for her business.

Add to that foundation the skills needed to build a reputation as a service-oriented travel agent:

1. Don't sell features, sell benefits—or as some agents put it, "Sell the sizzle, not the steak." This is the cardinal rule of a good travel consultant. Explain the features of the travel arrangements in terms of how they will benefit the client. Use everyday language; don't use jargon, even with the experienced traveler.
2. Avoid the common and costly error of assuming that the client is interested only in the least expensive options. Sell "up."
3. Follow up promptly with written confirmations, additional literature, and/or answers to specific questions raised by your client.
4. Notify the client of problems or delays at any stage.
5. Return every phone call and respond to every letter immediately.
6. Keep customers informed of impending rate changes, special promotions, new features, and industry news.
7. Never take an old customer for granted. Treat each one with at least as much respect and attention as new prospects receive.
8. Evaluate and try to correct customer complaints. Avoid using negative phrases: "We can't do that," "That's impossible," "It's not our policy." Make a special effort to call or write to principals and forward the customer's complaint. Send a copy to the customer and advise the principal that you are doing this. Even if nothing comes of your efforts, you are making friends for your company.

Sales techniques can be learned from books, seminars, or college courses, but we must keep in mind that a travel consultant does more then sell a product.

One of the main reasons a client/customer calls a travel agency is because he is looking for information and counseling. This is the *service* that the agency is really selling, and this is what should be promoted and advertised.

TELEPHONE PERSONALITY

One of the important requisites for a travel consultant is his telephone personality. It is through the telephone that many people first come into contact with the travel agency. Therefore, it is of great importance that this channel of communication be kept efficient and cordial. The majority of the consultant's time is spent on the telephone, either with clients or with carriers or other principals. Poor telephone manners alienate callers and destroy your company's image as "your friendly travel agent." Creating a good impression by telephone is more difficult than face-to-face contact, but a pleasant, unhurried, courteous manner will encourage the client to call again. Efficiency with a light touch is appreciated by the principals, but the wise guy or great kidder is not appreciated by a busy reservations clerk.

A good telephone voice is loud and clear, but pleasant. Smile when you answer the phone; even though the caller cannot see the smile, it is reflected in your voice. Avoid overfamiliarity, technical jargon, and slang. When calling to make a reservation or to check availability—in all areas, airlines, tour operators, hotels, car rentals, cruises, and so on—identify yourself and your agency then proceed with your request. Make sure that you have all the facts before you pick up the phone—names (first and last), addresses, phone numbers, number in party, dates of travel (also alternative dates and times in the event the first choice is not available), and any special requests.

Taking and giving messages can also make or break a sale. If the call you answer is for someone who is unable to take the call, avoid the blunt question "Who is this?" Use the more courteous "M_____ is busy just now; may I tell her/him who is calling?" Never hang up on a caller until the person he is calling has been advised that there is a call waiting; quite often the call may be from someone who is on the road and cannot easily be reached. When you have to put a caller on hold, do not forget him. A neglected call may mean a lost sale. Return to the caller every so often and ask if he can wait longer or wish to leave a message.

If you take a message, get all pertinent information on paper: name of caller (ask for the spelling even if it is a Smyth or Browne), phone number where the person can be reached (even if the caller is a personal friend or relative—he may be at a location unknown to the recipient of the message), date and time of call, full message, and the message taker's name or initials. Confirmations received from airlines or other travel principals should include the full name of the passenger, date of travel, and name of the agent who entered the original reservation. Do not hesitate to ask callers to slow down in order to get all these facts. It is the responsibility of the message taker to get the full message and pass it on to the right person.

When making a call to others who are out or unable to come to the phone, leave a message to have them call you back rather than hang up with the remark that *you* will call back. A name and number is usually sufficient. Quite often it may not be advisable to state exactly who you are or the company you represent. There may be occasions when customers would not want their employers or spouses to know they are planning a trip. Never call a customer at home unless you are directed to do so. This is where tact and diplomacy get full play.

KNOWLEDGE OF OTHER LANGUAGES

Another misconception that most people have about travel agents is that a knowledge of several languages is a basic requirement. This knowledge of other languages is helpful but is not essential unless employed in an ethnic agency (an agency that specializes in travel to a particular country). Even then, knowing the language of the customers is not as important as having the patience, compassion, and desire to be of assistance. English is becoming more and more the universal language. An agency can send an employee to escort groups to a foreign country without regard as to whether or not the person can speak the language of the country (although a few conversational words can help), as it is a law imposed by the tourist offices of most all foreign countries that the tour operator or wholesaler hire local English-speaking guides to accompany each group.

GEOGRAPHY

It may appear obvious that those who sell travel, whether domestic or international, should know world geography. Employers throughout the industry have been both shocked and dismayed when entry-level employees have no conception of the size or location of states in the United States, or of countries in Europe, much less have any knowledge of the continents of the world.

It should be routine to ask passengers to clarify their destinations. Are they going to Melbourne, Florida or Melbourne, Australia; London, England or London, Ontario, Canada? But when consultants themselves have a poor knowledge of geography and are unaware of duplicate city names, mistakes are easily made and are often difficult to correct.

A *current* world atlas as well as *current* road maps of the United States, Canada, Europe, and other regions are "must haves" in every agency's reference library. Agencies have been known to keep such references long past their usefulness. Years ago the *OAGs* (*Official Airline Guides*) included a large map insert of airline flight routes of the United States, which was very helpful in determining the most efficient routing and connections. The insert has been discontinued and flight maps are now included in their Travel Planners, but they are small and not as easy to read. Deregulation encouraged airlines to discontinue service to the smaller towns and cities. The experienced consultant can check maps and recommend alternative routings or methods of transportation, but the new employee

Figure 2-2 Visitors go nose-to-nose with the exotic wildlife in open, natural surroundings on special photo caravan tours through the San Diego Wild Animal Park. Photo courtesy of the San Diego Convention & Visitors Bureau and the San Diego Zoological Society.

may discourage business by telling the passenger that there is no way to get to his destination.

In-house geography training can be accomplished with the use of the geography quizzes that appear in *Travel Weekly* and *Travel Agent* magazines and enrolling employees in the destination specialist program offered by the Institute of Certified Travel Agents (ICTA). Also, in recent years a number of destination geography and travel and tourism books have appeared on the market. I have listed a few of them in the Appendix.

The good news is that geography is making a comeback in high schools as well as in colleges and universities. Enrollment in geography classes is increasing and many states are offering world geography classes as a separate course for the first time in 20 years. A great deal of the credit for this renaissance belongs to the Geographic Alliance Network, a collection of grass-roots organizations bringing together academic geographers, teachers, and others dedicated to improving geography instruction. These alliances, initiated by the National Geographic Society, sponsor geography workshops for teachers, develop classroom materials, lead public-awareness activities, and work with local, state, and national leaders to reform curricula. Begun in 1986 with seven alliances in six states, the network boasts an active membership of over 63,000 people—all working together to show that geography is an important tool for responsible citizenship, environmental awareness, and political understanding.

TRAINING

Travel agency personnel must possess more than willingness to work and a general education. Specialized training is becoming more and more necessary. The continuing growth of tourism calls for higher education, which should cover general and theoretical knowledge as well as specific technical education. The needs of the traveling public in accommodations, transportation, tour operations, and sales methods have created jobs and opportunities in the travel industry that did not exist before. Marketing research and automation, for example, require qualified personnel with a specialized knowledge. The experienced travel consultant is now sought by the airlines, tour operators, hotels, and cruise lines to fill important positions in their sales departments. They recognize the need to have someone in sales who knows the travel agency business. Opportunities are also available in federal employment as travel clerks and travel assistants for those with experience in interpreting and applying travel regulations and using carrier schedules and guides.

It has been said by many people in the industry that it takes five years to make a good travel consultant. Until recent years, when more travel schools were opened and more universities started travel education curriculum, the travel consultant learned the business from on-the-job training—by trial and error. This can be a slow and costly method (costly in the sense that an agency can lose business from the errors of an inexperienced employee). Also, most offices are too busy to provide supervision of a new employee. They find it more profitable to send a new employee to an entry-level travel agents' training school.

On the other hand, seniority does not guarantee efficiency and knowledge. A consultant could spend five years in a large agency and never learn much more than a small facet of the business. The consultant may have been a reservation clerk or employed by an agent who specialized in specific areas or types of travel, such as commercial accounts, vacation packages, cruises, and travel to Europe or the Orient. Travel schools can teach the basic terminology and use of reference books and computers, but the poise and savoir-faire of an experienced travel consultant is developed only from years of contact with the public.

The ideal training method should combine the classroom theory with on-the-job training plus as much personal travel as the student can afford. If travel agencies would cooperate with a state-licensed business school or accredited college and supply their services as instructors or guest speakers as well as provide internships for students, they would not only assure themselves of a source of trained personnel, but the entire travel industry would benefit from a more knowledgeable public.

TRAVEL/TOURISM COURSES OFFERED

Many travel schools are now reaching a more professional level with the help of ASTA's new category of members inaugurated in October 1986 for travel training schools. ASTA offers forums for educators as well as monthly bulletins and training aids for educators.

The Society of Travel and Tourism Educators (STTE), founded in 1980, is also dedicated to improving the quality of travel and tourism educators. Annual conferences and trade shows are geared toward keeping educators abreast of current events in the travel industry and refreshing their teaching skills.

Students would be wise to check the prospective school's standing by inquiring if the school or its instructors are members of either of the organizations mentioned above and checking with their local Better Business Bureau for a history of complaints. Potential students should also check if the school has been approved (licensed) by the state education bureau, to find out if the instructors have experience in the travel industry, and to compare the curriculum with what is being offered in other schools.

To satisfy requests from travel agents, most schools are now putting greater emphasis on basic training, such as learning to use the *Official Airline Guides* (*OAG*s) and other reference books, making the reservation, handwriting airline tickets (even though the office may be automated, emergencies will require the handwritten ticket), and how to sell and book tours and cruises. Selling techniques and product knowledge can be even more important than learning how to use a reservations computer. A good knowledge of the basics can lead to good prospects for management.

Visual training aids are now available to travel agents and travel training schools. ASTA sells video training tapes with supplemental workbooks, Amtrak and Eurailpass sell tapes on train travel, Alamo Car Rental Co. has a very good unbiased video on car rentals (free), many resort hotels provide free videos on their properties, Tauck Tours will send (free) a behind-the-scenes video on tour operations and free videos on some of their escorted tours, CLIA (Cruise Lines International Association) sells a complete program on selling cruises, and videos can be purchased from individual cruise lines.

Classes in tourism are offered in a growing number of accredited colleges and universities, the most notable being the University of Hawaii's School of Travel Industry Management; the George Washington University, Washington, D.C.; the Cornell School of Hotel Administration; and Canada College, Redwood City, California. Many of these courses specialize in hotel, resort, and restaurant management but are now including travel agent training and are using experienced travel industry personnel as instructors.

Many of the airlines also have travel agent training courses, such as TWA (Trans World Airlines) in Kansas and American Airlines in Dallas. IATA (International Air Transport Association) also has a training school for agents in Europe. These airline training classes are specifically for travel agency employees and concentrate almost entirely on airline reservations, ticketing, and tariffs. Although they are very worthwhile for the specific purpose of learning airline rules and regulations and airline computer training, this still leaves the burden of training a new employee in all other facets of travel agency business on the owner/manager of the agency.

Other countries are also feeling the pinch in the lack of experienced employees. Mainland China is now sending students to the University of Hawaii to receive training in tourism. Tourism institutes have been started in Cairo, Egypt; South Africa; Australia; Brussels, Belgium; Rome, Italy; Geneva, Switzerland; Israel; and Germany. A survey once made by the Board of Airline Representatives in Germany revealed that in many of the agencies visited, the staff had insufficient knowledge of the product they were selling. They have since installed an apprenticeship program whereby new employees have to work a specific number of years in a travel agency and pass exams supervised by the tourist board before they are officially a travel consultant.

PROFESSIONALISM: CERTIFIED TRAVEL COUNSELOR

Professionalism is the keyword in travel industry discussions all around the world. Travel agents in many European countries have to be licensed. In Tel Aviv, Israel, the Tourism Institute offers a *certificate in expertise* for travel agency work. The Israeli legislature makes it obligatory for every tour operator to employ at least one staff member who holds this expertise certificate. Spain and Iceland have introduced laws which provide that travel agency managers must pass examinations to prove their competence to hold executive positions. The British Institute of Travel Agents and the Australian Institute of Travel are sponsoring and promoting qualification programs for travel-proficient certification.

The Canadian Institute of Travel Counsellors, the only certifying organization for travel professionals in Canada, has been awarding the designation of *certified travel counsellor*, CTC, to individuals who fulfill their requirements. To be eligible for certification as a full member of the institute, industry members must meet the following requirements: (1) pass the qualification examination and (2) maintain full-time employment in a travel agency or in the marketing and promotion of travel for a minimum of three years. Graduates of travel programs approved by CITC as travel counsellor programs (qualification level) will be granted six months' credit toward the three years' experience required for full membership in CITC.

Both the CITC entrance examination and the CITC qualification examinations are offered twice yearly in various locations across Canada. The exams are held on the second Saturday in May and the last Saturday in October.

In the United States, the Institute of Certified Travel Agents (ICTA) was formed by a committee of leading executives in the travel industry to offer specialized professional studies to those seeking higher proficiency in the travel agent field. The ICTA idea was conceived by the American Society of Travel Agents (ASTA) during the presidential term of Dick Kerr and implemented during the term of Milton Marks in 1963. After the initial launching by ASTA, ICTA was incorporated as an entirely separate educational nonprofit organization (recognized as such by the Internal Revenue Service) and incorporated in the District of Columbia, where the administrative office was then located. The office is now located in Wellesley, Massachusetts.

The study program of the institute follows the pattern of other professional fields. There is first a rigid review to select qualified candidates. Then come the detailed courses of study, followed by inclusive examinations and preparation of a thesis (or they can submit a report after attending one of ICTA's seminars)—all leading to a certificate and the professional designation as a CTC. In effect, the institute is a postgraduate school. To be eligible, at time of certification applicants must have five years' full-time experience in a travel agency or in the marketing and promotion of travel. (Candidates meeting all other requirements prior to five years' experience are given a course completion certificate. Upon marking their fifth anniversary in the industry, they are awarded their CTCs.) Candidates study in their own geographical areas in one of two ways: They can join local study groups which usually meet weekly and prepare together for the examinations, or they can enroll in the independent study and testing schedule administered by the institute's staff. The CTC program takes approximately two years to complete.

In 1984, ICTA started a travel career development course, an intermediate training program. The course is geared for travel counselors who have worked for an agency for one year but are not ready for the CTC management course. This 20-week program can also be taken with local study groups or by independently studying the textbook *Travel Career Development* and taking a multiple-choice test based on the contents of the book.

Also new in 1984 was ICTA's risk management program, the first subject in a planned advanced study series. The course shows agents how to identify business risks and ways to eliminate, minimize, or bypass problems.

The trend toward greater professionalism in service industries, particularly in travel, is growing. In a *Travel Weekly* interview, Don Hawkin, a George Washington University professor of travel and tourism who has helped set up several certification programs, said: "Travel agents, hotel administrators, hotel sales executives, meeting planners and travel marketing executives have all established certification programs within the past few years. One reason for the surge in certification programs is a shrinking labor force. Travel will have to compete with other services for workers. The whole movement toward professionalism will make travel jobs more attractive."

The National Passenger Traffic Association (NPTA) in 1986 started offering their members (composed of corporate travel managers) a program of educational courses in conjunction with credit for experience and college studies leading to a professional designation as a *certified corporate travel executive* (CCTE).

The NPTA certification program is open to anyone in the travel industry. The program was set up and supervised by Jim Johnston, president of Educational Advisory Services in Philadelphia. Johnston stresses that the emphasis of the certification program is on management. Management courses allow travel managers to function better with upper management.

The Canadian Business Travel Association (CBTA) is looking toward the larger and older NPTA for guidance in gaining more recognition and educational opportunities for its regular and allied members. The CBTA's relatively small membership, which is spread over a huge geographical area, makes it much harder to carry on a concerted educational program. NPTA's plans for more self-study courses may help solve the problem.

Although airline deregulation in Canada has not turned the industry upside down as some believe it has in the United States, the ensuing increase in available air fares has focused attention on travel managers and their roles in business.

In 1985, Meeting Planners International (MPI), an association of over 7500 meeting planners in the United States and 21 other countries, developed the *Meeting Professional's Handbook* in response to the Convention Liaison Council's certification program, for which one may qualify by application and exam to receive a *certified meeting professional* (CMP) designation. People have been planning meetings since the begining of time, but the profession of meeting planning is relatively new. The meeting planner will be expected to thoroughly understand a variety of other services. These include such diverse areas as ground and air transportation, audiovisuals and production, promotion and printing, program development, and speaker contracting, special events, and so on.

Joseph W. Bow, CAE, CMP (a past president of MPI) prepared an article for *Hotel Sales and Marketing Association's Student Bulletin*, Vol. 2, No. 2 (May–June 1986), which is an excellent source of information on this new career of meeting planner.

QUESTIONS AND PROBLEMS

1. List the most important qualifications for a travel consultant.
2. How important are personal travel and a knowledge of languages?

3. What are some of the routine duties in a travel agency?
4. What is the most important requirement of a good salesperson?
5. Why is it important to know typing and office procedures?
6. In your opinion, what would be an ideal training program?
7. Prepare a simple geography quiz to test entry-level employees.
8. How can you qualify a travel agents' training school?
9. What are the requirements and qualifications to become a CTC? In the United States? In Canada?
10. What new certification programs have been created?

## chapter 3

Rules/Regulations Governing Travel Agencies

OBJECTIVES

When you have completed this chapter you will be able to:

1. Discuss the ways the travel agency is regulated.
2. Explain deregulation of the airlines and how it has affected the travel industry.
3. Explain how the Association of Retail Travel Agents (ARTA) opposed the airline control through ARC.
4. Describe the organization of the Airlines Reporting Corporation (ARC) and its primary function.
5. Describe the International Airlines Travel Agent Network and its function.
6. List the steps involved in applying for an appointment as an approved agent for the airlines.
7. Differentiate between an STBN and an ETDN.
8. Discuss the importance of location, size, and appearance of the business.
9. Decide on the advantages of buying an existing business.

INTRODUCTION

Travel agencies are much more regulated than most people realize. Starting the business involves more than just finding a good location and hanging a sign in the window. To sell airline tickets, the agency and its personnel must be appointed as a sales agent for the domestic airlines (United States, Canada, Mexico, and the Caribbean are considered domestic) through Airlines Reporting Corporation (ARC) and by the International Airlines Travel Agent Network (IATAN), which represents the International Air Transport Association (IATA) air carriers.

The agency must observe rules and regulations that govern every facet of the business, from the application for appointment down to rules for the storage of ticket stock. The three most important requirements to becoming an approved agent for the airlines are (1) adequate finances (officially, IATAN requires a financial statement reflecting a minimum of $30,000 in net worth and ARC requires a bond or irrevocable letter of credit in the amount of $20,000; (2) the manager or owner must have a minimum of two years' experience in a travel agency; and (3) a location that is available to the public.

In addition to conforming to airline rules, the owner must check on local community rules and state laws. Some cities and small towns require a new business file for a new occupancy permit, which requires them to conform to the local fire department and safety rules, and more states are passing licensing laws governing travel agents.

An attorney familiar with the travel industry and a good accountant who takes the airline rules seriously should be the first two people hired by the new agency owner.

DEREGULATION

Before deregulation, the Civil Aeronautics Board (CAB) controlled airline routes and fares. Consumers who wanted to fly from city to city could use any airline, but they all charged the same fare. On October 24, 1978, President Carter signed a law, the Airline Deregulation Act (based on a bill coauthored by Senators Howard Cannon (Nevada) and Edward Kennedy (Massachusetts), that phased out CAB's control over domestic aviation on December 31, 1984. The board indirectly regulated travel agents through its power to approve or reject ATC and IATA intercarrier and agency agreements.

The immediate result was the freedom given to the airlines to apply for new routes anywhere in the United States, or to discontinue nonprofitable routes as long as they give the Department of Transportation 30- to 90-day advance notice. Fares on some routes increased dramatically, while others plunged to their lowest level. The law also removed the airlines' antitrust immunity in intercarrier and travel agency sales agreements.

The CAB conducted a competitive marketing inquiry in 1981 to determine the validity of the airline sales distribution system by continuing antitrust immunity to airline interline agreements and joint accreditation of travel agents through the Air Traffic Conference. Judge Ronnie Yoder of the U.S. Justice Department heard the case and gave his recommendation on June 1, 1982 to maintain the system; however, the CAB's decision on December 16, 1982 reaffirmed its objective of complete deregulation. Although the CAB believed that this would benefit the consumer, they overlooked how the airline interline demise would affect travelers. They would no longer have their baggage transferred automatically from one carrier to another, and airlines would no longer honor each others' tickets on the same routes or alternate routes unless the carriers have an *interline agreement*. Joint fares may disappear. Separate tickets would have to be written for each change of carrier. There would be no protection if flights are canceled or oversold. Passengers would be on their own in making alternative arrangements, and refunds would be delayed or forfeited.

Deregulation also brought with it the reality that airlines can go bankrupt. Increased competition, revenue-decreasing fare wars, increased costs, and labor problems have forced a number of minor and major airlines into bankruptcy. Travel agents now have the added responsibility of helping clients minimize their losses. To protect clients against airline bankruptcies, travel agents should suggest that clients buy travel insurance that covers airline bankruptcies. They should encourage clients to purchase tickets with major bank credit cards, although this does not ensure protection. The credit card company may or may not protect them, even though the client notifies the credit card company that services were not rendered and requests that their account be credited for the amount of the ticket purchase. The present Fair Credit Billing Act does not require a credit card company to issue a credit or refund if an airline failure occurs more than 60 days beyond the date when the airline ticket charge first appeared on the consumer's credit card statement. The card-issuing bank or company then has 30 days to make the correction, usually through a credit to the cardholder's account.

In 1978 there were 36 certificated scheduled carriers. During the 10 years following deregulation a total of 210 carriers received new operating authority; however, over 200 ceased operations, merged, liquidated, or were decertified, leaving 73 certificated carriers in 1990. The top seven of these carriers control nearly 95 percent of the traffic.

The success of these few does not compensate for the myriad of problems created by the increase in passenger traffic. During the first 10 years of deregulation the number of passengers jumped from 246.7 million to 415 million. Projections say that the number will rise to 685 million by 1998, but the recession and the Persian Gulf War in 1990 brought a $2 billion loss to the airlines, the worst year financially in their history.

High on the problem list are airport congestion, an overburdened air traffic control system, crowded aircraft, and poor service, ranging from lost luggage, overbooked flights, and late departures, to rude and arrogant behavior from airline employees. The drive to reregulate the airlines gained new support in May 1991 when congress members introduced the Airline Competition Enhancement Act of 1991, which would mandate new government controls over computer reservations systems, and the Transportation Department would be charged with tightly regulating the prices that carriers charge competitors when selling gate spaces, landing slots, and international routes. The idea is to make it easier for smaller carriers and new airlines to gain entry.

Finally, the bill would clarify the existing law to allow foreign companies to hold a 49 percent equity investment in a U.S. carrier, although they still would be limited to 25 percent of the voting control. Relaxing the ban on foreign investments will eventually remove the ban on cabotage (the right of a foreign airline to carry passengers between two domestic points in the United States). Removing the ban on cabotage would provide U.S. airports with an entirely new set of customer airlines and they would have the means and the motivation to invest in new gates and runways to accommodate this new business.

Removing the barriers to foreign investors and cabotage should benefit American carriers by encouraging foreign countries to remove similar restrictions and will provide access to the lucrative routes between the world's major cities.

AREA BANK SETTLEMENT PLAN

By eliminating the agency system as it formerly existed, the Air Traffic Conference and the area bank settlement plan (ABSP) were also phased out. The ABSP provided the convenience of having a central clearing house for both the airlines and travel agents in the reporting and payment of ticket sales. The travel agents submitted sales reports once a week and the ABSP sorted the tickets and forwarded payments to the individual airlines. ARC has taken over ATC's responsibility to supervise and check the reports sent to ABSP and to followup if or when there are irregularities or late remittances.

In the spring of 1983, the American Society of Travel Agents (ASTA), the Association of Retail Travel Agents (ARTA), the Air Traffic Conference (ATC), and almost all of the individual airlines joined together to get the U.S. Congress and Senate to consider the Air Traveler's Security Act of 1983, introduced into the Senate by Senator John Warner (Virginia) and others. The corresponding bill was introduced in the House by Representative Glen Anderson (California) and others. The bills hoped to overturn CAB's competitive marketing decision and give continued antitrust immunity for the ATC and IATA travel agency programs and prevent nonaccredited outlets from making airline sales. The committee bill contained a policy statement that consumer welfare, tourism promotion, and professionalism and financial stability in airline marketing require continuation of cooperative airline working arrangements.

However, early in 1984, the Air Transport Association (ATA), of which ATC is a subsidiary, started preparing a contingency plan in the event that CAB or the pending legislation did not extend the antitrust immunity. This contingency plan was developed without participation or knowledge of any travel agency representation. Their plan, announced in June 1984, provided for the establishment of a separate corporation, Airlines Reporting Corporation (ARC), consisting of no more than 30 stockholders. These stockholders are limited to passenger airline members of ATA. The corporation is operated much like any industry-owned corporation. Its principal customers are the airlines, both domestic and foreign, although its services are available to nonairlines such as Amtrak or other travel suppliers. Travel agents do not have a direct role in administering the affairs of the corporation but have an advisory role through the establishment of an advisory council. The corporation replaced, in its entirety, the current air traffic conference agency program, including the area bank settlement plan. The announcement of the new corporation killed the Air Traveler's Security Act.

In the meantime both the Senate and the House commerce committees voted in July 1984 to transfer most remaining CAB authority and rules to the Department of Transportation (DOT). This gives DOT authority to protect airline consumers and police against unfair industry practices. In addition, all CAB rules governing charters, in-flight smoking, baggage liability, denied boarding compensation, deceptive advertising and reservations systems bias transferred intact at year's end. Both the House and Senate bills gave DOT the authority to grant antitrust immunity to joint industry ventures, which include the joint travel agency programs. Despite the transfer of that authority, the ATC and IATA travel agency programs still lost their antitrust immunity on January 1, 1985.

ARTA–ARC AGREEMENT

The Association of Retail Travel Agents (ARTA) opposed total airline control through ARC and filed a lawsuit against ARC in September 1984 seeking a permanent injunction dissolving ARC on the grounds that it violates antitrust laws. ARTA's president, Ronald Santana, said the entire goal of the ARTA suit is to improve travel agent input into the sales system and gives agents some control over their own business lives.

In a preliminary decision in February 1987, U.S. District Court Judge Louis Oberdorfer ruled that three features of ARC violate antitrust laws: (1) the uniform seven-day remitting cycles for travel agencies, (2) the requirement for each agency to post a bond or letter of credit, and (3) the requirement that a new owner of an agency must assume the old owner's ARC obligations in a change of ownership.

On the morning of March 30, 1987, ARTA and ARC agreed to settle out of court after ARC agreed to eliminate certain practices that ARTA found objectionable. With the ARTA–ARC agreement endorsed by Judge Oberdorfer, the major agency associations gained the right to appeal virtually all industry-wide ARC decisions affecting existing agents through a neutral arbitration panel. The agreement also called for Judge Oberdorfer to have ongoing oversight of the restructuring of ARC.

ARC repealed its system of late remittance charges for dishonored sales report drafts and other remitting violations and replaced this with a system of assessments on agents based on actual costs to the carriers of the remitting violations.

ARC now gives agents reasonable advance notice of agency audits and will limit the circumstances under which it picks up an agent's ticket stock and validation plates.

ARC also eliminated the requirement that new owners assume the obligations of their predecessors. A person interested in buying only the assets of a travel agency can now do so without being held responsible for the liabilities of the agency.

A review procedure known as the *travel agent arbiter program* was established on January 1, 1988. The program is operated by an independent entity known as the Office of the Travel Agent Arbiter, headed by a person holding the position of travel agent arbiter (TAA). The position of associate travel agent arbiter (ATAA) was established to provide prompt expansion capability should the volume of business of the TAA office need such expansion. The TAA and each ATAA are selected, and the term of office is established, by the Joint Advisory Board–Agent Reporting Agreement (JAB–ARA). Neither the TAA nor ATAA nor any employee of the Office of the Travel Agent Arbiter can be an employee of ARC or of any carrier or of any agent or organization or association of agents.

ARC's board of directors established a committee of six, composed equally of airline and agent representatives (one of which shall be a representative of ARTA) known as the TAA Oversight Committee. The committee oversees the budget and administration of the TAA office on a day-to-day basis.

Two seats on ARC's joint advisory board (JAB) are assigned permanently to the two largest national trade associations of ARC-accredited agents, which are membership organizations, duly organized and constituted as nonprofit organizations. (The two are ARTA and ASTA.)

Detailed information on the travel agent arbiter program, its jurisdiction, rules, and procedures, are provided in the ARC's *Industry Agents' Handbook*. The handbook is sent to all travel agents on ARC's list and is issued twice a year.

ARC STRUCTURE AND ORGANIZATION

The *board of directors* is the highest decision-making body in ARC. The ARC board consists solely of airline representatives and meets about four times per year.

The *ARC advisory council* consists of 12 travel agent representatives. This group never actually meets as a group. Instead, each of the 12 agency organizations is permitted to give views to the ARC board of directors before each ARC board meeting. Agents are excluded from the remainder of these meetings.

The *ARC joint advisory board* (JAB) consists of six airline and six travel agent organization representatives. The JAB meets to discuss suggested changes in the ARC rules that affect travel agents, with an ARC official serving as chairman of the group. Under ARC rules, the ARC board can never change any rules that affect travel agents unless the JAB has first considered them. Recent changes in ARC as a result of the ARTA–ARC lawsuit settlement have given the JAB additional powers, such as selecting the members of the IAP and the TAA, subject to ratification by the ARC board of directors.

Joint working groups (JWGs) are subcommittees of the JAB, established to develop details on many of the programs that are the responsibility of the JAB. Currently, there are three active JWGs working on details of the ARTA–ARC settlement in the areas of arbitration, reporting and remitting alternatives, and bond alternatives.

The *Independent Arbitration Panel* (IAP) was established in 1988 as a result of the ARTA–ARC lawsuit settlement. Three panelists were selected to serve on the new panel empowered to review decisions made by ARC's board of directors. These can be appealed by at least two agency associations.

The appointments were endorsed unanimously by JAB and ratified by ARC's board. Panelists meet at various locations when the need arises.

The *travel agent arbiter* (TAA) replaced the travel agent commissioner to resolve disputes between individual agents and ARC or a carrier. Travel agents and ARC share the expenses of the arbiter's office equally, whereas the commissioner's office had been totally financed by ARC. Along with the broadened powers to hear agency complaints against carriers, the arbiter will continue the commissioner's basic mission of handling the most serious cases of retailer breaches of the agency agreement.

AIRLINES REPORTING CORPORATION

Whereas ARC reviews and processes applications from travel agents, the primary purpose of ARC is to distribute, process, and account for ARC and non-ARC traffic documents on behalf of its carrier customers and their agents. The original retail or distribution entities for which the corporation undertook services on behalf of its airline customers were (1) full-service industry travel agencies, (2) restricted-access agencies, (3) in-plant agencies, (4) IATA-only travel agencies, (this category is now discontinued) and (5) "other persons." (The former ATC program dealt only with industry-wide travel agents.)

A full-service industry travel agent is basically the same as the former ATC-approved agent, although ARC standards for approval are less restrictive. To be approved, an applicant would need to meet minimal airline ticketing and sales or managerial requirements; would no longer be restricted on "self-sales" (ATC barred an agency from doing 20 percent or more of annual airline business as self-sales—however, the individual airlines continue to restrict self-sales); report and remit sales every seven days, although individual airlines can extend remitting time through the direct form of payment (DFOP) option; carry a bond in the minimum of $20,000 or may substitute an irrevocable letter of credit in the same amount for the bond; and pay an application fee and an annual fee per location.

Restricted-access agencies must meet all requirements for a full-service agency except that it is not open and freely accessible to the public. (ATC had no such classification.)

In-plant agencies are any agencies located on a customer's premises primarily to serve that customer, which can include a *home* or *branch office*. (ATC permitted in-plants as branches only.) ARC now classifies this as a *customer-premises* location. (IATAN does not have an in-plant category.)

IATA-only agencies were those that had IATAN but not ARC accreditation. This category has been discontinued.

"Other persons" includes any industry agency or other ticketing outlet (and need not meet ARC accreditation standards) which obtains the ticket stock of a particular airline and which reports sales on that carrier every seven days through the area settlement plan. Remitting can be made directly to the airline(s) under the DFOP (direct form of payment) option. (ATC had no such category.) The sponsoring airline pays an annual fee to ARC for each "other person" using the area settlement plan and the sponsoring airline is responsible for collection of other persons' remittances.

Although the CAB's decision in 1982 and the new ARC give the airlines the freedom to appoint nonaccredited outlets as their online agents (the "other persons" classification), none of the carriers have done so.

In 1985, ARC approved the agents' use of satellite ticket printers (STPs) at their business account locations; however, there are specific rules and procedures to follow if an ARC listed agent wishes to avail itself of this method of ticket delivery. An STP has a very limited purpose. It is intended solely for the delivery of ARC traffic documents (airline tickets) to another location by installing a ticket printer at the customers' location which is controlled by the agents' home office or branch office. The agent's and auditor's coupons are generated at the agency, while the flight and passenger coupons are spit out of the printer at the client's office. Printers are linked with on-site offices through dedicated or dial-up telephone lines.

An application accompanied by a nonrefundable fee is required to apply for an STP. General information for an authorized STP location and a copy of the "Supplementary Agreement Covering a Satellite Ticket Printer Location" is included in the ARC handbook.

The major drawback to the STPs is ARC's stipulation that the agent will be held totally liable for the ticket stock at the STP location. An airline would have every right to insist on payment for misused tickets at the STP. If the STP location is open to the general public, the STP, including its in-use supply of ARC traffic documents, must be completely enclosed in a steel security container or an acceptable equivalent thereof. This makes it necessary that the agent arrange an agreement with the client to share the responsibility.

Although it is easier to get ARC approval for an STP and avoids the problems of installing customer-premises locations, the expenses involved may outweigh the benefits. Equipment costs, phone lines to STPs, dial-up phone charges, office space rentals, and the salary of an employee to monitor the machines have to be considered. Frequent malfunctions have also been reported as a primary disadvantage of STPs.

As the number of STPs grew, they generated a new type of ticket delivery. A number of companies turned themselves into satellite ticket printer networks (STPNs). For a fee, agents could contact a company and arrange to have a ticket delivered at a specific ticket printer site (usually an airport location) for pickup by a client. The agency makes the reservation but must release the passenger name record to the STPN, which prints all the coupons. The agency receives the commission from the STPN minus the delivery charge.

To operate a STPN, a company must get ARC accreditation as a travel agency, since only appointed agents can have satellite printer sites. For this reason, some agents are reluctant to use STPNs, as they are seen as potential competitors.

ARC is now considering a new category: electronic ticket delivery networks (ETDNs). Like STPNs, ETDNs would be networks of attended satellite ticket printers around the country that could be used by accredited agents, for a fee, for ticket delivery. They would not be accredited travel agencies in the traditional sense. To protect ARC, a letter of credit or bond is required in the amount of $50,000 for the first ticket printer location, plus $5000 for each additional location.

An agency using an ETDN's services would issue the ticket itself in its own name. The agency would have total control over collecting payment from the passenger and reporting and remitting to ARC. An ETDN would be valuable when agencies do not want to make the investment to buy STPs or do not have clients big enough to justify them.

A number of companies wanted to become ETDNs, but the computerized reservation system (CRS) vendors will have to reprogram to accommodate them. So far, no CRS has announced firm plans to accept ETDN transmissions.

ARC BOND AND INDEMNITY PROGRAM

A satisfactory credit standing is one of the most important single qualifications for appointment in either one of the airline corporations. In 1963, ATC started the agent bond requirement. Previous to this, trust accounts were maintained by the agent in the name of each conference wherein the net amount of the ticket was deposited and withdrawn only at the time the sales reports were made every 15 days. At present, new applicants must submit, along with their ARC application, a bond in the standard ARC form in the minimum amount of $20,000, or a written statement by a surety company confirming that the required bond will be issued in the near future. The surety must be listed as an acceptable surety in the *Federal Register* published by the Department of the Treasury. If the written statement is submitted in lieu of the bond, the application cannot be finalized until the actual bond is received. ARC must receive the signed *original* bond. The bond guarantees that the agent will remit all amounts due the conference members under his sales agency agreement.

After the first year in business, the agent must increase the bond to cover the average monthly cash sales of all air transportation, domestic and international, for the 12-month period preceding the bond renewal date up to a maximum of $70,000. A minimum of $10,000 is allowed for agencies approved before March 1, 1987 that have been under the same ownership for at least two years. The minimum for new agencies, and agencies that have an approved change in ownership after March 1, 1987, will be $20,000. The agency may, however, whenever its 12-month experience so warrants, adjust the bond or letter of credit downward, but in no event below the minimum of $10,000 or $20,000, whichever is applicable.

The agent can elect to substitute the ARC bond with an *irrevocable bank letter of credit* in the bond amount. The letter of credit is to be used as a replacement, not as an addition, and the agent must use one or the other, not a combination of both. The ARC bond is a performance or financial guaranty type of bond. The irrevocable letter of credit is a guarantee of payment issued by a federally insured lending institution.

Bonds are to be procured and maintained without expense to the ARC and/or its members. The bonding company assumes the responsibility of investigating and passing judgment on the agent's credit. Surety companies are getting stricter in the requirements for issuing the ARC bond. Some companies request a commercial letter of credit in the full amount of the bond. Others will accept a letter of credit for 50 percent of the bond amount, or will issue the bond when they receive an indemnity agreement signed by each owner and/or stockholders and their spouses plus copies of personal financial statements for each owner and/or stockholder. In addition to the financial statement of the business, confirmation of all bank balances on the bank's letterhead must be sent with the bond application.

Under current rules, agents are required to review their bonding coverage at least once a year, but must at no time let bonds fall more than $2000 below the required amount. ARC started a monitoring program in 1977 by running computer checks on a quarterly basis and found that about 10 percent of the appointed agents were carrying bonds below the required amount.

ARC does not expect an agent to maintain a bond or letter of credit in excess of the required amount and will now notify agents once a year whether their bonds are too low, too high, or just right. Although it is the agent's responsibility to maintain proper coverage, ARC will advise any agent found not doing so at least 90 days in advance of the anniversary date of such instrument.

If ARC determines that the agent has failed to adjust the bond or irrevocable bank letter of credit by the anniversary date, ARC will immediately so notify all carriers and the agent and will send an airline sales representative or someone from Equifax to remove all ARC accountable documents and airline validation plates and the agent cannot issue airline tickets until the bond is renewed or increased.

However, as a temporary measure to avoid the withdrawal of ARC traffic documents and airline identification plates, the agent may assign, in a form acceptable to ARC, a certificate of deposit in the amount required until they can arrange renewed coverage, thus preventing a loss of business when the ticket stock and plates are removed. This will be accepted by ARC *as a substitute for a period not to exceed 30 days from the date of the cancellation*; otherwise, ARC will terminate the agent's agreement.

Bond coverage in excess of the minimum is waived by ARC if the agent submits to ARC annually a current balance sheet, certified by a certified public accountant to present fairly the financial position of the agent, which establishes that total assets available for satisfaction of debts exceed liabilities by at least $100,000, and the credit rating of the agent, if published by Dun and Bradstreet or other recognized credit-rating agency, is shown as "good" or higher.

INTERNATIONAL AIRLINES TRAVEL AGENT NETWORK

In November 1984, IATA formed two new corporate bodies, to be known as Passenger Network Services Corp. (PNSC) and Cargo Network Services Corp. The new corporations were not intended to be substitutes or the competitive answer to the Air Transport Association's Airlines Reporting Corporation (ARC); however, because of the loss of immunity in the U.S. agency system, the PNSC was formed to endorse and supervise the travel agencies on behalf of their member international airlines. The PNSC began full operations in May 1985, trading throughout the United States under the name International Airlines Travel Agent Network (IATAN). The trading name identifies network travel agents with the IATA organization and its listings of recognized sales outlets worldwide.

The corporate board of directors meets regularly to consider agency standards and other policies and the seven-member executive committee, more frequently, as circumstances warrant. In the past, IATA met once a year with a group of airline representatives. Three directors were elected from the ranks of travel agency executives and also serve on the executive committee.

Figure 3-2 American Airlines—Airport ticket counters.

IATAN forms the link between its 201 international airline customers and their appointed agents. It acts on behalf of its subscriber airlines to appoint U.S. agents according to each airlines' own standards. It also seeks to maintain professionalism among travel agents by endorsing them as official international airlines travel agents.

Whereas the international airlines participating in the old IATA program collectively set standards for agents to represent them all, IATAN provides the machinery to enable airlines to appoint agents according to any standards they may individually wish to apply.

The system is flexible. Many of the subscribing airlines have elected to adopt IATAN endorsement standards as their own appointment standards, whereas other customers have introduced different requirements. The airlines can choose only those agents who meet their particular standards to represent them in the U.S. marketplace.

IATAN standards for airline appointment tend to be high. IATAN assesses agent financial capacity, ensuring that the applicant has adequate working capital to support a head office and enough extra to support branches, if it is the agent's intention to operate them. Agents have to have enough invested in the business to ensure their commitment to its success.

Unqualified staff can make mistakes that inconvenience passengers and cause trouble for airline check-in and handling staff, so IATAN is concerned that those who work in the business are properly qualified.

When an agency applies to become an appointed representative of the international airlines, and its qualifications have been verified, IATAN approval is a two-step process. Agencies get a certificate of endorsement by the corporation; then the application information is checked by computer against each airline's appointment standards. The computer prints out a certificate of appointment for the agency listing all those airlines whose standards it has met.

A new service, called AEROFAX, was introduced by IATAN to send bulletin mailings to its members quickly and efficiently. Instead of being mailed, lists of sales intermediaries, endorsed agents, branch office openings, changes in status, and so on, are relayed by teletype to the airlines' U.S. regional or field offices on the same day that they occur.

IATAN will continue to verify their standards with their program of reinspecting agencies to ensure that they are living up to personnel, location, financial, and other standards.

A number of industry leaders have started questioning the need for the IATAN appointment when the ARC accreditation is all that is needed to issue tickets and report sales remittances for bookings on the world's major airlines, making IATAN's cumbersome and costly appointment procedures redundant. Most agents do not realize that even though they may have the ARC and IATAN appointments, the individual airlines have the final decision as to whether or not they wish to do business with the agent and pay commission on sales.

IATAN's answer points out that an IATAN agent has the legal right to ticket on all IATAN's international customer airlines, and it results in having to handle only one contractual document to deal with each airline. IATAN endorsement is seen by its customer airlines as a dependable means by which travel agents can be measured to a professional standard.

IATAN endorsement standards are also significant to the traveling public, as a display of the IATAN window decal and the IATAN logo on the agent's business stationery and press releases announces to the public and to industry partners at home and abroad that the agent is a bona fide, full-service travel professional with validated qualifications to sell international air travel.

In my opinion the IATAN appointment is important to the new agency and to the agencies that specialize in international travel. The new business needs the support of the IATAN appointment until a good rapport has been established with both the travel industry suppliers and the traveling public. The established international travel agent needs the support and contacts gained through membership with the International Air Transport Association (IATA), which continues to administer a worldwide agency program outside the United States.

IATAN FINANCIAL REQUIREMENTS

At the present time, IATAN does not require a bond in the United States, and for that reason, they are more concerned about the agent's financial stability. In addition to the completed questionnaire, the applicant must present a *sworn*, current financial statement prepared in accordance with standard accounting practices showing that the agent is solvent and of a satisfactory financial standing, and a letter from the agent's bank verifying the balance in the account. The applicant's *working capital* must be adequate, and to be considered adequate, the current assets must exceed the current liabilities by an amount of not less than $25,000, plus $5000 for each additional branch office.

The investment of the principals in the agency must not be less than $30,000 in *tangible net worth*, whether it is a stock corporation, nonstock corporation, partnership, or proprietorship. Tangible net worth is calculated by summing up the paid-in capital, net income/loss, less drawings, less intangible assets.

Unofficially, both ARC and IATAN recommend a minimum startup figure of $50,000. More is needed if new agents plan to specialize in commercial business. They will have to cover the costs for additional employees, CRTs, and enough funds to cover the accounts receivable, as most business will ask for 15 to 30 days' time to pay for their travel, even though they know that the agent must pay the airlines every seven days.

THE NEW TRAVEL AGENCY

"What do I have to do to start a travel agency?" This question is asked quite frequently of anyone connected with the travel business. It is not an easy question to answer and it cannot be done in just a few words or a few paragraphs. This chapter was written as a guide to prospective travel agency owners and as an explanation to new employees on how the agency began.

To operate a *full-service travel agency* you must have the airlines' approval to issue tickets on your premises, and to receive that approval you must be appointed by the Airlines Reporting Corporation (ARC), which replaced the Air Traffic Conference (ATC) and the International Airlines Travel Agent Network (IATAN) and placed on their *agency list* as an endorsed entity who has been appointed by ARC/IATAN as the airlines passenger sales agent for the purpose of selling air passenger transportation. Only authorized locations may receive commissions for the sale of airline tickets.

Most of the emphasis on the new travel agent is placed on applying for and receiving the airline appointments as soon as possible. This is primarily because the airlines authorize a complete investigation of the new owners—and the other industry segments (tour operators, hotels, etc.) know that if the applications are accepted without question, you have a good chance of receiving the airline appointments and therefore will be a good potential business outlet for them.

The travel agency must be open for business at the time the completed applications are sent to ARC/IATAN. Adequate finances, an attractive office available to the public, qualified personnel, and the willingness and ability to promote and sell travel are the major requirements. Quite often it takes from two to six months for ARC (IATAN takes 30 days, provided that the application is routine) before the new agent can accumulate all the supporting documents that are needed for submission with the applications (see the "Checklist of Procedures" later in the chapter) and receive approval. During this time there will be no income from airline sales, as the new agent is on a retroactive commission basis only after the applications are accepted by ARC and IATAN. However, the agency can sell and earn commissions during this period on hotels, car rentals, tours, and cruises.

PERSONNEL REQUIREMENTS

Experienced personnel is the second most important requirement by all the conferences, airlines and others (the most important is the financial criterion). This is just plain common sense, as no business can survive without an experienced staff to take care of customers. The owner of a new agency who has had no previous experience in the travel industry must be prepared to face resentment and antagonism from other travel agency owners, skepticism and mistrust from the airlines, and a slow response from the public. Absentee owners, especially, are looked on with disfavor by almost everyone in the industry. If owners have other full-time jobs or other business ventures, they are suspected of entering the travel business solely for the travel benefits (although these have been reduced drastically).

ARC, IATAN, CLIA, and Amtrak have similar personnel standards. One person, either the owner, partner, officer, or manager (referred to as the *qualifier*) must have a minimum of two years' experience of full-time employment as a travel counselor or a manager in the travel business. This person or qualifier must have full responsibility and exercise daily supervision of the agency, must be employed full time (at least 35 hours a week), must demonstrate a working knowledge of the ARC and IATAN travel agents handbooks, and must be capable of successfully completing written questionnaires on both. (ARC sends the exam with the application.) In addition, the qualifier or another full-time employee of the applicant must have one year's experience (within the past three years) in airline passenger ticketing in the full-time employment of either an ATA or IATA member airline, or a travel agency included on the ARC or IATAN agency lists. Any job with one employer for less than six months will not be considered toward meeting this requirement.

Again, it is a matter of using common sense to have a minimum of two experienced people in the office. While waiting for the listing (endorsement), tickets will have to be picked up from the airline ticket offices or the nearest airport, and quite often airline ticket agents are not familiar with new agency procedures. It takes an experienced travel agent to explain it to them. Absences due to illness or for other personal reasons could also result in leaving the office without an experienced travel consultant on hand to take care of business. Much harm can be done to the agency, the airlines, and to travel agents in general when an inexperienced employee gives a customer inaccurate or incomplete information. An experienced manager will not only protect the owner from costly errors, but will protect the airlines' interests as well. Also, there is no lack of work to keep two people occupied. Although business may be slow coming in, the new agent must write or call hundreds of airlines, steamship lines, bus companies, car rental companies, hotels, resorts, and wholesale tour operators for current brochures and rate sheets. As these brochures start arriving, there is then the time-consuming job of stamping them with the agent's address and filing the literature. These brochures are the agent's inventory and selling tools. Lack of a brochure can cause a lost sale. The general public insists on seeing the rates and arrangements offered to them in print, preferably in a published brochure.

LOCATION

Years ago new travel agents had to prove a need for an office in the area where they wished to locate when they applied for airline appointments. This need clause was thrown out when some applicants argued successfully that it was a restraint of trade. Applicants are now free to open a travel agency wherever they please provided that the location is easily accessible to the general public.

To be included and retained on the agency list, ARC requires that the applicant must meet each of the following qualifications:*

1. The place of business must be engaged primarily in the retail sale of passenger transportation and must be clearly identified as, and held out to the public to be, an office for the sale of air transportation and ancillary services.

2. The agency must be open for business and easy for all the general public to find and enter without hindrance.

3. The agency does not have to be open for business while the application is pending, but the application must provide details as to the precise location and staff and the date the location will be open with qualified personnel. ARC traffic documents will not be provided until the agency is in full operation with qualified personnel.

4. If the location is open at the time of application, applicants can serve their customers by buying tickets directly from the carrier(s), or through the use of exchange orders that some carriers provide. Applicants should check with each carrier to determine how it wishes business to be conducted until ARC tickets are provided.

5. Each carrier establishes its own commission policies. While the application is pending, ARC will not answer questions pertaining to commission structure. All such inquiries should be directed to the specific airline.

6. Every ARC industry agent location must have an off-premises bank safe deposit box or equivalent facility for the storage of excess traffic documents. An agent is permitted to keep 80 manual traffic documents, or the average weekly number of manual ARC traffic documents at that location during the preceding calendar year, on the agency premises when it is unattended by agency personnel. But those traffic documents must be kept in a locked steel container, separate from the carrier identification plates. Automated agencies may have 200 tickets per printer on the premises, plus 600 in storage, or 200 per printer, whichever is greater.

IATA's requirements for the applicant are very similar to those of ARC. The wording and format on the applications may vary, but the information accumulated for one can be used for both. Soon after ARC and IATAN receive the applications (and I would suggest that these and all correspondence to the airline corporations be sent by certified mail with a return receipt requested), the applicant will be advised as to the date that they are placed on a *retroactive commission basis*. The airlines are notified of the new agency application. The corporations will then request an inspection and credit check through an outside auditing firm, usually the Equifax Co. (IATAN has its own field representative inspector.) The object of the inspection is to verify all facts given in the application. The airlines will send their sales representatives to make a report for their own records. Everyone will be on the alert for discrepancies in the applications and whatever is observed on the premises. Until approvals are received, the agent will be on probation and every move he makes will be noted, not only by the sales reps, but also by other travel agents. If the airlines or conferences receive a letter of complaint from another travel agent, they have to investigate even if they know the letter was sent by a chronic complainer or an agent worried about the new competition.

*This checklist is adapted from the ARC, *Industry Agents' Handbook*, Washington, D.C., Sec. 80, Attachment B, April 1991.

Suburbia or Metropolis

There are many widely differing opinions on the subject of the right location for a travel agency. The decision rests on the agent's personality, the business contacts, or following that he may already have, the character of the neighborhood involved, and of course, the operating budget.

Successful agencies can be found in farm towns, college communities, ethnic neighborhoods, industrial areas, apartment house complexes, downtown business districts, shopping malls, department stores, resort areas, medical buildings, and hospital zones. A location in an area that draws the public for commercial or social activity gives the best exposure when the business is new. After agents are established, they may sometimes find that they can do with less exposure and concentrate on repeat and referral business or commercial accounts and can move to a lower-rent district.

Shopping center locations can be very advantageous in terms of the convenience and comfort of the customers, as well as those of the owner and staff of the agency. However, operating costs are usually high, and unless the agency is located centrally, it may be buried in the back where few shoppers will see it. Kay Showker, *Travel Weekly*, surveyed agencies in suburban shopping centers throughout the United States. "Selection of the 'right' center is the key to success. Decisions should be based," she said, "on a careful study of the type of center, presence of quality stores, potential growth of the surrounding area, income range of center patrons and cost."

Although many agents believe that it is usually the woman in a family who buys travel, statistics have shown that generally, men make the final decisions on cost and destination. The majority of men living in the suburbs earn their living in the city, where the companies they work for often have their own traffic department or travel agent. If not, there may be a number of travel agencies or airline ticket offices within walking distance, very convenient for lunch-hour travel arrangements or for picking up brochures to be booked with the local travel agent, but the reverse happens just as often. The wife will bring home the brochures from the neighborhood agent and husbands book it downtown.

Another obstacle the suburban travel agent faces is the belief that some local residents have that the suburban agent is not as experienced or does not have the contacts that a downtown agent has. Suburban agents must work twice as hard to convince the general public of their professional competence. They also face the problem of hiring competent personnel who are willing to relocate in the suburbs. Most younger agents prefer working in the downtown area, where all the "action" is. If agents are fortunate enough to find qualified employees in their neighborhood, they face the problem of evening business hours. Downtown agents observe the same business hours that other businesspeople have, and logically, the shopping center agent will try to observe shopping center hours. It is difficult, however, to find personnel to work evenings. Many agents solve the problem by remaining open evenings by appointment only, but oddly enough, clients do not want to impose on the agent by making him work overtime and prefer an agency that has established evening hours. Evening business hours and availability on Saturdays are almost necessities for suburban agents and can be very profitable, as those are the best times for persons employed full-time and families to come in together and finalize their travel plans.

Other factors to consider in selecting a location: street level or inside; department store tie-in or independent? Department store locations can be very beneficial. You have a built-in market with the department store employees, especially the buyers; customers can use their store credit card to charge their trips; low-cost advertising and promotions by using the store's display and graphic arts facilities and their volume discounts with the newspapers. Identification with the store name is a distinct advantage—especially to a new operation. But selecting the right store is important. A large department store with thousands of customers may not actually be a good selection for a travel agency if the store specializes in low-cost or discount items. However a high-quality store could bring in many affluent travelers that the agent normally would not have reached.

The drawbacks to a department store location, and to some extent the suburban shopping center, are the necessity of observing store hours, customers who are just killing time while waiting for someone else, or weary shoppers who are simply looking for a chance to try out your comfortable chairs. There may also be less room for expansion, and the department store may consider the travel agency as simply another customer service, assigning it space that is not as convenient or visible as the owner would prefer.

An ideal location for a suburban agency would be close to, but not directly involved with, a high-quality shopping center, a street-level location with large window display area, ample parking area, and accessibility to local transportation systems.

Before making a final decision on a location, ask a few questions about the space. Is there room for expansion? Do not start with a location that is just barely adequate for the first year or two. Remember that every time a business moves, it is like starting a new business. Conferences must be notified of the change in location, stationery and business cards changed, and phones transferred (and if the office is computerized there could be weeks and even months before the new service is available). Customers will be lost unless you relocate in the immediate area. Is there adequate room for office equipment, file, and storage areas? Are there enough phone and electrical outlets? What are the building regulations for indoor or outdoor signs? Is there ample space for a window display? And don't neglect the employees' comfort and convenience. Is there at least a small area for a rest room, for coffee breaks or lunch hours? Make a list of the desired objectives and, if necessary, consult an architect or interior decorator for suggestions on the most efficient use of space.

Size and Appearance of the Premises

Standards never have been set concerning the premises or size of the agency, but agents have been refused appointments because the premises were too small. A good rule of thumb would be to provide space for at least two travel consultant's desks with seating space for at least two customers at each desk; a reception area with seating space for several waiting customers; space for at least five filing cabinets and a safe; a storage area for display material, posters, and seldom-used brochures; and if the premises are large enough, space for a private office and a conference room for large groups.

Automation is almost mandatory now unless the new agent plans to specialize in vacation/leisure travel. Commercial accounts have been known to refuse to do business with a travel agency that is not computerized. A suggested procedure would be to start with the minimum required two CRTs (cathode ray tube—the monitor or screen) and one printer. The CRTs could be placed on swivel-topped tables between desks and available for use by more than one person.

Room must be allowed for brochure display racks. An open display of brochures is not only a convenience to the staff and its customers, but is also a good advertisement of the variety of tours, cruises, and so on, that you have to offer. This is also an important check point for sales reps on their inspection reports, as they too see the open display of brochures as a good advertisement for their airline. An inexpensive but impressive method of display is the use of pegboards on one or more walls of the agency with the appropriate metal brackets to hold the brochures. Metal racks or made-to-order wood frames are also attractive and efficient.

The office should be clean, bright, uncluttered, and present a picture of businesslike efficiency on the part of employees and owners. Bookcases, shelves, or special file drawers should be provided for the large quantity of reference books and bulletins the agent uses in her daily work. Some agents will go to extremes and refuse to display travel literature. This, however, goes against the requirement that the premises should be suitably identified as those of a travel agent.

"OTHER" APPOINTMENTS

There are two other conferences important to the full-service travel agency. In June 1984 the Federal Maritime Commission approved the merger of the Pacific Cruise Conference and the International Passenger Ship Association into a single national body under the name of the Cruise Lines International Association (CLIA). CLIA will now include membership to steamship lines with cruise ships of less than 2500 tons carrying fewer than 100 passengers (formerly prohibited). Qualified travel agencies will now automatically represent all CLIA member lines and can display the CLIA emblem. Under the unified CLIA, agents will pay less each year for the new bonding/representation service, but CLIA is planning more benefits and features to agents displaying the CLIA seal. At the same time, the new CLIA agreement does not prohibit cruise lines from paying commissions to others not on the master list of commission-worthy agencies. Even before the merger, CLIA was actively assisting travel agents in promoting cruises and in educating both owner/managers and staff in selling cruises.

Seminars, video training tapes, films, and brochures are available to agents throughout the United States. Cruise sales are becoming a major factor in the profitability of more and more travel agencies, and CLIA is renewing their efforts to expand the cruise revolution.

CLIA developed new rules for affiliate agencies effective July 1, 1991 for new applicants and January 1, 1992 for renewals. Although 90 percent of CLIA's affiliates are full-service agencies that operate at retail locations, 10 percent are cruise-only agencies, and half of the cruise-only group operate office locations from residences. CLIA and the industry associations that worked with CLIA in developing new membership requirements were not objecting to people operating out of their homes; the new requirements are simply a part of the process to better define travel agents, in the interests of professionalism.

CLIA agencies must now prove to be in compliance with federal, state, and local municipal laws with copies of whatever it is that legitimizes the location: a commercial license, a vendor's license, or a zoning certificate. They must also furnish information on the type of ownership, type of agency insurance, whether the agency has a corporate letterhead, whether it has a designated and promoted phone number, type of advertising, number of employees, and a breakdown of business (leisure, corporate, individual, and group).

The National Railroad Passenger Corporation (for some strange reason, known as Amtrak) also requires an application to become an approved agent to sell rail tickets and tours and earn commissions on these tickets. In recent years, however, Amtrak has been advising new applicants to wait until they receive their ARC approval before applying for the Amtrak appointment, which will then be approved automatically.

Amtrak has three tiers of agencies and the commission structure ties in with the three tiers: (1) top-producing agencies, averaging $50,000 annually, qualify for override agreements and deal firsthand with Amtrak sales personnel; (2) agencies that produce $10,000 are served by telemarketing sales representatives; and (3) agencies averaging $1000 in sales are covered by direct mail. Agencies in the third category receive books such as *Amtrak's America Travel Planner* but are not regularly visited by sales reps or called by telemarketers. Overrides are not based solely on past sales. Amtrak will work with agents who are willing to market rail travel aggressively and will provide them with cooperative advertising, seminars, joint promotional events, and additional commission. Not all travel agents are interested in selling rail travel, but having an alternative method of transportation available during airline strikes or winter storms has often paid off. Amtrak is a member of ARC and can be booked and ticketed in the same manner as airlines. Roughly 75 percent of the agents booking Amtrak used their CRTs.

To be appointed as an agent for all of these conferences, a completed application, a current financial statement, fees, bonding, personnel, and security requirements must be met. In recent years both ARC and IATAN have requested an advance payment of a nonrefundable fee before they will mail the applications. (Check the Appendix for current addresses.) The ARC fee includes the cost of a current copy of the ARC *Industry Agents' Handbook*. The handbook contains all the instructions, procedures, rules, and regulations governing operation of an ARC-appointed travel agency as well as the ticketing and sales report rules. Special attention should be paid to Section 80, which deals with the agent reporting agreement. This section contains the qualifications for inclusion and retention on the agency list.

IATAN will also send a copy of their *Ticketing Handbook*, *Travel Agent Handbook*, and an information sheet, "Standards of Endorsement as an International Travel Agent," which contains the details on how to become a part of the network.

Many large, well-established tour operators will not recognize a new travel agent until the agency has received approvals from at least two of the carrier corporations. They will withhold placing the agent on their mailing lists until the agency is established.

The bus transportation companies and the sightseeing bus companies are not as strict in recognizing the new travel agent as are the airline corporations. However, they, too, will make an inspection of the applicant's premises and may ask to have an application completed and sent to their main office. The travel agent then has the option of becoming a *ticket agent* and actually issuing bus tickets in his office, or becoming a *letter agent*, whereby the bus company's ticket office issues the ticket and mails it to the agent with an invoice for payment due, less commission. Unless the travel agency is located in an area far from a bus station, few agents will ask to be ticket agents. The added expense of providing security for ticket stock on the agent's premises is seldom worth the commissions earned.

Car rental companies, hotels, and resorts—both domestic and international—will accept requests for reservations from new agencies provided that they are open for business. Since most of the industry is now computerized, they will ask for the ARC or IATAN identification number (actually, it is the same number for both—a unique worldwide system for identifying specific locations) to be used as a *record locator* (the record consists of the travel agency name, address, and phone number, which will be displayed when the ARC or IATAN ID number is entered in the computer). Obviously, if the agency has not yet been assigned a number by ARC/IATAN, they will not have an ID number; therefore, each principal will assign a temporary number to the applicant until they have received the ID number from either ARC or IATAN.

STATE LICENSING

A growing number of states in the United States are considering the licensing of travel agents. The main objective in licensing is to weed out the "fly-by-nights" who advertise travel and use a post office box number for an address or a telephone answering service as their office. It is incredible how naive the public can be at times. They will send payment for a charter, tour, or cruise without knowing if the operator is a legitimate travel agent. The operator collects the money and leaves town, or worse, will pay the airline for one-way passage only, leaving the passengers stranded at their destination. Ironically, the media will blame the travel agent. They, too, do not bother to find out if the seller was a bona fide travel agent.

Most travel agents would prefer a form of accreditation or licensing if this could come from a professional association of travel agents rather than through any kind of accreditation by federal or state government. A lack of professional standards and requirements damages consumer confidence. The CTC (certified travel counselor) program, through the Institute of Certified Agents (ICTA), is a good program, but neither the CTC program nor membership in ASTA (American Society of Travel Agents) or ARTA (Association of Retail Travel Agents) have the recognition they deserve. If these three groups could get together and establish accreditation procedures and develop professional standards for all travel agents, they would also strengthen the agent's ability to lobby the government for more policies that would benefit all travel agents.

California, Florida, Hawaii, Iowa, Maine, Massachusetts, New Jersey, New York, and Ohio are among the states that have passed legislation or are in the process of licensing travel agents. Some states are considering testing agents (the question is: who would make up the exam and administer it?); others require only the registration of the travel agent after they receive the ARC appointment. Some states are also regulating deposits and refunds; others are only interested in ensuring that all travel sellers are registered.

Ohio's registration law became effective in 1977 and was amended in 1979 to include the requirement that travel agents and tour promoters include their registration number in all advertising and other solicitation materials. As a result of this change, the Ohio newspapers refused to accept advertising from retail firms without registration numbers, forcing travel agents to register. Other states are copying this rule. Only wholesalers that sell through retail agents are exempt. Another amendment in the Ohio bill affects travel firms that do not hold ARC or IATAN appointments or an ICC (Interstate Commerce Commission) bus broker's license. Such nonapproved firms are required to post a $50,000 bond or provide a financial guarantee in the same amount.

"WILLINGNESS, ABILITY, AND ACTIVITY IN PROMOTING AND SELLING TRAVEL"

The heading above represents what was once a major requirement of the airline conferences in granting approval to an applicant. It is no longer an official requirement, but unofficially, the airlines will look more favorably on an agent who is actively promoting and selling travel than one who is content to sit back and wait for business to walk in. The travel industry is always ready and willing to support the promotional efforts of the travel agent by furnishing brochures, posters, window display material, and sales representatives who are available to speak to groups at private meetings or at film shows open to the public.

PROPRIETORSHIP, PARTNERSHIP, OR CORPORATION?

Your accountant and lawyer can best advise you whether to start as a proprietorship, partnership, or corporation. Above all else, do not start a business without professional assistance with the numerous legal routines that must be followed in today's business world or without the installation of an efficient and easily maintained bookkeeping system.

Both an accountant and an attorney are important in the formation of the travel agency. The financial statements required by ARC and IATAN and the bond applications must be prepared by a professional accountant. The statement must show the minimum required in working capital and net worth.

Some accountants do not take these requirements seriously and consequently, cause their agent clients unnecessary delays and expense in obtaining credentials. Two of the travel agencies I was personally connected with were refused approval by IATA because of inadequate finances. After studying the financial statements, it was discovered that one accountant had listed a long-term liability as a current liability, which naturally threw the current cash flow in the red instead of the black. A second accountant listed the owner's investment in the business as a loan to the corporation instead of showing it as paid-in surplus which made the net worth of the agency consist only of token shares of stock issued to start the corporation.

Since the travel agency must be open for business at the time the applications are submitted, an attorney is important to assist owners in deciding on the type of organization and in drawing up employment contracts, checking the lease, and filing the necessary forms with the state and federal governments.

Many factors can determine the selection of the form of organization. A mom-and-pop travel agency may not find the corporate form of organization suitable to its financial needs, while a company composed of several unrelated owners may find that a corporation best suits its needs. The following brief descriptions may assist you in deciding which form of organization is best.

Liability of Owners for Business Debts

Both sole proprietors and partners are fully and personally liable for business debts of their companies. In contrast, a corporation has a legal existence separate from its owners and has *limited liability*. However, the owner/manager of a small corporation is likely to find that limited liability is more characteristic of textbooks than of real life. Creditors may ask the stockholders to sign as personal guarantors, accepting the same liability as if they were operating as sole proprietors. Limited liability is based on the amount of capital invested in the corporation, so a family-owned corporation could be held liable for all its debts.

Transferability of Ownership

Sole proprietors have the most flexibility, but if they wish to sell their interest, they may have to search long and hard to find a buyer. If they want to sell only part of their equity, they must seek a suitable partner. Partners cannot transfer their interest to another partner. The remaining partners in the business have a right to choose who they want and need not accept any buyer. The stockholder of a corporation does not need the approval of other owners to sell his or her share unless the stockholders have a written agreement to offer their stock to the other stockholders first. If no such agreement exists, there is the danger that shares of stock may suddenly be sold to incompatible strangers. Another danger the majority stockholder should be aware of is that if too many shares are sold to others, the majority stockholder could become a minority stockholder and lose control of the business.

Tax Advantages

There may be some tax advantage to starting a new business as a proprietorship and then incorporating at a later date. Many accountants and lawyers recommend starting a corporation and notifying IRS (Internal Revenue Service) that the corporation wishes to apply as a *Subchapter S corporation* for tax purposes, provided that this is a domestic corporation and there are 35 or fewer stockholders who are all U.S. citizens. Under subchapter S, a corporation's losses can be applied proportionally against the stockholders' personal income.

It is more expensive to form a corporation than a sole proprietorship or partnership, but an experienced corporation lawyer can save thousands of dollars for the owners. Don't skimp on lawyer or accountant fees. It saves time and money in the long run.

The decision on which type of ownership you want should be made as early as possible. It is best to avoid subsequent changes in legal status. Any changes in legal or beneficial ownership or in corporate status (except in minor changes in ownership that do not result, singly or cumulatively, in a substantial transfer of stock, 30 percent or more, or result in transfer of controlling interest to a person in whom such controlling interest was not previously vested) must be reported to all the conferences 30 days in advance and may require new applications, bond, and appropriate fee as may be requested.

Control

Sole proprietors (commonly known as mom-and-pop agencies) or partners can be sure that they will retain control or at least partial control of a business. Partners can force an end to partnerships rather than share control with someone they do not like or trust. In contrast, a corporation continues even though stock ownership may change, and control is usually held by the majority stockholder, although a chairman and board of directors may actually manage the company.

Corporations are also subject to more external control, restrictions, and report requirements from government agencies than are proprietorships and partnerships. However, corporations are more manageable than partnerships or sole proprietorships in connection with estate planning and probate. If one of the principals in a partnership or proprietorship dies, the airline corporations require an immediate change of ownership application to be completed; if a stockholder (with 30 percent or less ownership) dies or sells out, the business continues as usual.

Maneuverability

How quickly can the business organization respond to changes in its environment or to internal needs? The sole proprietor needs to consult no one. Partners, on the other hand, may need to consult other partners, while corporate officers may need to obtain approval from their directors, possibly even their stockholders. It may be necessary to amend bylaws before action can be taken. Of course, the speed of decision depends partly on the side of the organization, but the form of organization also establishes certain rules and regulations that affect the maneuverability of management.

ELIGIBILITY FOR COMMISSIONS

Now that you are open for business and have sent in all of your applications, you will enter into that nerve-wracking waiting period that all new agents have to go through. Upon receipt of the application, ARC will notify all members and will order an investigation (now handled by an outside investigative firm) to verify the statements in that application and determine whether there is any reason to believe that the applicant does not meet the requirements for inclusion on the agency list. Upon completion of such investigation, but never sooner than 30 days or more than 90 days after receipt, and if the investigation shows that you meet all requirements, ARC shall enter into a sales agency agreement with you and will place your name on the agency list. All members are notified of the date on which the agreement is completed.

In the event that the application is disapproved and applicants disagree with the decision, they have the right to a request for review by the travel agent arbiter (rules and procedures are provided in Section 100 of the ARC Handbook). Within 15 days after the applicants' receipt of notice of disapproval from ARC, applicants shall notify ARC and the arbiter by certified or registered mail of their request for review. If the arbiter's review also goes against them, they have the right to seek judicial relief. However, this can be an expensive, long-drawn-out proceeding and would not be worthwhile unless applicants have some very convincing evidence to substantiate their request.

IATAN's procedures are quite similar to ATC's. Upon receipt of a completed application form for endorsement by the network and appointment as an agent by subscribing airlines, the information is verified by an IATAN field representative. The verification process determines whether or not an agency meets IATAN's endorsement standards of staff and managerial experience, financial stability and integrity, security precautions, and the like. The procedure includes a financial review and an inspection of the applicant's premises.

When an applicant agency is informed that it does not qualify as an IATAN-endorsed agent, it is advised at the same time that it may apply to the IATAN commissioner within 30 days for a review of the network's findings. Similarly, an agency whose endorsement has been withdrawn is allowed 30 days to apply to the commissioner for an evaluation review.

When an applicant or agency requests such a review, it is sent a consent agreement in which IATAN agrees to be bound by the commissioner's decision. It also receives a form of notice to be filed with the commissioner to initiate proceedings, along with a copy of the rules for appeal.

As soon as the new agent is advised of the approvals, the owner and/or manager can start claiming their retroactive commissions from the individual carriers on their airline sales. Whether or not an agency receives retroactive commissions (that is, commissions on air sales between the time their application is acknowledged and the time they are actually approved) depends on the individual airlines. The airline corporations notify all of their members when the applications are received; and if the sales representatives feel that their airline will want to do business with the agent (even though an applicant is approved by ARC and IATAN the individual airlines still have the right to refuse to do business with an agent), they will arrange to have air transportation exchange orders (envelope type) issued to the applicant.

This is a standard industry form, designed primarily for verification of sales made while the application is pending approval. The exchange order may only be

Figure 3-3 Air Canada—Boeing 767.

used on sales made on the carrier that issued the form; in no event may the exchange order of one carrier be drawn on another carrier. After the airline reservation is made, the form is completed, check is enclosed, and the copy of the exchange order is kept by the travel agent. The exchange order can be given to the passenger to present to the airport ticket agent and receive the ticket, but most agents will go and pick up the ticket and then give it to their customers rather than cause them delays or problems.

Copies of the exchange orders are needed when claiming commission on these sales. If the individual carriers do not use the exchange orders, they will ask the agent to keep a record of sales listing ticket numbers, amount, destination, name of passenger, and amount of commission due. If exchange orders have been issued, the carriers are committed to paying the retroactive commission even if the corporations eventually disapprove the applications.

BUILDING THE BUSINESS

The first concern in starting a travel agency, or any type of business, is establishing personal relationships with all community centers: chambers of commerce, social clubs, senior citizens' organizations, banks, hotels, churches, synagogues, bars, neighboring businesses, local theater groups, musical groups, and book discussion groups. A new enterprise cannot afford to just open the door and wait for customers to walk in. Owners and/or managers must go out and introduce themselves and let people know they are open for business. They should include the names of all local clubs and organizations on their mailing list, send personal letters to the presidents and/or the program committee chairpersons, and offer their services for film shows or lectures on travel. Films or videos of all parts of the world can be obtained free of charge from the airlines or local film libraries.

Audiovisual shows on the agency's own premises, if it is large enough to accommodate at least 50 people, or in a nearby hotel, church, or bank conference rooms, are good ice-breakers. Keep the show in the office or as close by as possible and encourage people to come in and browse around. Serve refreshments, but keep them simple. Elaborate buffets may discourage people who do not want to impose on the agent's hospitality or who may feel that in accepting the agent's generosity they are obligated to make their travel arrangements with him or her. Never make a sales pitch at these shows unless requested. The soft sell is best in selling travel. Use the film shows simply as a means of introduction, but let the audience know that you are available for consultations on their travel questions.

Invite sales representatives from the airlines that service the area your film is promoting. Allow them to pass out literature from their airline, but tell them also to soft-pedal the sales talks. Have a drawing for door prizes after the show (the entry blanks will serve the double purpose of furnishing a head count of the audience and can add to your mailing list). Ask the carriers to donate flight bags or other give-a-ways for the drawing or purchase inexpensive novelties. On several occasions, when nothing else was available, pineapples, coconuts, and oranges were appreciated by the audience.

Every agent should join their local chamber of commerce. Members of the organization are more than willing to help a new agent get established in the community. They will refer clients to you and give you leads on promotional activities in your area. You can reciprocate by keeping on hand a supply of general information brochures and maps of your city and state to give to out-of-state visitors.

Invest in every form of advertising media available. Small ads that appear every week will pay off much more than one large ad that may appear only once a month. Advertising results cannot be measured immediately—the effect is cumulative. Repetition builds up the response from each succeeding advertisement. Giveaways such as pencils, pens, scratch pads, luggage tags, rain bonnets, or other novelties will also help spread the word. New agents must face the fact that they must sell themselves and their businesses day and night until their efforts begin to pay off.

CHECKLIST OF PROCEDURES FOR OPENING A TRAVEL AGENCY

1. Find the right location.

2. Decide on the name and the form of organization you will use and have your lawyer prepare the necessary papers. Make sure that the word *travel* appears in the firm's name or that it somehow informs the public that this is a travel agency. The name selected should be double checked to make sure that it does not resemble that of an airline or an existing agency in your state (or province).

3. Have a CPA prepare the financial statement on the official forms requested by ARC and IATAN, as well as several copies of the CPA's own form. You will need the extra copies to include with your applications for the other organizations and the ARC bond application.

4. Have your accountant apply for the federal employer identification number (this is a requirement on applications), and notify other government tax offices. Have the accountant set up the bookkeeping system and make sure that a method of recording all airline sales, whether or not they are commissionable, is started and maintained from the first day of business. Copies of this record will be needed to request retroactive commissions and can be used as proof of productivity, if necessary.

5. Open a checking account and a savings account in the name of the travel agency. Order a supply of checks. Voucher checks with two copies are recommended. They are a little more expensive, but the time and labor saved just from eliminating accompanying letters are worth the additional expense. Also, the extra copies are necessary documents for your customer's file and the bookkeeping file.

6. Order phones and apply for listings in the Yellow Pages. Order the full number of phones and lines you will eventually need in the office. The monthly charges for additional phones and lines, even over a year's time, will not be as high as the installation charges if you discover that more are needed later. Two lines with pushbuttons, a hold feature, and lights are the minimum number recommended. You can, of course, buy your own phones, but check all options before making a decision. In some areas, leasing may be less expensive than buying.

7. Order stationery, envelopes, business cards, invoices (four-part), speedy memos, and announcement cards or letters. Here also, it is more economical to order more than you think you will need rather than incurring delays and additional charges by reordering later.

8. Order a permanent sign for window or outdoor use if applicable. This also is one of the "must haves" on the IATAN/ARC endorsement checklist. If your agency is in an office building, make sure that your name is included in the building's directory as well as being placed on the door.

9. If you have not already done so, send for applications from ARC and IATAN. ARC now has a computerized application kit, but a printed copy must still accompany the diskette.

10. Apply for the ARC bond in the minimum amount required. This is a requirement; ARC approval depends on it.

11. Request letters from former employers or business associates, certifying to the previous work experience of the individual(s) being relied on to meet the experience requirements.

12. Have a photographer take several photos of both the interior and exterior of the agency—the exterior shot should show the entrance to the office. Snapshots are acceptable, but have enough copies made to send one set with each application.

13. Send for subscriptions to the *Official Airline Guides*, *Steamship Guides*, *Travel Planners*, and other reference books and travel trade publications listed in the Appendix. There are three major travel trade newspapers and magazines and it is worthwhile to subscribe to all three, *Travel Trade*, *Travel Weekly* and *Travel Agent*. The cost is nominal, and even though there may be repetitions of the news items, each of these publications has good feature writers and supplemental editions of sales guides which are invaluable. Allow at least four weeks for delivery of the first copy of each.

14. Order desks, chairs, file cabinets, brochure display racks (another "must" on the inspection report), and other office equipment. At least one typewriter with a 13- or 14-inch carriage and an adding machine or calculator (with tape) that shows a credit balance is essential. A copying machine, postage meter, and checkwriter are useful but not absolutely essential for a small office during the first year.

15. Order insurance and employee bonds. Most insurance companies now offer a package to businesses that covers all the essentials. Check on extra expense coverage rather than business interruption insurance. Extra expense is more practical for a service business that might operate from other locations if the building is destroyed by fire or natural causes.

16. Send a combined letter of announcement and request for brochures and current rate sheets to all airlines, steamship lines, bus lines, car rental companies, tour operators, hotel representatives, hotel chains, major individual hotels and resorts, and tourist boards. Use the *Travel Industry Personnel Directory* published annually by Fairchild. This mailing can be done most inexpensively by using preprinted postal cards or a form letter.

Figure 3-4 Reprinted by special permission from California Parlor Car Tours. (All rights reserved.)

Chap. 3 / Rules/Regulations Governing Travel Agencies

17. Prepare a customer mailing list and send an announcement letter or card to prospective clients. Mailing lists can be purchased or borrowed from churches, businesses, or social clubs or purchased from companies that specialize in preparing selected mailing lists. *Suggestion*: Include a return-addressed, postage-paid card (business reply card) asking the prospects if they would like to be included in a permanent mailing list and whether they need any travel information at the present time. This requires the purchase of a business reply permit from your local post office. The cost is small and postage is not paid until the card is returned to your office.

18. Send news items about your opening to all local news media and to all the travel trade publications. The trade papers are interested only in the basics—who, what, where, when; but try to find an interesting angle to attract the local papers. Send black-and-white photos of the agency, the principals, and of the open-house party or drawing (if you have one).

19. Open-house parties: one for the general public, one strictly for travel industry personnel. Invite the district sales managers and sales representatives of all the airlines that use your local airport as well as the representatives of the international carriers that you feel you will be using in the future, whether or not they have a local office. Do not omit the steamship lines, tour operators, car rental companies, bus lines, and hotel chains. They all have sales representatives who make personal calls on travel agents. If they are invited several weeks in advance, they will try to schedule their sales calls to attend your open house. Do not worry about being overcrowded. The majority of invited guests will probably send their regrets. People in the travel industry do a lot of traveling themselves, so they may not be able to attend but will be pleased that they were invited. Many agents prefer to wait until they get their approvals before they have an open house, but the sooner a new agent gets to know the people he or she will be working with, the better for business.

   Most important, address the invitations to the district sales manager of each office. This will give them the opportunity to make an informal inspection of your premises. Have the party during the day. You will get a better response as the sales representatives will then come in on company time instead of on their own time. Keep it simple: wine and cheese or a coffee klatsch with a variety of pastries.

   There are a number of good ideas that could be used for the open house for the general public. A drawing for free prizes is one of the best, as this will not only bring people in to sign up for the drawing but will also provide you with additional names for your mailing list. Prizes can range from flight bags donated by the carriers to a free weekend donated by a resort. (Newly opened hotels or resorts are the best prospects to solicit free-weekend prizes.) Both the carriers and the hotels are glad to cooperate with such promotions if they are assured that they will be included in the publicity and advertising.

BRANCH OFFICES

After an agency has been approved and is prospering, the owners may decide to expand by opening a branch, or perhaps they have several large commercial accounts on the other side of town or in an area that has a good potential for future sales and could be better serviced with an office in that vicinity. Owners have also opened branches in order to keep good employees they are unable to promote to higher positions in the main office. Whatever the reason, owners should carefully investigate the branch location and be prepared to spend almost as much in establishing the branch as they did in opening the main office.

It may not take as long to make a profit at the branch because it will have the advantage of trading on the main office's reputation and advertising. It will be able to obtain the airline tickets, at full commission, from the main office while waiting for the approval for the branch. Branches must be wholly owned by the main (or home) office. ARC will not approve a branch unless the home office has full financial and legal responsibility for the administration, staff, liability, maintenance, and operational costs of the branch location.

The same procedures used to open the home office are used for a branch office, with these exceptions: No new sales agency agreement is required. The agreement signed for the home office covers all branches. No separate bond has to be posted for the ARC at this time. The amount of the existing bond would be computed on the basis of the volume of business in both the home and branch locations and increased accordingly. IATAN requires that the working capital shown on the home office financial statement be increased by a minimum of $5000 for each branch. The other procedures remain the same:

1. The standard applicant questionnaire, properly completed and signed by the owner, officer, or other authorized official.
2. Interior and exterior photographs.
3. A current financial statement of the home office.
4. A check for the fees requested for a branch office.
5. Letters from former employers or business associates confirming the employment experience of the branch manager.

After the applications for a branch office are submitted, the airline corporations will advise of the approval or rejection within 90 days.

In-Plant Branch Locations/Customer-Premises Location

Many large corporations have departments within their companies that make all the travel arrangements for their executives' and salespersons' business travel. Such a department is usually referred to as an in-house travel department. The in-house travel department does not receive commissions on airline tickets issued at the corporate location but does receive liberal credit from the airlines. They are usually billed every 30 days. Most of these companies are automated and the airline that furnishes the automation and/or the ticket stock does the billing.

In-plants, now classified by ARC as customer-premises locations, are actual branches of appointed agents who open offices on the premises of their customers so that they can service these accounts more easily and efficiently. The customer-premises location earns 3 percent commission and is usually staffed by the customer. Until 1979, when CAB's decision to permit reimbursement of corporate salaries by the in-plant operator went into effect, there were few in-plants in the United States. This decision opened the door to make the in-plant a financial advantage to the customer. It has the convenience of tickets issued on the premises and the ease of maintaining travel cost control.

Despite the low commissions, customer-premises locations benefited travel agents by guaranteeing them exclusive business with a company whose travel budget might run into the millions. Additional income is earned from hotel and car rental reservations, employee vacation travel, and arranging sales conventions, meetings, and sales incentive programs for the customer. The number of in-plants approved by ATC peaked at 600 in 1983. Since then, many in-plants converted to full-service agencies or discontinued when ARC approved the STPs (satellite ticket printers) in 1985. The number of satellite ticket printer locations grew by 49.2 percent during 1990, and they now represent 15.6 percent of all U.S. travel agency locations.

The in-house travel departments have their own association, the National Passenger Traffic Association (NPTA), which has been lobbying for a number of years to force airlines to pay them commissions. However, the airlines had been adamant in their refusal (they felt that in-house travel departments were customers and not distributors) and even threatened to discontinue the 3 percent commission paid to in-plant locations. For this reason a large number of in-plants converted to fully appointed branches. The big stumbling block to conversion is the rule that full-service branches must be available to the public without forcing customers to go through any security measures other than a check-in at the entrance. It must occupy a separate premise identified as a travel agency by a sign on the door. It must prove to ARC that its operation is now changed to one serving the travel needs of the general public. Location must now have experienced personnel required for full-service branches and must comply with the security requirements for the ticket stock and the financial requirements (bond or letter of credit).

As a full-service agency or branch, these offices would qualify for the full amount of airline commissions. Although to satisfy the U.S. Justice Department, ARC has removed the percentage limits on self-sales (tickets sold to the agency or financially related entities), the major carriers will continue to observe the former ATC standards, which barred an agency from doing 20 percent or more of annual business with an entity that has a financial interest in the agency.

However, with the new ARC accreditation rules, the corporate accounts can now apply for a *restricted access location* as a home office as well as a branch office of an established agency. Commission payments would remain at 3 percent unless a higher percentage is negotiated with the individual airlines.

The location need not be open to the public and, at present, does not need a managerial qualifier but must have a ticketing qualifier (an employee who has a minimum of one year's experience in airline ticketing), who can be an employee of either the travel agency (if it operates as a branch) or host corporation. (ATC had no personnel requirements.)

BUYING AN EXISTING AGENCY

Buying an existing agency does not eliminate any of the aforementioned steps in starting a new business. The established owner must give all the trade organizations a minimum advance notice of 30 days that he is selling his business and request the change-of-ownership application. The application consists of a questionnaire very similar to the new agency application, but it also requires an inventory of all accountable ticket stock and airline validation plates, a new ARC bond or a notice that the present bond has been reassigned to the new owners, a current financial statement, and personal history forms completed by each owner, officer, director, and manager for the new ownership.

The biggest advantage of buying an existing agency is that business can go on as usual; sales can be made and commissions collected on these sales while waiting for the approval of the change of ownership. There also are the advantages of acquiring an experienced staff, established clientele, and having travel literature and reference books on hand for immediate use. This is supposing, of course, that the seller has an up-to-date, profitable agency for sale.

The disadvantages can, however, often outweigh the advantages. The financial requirements and the personnel experience requirements are adhered to strictly by ARC and IATAN when considering the request for change of ownership. Buyers must make sure they can comply with these requirements before they complete the purchase. They should also have their accountants check the books and contact all the suppliers to make sure that there are no outstanding debts against the existing ownership or have an indemnification clause added to the purchase agreement from the seller to the buyer, protecting the new owner against debts that may surface later. Further, a buyer should spot check the customer files to determine if they are active accounts or whether the business had deteriorated due to poor service. It may prove more difficult to overcome a bad reputation than to start a completely new agency.

If the new owners are contemplating a change of name and/or a change of location, this is all best done at the same time as the change of ownership. Regulations require a 30-day advance notice for every change.

To protect both the buyer and seller as well as the industry suppliers, a contract should be drawn up setting out in detail the terms and conditions of sale. A deposit should be paid to the seller when the sales agreement is signed, possibly a non-refundable deposit, and the remainder of funds placed in escrow with the understanding that these funds will be disbursed when the buyer receives the ARC and IATAN endorsement of the transfer of ownership.

There should be a written inventory of all the assets of the agency, signed by both parties, and attached to the contract of sale so that there can be no misunderstanding as to exactly what is included in the sale. The inventory should include stationery and other imprinted office supplies unless the buyer is planning on changing the name and/or the location of the business. It might also be worth while to include prepaid expenses such as insurance, subscriptions, and deposits. Most important, the airline ticket stock inventory should be verified by both parties at the time the sales agreement is signed and again when the change of ownership is approved by ARC and IATAN.

The seller should request the buyer's guarantee, in writing, that the buyer will not use information received on the seller's financial statements, customer lists, or other data that the buyer has seen during negotiations in the event the sale is not completed. A buyer should request signed statements from the seller that there are no pending, threatened, or current legal matters or ARC or IATAN proceedings against the sellers or their agencies.

Purchase agreements should include decisions on the collection of customer accounts receivable and refunds or adjustments due to the agencies from trade principals. Should buyers agree to buy these receivables or collect the monies and forward them to the seller? Commissions earned on confirmed air reservations or tour or cruise bookings may pose problems as to how they should be divided unless provisions for them are included in purchase agreements. Generally, if the booking is approximately half or three-fourths completed with some monies received from the customer, the commissions should go to the seller; if reservations only have been made, the seller should get a percentage of the earnings as negotiated with the buyer.

Purchase agreements should also stipulate dates when buyers could have access to the premises before the conclusion of the sale and written assurances from buyers that the overhead expenses, such as rent, salaries, insurance, and phone bills, would be prorated from that date and the close of escrow. The purchase agreement should also cover the distribution of commissions earned from sales brought in by the buyer, completely independent of the seller's normal business or promotional efforts during the interim.

Agency sellers are advised to check the prospective buyer thoroughly. Don't give up possession or control of your travel agency unless, and until, all details have been worked out and agreed to in writing and until the buyer has received agreement for the change of ownership from ARC and IATAN. Remember, the seller is held legally responsible for the agency and the ticket stock until the change of ownership is approved.

Noncompete pacts in the purchase agreement are becoming more common. The most aggravating problem for new owners is sellers who leave and compete against them, often taking away important clients. Most court decisions in cases involving noncompete agreements say that no one has the legal right to force someone not to work, but buyers of travel agencies have the legal right to say that sellers cannot compete in the same vicinity. The agreement must, however, be limited to a relatively small area—perhaps the city limits in a small town or 2-mile limit in a larger city. It must also have a time limit, perhaps six months to two years. It cannot permanently keep someone out of the market.

Determining Market Value

There is no set formula for determining the market value of a travel agency. As with other business sales, the location, personnel, volume of previous business, and potential for new business must be among the prime considerations. However, when purchasing a retail travel agency, the number of industry appointments held by the agency is often the deciding factor. If the agency holds the ARC, IATAN, and CLIA endorsements, they can easily be changed, and if the buyer desires, they can be moved to another location and the name can be changed. The advantage of buying appointments is that the business continues while the changes are made and saves the buyer a minimum of $25,000 in start-up costs. Most newcomers in the field prefer to buy a going business rather than start from scratch.

Establishing the true value of a travel agency can be very difficult. Quite often it may just boil down to how much the seller wants and how much the buyer is willing to pay. The average agency owner is apt to want too much money, often because he has the wrong concept of valuation. Sometimes it is because the agent paid far too much for the agency when it was purchased. Since a travel agency is a service business, the value depends on the volume of business generated during the past two or three years—whether it has been increasing steadily—the quality of its staff—whether the key personnel will remain—and the potential for further growth. A good mix of vacation/leisure travel, group/commercial business may be more advantageous than an office that specializes in only one area.

An examination of the profit-and-loss statements will not always give a true picture. For tax reasons, most small agency owners prefer not to show a large profit. It would be better to check the gross commissions earned (airline commissions can be checked easily by examining the previous year's computer printouts for the weekly airline reports to ARC), other commissions would show up in the check disbursement records. If there has not been a dramatic shift in earnings during the past two or three years, the value can be determined by taking between 70 to 130 percent of the annual gross commissions, depending on the location, staff, and growth potential. Another method often used is to take a percentage of the previous year's sales—between 6 and 10 percent, depending on whether the agency has been operating in the red or showing a profit.

There is no denying that retail agencies are worth more today than they have been in the past. Their share of airline ticket sales alone has been increasing steadily and more and more vacation travelers prefer to turn their travel plans over to the professionals. Since a travel agency is a service business, the responsibility of maintaining and increasing business will continue to depend on the quality of service provided by the owners and staff. A travel agency is no better than the people working in it.

FRANCHISES

The only thing I can say about franchises is: DON'T. Don't waste your time or money. Franchise operators are charging between $10,000 and $45,000 just to help you find a location and hire a manager. The franchisee will still have to conform to ARC bonding rules and the IATAN endorsement standards. Unfortunately, their slick presentations appeal to experienced business people who mistakenly believe that travel can be sold like hamburgers or buckets of chicken. Standard uniforms and stationery may be very attractive, but a good artist could do the same for you at less cost. Franchisers not only collect a fee up front, but also take a percentage of sales each month plus a fee for advertising that seldom materializes. They promote the idea that their franchisees can sell specific tours that pay more commissions, but neglect to say that any agency can do that by joining co-ops and consortiums that do the same thing at a much lower fee.

CO-OPS AND CONSORTIUMS

To join or not to join—that is the question most frequently asked since deregulation. The increasing economic pressures caused by low commission earnings on discounted air fares, competition from new agencies, and competition from agencies that do belong to consortiums or co-ops are reasons given for considering the question of joining.

The pros and cons are debated by all, from the small agencies to the mega-agencies. There is no denying that there are advantages in a membership, but the agent should check carefully to determine if the expenses are worth the advantages. Initial consortium membership fees run from $100 to several thousands of dollars. Some require stock purchases and service fees in addition to the annual fees.

The cooperatives/consortiums' original aim was to negotiate with travel suppliers toward a sliding commission scale that would put members in a higher bracket than they could have reached on their own. They started with tour operators and then branched out to include hotels, car rental companies, cruise lines, and airlines. In return for an agency consortium agreeing to give sales/marketing support to a particular supplier—in preference to competitors—the *preferred supplier* is expected to offer commission overrides based on volume as well as other marketing benefits.

The preferred supplier relationship can be beneficial to both the supplier and the agent. The suppliers realize that higher commissions are a small price to pay if they can achieve a substantial increase in the marketing/sales efforts of their products. Agencies can become more profitable, but only if the consortium's list of suppliers includes those they would normally use. A large override on a product that the agency does not sell will not do it much good.

The secret to success lies in an agency's ability to select the consortium with the preferred supplier list that fits its type of operation and can easily provide them with total marketing/sales support. There are a number of other questions that agents should ask before joining a consortium.

Have the leaders had practical experience in the operation of a retail travel agency? Does the consortium have local paid representatives in a regional office to serve my area? Are new suppliers being added, or is the supplier list declining? What size are the member agencies, and would my agency share common interests? (The flow of information between agencies is an important part of belonging to a consortium.) What kinds of services offered are also a big factor, especially if an agency's clients need those services, such as an 800 emergency number or a negotiated rate program for hotels.

For the preferred supplier relationship to succeed, the owner/manager will have to consider a monetary and/or other incentives to employees in return for directing clients to the agency's preferred list. This is usually done by offering the employees a share of the override or a flat dollar amount per sale or offering a variety of travel prizes for the top-producing employees who reach or exceed the quotas.

A list of co-ops and consortiums is provided in the Appendix.

QUESTIONS AND PROBLEMS

1. Name some of the rules and regulations that affect the travel agency.
2. When did deregulation begin?
3. How did deregulation affect the airline passenger?
4. What is cabotage?
5. What are the requirements for obtaining an ARC bond, and what is the purpose of the bond?
6. What is ABSP, and how does it affect the travel agency?
7. What are the duties of the travel agent arbiter (TAA)?
8. List the entities that fall under the ARC jurisdiction.
9. What is IATAN? What are their financial requirements?
10. What is the very first step in starting a travel agency?
11. What are the qualifications ARC requires for an applicant?
12. What are the personnel experience requirements?
13. What are the advantages of a suburban location?
14. When are the travel agents eligible for commissions? Can they earn any income before they receive their airline appointments?
15. Name the other endorsements important to the travel agent.
16. Choose the type of organization you would have in a travel agency—proprietorship, partnership, or corporation and give your reasons for that choice.
17. How would you introduce a new business to the community?
18. When would you advise opening a branch office?
19. How would you determine the market value of an agency?
20. Would you join a co-op or consortium? Why?

chapter 4

The Travel
Agency Manager

OBJECTIVES

When you have finished this chapter you should be able to:

1. Describe the abilities needed for a travel agency manager.
2. Compare problems encountered in a travel agency with those in other types of businesses.
3. Understand the importance of advance scheduling and planning in the travel agency.
4. Prepare a compensation program to motivate employees.
5. Discuss the feasibility of "flexible" office hours or employees working at home.

INTRODUCTION

Just as the manager in any other business enterprise, the travel agency manager should be concerned first and foremost with perpetuation of the business through ensuring a reasonable profit from sales and maintaining an efficient operation at a low cost to the owners. The human element is the key to maximum effectiveness in management. The very term *management* implies the skillful leading and handling of personnel. In this respect, management must be seen as including job skill, job management, and people management.

Good management requires continuous executive interest, participation, and encouragement at all levels, from the owner of the business to the immediate supervisor. Management throughout the organization tends to reflect the people at the top. For this reason, the manager must personally understand the essentials of good management and must apply them skillfully. He or she must set the example for the others to follow. While a particular manager may be highly effective as a travel salesperson, subordinates may leave much to be desired. The manager must then provide the leadership and the opportunities for constant improvement. To do so may take time away from direct attention to sales, but experience has shown that this is time well spent.

THE MANAGER'S RESPONSIBILITY

The job of manager involves the making of decisions on a wide variety of problems and the assumption of a multitude of responsibilities. Managers are responsible for the selection, instruction, and guidance of subordinates; for developing efficient teamwork; and for assuring effective communication and control within an agency. They must always have the vision to foresee and meet changing conditions. They must develop a keen sense of proper timing. They are also responsible for building and strengthening the morale of an organization.

The manager of a travel agency is often the top salesperson of the office. While superior performance should be recognized and rewarded, and while the manager should be the best informed person in the office, it is a well-known fact that good salespeople seldom make good managers or administrators. Although working experience in a travel agency is a very necessary requirement, the manager also needs business training in management and administration. Quite often the difference between a profitable business and one that is barely covering expenses is the quality of management skills.

The SARC (Systems Analysis Research Corporation) report to the travel industry can be used as a good definition of the manager's duties:

All travel agents have three roles. Primary is the role of serving the travel needs of the public; next comes the role of representing the principals; *the third role is as a businessperson with the necessity to remain in business* [italics added].

Travel agents should be in business to make a living and a reasonable profit regardless of any travel privileges and other fringe benefits which may be available. They must perform all the normal functions of a business; issuing tickets and vouchers, making reservations, providing personnel and counter space for the public, keeping accounts and records, making credit available, paying the rent, hiring and paying personnel, taxes and all the rest.

One historical function of travel agents, shared with most businesses but few of the professions, is advertising and promotion. Doctors, lawyers, and other professions are usually prohibited from direct advertising and promotion. Travel agents, however, promote both in the interests of informing the public and representing their principals, and do so through direct mail, advertising in newspapers, TV, radio, magazines, the Yellow Pages, outside solicitation, lectures and films to groups, telephone contacts, and all other means.

Thus the travel agency manager bears a heavy responsibility not only to the public, the principals, and the employer, but also to the employees, who will depend on good leadership and guidance. Monitoring and motivating employees are key responsibilities.

ABILITIES NEEDED FOR MANAGEMENT

The manager's duties call for many well-developed abilities. Of the greatest importance is an ability to *understand people*—to size them up, to judge their abilities and character, to sense their real motives—and to motivate them to the desired goals (it may be the goal of bringing in more business from the public, or bringing out the greatest potential of service from the employees). Mature judgment is needed in dealing with the many complex issues faced. Making decisions requires courage to act promptly and decisively, particularly in emergencies. The courage to act also entails the courage to make mistakes and to admit that mistakes have been made when they do occur. Imagination and resourcefulness are also invaluable in meeting new conditions and never-ending complexities involved in the travel industry. To maintain a healthy balance, a person entrusted with the responsibilities of management must have strong moral stamina, without which he cannot make courageous decisions, endure criticism, or bridge misunderstandings.

Managers are given the opportunity to exercise leadership. That leadership does not become effective, however, until it is accepted by everyone in the organization. The authority to make such leadership accepted has to be won rather than received as a gift or reward for other services. Only as a manager's performance and demonstrated ability merit and gain that acceptance and respect of others does his or her leadership become a vital directing force. Managers should be leaders, not bosses. Discipline that is too rigid creates fear, suspicion, hatred, resistance, and other negative attitudes. Becoming skilled in the essentials of good management will do much to promote acceptance.

GOALS AND REWARDS

Thus management becomes a challenging responsibility. It involves guidance, leadership, and control of the efforts of a group of individuals toward a common goal. Effectively applied, it results in getting something worthwhile done well through other people with maximum dispatch and minimum expense.

While the financial compensation in most travel agencies is low compared to other industries, a successful manager usually enjoys other rewards, such as the personal prestige and satisfaction that comes from a job well done. The opportunity of meeting and knowing people from all over the world and the knowledge that his or her efforts, small as they may be, are helping to bridge the gap in understanding and knowledge between peoples and nations can also be sources of real contentment.

THE PLANNING PROCESS

Managers must shape their organization's programs to meet both present and future needs. They must develop long-range plans and goals. Managers who know what their objectives are, what steps are necessary to achieve them, what goals must be reached, and what resources will be required are certain in the long run to accomplish more than anyone who operates on a day-to-day, catch-as-catch-can basis.

The planning process and, in fact, the process of decision making generally should be based on an analytical approach. This involves several essential steps:

1. *Clarify the problem.* Visualize the present situation or condition which requires solving or improving. Be creative. Often there can be more than one solution.
2. *Establish sound objectives.* Such objectives should be in terms of results desired within the framework of your company's goals.
3. *Get the facts, feelings, and opinions.* Before a situation can be corrected or improved, it must be determined what caused it. Without all the available, pertinent facts, an ill-considered or inadequate action may be taken. Feelings and opinions of persons involved, or who may be affected, should also be considered carefully. They not only disclose otherwise unknown causes and possible solutions, but contribute to conditioning those affected to accept final decisions when they know their feelings have been taken into account.
4. *Analyze and evaluate the facts.* After the facts are obtained (including the feelings and opinions), they should be analyzed and evaluated to determine the basic issues of the problem under consideration. Such a review will also suggest various alternatives to be considered. Analysis requires objectivity, together with a willingness to give up cherished or preconceived ideas, and acceptance of new conclusions if needed.
5. *Determine actions to be taken.* Consider the various alternative solutions or possible actions. Review their advantages and disadvantages. Weigh these actions against the objectives established to determine which actions will achieve the conditions desired with respect to personnel, money, materials, and service. Do not jump to conclusions, but once you are sure of a safe, effective course, take necessary action. Do not procrastinate, but watch your timing. Delays can be costly.
6. *Set goals.* Determine the major steps necessary to carry out the course decided upon. Then establish tentative target dates when these steps should be completed. Be flexible, but stand behind your goals.
7. *Prepare plans.* Work out the actions necessary to achieve the goals that have been established, the methods to be used, and the resources needed. Particular attention should be given to interrelationships between different parts of the plan, so that a closely coordinated course of action will result.
8. *Check results.* Plans are not self-executing. Check from time to time to learn what action is being taken. Make sure that it is producing the desired results.

THE OPERATING BUDGET

The manager has a basic obligation to be economical. Budgeting essentially is a technique of program planning, since the allocation of funds determines what is to be done. The preparation of the budget affords an opportunity for annual review of objectives and work plans. In the preparation of the budget, careful attention should be given to the relationship of benefits and costs. In some activities, this can be calculated fairly closely; in others, such as advertising and promotions, only a general estimate can be made. Even here, however, the process of weighing costs against long-range benefits can be helpful in determining whether a particular activity should be undertaken. One of the major responsibilities of the manager is considering and recommending program priorities. This means seeing not only that functions which have outlived their need are discontinued, but also that functions of low priority are not continued while programs of high priority are neglected.

Prospering in a recessionary economy is a real challenge in the travel industry, as travel is one of the first items to be cut back or eliminated by both business and vacation clients. During stressful periods, management should go back to the basics of examining the costs of doing business, avoiding overextension, and using slack time to motivate and train employees and should look for ways to improve public image. Savings can be realized simply by checking on purchasing policies on office supplies, postage, and trade subscriptions. Employees should be encouraged to act like customer service fanatics; everyone should make customer service a high priority.

Past experience is the usual criterion used in preparing the budget. However, in a travel agency, the manager must also keep a close watch on coming events or trends in the industry as well as to weigh the end results of previous years. Statistics on travel agency operations are given in the various travel trade publications from time to time, and while they may be helpful in matters of comparison, they cannot be used blindly as criteria for individual offices. There are so many variants to be considered in making comparisons: location, size of staff, type of business (commercial accounts, ethnic groups, etc.) However, percentages used by other agents may serve as a guideline in preparing the budget.

ORGANIZATION

The first step in organization involves analyzing and clarifying purposes and functions. Basically, organization involves division of labor, that is, dividing the whole job into workable parts. While encouraging specialization, it emphasizes the need for coordination to ensure that the parts work together smoothly. Travel consultants tend to want to be sufficient unto themselves. To a certain degree, this is necessary and even desirable. Experience indicates that good management is hardly possible if the manager attempts to hold authority closely. Managers must permit, even require, their subordinates to assume responsibility for many important decisions while working on a client's travel plans. Referring matters to a manager for decisions

Figure 4-2 Celebrity Cruises MV Horizon.

necessarily means delay and may result in those decisions being made by persons not sufficiently familiar with the situation.

The establishment of carefully thought out objectives, goals, plans, policies, and standards will give members of the staff the confidence and security needed to perform more efficiently. Freedom to act within their limits can then be granted with greater safety. At the same time, the manager is freed from the paralyzing necessity of approving individual actions of subordinates and can concentrate on the essential tasks of management. The manager's job is to see that essential things are done and to provide the facilities for a good working climate. Good managers observe two guidelines when they distribute or delegate work to others: (1) delegate work that another person can do to good advantage, and (2) delegate work that the manager would do only at the expense of something more important. It is not good management to turn over a job to a subordinate and leave the manager idle and unproductive.

Work programs should be scheduled within the framework of an agency's long-term plans. Almost any activity, including the manager's work, will benefit from some degree of scheduling. In a smaller agency, routine duties could be assigned on a rotating basis, weekly or monthly, among staff members. The larger agency can afford specialists for specific duties or geographical areas. Work schedules should be double-checked to avoid unnecessary duplication of activities. Confusion as to who is responsible for what, or to whom, will inevitably result in inefficiency. Effective organization is one of the major tests of good management.

Basically, all work may be divided into two broad categories: (1) routine—work that can be performed by almost everyone in the office (such as sorting the mail, stamping and filing brochures, preparing a mailing, follow-up on inquiries); and (2) creative—work that involves using judgment, initiative, or speculation (such as preparing a sales promotion program, writing ads, plotting a group tour itinerary, or working with commercial accounts on their sales incentive programs). Good managers will divide their work into these two broad categories. They generally should not waste energy on the one and not delegate the other, unless they can effectively organize a deputy's capacity for doing it, and then only if it pays. Good managers may safely delegate only as long as, by so doing, they are left free for the more important, more profitable decisions. Failure frequently results from keeping too much for themselves or delegating the wrong kind of work. The character of the work, rather than its complexity or the amount of money it involves, should determine what kind of work may be safely delegated. Success depends on learning to share responsibilities skillfully.

Delegation gets employees involved, and when they sense that the manager is interested in helping the employee advance, they will respond with good work. Good managers will make sure that they have one or two employees capable of succeeding them while they are on the road or ill. Large agencies may give them the title of assistant managers, while the smaller office may just designate the employees who will take charge when the manager is out.

RECRUITING NEW EMPLOYEES

One of the manager's most important tasks is to recruit and develop good employees. Management implies consideration of the human being as a valuable resource. People must be recognized as human beings having, unlike any other resource, personality, citizenship, and control over why, how much, and how well they work. They also require motivation, participation, satisfaction, incentives and rewards, leadership, status, and usefulness. Management alone can meet these needs. Successfully met, happy productive workers result and contribute to effective, profitable service rendered.

The attitude of managers (as well as owners) toward employees will greatly influence the spirit and productivity of the entire office. Too close supervision tends to lower production. Employees usually do better work when they have some degree of freedom in determining how to do their jobs. There must be a genuine interest on the part of the manager in the welfare of those who work under them—basically, application of the Golden Rule. A few essentials are:

1. Familiarize new employees with the office and what is expected of them. Give them a copy of your office manual. If your agency does not have a manual, put one together. Ask the staff to assist you.
2. Provide adequate equipment and good working conditions.
3. Challenge employees to improve themselves by providing incentives, financial or otherwise.
4. Help them advance. Never stand in their way.
5. Give credit when and to whom due.
6. Share responsibility for mistakes made and help prevent them.
7. Be loyal to employees under pressure or criticism.
8. Reprimand employees in private and only when necessary.
9. Let employees know in advance of organizational and work changes, and brief them on special sales promotions before they are publicized. The most profitable businesses are those which follow a program of keeping their employees fully informed.
10. Assist in comparable placement elsewhere when forced to cut back in staff.
11. Treat employees considerately, firmly, and justly. Do not show favoritism.
12. Let employees share in planning what is to be done and when decisions are made, explain why.
13. Show sympathy and helpfulness in time of difficulty.
14. Be an interested, sympathetic listener and always get both sides of the story when disagreements arise between staff members.

The example set by managers is undoubtedly the most effective means of developing a tradition of fair and courteous treatment of the public. If managers are deeply concerned about observing the principles of good human relations in dealing with the public and with the employees, it is likely that those who work under them will be similarly concerned. Employees will only extend the kind of consideration they receive.

Standard policies and standard methods should be set up in writing to establish good internal control in office procedures. Control means evaluating job progress and results. It means control of facts, not control of people. Standard policies affect control through applying a sound decision consistently to meet recurring situations or circumstances. Standard methods should represent the best way to do a specific job. Those policies and methods should be determined in cooperation with the employees who will actually do the work. If an office manual does not exist, draft one, or if it does, call a staff meeting to suggest changes and/or improvements. The most efficient method possible, if imposed on employees who are not sympathetic, may prove to be the least efficient in practice.

The process of selecting travel consultants may vary greatly among the agencies, depending primarily on the functions to be assigned to them. The term *travel consultant* is often applied to all employees, although their duties may involve more secretarial, clerical, bookkeeping, or ticket-writing duties. Granted, it is difficult to measure the knowledge of the applicants even though they may have previous travel agency experience (unless they have completed the management course or the travel career development course offered by the Institute of Certified Travel Agents). There are many characteristics that the manager can look for when interviewing an applicant.

Voice, good grammar, enthusiasm, initiative, tact, resourcefulness, imagination, and analytical skills are necessary in the initial discussion with the client to determine their travel needs. Persuasiveness, persistence, tact, confidence, knowledge, and consideration are needed to answer or forestall objections and to close the sale. Orderliness, honesty, and attention to details are the characteristics required to follow through and process the sale. Following-up with customers to make sure that they received good service during their travels requires friendliness, personality, helpfulness, and courtesy.

The characteristic most needed in the travel agency is tact. Tact is defined in the *American College Dictionary* as: "Keen sense of what to say/do to avoid giving offense; skill in dealing with difficult or delicate situations." (Synonym: tact, address, poise, savoir faire; well-bred skill or grace in behavior). Sometimes it takes exceptional self-control when dealing with the obnoxious customer, or when maintaining composure in an uncongenial office. (Travel agents are only human; quite often stress and fatigue during the busy seasons can affect even the most cheerful personality.) Even when clients are entirely unreasonable, an effort must be made to understand their point of view and then explain the other side of the situation. Arguments can lose sales and possible future business. The best test of creative selling is the mature and diplomatic handling of difficult situations.

Another important quality to look for in prospective sales people is their genuine fondness for people. One who is active in social and civic organizations will not only be more adaptable in a busy office, but will also have more contacts for promoting and selling travel.

Actually, recruiting of new employees in most agencies is usually left to chance, or to following up leads from friends, customers, employees, and the airline sales representatives. Most agents hesitate to advertise because they do not want to take the time to weed out possible replies from those who have no previous experience but want to learn the business. One mistake agents make, when they do advertise, is in using a blind box number instead of their own phone number or address. Box numbers discourage most consultants from answering. Consultants, who are presently employed in a travel agency but are interested in making a change, would not want to reveal their interest until they know who is advertising.

An ad in the classified section of a morning newspaper usually brings the best results in recruiting employees. A successful ad should include the address or general location of the office. This will immediately eliminate inquiries from those who would not be interested in working on the other side of town, unless your offer is too good to pass up. This type of ad may bring in qualified applicants who have recently moved into town and have not yet made any contacts in the local travel community. It will also attract airline employees who would like to learn more about the travel agent to increase their knowledge and experience for future advancement with the airlines or who have plans, upon retirement, for opening an agency of their own; or those who would like to try the variety and excitement in a travel agency office.

Employment agencies may try hard to fill the vacancy in your staff, but the applicants referred by them are usually qualified only as receptionists or secretaries. Unless an employment agency has a good knowledge of the travel industry, it is likely to have the same misconceptions about the work that the general public has.

The established agent can also consider applicants whose former experience has been as travel clerks or traffic managers in large corporations and former executive secretaries who are accustomed to making airline and hotel reservations for one or more executives and salespeople who are constantly on the road.

There is such a severe shortage of experienced travel consultants throughout the United States that travel agents are using more creative methods to attract or keep employees. An agent in California tried tempting new employees with a bonus of $2000 to sign up with his agency and offered a bonus of $1000 to each employee who found a recruit. He filled four positions but still had six open. Other agents are turning to the over-50 group, retirees and empty-nest parents. Surveys have shown that mature workers are more reliable, there is less absenteeism and tardiness, and contrary to general opinion, they can and will learn new skills. A major airline automation instructor said that classes of students in the older age group, 35 and up, did better in learning and retaining their lessons than did younger groups. Older salespeople are also better suited to sell travel to their contemporaries on the other side of the desk.

The fear of losing experienced employees to pregnancy and child-care problems has initiated a trend toward work-at-home offices. Agents are installing CRTs, phones, and reference material in the employee's home. A co-worker in the agency is assigned to each at-home employee to do the ticketing (there is no ARC stock in the home) and to keep them up to date on mail and phone messages. Naturally, this requires a lot of trust between the manager and employee, but it can be beneficial to both. The agency can expand its work force and the employees can stay home and raise their families.

Travel schools are becoming increasingly important as a resource for entry-level employees, as well as providing training for new employees who have demonstrated the capability to become worthwhile additions to the agent's staff.

TRAINING

An effective training program could be set up in an individual agency with the use of a buddy system. A more experienced employee can be designated to help and guide a new member. The training program can consist of three stages: (1) the *orientation* stage, in which a trainee is familiarized with the staff, the office, and the bookkeeping and selling procedures. This is usually followed by (2) a *selling training* stage, during which specific selling and computer techniques are given to the trainee. If an agency is computerized, the trainee can be sent to an airline computer school; or if the trainee has had some experience with computers, he or she could brush up by going through the programmed computer training on the premises. Airlines also offer special training sessions for travel agents at their training centers. Finally, there is (3) the *on-the-job training* stage, which may involve personal contact with the customers under close supervision of the buddy or manager.

Training is not useful only for beginners; it is often necessary and desirable at many times during the consultant's career. The many changes in fare structures and validity dates alone make it imperative that the entire staff and the outside salespeople in the agency be kept aware and up-to-date so that they can give clients the best possible choice for their travel needs. Selling techniques must also be reviewed. It is the manager's responsibility to make sure that bulletins from the carriers and others are passed around to everyone or posted on an interoffice bulletin board.

Good sales training increases the efficiency and skill with which salespeople perform their tasks. The results are increased sales, lower turnover (as a result of higher morale), and a reduction in the time needed to reach peak efficiency. To do a good selling job, the consultant must have a working knowledge of all available sales aids. Besides the *Official Airlines Guides (OAGs)*, *Steamship Guides*, and *Railway Guides*, most agents will also subscribe to one or more publications of hotel listings. All the conferences—air, steamship, and rail—furnish agents with their handbooks on travel agency procedures and their own rules and regulations. These are the basic reference books for all travel agencies, large or small, and each person in the agency should be well versed in their use. Even if an agency is computerized, there will be occasions when computers are down and the staff must turn to the OAGs for flight information or to hand-write a ticket.

Excellent sales materials and reference books are distributed free of charge by the individual airlines, hotel chains, and tour operators. Tourist boards of all 50 states, the Caribbean islands, Canada, and most foreign countries are only too glad to furnish agents, at their request, with general information brochures, maps, and posters. These can be invaluable to consultants who have not yet visited that particular destination, as well as for the customer who is booking a trip to an unfamiliar area. All of these sales aids should be studied carefully and filed for easy accessibility. The agent who lacks organization and has to fumble through drawers and shelves for pertinent material is not likely to inspire confidence in the customer waiting for information.

Familiarization (fam) tours and travel industry seminars are very important sales aids. An area can be sold much more effectively if the travel consultant has visited there personally. The owner/manager should send the staff, on a rotating basis, on as many fam trips as possible. Some agencies will pay all costs as well as salary while agents are out of the office; others will share the costs; still others will allow their staff unlimited (paid) time off to attend seminars or fam trips but employees pay all costs involved. Consultants should be encouraged to make a full report of their impressions and knowledge received during their participation in fam trips or seminars.

There are also seminars and trade shows held locally by carriers, tourist boards, and tour operators. It should be part of a company's policy to send at least one person to attend each local seminar and then report to the rest of the staff. Evening seminars may bring up the question of overtime pay. Most agents will post the invitations on their bulletin board and leave the decision to attend up to individual staff members. Breakfast or luncheon seminar attendance usually requires the manager's permission since these run into company time.

Other good sources of sales and training aids are travel trade publications. A subscription to at least one of the trade newspapers should be given to each employee. Receiving the latest news when it is fresh, rather than waiting their turn for the office copy, is worth the cost.

Although there is no question that travel agency business needs more aggressive sales-oriented people, the aggressiveness should be directed outside the office—toward building up business with more creative sales promotions. Managers who encourage competition rather than cooperation among their employees will soon find that competition often turns into resentment. This results in discord among the employees. They neither care to, nor want to, help one another get things done. The goal that should be set for an office should be that of increasing the overall business of the agency rather than that of increasing the person's quota. Rewards should be given to competent employees, but they should be based on individual merit, which naturally encompasses productivity, cooperation, originality, and creativeness.

COMPENSATION AND MOTIVATION

Careful recruiting, selection, and training can increase the efficiency of the office staff in performing the numerous functions that are required, but they do not guarantee that the consultants will be motivated to perform them. Money and promotions are rarely enough to keep people motivated for the long term. Consultants also need the satisfaction that results from doing interesting, challenging work. The agency's compensation plan and nonfinancial incentives (pride in a job well done, the respect of a consultant's friends and associates, etc.) are the principal means by which management can help to ensure that their staff is highly motivated.

As the years go by the work force is changing. To find and keep qualified people, managers will have to offer prospective employees greater flexibility. Bureau of Labor Statistics indicate that the U.S. work force will experience significant demographic changes over the next 10 years. The share of employees aged 16 to 24 is expected to shrink, while the share of employees aged 25 to 75 is expected to increase. More immigrants, both legal and illegal, are entering the work force. By the year 2010, ethnics and immigrants will comprise five-sixths of the available labor pool. Agencies will also be greatly affected by the number of functionally illiterate employees entering the work force. Aging, ethnic diversity, needs of working mothers, and training and career development programs will require new management policies to meet the needs of employees.

Determining the amount of compensation and bonuses to be paid to the staff is a major problem in most agencies. Management must take into consideration the number of functions the person will perform, the earnings of consultants employed by competing offices, and the potential profitability of the entire agency.

To have sufficient income to compensate employees adequately—and to leave a reasonable profit for the owners—each person in a travel agency should produce approximately two and a half times their combined salary and fringe benefits in commissions. To evaluate productivity in a businesslike manner, it is wise to record each person's commissions and thus determine compensation.

A record of sales by individual employees (discussed further in Chapter 5) will enable management to see the production of each year's sales in order to recognize those employees who are constantly improving their own record. Bonuses in proportion to the increase could then be paid at the end of each year. However, management should also emphasize that bonuses paid would be in proportion to the profits earned by the entire staff.

Much research on management–employee relationships has brought out the interesting conclusion that nonmonetary incentives can be more important than physical factors, working conditions, and even the amount shown on the paycheck. Violation of any of the essentials of good management can impair morale. For example, lack of planning, organizational squabbles, failure to state clearly what an employee is supposed to do, poor communication, failure to provide needed equipment, undesirable working conditions, inefficient methods, and unequal or arrogant treatment all affect the spirit of an agency.

Good managers must also guard against accepting recognition, praise, and even outright flattery for themselves rather than for their position. They must avoid the temptation to claim all the credit when business is good and to pass the blame to subordinates when things go wrong. Managers must always present a self-confidant, even-tempered image to the public and their employees. The good of the company must come above personal pleasures or conveniences. If fatigue, boredom, or disagreements with staff members or superiors become too apparent, there is either something wrong with the agency, or the manager is in the wrong profession.

STAFF MEETINGS

Staff meetings for the purpose of discussing new fares, regulations, tour offers, stimulating ideas, suggestions on internal problems, and to obtain the judgment of the staff are an essential tool of management. They keep both manager and employees well informed and open up the channels of communication. Sales representatives from airlines, steamship lines, and other travel industry principals welcome the opportunity to make their sales calls to an agency at a time when the entire staff is available. As a general rule they should be held at least once a month on a set day and for a fixed length of time. To avoid overtime problems, some agents schedule staff meetings either one hour before opening or one hour after

Figure 4-3 Moni Roussanoo Monastery/ Meteora.

closing and allow participants to take an additional hour for lunch (spaced throughout the week).

Managers need to develop skill in guiding discussions at the staff meeting to bring out important points, obtain the real views of all participants, and restrain monopolization and irrelevant talk. There is sometimes a tendency for one or a few persons to dominate in the discussion, especially if it falls in their area of responsibility, and for the others to agree without giving the problem real thought. Decisions arrived at in the meeting or afterward should be clearly stated, in writing, if possible.

Managers bear full responsibility and must therefore retain control and ultimate authority. Staff meetings are essentially advisory in character. Participation must not mean indecision or lack of leadership on the part of the manager or unwillingness on the part of the employees to accept his decisions. However, managers will profit from the joint efforts to discuss and solve problems.

There is a wealth of ideas in the minds of employees as to improvement that could be made, especially in their own field of operations. However, employees will not willingly part with their ideas unless they feel that their suggestions are wanted and will be recognized properly and fairly. Whenever possible, employees should be encouraged to submit their ideas and rewarded, either financially or with the title "Consultant of the Month" or whatever suits the occasion.

In the final analysis, managers have the responsibility to represent both the principals and public, and have the ability to see things as a whole. They must have a genuine concern for the rights and interests of both their superiors and their subordinates, together with integrity and courage to do what seems right.

TRADE ORGANIZATIONS

Travel agencies are not unionized, although several unions have attempted to do so. I doubt if a union could succeed in organizing travel consultants, as there are so many variables in this industry and unions could not possibly increase the fringe benefits of travel, as these come from the principals, not from the individual employers, although employers may make the final decision as to who can or cannot receive these benefits. There are, however, two organizations of travel agents that protect and promote their mutual interests: ASTA (American Society of Travel Agents) and ARTA (Association of Retail Travel Agents). ASTA and ARTA were formed for travel agency owners and managers, although both permit agency employees to join as junior or associate members.

ASTA was started in 1930 by 15 New York–New Jersey steamship agents. At that time the name was the American Steamship and Travel Agents Association—airlines were not very important in those years. In 1941, ASTA changed the name to American Society of Tourist Agents because the original name gave too much prominence to steamer services, with no recognition of aviation or other operators. It was subsequently changed to the present name. Airlines, tour operators, car rental companies, hotels (individual properties and chains), and other principals in the travel industry are accepted for allied membership. The organization started with four categories of membership: active, associate, junior, and honorary. ASTA has since added a number of associate and allied categories, including a category for travel schools, but from the very beginning only the active members have had voting rights.

Membership in ARTA, which began in 1964, is limited to travel agencies and employees only. The agency must hold at least two industry conference appointments (one must be ARC) and do at least 70 percent retail business. Employees can sign up individually even if their employer is not a member of ARTA. Inside salespeople must have a minimum of one year's experience and be included on the ARC or IATAN eligibility list; outside salespeople must have three years' experience.

Both organizations offer seminars and fam trips to their members. ASTA and ARTA offer reduced rates for the ARC bond, provided that the agency has been a member for a minimum of one year. ASTA also offers group rates on hospitalization insurance and on errors and omissions insurance. Both ASTA and ARTA have been actively lobbying in Washington, D.C. to improve the travel agents' position in the travel industry. Membership to either of these organizations is, of course, optional. It is up to the discretion of the owner and/or manager to decide which one to join. They all stress the idea that "unity is strength" and that with the many changes that may come in the future it would be advantageous to the agency to join either ASTA or ARTA, if only to be kept up-to-date on what is going on in the industry. As *Travel Trade* magazine says: "Be a VOICE, not an echo."

Estimates of the number of commissioned or outside salespeople range from 165,000 to 200,000 and a number of organizations have been formed to appeal to these salespeople. Some charge membership fees and offer to help them start a travel agency at home, but what they are actually offering is the position of commissioned salesperson. Others are similar to co-ops and promise educational seminars and reduced-rate travel or fam trips to their members. A few are legitimate organizations that are interested in improving the status of the outside salesperson. I believe that individual travel consultants would gain more from membership in ARTA or ASTA. They would qualify for the fam trips and seminars held by each organization and receive current newsletters and bulletins in their own name.

QUESTIONS AND PROBLEMS

1. Describe a "good" manager.
2. Should the top salesperson automatically be promoted to manager?
3. What does SARC have to say about the three roles of a travel agent?
4. Can you add any additional abilities needed for management—specifically for a travel agency?
5. List some objectives a travel agency manager may set for his staff.
6. What methods would you use to recruit a new employee?
7. If you were a new employee in a travel agency, what would you like to know on your first day in the office?

8. How would you, as the manager, keep the staff up to date on industry happenings?

9. Which method would you recommend to determine an incentive bonus for employees: a bonus based on individual sales, a bonus based on the overall increase in sales, or a combination of both?

10. Describe a successful staff meeting in terms of participation by the staff and accomplishments achieved.

11. How long do you have to be employed by a travel agency in order to join one of the trade organizations?

chapter 5

Office Procedures

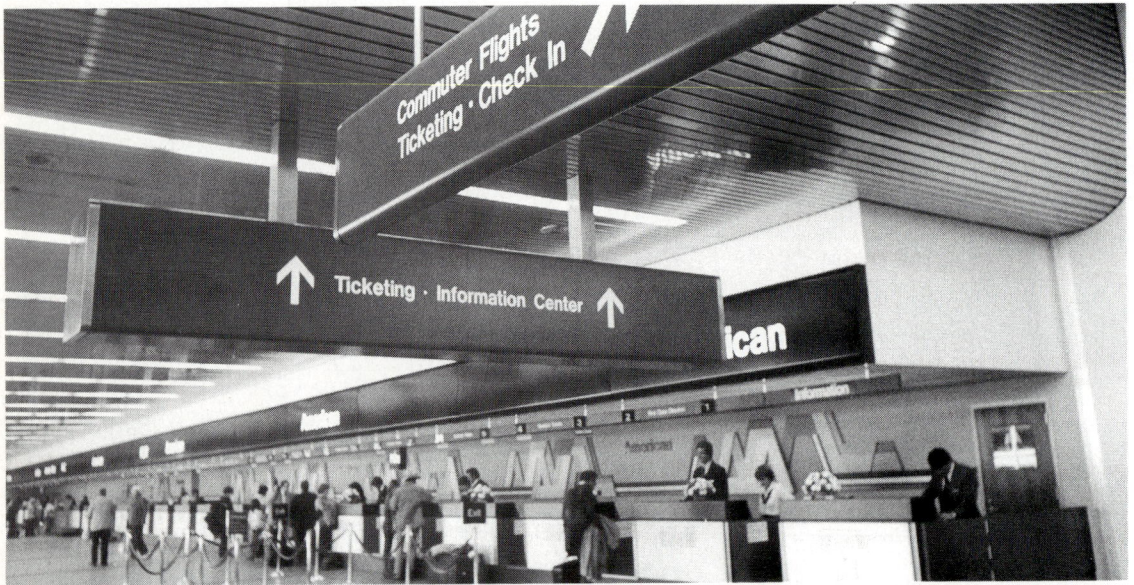

OBJECTIVES

When you have finished this chapter you should be able to:

1. Discuss the importance of keeping accurate financial records.
2. Explore back-office automation systems for a travel agency.
3. Compare preprinted form letters with standard formats used with word-processors or manually typed.
4. Suggest methods of filing and displaying travel literature.

The travel agent is in a service business and, as in most service businesses, time is the most valuable commodity. Since his time is valuable and the profit margin is low, the agent must make sure that every moment spent in the office is put to good use.

During the slow selling seasons, the staff can take a breather and catch up on paperwork. (Slow seasons may vary, depending on the kind of business the agency is in. The vacation/leisure travel market usually slows down in September/October, and January/February; the commercial market may be slow in summer and picks up after vacations are over and the businesspeople start on their sales calls, conventions, and meetings.) During this time the files are brought up to date by weeding out the expired brochures, mailing lists are checked to make sure that names have been added from the completed customer file and inquiry file, the computer client profiles are checked to make sure that they contain current data, plans for the coming year are formulated, promotional letters are composed, and customer mailings are prepared.

This slack time is also the time for management to analyze the previous year's business and determine what improvements are needed, and where. It is commonly known that there are two methods certain to make more money: (1) by increasing sales without increasing the overhead, and (2) increasing income by reducing overhead.

One of the best methods of reducing overhead and increasing income is to modernize the bookkeeping and office systems. A simplified bookkeeping system that is easily understood and maintained by all members of the staff and still provides management with the information needed should have top priority. Office forms should be reduced to a bare minimum. The less paperwork the consultant has to handle, the more time he will have to promote and sell travel. Although, paradoxically, quite often a slight increase in paperwork can reduce time and effort spent later in locating meaningful information. It is impossible to pinpoint the amount of profits that result from an efficient office system because the results depend on how effectively operating managers use the information provided for them. Nevertheless, the office function can and should be a positive source of company profit.

The Small Business Administration (SBA), as well as many certified public accountants (CPAs), believe that the major reason for a business failure is lack of knowledge (of the business) by the owner and/or manager. The other reasons have been tabulated by the *Journal of Accountancy* as follows:

1. Inadequate records
2. Inaccurate information as to costs
3. Insufficient long-term or equity capital
4. Faulty purchasing practices
5. Faulty sales policies
6. Lack of inventory control, etc.

In a study of small firms that had declared bankruptcy, three kinds of management errors showed up repeatedly:

1. Poor financial planning because of inadequate records or a failure to use the records available.
2. Poor sales management and market analysis.
3. Poor general administration, culminating in added expenses not offset by additional revenues.

The study left little doubt that inadequate and misleading financial records cause more trouble than any other error of management. Nowhere was there evidence of failure because of a breakdown of the accounting function. The difficulties arose because of management's failure to use accounting. There was, in fact, real evidence that where new management established adequate record keeping, the change from loss to profit was sometimes dramatic. This would indicate that business success is directly related to the full use of adequate records.

Many agencies have regarded record keeping as a necessary evil rather than a positive aid. A careful analysis of sales, commissions earned, and the expense incurred in making those sales would enable management to decide whether the income obtained from a particular activity was really worth the effort and expense involved. Quite often, a seemingly large profit from a group tour, for example, was dissipated by the amount of time spent; by the cost of mailings, advertisements, giveaways, and special services given to the tour members. New agents may encourage business they perform at a loss, or may give away transfers and sightseeing side trips in the mistaken belief that this will build goodwill and recognition for their office. However, when the time comes to charge for their services, those customers will then feel they are being overcharged and imposed upon.

It must be conceded that the pressures of day-to-day business will leave little time for bookkeeping entries, especially in smaller agencies that do not have full-time bookkeepers on their staffs. However, a knowledge of the basic principles of accounting and bookkeeping, and a close adherence to the policy of registering all monies received and paid out in full detail, will enable even a part-time bookkeeper or accountant to keep the records up to date with a minimum of time and effort.

The aim of a good system should be to help management achieve its objectives and avoid dangerous moves, not to bog the agency down with mountains of useless facts, no matter how well organized. Top management is not the only level where information is needed or desired. All personnel in a travel agency must be provided with reliable facts. This puts managers in a critically important spot. They must keep pertinent information flowing through all channels with a minimum time lag. The system is no better than the people assigned to its operation. If employees lack understanding of the system's purpose, or if they resist innovation, the system will break down. Cooperation from each person on the staff is essential, especially if the agency has moved out of the small business category and installs an automated accounting system.

Although the owner and/or manager will seldom be involved in the actual bookkeeping and accounting process, they should know the accounting standards and terminology in order to better understand and read the financial statements and other reports that may be generated by their accountants.

ACCOUNTING STANDARDS

The art of accounting is the charting of the course of business. It was born of necessity when people first began to trade. It was necessary for bankers and merchants to have a practical and simple means of recording changing relationships with debtors and creditors. It was necessary for the adventurers in trading expeditions to far-off places to have knowledge of the outcome of ventures. The principles of modern bookkeeping began to emerge as business became more complex and grew in volume.

Professional accounting services are now needed in every type of business, due to the increase in the governmental reports. Financial statements that were originally for the exclusive benefit of owners and managers—and a closely guarded secret—became the basis for taxation and regulation of business by government.

The primary concern of accountants is to report and interpret the past so as to throw light on the future. They prepare financial statements not only for the benefit of management in formulating future plans and policies, but also for the many federal, state, and city income tax reports now required by the government. Good accountants will consult with management and set up the bookkeeping system best suited for that particular type of business. They must examine each transaction involved in the operation of the business to determine the most efficient method of gathering the information needed and to record it properly. The best system is one that can accomplish these objectives without adding substantially to the work load of the staff.

Office systems tend to differ from agency to agency, depending on policy, assignment of responsibility, the degree of specialization, and other factors. Before a new system is installed, the owner and/or the manager should analyze all past business and define the objectives. A new agent may keep more detailed records during the first two years of operation until it can be determined which are necessary and which can be discarded.

Financial Statements

The financial statements needed by the average travel agent can be reduced to two basic reports: the balance sheet and the profit and loss statement on a yearly basis (for income tax reports), and a simplified profit and loss (or cash flow) statement on a monthly or quarterly basis. A small agency with two to five members on its staff can easily manage with a quarterly statement to coincide with the quarterly payroll reports.

The *balance sheet* shows the financial position of a business as of the close of business on a certain date by presenting its assets, its liabilities, and the equity of owners. The traditional, most-followed form of the balance sheet is the *account form*, with assets on the left and liabilities and owners' equities on the right. (In British and continental practice, the order of assets and liabilities is usually reversed.)

This statement of financial position logically sets forth the relationship between the assets available for use by the company and the sources of the funds from which the assets are acquired. The three major sources are (1) money borrowed from creditors, (2) money provided by owners (in a corporation they would be shares of capital stock issued by the firm), and (3) money earned by the company. The accounting equation is as follows:

$$assets = liabilities + owners' \ equity$$

In this equation, liabilities are amounts owed to creditors, and owners' equity consists of capital stock (amounts contributed by owners at time of investment) in addition to retained earnings (amounts earned from customer service, now belonging to the owners and left in the enterprise as additional investment).

The *profit and loss statement*, also known as the *income statement* or the *statement of earnings*, contains a summary, for a given period of time, of the income of a business and the expenses incurred in earning that income. The expenses are deducted from the income to obtain the difference called the *net income* or *net loss* for the period—net income if the income is greater, and net loss if the expenses are greater. Since 99 percent of the travel agent's income is composed of commissions earned, this should be broken down by category (i.e., airline, cruise, land, etc.). The agent can then determine which areas are the most profitable and which areas need working on.

Since the travel agency is a service organization, it does not produce or handle any tangible product (i.e., something that can be stored and sold to customers in a later period). The absence of a product reduces the usefulness of earnings computations as a measure of performance because a large share of the costs are *period* rather than *product* costs. This means that many of the costs are considered to be expenses in periods in which there is no clear identification with the earnings of that period. For example, a considerable amount may be spent for sales promotions and advertising of a tour that may not be finalized until months later. Other costs may consist of a year's supply of stationery and other office supplies, luggage tags, and so on. Some of these costs could be entered in the journals as prepaid expenses—however, this would necessitate an inventory tally and a general journal entry at the end of each accounting period to determine the amount expensed (or used) during that period. Unless very large sums are involved, the additional bookkeeping would not be worth the time and effort needed.

Costs and Income

Often, the dollar value of the services performed for a client cannot be determined until the services have been completed, possibly not until after several months have passed, as in the case of hotel or car rental commissions. Again, quite often, commissions are deducted from payments made to tour operators or cruise lines for travel that will not culminate anywhere from 30 days to six months after payment was received. In the meantime, the client may cancel and request a refund. The refund would then reduce earnings in an otherwise highly productive month. Most agents use the cash system, where income is recorded only when it has been received. All this must be taken into consideration when preparing or analyzing an income statement for a travel agent.

Agents' income is derived from commissions on sales and from service charges or cancellation charges levied against clients. In most cases the commission is deducted at the time payment is forwarded to the suppliers and principals on behalf of the client. The general practice among most agents is to forward payments only after monies have been received from clients. In the event that payments are forwarded before a collection has been made from the client, the entire amount would be charged to accounts receivable at the time payment is sent, to properly record the sales and commission earned.

Costs incurred by agents in conducting their business may be grouped in two classes: costs that can be *directly related* to sales, including advertising, sales promotions, giveaways such as flight bags, luggage tags, passport holders, bon voyage gifts, calendars, and pens, and salespeople's salaries and educational expenses; and costs *not directly related* (overhead), such as office rent, postage, utilities, and salaries of officers and nonsales personnel.

TERMINOLOGY

Accounts payable reflects claims of suppliers and principals. This item represents the company's position as a purchaser of goods and services, whereas accounts receivable represents its position as a seller. Deposits and payments from customers that are not forwarded immediately to the principals would be reflected in accounts payable on the balance sheet.

Accounts receivable are monies owed to the company by its customers. These accounts are the result of normal operations and seldom are documented by formal evidence of debt. A debt evidenced by a promissory note or some other formal document normally is reported in *notes receivable*.

Accrual basis accounting recognizes revenue when a product is shipped or a service is rendered rather than when the amount is collected. It is used by accountants to match revenues with expenses when determining income.

Accrued expenses such as payroll taxes payable to the federal and various state and city governments, real estate taxes, personal property taxes, and wages, are incurred expenses for which payment has yet to be made.

Assets are the objects used by the company in the conduct of its business activities. Assets are held because they will benefit the revenues of a future accounting period. For example, cash can be used to acquire commodities and services. A building, or furniture and office equipment, can be used by a business in future operations. The dollar value given to assets on the statement is the original cost minus the accumulated depreciation and amortization. They are generally listed on the balance sheet in order of liquidity, from cash to long-term assets. Assets consist not only of cash, buildings, furniture, and fixtures, but also investments, prepaid expenses, and accounts receivables. Prepaid expenses normally are those that will be used up in the near future. Insurance premiums are most commonly designated as a prepaid expense.

Break-even point is the point at which income covers the expenses.

Capital stock generally represents the amount received by a corporation from the sale of stock. In a small or family-owned corporation, this would be the owner's investment.

Cash basis accounting records sales or revenues only when the cash is collected and recognizes expenses only when they are paid. This does not give an accurate picture of the economic results of operation, but is used when allowed, for tax purposes, as it results in a lower tax in most cases. Most service-oriented businesses are allowed to use cash basis for tax purposes.

Current assets and current liabilities are assets and liabilities that will be liquidated within a year. The relationship of current assets to current liabilities gives valuable liquidity information.

Income is generally referred to as net income, profit, or the "bottom line" rather than gross income. The sales or gross income can be called either sales or revenues.

Liabilities represent amounts owed to persons outside the business. Liabilities that come due within the year, and that are expected to be paid with current assets or by the creation of other current liabilities, are classified as *current liabilities*. Amounts owed that do not become due within one year are classified as *long-term liabilities*.

Owners' equity represents the amount invested by the stockholders in the total assets either as an initial investment or through earnings retained in the business.

Retained earnings is the total amount of all current and prior period earnings that have not been distributed to the owners in the form of dividends. Each year this amount is increased by profits (decreased by losses) and decreased by any dividends paid. This money is usually set aside for future expansion or to pay off long-term liabilities.

Working capital represents current assets less current liabilities.

TRANSACTIONS AND THE BOOKKEEPING SYSTEM

Before financial reports can be made, the individual *transactions* must be recorded. Before the transactions can be recorded, they must appear on a business form of some kind. The average travel agency could have hundreds of transactions in a month's time. In essence, almost every business action results in a transaction. Accounting reports are the summarized results of transactions. Summarization is accomplished by a bookkeeping system that records the financial results of a transaction as it occurs and then processes the information to enable the accountant to prepare reports periodically. A bookkeeping system can take many physical forms. It could be a roll of cash register tape, files composed of invoice copies, punched cards, a tape, or a diskette in an electronic data processing system. However, the basic functions of journals and ledgers are maintained in all these systems.

Journals are often called the books of original entry. The transaction is first recorded in a journal; the information in journals is summarized periodically, usually on a monthly basis, and transferred to a *ledger*. A ledger actually is a filing index for information to be used in accounting reports. The bookkeeping system is a tool to help achieve the end product, the accounting report. A good system is also a storehouse of data that is easily available to all members of the staff for future reference.

Invoices and Voucher Checks

The information found in the sales and receipts journal is recorded therein from the use of an *invoice* or some form of sales slip. The recording of the amount of a transaction in a journal is called an *entry*; its transfer in detail or total to a page in a ledger is a *posting*. For every transaction or group of similar transactions there must be an entry; for every entry or group of similar entries there must be a posting.

The sample bookkeeping and office system described in this chapter is based on the use of just two pieces of paper: consecutively numbered invoices in four parts (or more if needed) and the use of voucher checks in a minimum of three parts:

1. The original (usually white) invoice copy is used for the client receipt.
2. The second copy (usually yellow) is placed in the client file, or attached to the reservation sheet if it is a simple transportation or hotel sale, then filed alphabetically by client name when the file is completed.
3. The third copy (usually pink) is the bookkeeping and bank deposit detail.
4. The fourth copy (usually gold) is filed numerically if it is a cash (check or credit card) sale or placed in an accounts receivable file if payment will be received at a later date. When payment is received, the gold copy is then removed and placed in the numerical file and a notation is made to record the payment.

The second and equally important piece of paper in this system is the *check voucher* copy. The use of voucher checks in three parts combined with the numbered invoices guarantees a foolproof method of accounting for monies received and monies paid out. The check itself is the original, which is mailed or given to the payee. The second copy is used for bookkeeping purposes, and the third copy is placed in the client's file or attached to the reservation record.

When transactions are completed and the client's records are prepared for filing, it is a simple matter to reconcile the monies received with the tickets issued or payments made on their behalf by checking invoice and voucher copies included in their records. This system is also ideal for data processing, as an additional copy of the invoice and check voucher could be ordered and used for data entry. These copies can be coded with account numbers and amounts by a bookkeeper or accountant (or even by the travel consultants if they are given a chart of accounts and instructed in its use).

All transactions in the office should be recorded on an invoice even though there may not be any physical handling of money in the transaction. All monies received for deposit to the company account *must* be recorded on an invoice. This point must be emphasized because it is here that most errors are made. The *exact* amount of money collected (to be deposited) from the client should be shown on the invoice with a qualifying statement if the amount collected is either less or more than the amount due. (A refund may be due if the amount is higher, or the balance may have to be placed in accounts receivable if the amount is less.) The explanation could be typed separately on the office copies if you would rather not have this shown on the client's copy.

Placing as much information as possible on the invoice and the check voucher will not only keep the customer and principals well informed but will also eliminate unnecessary work for the bookkeeper and accountant when the entries are made in the journals. Ticket numbers, date of departure, itinerary numbers, dates reserved, number of people in the party, names and ages of children in the party, type of room and meal plan desired, number of nights (if a hotel reservation), date of sailing, ship's name and cabin number (if a steamship reservation), and so on, should appear on both the invoice and the check voucher. If these source documents are not complete, the bookkeeping system cannot perform its principal function—to gather information correctly!

A central location (usually in the safe or a file case with a lock) should be decided upon for the filing of the invoice bookkeeping copy and the money received during daily activities. When the time arrives for the bank deposit to be made, the invoices are first put into numerical order (including the credit card sales and the accounts receivable sales), then an adding machine tape is run on the cash/check totals and attached to the batch of invoices. The money is then listed on the deposit slip and added, and this total deposit should agree with the invoice total. This step should not be omitted because it is here that discrepancies can be found and corrected. Occasionally, a customer may put the incorrect amount on the check or decides to make a partial payment instead of the full amount due.

The deposit slip is made up in duplicate, and after the deposit is made, the duplicate deposit slip is attached to the batch of invoices and placed in the bookkeeper's file until the invoices have been recorded in the journal. For a good internal control of cash, a daily deposit should be made even though it may consist only of the total of one or two invoices. (Customer's checks have been known to "bounce." The sooner they are deposited, the sooner this will be known.) After the invoices have been recorded in the journal, they are filed in date order (date of deposit). The completed customer file is in alphabetical order, the gold copies in numerical order—thus giving the office a good cross-reference system whereby an invoice can be located by customer name, invoice number, or date.

An additional cross-reference can be made by noting the invoice number on the agent's copy of the tickets issued. If the airline sales report total does not agree with the journal's total of airline sales for that period, it can be determined quickly if an invoice was written for each ticket by auditing the agent's copy of the airline report. The most common error occurs when a rush ticket is delivered or given to a commercial account, and it is not recorded on an invoice.

Also in the interest of good internal control, all money paid out of company funds should be made by a company check. This includes all payments made to suppliers and principals, customer refunds, and reimbursements made to staff members for expenses incurred on behalf of the company. A check should never be made out to cash except when reimbursing the petty cash fund, and then expenses should be itemized on the check stub or voucher.

Journals and Ledgers

Basic books for this bookkeeping system are:

1. Sales and receipts journal
2. Check disbursement journal
3. General ledger
4. Payroll ledger
5. Accounts receivable ledger
6. Airline sales recap ledger
7. Tour operator sales recap ledger
8. Record of sales by individual employees

The column headings in the sales journal and the disbursement journal are almost identical (see Illustrations) so that the accounts can easily be reconciled at the end of the month. Reconciling the accounts at the end of the calendar month for all sales—and at the end of each reporting period for airline sales—plays a very important part in correcting errors and discrepancies between receipts and payments while the transactions are still fresh in everyone's memory.

The sales accounts should normally "zero out" at the end of the period. If an account continues to show a balance for more than 60 days, the bookkeeper or accountant should notify management to investigate the reason for the outstanding balance. Quite often this happens if money from a client has not been forwarded to the principal, or an airline ticket has been paid for but not issued, or a payment was forwarded to a principal before the money was received from the client and an invoice was not written to record this to accounts receivable.

All invoices should be recorded in the sales and receipts journal in numerical order. (Dates will automatically follow suit if invoices are not written out of sequence.) All numbers must be accounted for even if the invoice is voided. (The staff must be advised that all copies of invoices and checks must be saved and filed even if they have been voided.) By using numbered invoices and recording every number, the chances of fraud or dishonesty are lessened and it is easier to catch duplications or other errors.

Sales and Receipts Journal

The following is a sample of the information that could appear under the column headings in Figure 5-2:

1. Date of invoice.
2. Invoice numbers in consecutive order.
3. Name of client or other source of receipt of money. Enter VOID if the invoice was voided due to a typing or clerical error.
4. Total receipts: enter the *exact* amount collected.
5. Memo bank deposit. Enter the amount of money deposited as shown on the duplicate deposit slip for that date. If more than one bank is used, separate columns should be headed for each bank account.
6. Airline sales, standard ticket. Enter all sales transactions issued on a standard ticket. This will include tour orders, MCOs, refunds, and debit or credit memos from the airlines as well as tickets issued for straight transportation. If space permits, a second column under this heading could be used to separate the tour order and MCO sales from all other standard tickets.
7. Airline code and/or commission code. The main purpose of showing these codes is for easier cross-referencing at the end of the month between sales and disbursements. A recap at the end of the month will supply a quick estimate of amount of business done with each airline and the percent of commission earned on each sale, although this information is given on the computer printout of the ARC airline report.
8. Other airline sales. Enter sales made to airlines not on the ARC standard ticket plan or when the agent does not have the airline identification plate and prefers to pay the airline by exchange order or invoice, or uses the airline's own ticket stock and reports directly to the airline.
9. Credit card sales. Enter the sales paid by credit card. (Credit airline sales; debit credit card sales. This enables the agent to keep track of all airline sales.)
10. Land arrangements. Enter all sales for tours, hotels, car rentals, greeter services, city sightseeing trips, and so on. These items may be entered

in separate columns if there are enough transactions in each category to make it worthwhile; otherwise, each transaction may be coded (i.e., T for "tours," H for "hotels," etc.) and recapped at the end of the month to get the total sales for each category.

11. Steamship sales. Enter cruise or transportation sale via ship, including port taxes.

12. Rail/bus sales. Enter amount collected for transportation (code R for "rail" and B for "bus"). Tours featuring rail or bus would normally be entered under land arrangements.

13. Miscellaneous sales and/or other income. Enter travel services or sales to customers that are not listed in any other category and will earn a commission for the agent (e.g., travelers' insurance, travelers' checks/ money orders, gift certificates, gift parcels, bon voyage gifts). This account may also be used to record service charges and cancellation fees, which are retained by the agent.

14. Details (description). This space is used to record ticket numbers, name of tour operator or steamship line, or any other details that help in cross-referencing the monies received and payments made to the principals.

15. Suspense account. The majority of entries in this column will be entries made to record refunds received from tour operators, hotels, or other principals (other than standard ticket refunds) which will be immediately forwarded to the customer. This column also will be used for recording money received for flight bags, books, or sales that will not earn a commission for the agent. As the term "suspense" indicates, this money will simply be in and out of the checking account and the transaction normally will not affect any of the sales or expense accounts. This account may also be used to enter deposits received from customers for future sales which will not be immediately forwarded or applied to a sales transaction. Strictly speaking, these deposits are normally entered as a credit to accounts receivable; however, this may complicate the accounts receivable account reconciliation. Also, it is easier to keep track of such deposits in the suspense account. A good example of the use of the suspense account is when an agency is wholesaling its own tour. A separate page should be used in the general ledger to record deposits and payments received for this tour until such time as the agency is ready to forward payments to the carriers and principals involved with the tour.

16. Accounts receivable. A double column will be needed for this account. The debit (DR) column should show the exact amount of money still due from the customer in the event that full payment was not received, or the total amount of the sale (which will be paid at a date later than the date the ticket was issued or payment was forwarded to a principal). The credit (CR) column will show the money received from customers on these charge sales, which are sales payable to the agent (not credit card sales, which are sales payable to the organization that issued the credit card and are charged through the airlines or other principals that accept the cards).

17. General ledger. Transactions that cannot be classified as sales but will affect expense accounts, such as money received from the customer for a phone call or cable made at the agent's office, are recorded in the general ledger. (This would be a credit to the phone expense. Telephone calls or cables sent by a tour operator and shown in the customer's invoice would be included in the amount paid for land arrangements.)

18. Details. This space is used for explanations on entries made for the general ledger and accounts receivable.

19. Commissions earned. Two columns should be used for this account unless space is limited. The debit column is used most often to record debit memos from the airlines for unearned commissions. (For debit memos to record the lost commissions, credit the standard ticket sales account to record the money due the airlines.) Also use the debit column to record small amounts that were undercollected from customers against commissions earned rather than spending time and money in billing them for amounts of $1 or less. Commissions received by a separate check from carriers or principals, usually hotels and car rentals, will be credited to this account. A total of the commissions earned columns in the sales and receipts journal and the check disbursement journal will give management a quick monthly income tally.

Check Disbursement Journal

The following information should appear under the column headings in the check disbursement journal (see Figure 5-2):

1. Date of check.
2. Check number.
3. Name (to whom money is paid).
4. Amount of the check.
5. Gross sales paid on standard ticket plan (before commissions or credit card sales are deducted).
6. Gross airline sales not on the standard ticket plan.
7. Credit card sales. Sales paid by credit card on the standard ticket plan.
8. Land arrangements. Gross sales.
9. Steamship/cruise. Gross sales.
10. Rail/bus. Gross sales.
11. Miscellaneous sales. Gross sales of travelers insurance, etc.
12. Details/description. Enter customer's name or other pertinent information needed to cross-reference the transactions.
13. Suspense account. The same amount as that entered in the sales and receipts journal should now be debited in this account. Recall (lost) commission will be debited to the commissions-earned column in the case of refunds from suppliers who deducted the commissions originally taken when the money was forwarded to them. The customer usually gets a full refund; however, some agents are now charging the customer for their (the agents') lost commission on a canceled sale.
14. Accounts receivable. Entries that will affect the customer's account.
15. General ledger accounts. Enter expense items (with appropriate explanation) that may occur once a month or less, such as rent, utilities, or quarterly government taxes.
16. Commissions earned. The amount shown in this column (usually a credit) and the check amount should equal the gross sales.
17. Expense accounts/payroll accounts. The number of columns used will be determined by the activity in each account. The most commonly used expense accounts are: office supplies, advertising and sales promotions (can be combined), outside services (commission salespeople), postage, dues and subscriptions, utilities, telephone, rent, donations, miscellaneous expense, and educational expense (this account heading replaces the familiar term "travel and entertainment"). Since "travel" charged to the organization by owners, managers, and employees is usually for agent's familiarization trips and seminars, this could be more correctly

SALES AND RECEIPTS JOURNAL

Date	Inv. No.	dr Cash	Memo Dep.	cr Std. Ticket Sales	cr Other AL Sales	cr Land	cr Steam Ship Sales	cr Rail Bus	cr Misc. Sales	Detail dr/cr Sus-pense Acct.	dr/cr Accts. Rec.	dr/cr Gen. Ledger	Detail dr/cr Com-missions

CHECK DISBURSEMENTS JOURNAL

Date	Ck. No.	Name	cr Cash	dr Std. ATC Tickets	dr Other Air-Lines	cr Credit Card Sales	dr Land Sales	dr Steam Ship Sales	dr Rail/ Bus	dr Misc.	Detail dr Sus-pense Acct.	dr Accts. Rec.	dr Gen. Ldgr.	dr Com-missions	*Expense Accts. **Payroll dr & cr

Figure 5-2

*Expense accounts such as office supplies, advertising, utilities (where there would be more than 3 or 4 entries during the month). Single entries such as rent, phone, subscriptions, can be entered in the General Ledger Account.

**Payroll accounts—gross pay, FICA, withholding tax, city tax and state tax—can be included in the Check Disbursements Journal when there are 5 or less employees. A larger staff may necessitate the use of a separate Payroll Journal.

listed as educational expense. Entertainment of clients would be more appropriately classified as advertising or sales promotions.

General Ledger

The general ledger is composed of classified pages on which appear the summarization of the transaction data for each account. The sales, commission earned, and the expense accounts often are called *nominal accounts* because at the end of the year the total money amounts reflected in them are transferred to a single net result or profit and loss account.

In addition to the nominal accounts, there are real accounts which are maintained throughout the years. Some of them are constantly changing (like cash) each day, week, or month; some increasing; others remaining the same. The real accounts separately reflect such items as cash balances, amounts owed by customers (accounts receivable), and the cost of office fixtures and other property to which the establishment lays claim—all these are assets or things owned. A second class of real accounts reflects the liabilities or the amounts owed to creditors for services received from them but not yet paid for (e.g., deposits and payments received from customers but not yet disbursed) and to owners of the business for their original investment and for the retained profits that increase their investment.

Posting the summarized account totals from the journals to the ledger should be the responsibility of an accountant. An experienced accountant can save hundreds, perhaps thousands of dollars for the company simply by posting the expense in the proper account. Also, it is a well-known fact that it is easier to catch another's mistake than it is to catch your own. No matter how conscientious the bookkeeper may be, it is best to have an outside accountant come in to post the journal entries to the ledger and prepare the financial statements.

Simplified Profit-and-Loss Statement (or Cash Flow Statement)

A profit-and-loss statement may be prepared by the bookkeeper at the end of each month after reconciling the accounts in the sales and receipts journal and the check disbursement journal without waiting for the accountant to come in. This simplified statement may not be totally accurate according to strict accounting standards, but it would give management an immediate picture of the sales and commissions earned during the previous month.

In modern accounting this type of statement can also be referred to as the cash flow statement. The first item in this report would be the totals of the commissions-earned columns taken from both the sales and receipts journal and the check disbursement journal broken down by sales categories (i.e., airline, land, cruises, etc.). Expenses are picked up from both journals. Monthly profit or loss is found by subtracting all expenses from commissions earned. Sales account totals would be itemized from the check disbursement journal, since this journal reflects the completed sales. Commissions earned by category could be shown on the same line as the total sales by category, thus enabling the comparison of sales and commissions.

The outstanding accounts receivables and accounts payables will then be summarized and aged (show the date of original entry). This cash flow report will not reflect accruals, depreciations or tax expenses, but as stated earlier, it will give management a quick summary of the month's transactions.

Accounts Receivable Ledger

Most agencies try to keep their charge sales at a minimum. Airline tickets must be paid whether or not the agent has collected from the passengers, and since this payment can amount to a good-sized figure, most agents cannot afford to have their operating money tied up in accounts receivable. Delinquent travel bills are difficult to collect. Once the trip is over, clients do not feel that travel debts are as important as their other bills. Agencies that specialize in commercial accounts (that pay by statement once or twice a month) will definitely require an accounts receivable ledger or some method of control over charge sales.

The ledger method consists of a separate binder, or subdivision of the journals, that contains individual ledger sheets for each customer wherein entries are made from both the sales and receipts journal and the check disbursement journal of all transactions affecting the account (manual method) or (if computerized) a separate listing in the accounting program. These entries should be posted daily, if possible, in order to keep a current balance for each customer at all times. At the end of the month, a total is taken of the outstanding charges, which should agree with the accounts receivable account total in the general ledger. Discrepancies should be checked out immediately as they can affect other accounts. For example, a voided ticket was not removed from accounts receivable, or a credit card sale was entered as a charge sale.

Detail or Recap Ledgers

The airline sales recap (recapitulation) ledger is necessary for new agencies. During the waiting period for appointment approval, a new agent should keep track of all airline sales (even though they may be noncommissionable). This record should show a breakdown by airline, destination, fare, date of sale, name of passenger, ticket numbers, and amount of retroactive commission due the agency. The information contained in this ledger will then be used to supply proof of productivity to the conferences and will be used when requesting payment of retroactive commissions earned.

A separate ledger can also be set up to keep a record of sales according to tour operators. This record is useful in keeping track of sales made to tour operators who maintain quotas for travel agents and pay additional commissions (overrides) when those quotas are exceeded. Most tour operators (wholesalers) automatically send the agency a check for their override at the end of the year. Some will increase the commission as soon as the quota is met, but if agents know they are nearing the sales quota, they may be able to steer additional business to that particular tour operator and thus be sure of their override.

Record of Sales by Individual Employees

This record is usually maintained by agencies with a large staff to determine the productivity of each travel consultant. This information is useful for payroll and bonus purposes and is an aid to management in decisions involving personnel: Should the size of the staff be increased or decreased; are the profits equal or higher than the cost of maintaining each employee?

OFFICE FORMS

The most commonly used business forms in a travel agency, other than the invoices and voucher checks, are:

1. Reservation information (sheets or cards). An $8\frac{1}{2}$- by 11-inch sheet provides room for hotel, tour, car rental, steamship, or bus details as well as providing for a lengthy flight itinerary. A file card is often used for simple air travel, but in the interest of consistency and elimination of duplicate file systems, it is preferable to use either one or the other rather than both. This form can be ordered from printers who specialize in travel agency forms, or

AGENT _____ **ORDERED BY (SECRETARY/SELF)** _____ **DATE OF REQUEST** _____
PASSENGERS NAME/S & ADDRESSES(Age of children)   **CONTACT PHONE NO'S**
                                          B—BUSINESS   H—HOME

_____

_____

_____

_____

_____

CHARGE/DELIVER TO _____ **CREDIT CARD#** _____

                                                  EXP. DATE _____

Ticketing Date _____ Ticket No's. _____ **RESERVATIONIST SINE** _____

FROM	TO	Fare Basis	Via	Flt. No.	Day	Date	LEAVE	ARRIVE	OK	REMARKS

TOUR NO. _____ **TOUR OP./AL TOUR DESK** _____ **PHONE** _____
HOTEL/CAR RENTAL REPRESENTATIVE _____ **PHONE** _____
STEAMSHIP LINE/RAIL/BUS LINE _____ **PHONE** _____

HOTEL/CAR/CRUISE REQUIREMENTS						
Hotel/Car/Ship (Name-type)	Destination City	No. of Nights	Room Type	Dates Ar./Lv.	Rates or Meal Plan	REMARKS

Figure 5-3

a variation of Figure 5-3 can be customized by your local printer or run off on your own copying machine. Since it is a form used only by the office staff, it does not have to be elaborate or expensive.

    Computerized agencies are advised by the airlines that this paper is no longer necessary; however, I disagree with that theory. A reservation information sheet (or card) is still needed, especially when the computers are down and a passenger needs fast answers about his or her flight schedule, or when an error was made and the record cannot be located. It takes only a few seconds to jot down the PNR (passenger name record) and the record locator

Chap. 5 / Office Procedures

number. It must also be kept in mind that computer records are not permanent.

2. Itinerary draft worksheet. An itinerary draft worksheet for group tours or FIIs (foreign independent itineraries) in calendar form or report form is another item used strictly by the office personnel and can be ordered from a printer or originated in your own office.

3. Reservation confirmation. This can be a preprinted form which is sent to the customer to confirm the arrangements made for him or it can be an individually typed letter. Preprinted forms can save time, but there are occasions when a personal letter is more impressive and effective.

4. Reply message forms (multiple message forms). These are printed three-part forms with space allowed for the receiver to answer and return to the sender. The multiple message set also comes in four parts, enabling an agent to give the customer a copy. This form is especially useful for last-minute hotel or car rental reservations when the customer is departing before a confirming reply could possibly be received from the principal. This form should be used only for correspondence within the industry. Correspondence with clients should always be on the company's letterhead stationery or memos.

5. Hotel reservations request. There are several variations of printed forms to send to hotels, but they do not always provide enough room for special remarks or instructions. The multiple message forms are more useful for a detailed reservation. Actually, few hotel reservations other than international are still made by mail; 99 percent of hotel reservations are made by phone to a toll-free number either directly to the hotel or to a hotel representative.

6. Travel vouchers. These are used when the agent prepays hotel or other travel arrangements to the principals for his own group tours or independent itineraries. The tour operator/wholesaler usually will provide the travel vouchers when a package tour is sold to the customer. Vouchers are given to clients to present to the hotel or car rental company when they check in. One copy is sent to the principal with the payment (less commission) and one copy remains in the client file.

7. Many other printed agency forms and form letters are available from travel agency printers or can be made to order by the agent's own printer to eliminate time spent in letter writing. The majority of these forms are useful and timesaving, but the agent may start relying too much on form letters and lose the personal touch that is so important in the relationship between the customer and the consultant. The exception would be in the use of a PC (personal computer) and a good word-processing program to create form letters that can be personalized with the mail-merge program.

The Mines Press, Inc. in New York has an excellent supply of timesaver forms (4 by 8½ inches) designed for travel agents. Some are: "As You Requested" (to be enclosed with brochures or information requested by phone or mail), "Short Notes" and "Speed Messages" (ruled or blank), "Change of Plans" and "Cancellation of Room Arrangements" (to be sent to suppliers), "Check Transmittal Memorandum" (if the agency does not use voucher checks), and many others. Samples will be sent by Mines Press upon request.

There are many other forms and form letters that could be used in an agency. One of the more important ones could be the "Commission Reminder" letter or card sent to hotels, car rental companies, or other principals where a reservation only was confirmed for the customer and payment was made directly to the principal. A "Commission Due" file should be maintained for this type of travel arrangement and a reminder sent to the principals 30 days after travel has been completed.

One of the major complaints of most travel agencies is the outright refusal or late payment of commissions earned through hotel and car rental reservations. In an effort to help agencies with this problem, Travel Trade Publications initiated a *commission bypass collection program*. They designed a letter, S.O.P. (standard operating procedure), that agents can copy or modify and send to late payers with a copy to the *Travel Trade* Bypass column. If the agents do not receive their commissions within two weeks, they notify *Travel Trade* to publish the company's name in its travel agency bypass and noncommission payers' column. The program has been highly successful, and during the two years that it has been used, over 5000 travel agents have received well in excess of $600,000 in past-due commissions. *Travel Trade* now reports that they receive more "thank you" letters from agents than requests for a copy of the S.O.P. letter.

8. Stationery and envelopes. The travel business is mainly a luxury business and must foster that image in every way possible. A simple but attractive and distinguished letterhead on good bond paper for your stationery and envelopes used for all customer mailings is essential in promoting that image from within. Paper is cheap compared to the cost of other advertising. First impressions are usually lasting. Quite often the first contact with a customer is through a mailing of brochures or information requested by telephone or mail. In these cases, an envelope of poor quality with a stamped or badly printed letterhead will not create a very good image.

Savings on stationery and supplies can be accomplished in a number of ways. For example, good-quality paper should always be used, but in smaller sizes for shorter messages. In many instances, agencies use postal cards (with preprinted message and return address) to request brochures, availability information, or replies to their suppliers and principals. The use of disposable carbons (carbon sets) instead of onionskin and regular carbon paper will save both time and money. Offices equipped with a copying machine can save time and money by photocopying written replies on incoming letters. The copy is put into the agency files and the original letter is mailed. Copying machines can also be used when it is necessary to send a follow-up on a request for information. The carbon of the first letter is photocopied and sent to the addressee (with the current date). This usually brings an answer and no extra typing is necessary. Of course, this can also be accomplished by adding an additional carbon when typing the original letter, but it cannot always be predetermined when the additional copy will be necessary.

Fax (facsimile) machines are now used almost universally in the travel industry. The initial output may be high; the average-size unit for a small office costs approximately $1195 per unit. Paper costs average between six and nine cents for receiving a message, and sending a message is approximately the cost of a phone call. However, the convenience of sending and receiving written material within a few hours may be well worth the cost.

Further reductions in cost and faster service can be accomplished by answering letters by telephone whenever possible. Another important method of time and cost reduction is a properly equipped workstation for each travel consultant. Additional subscriptions to the OAGs and other frequently used reference books will be more economical in the long run than attempting to use one set of books for the entire staff. Hundreds of dollars (in time and aggravation) can be saved each year if consultants do not have to leave their desks to search for a guide or to borrow someone's stapler or dictionary. Supplies of ticket stock, invoices, and voucher checks, and the brochure files—items that cannot be distributed among all employees—should be in a centrally located area easily accessible to all.

Some firms have found it economical to enforce the rule "no supplies for personal use." Petty pilferage of postage stamps, rubber bands, pens, pencils, paper, and so on, by employees adds up to a substantial inventory loss in many offices during the course of a year.

Postage is an unavoidable expense in a travel agency, but postage and mailing economy is possible and profitable. Mechanized mailrooms, including automatic folders and inserters, staplers, and postage, can save money for large offices; so can the "free ride" method of mailing. According to post office estimates, the average first-class letter weighs less than a half-ounce, yet senders are entitled to one ounce's worth of letter transportation for each stamp. The wise agent could use his other half-ounce with "free ride" material such as "stuffers" provided by carriers and tour operators, or a general information or city sightseeing tour brochure relating to the client's destination.

Keep in mind that no matter how much is spent on good-quality paper, engraving, and postage, if the letter is not carefully constructed and neatly typed, everything else is worthless. Therefore, it is important that every letter that goes out of the office be clean, attractive, and error-free.

RETAINING ARC RECORDS

Questions often arise about how long records and paperwork used in the course of conducting a travel agency should be kept. The airline conferences require that airline sales reports and supporting detail (agent's coupons, debit and credit memos, reservation records, client files, etc.) must be kept for a minimum of two years.

The schedule in Figure 5-4 lists the minimum periods necessary to comply with federal, state, and municipal law for other documents and office records.

THE BASIC SYSTEM OF TRAVEL AGENCY FILING

In addition to the records mentioned previously, and the completed customer files and the check voucher file, the travel agency has the unique problem of obtaining and filing the enormous quantity of brochures needed to service their customers. There have been many discussions and many articles written concerning the quantity and selection of brochures to be kept in agents' files. This is a decision that should be made by individual agents. You must keep in mind, however, that the brochures are both your inventory and your selling tools. Travel customers expect agents to present them with brochures on particular tours or destinations they are inquiring about. If those brochures—or some tangible evidence that the agent is capable of taking care of his request—are not immediately forthcoming, the customer may well walk out to look for an agent who can supply them. The general public has the misconception that only the agent who advertises a tour and has the brochures to give to them is authorized to sell that tour. Only experienced travelers know that any agent can sell any tour that is advertised.

The large volume of brochures that once overflowed on agents' desks has now decreased. Carriers and tour operators are now mailing only one or two copies of their brochures, accompanied by a self-addressed order card. This gives agents the opportunity to request only the material they feel is needed in their office and still have a copy of each selection on hand in the event that a customer requests information on an area the agent does not normally service. Since travel agents are expected to know everything, they cannot afford to neglect any geographic area or special-interest tour. They may get only one inquiry a year on this area, but that one inquiry may turn out to be a $5000 order.

Many steamship lines will no longer do a general mailing of new brochures; they will wait for a brochure request from the agents. Several brochure mailing services (such as Western Folder) are now being used by carriers and others to send brochures to agents. An order folder is sent to agents, who then select only

RECORDS RETENTION TIMETABLE

Types of Records	Period to be Retained
ACCOUNTING RECORDS	
General Ledger, Subsidiary Ledgers and General Journal	Permanently
Cash, Sales, Disbursement, and Payroll Journals	Seven years
Copies of the annual financial statements of the business	Permanently
Cancelled checks and bank statements	Three years
Vendors' invoices, purchase orders and other related records	Three years*
Sales invoices, credits, customers' correspondence and other related records	Five years**
Internal accounting reports, such as operating analyses, budgets, and comparison reports	As long as useful
TAX RETURNS	
Federal Income, State Income, City Income	Permanently
State Corporation Franchise	Five years
State Personal Tangible and Intangible Personal Property	Five years
State Sales and Use Tax	Four years
Federal, State, and City reports relating to employees' income taxes, Social Security taxes, Unemployment Compensation taxes and Workmen's Compensation reports	Four years
PAYROLL AND RELATED RECORDS	
Employees' individual earnings records	Four years
Employees' time cards or time sheets	Seven years
Employees' familiarization trip authorizations	Two years
Retirement and pension plan records, including deduction authorization records	Permanently
Employment contracts, group insurance records	Permanently
OTHER SALES AND PURCHASING RECORDS	
Bulletins and memos from carriers and principals	As long as useful
Sales analysis reports and records	As long as useful
Correspondence with vendors, vendor quotations, etc.	As long as useful
General correspondence	As long as useful
Customer mailing lists	Clean every 2 years
CORPORATE RECORDS	
Certificate of incorporation	Permanently
Charter	Permanently
Constitution and by-laws	Permanently
Resolutions and minutes of directors' and stockholders' meetings	Permanently
Authorizations and appropriations	Permanently

*Maintain in a permanent file the vendors' invoices covering acquisitions of property, plant, and equipment, and other expenditures of a permanent nature.
**Retain paperwork on uncollected or litigated items.

Figure 5-4 Information courtesy of Michael Business Machines.

the brochures they want to use in their offices. Suppliers ship all their brochures to the mailing service, and the agent's order is filled and sent in one shipment.

Many agents are now using some form of wall display racks or pegboard and brackets to file tour or package brochures, reserving their file cabinets for hotel, general information, and special-interest brochures. These wall displays can play an important part in the decor of your office. There is no denying that the majority of brochures are attractive and colorful. Wall displays are also a convenience to both staff and customer. However, the brochures must be filed just as carefully on the wall as they are in the file cabinet. They should be grouped in geographic or special-interest areas, and care must be taken to keep only current copies on display. As new copies arrive, the outdated literature should be discarded.

Maintaining a supply of hotel brochures is another source of contention. Some agents feel that they are a waste of space, but a package or group tour sale is easier to sell when customers are shown detailed brochures of the hotels they will be visiting. Since it is impossible to maintain a file of brochures from every hotel in the world, it is more advisable to request brochures and rate sheets from only the major resort areas and most popular hotels in the larger cities. Other hotel brochures can be requested as needed.

Suggested Method of Filing Travel Literature

A. By Area
   1. United States and Canada
      a. Individual states or provinces
      b. Subdivide by major cities and resort areas
         1. Hotel and resort brochures
         2. General information brochures
   2. Europe and Asia
      a. Individual countries
      b. Subdivide by major cities and resort areas
         1. Tours
         2. Hotels
         3. General information
      c. Specific area tours
         1. Mediterranean
         2. Eastern Europe
         3. Scandinavian countries
         4. British Isles
         5. Holy Land
         6. General Europe
   3. Bahamas, Bermuda, Caribbean, Virgin Islands, West Indies
      a. Tours
      b. Hotels and resorts
      c. General information
   4. Mexico, Central America, South America, Africa
      a. Tours
      b. Major cities: hotels
      c. General information

Special-Interest Tours and Information
   1. Art and music
   2. Campsites: United States & Europe
   3. Gambling resorts/casinos
   4. Garden tours: United States and Europe
   5. Health spas: United States and Europe
   6. Honeymoon package tours and hotels
   7. National parks: United States and Canada
   8. Nevada: Las Vegas and Reno
   9. New England tours
  10. New York City show tours
  11. Niagara Falls, United States and Canada
  12. Rail tours (could be combined with rail—general information)
  13. Scuba diving and water sports
  14. Skiing: United States, Canada, Europe, others
  15. Special events: Mardi Gras, Rose Bowl, etc.
  16. Sports
      a. Fishing resorts
      b. Golfing resorts

       c.   Hunting camps/safaris
       d.   Tennis resorts
  17.   Student tours: United States and Europe
  18.   Youth/adult hostels: United States, Europe, others

Carriers and Other Services
   1.   Airlines
       a.   ARC and IATAN (appointment files)
       b.   Scheduled airlines
       c.   Charter (nonscheduled) airlines
       d.   Air taxis; helicopter services
   2.   Bus (motorcoach) lines: United States
       a.   Transportation
       b.   Sightseeing companies
       c.   Charter services
   3.   Bus (motorcoach) lines: Europe and others
   4.   Car rental companies: United States
   5.   Car rentals/purchases/shipping: Europe
   6.   Car rentals: other areas
   7.   Rail/Eurailpass: Europe
   8.   Rail: United States (Amtrak)
   9.   Steamship lines
       a.   Passenger lines: cruises
          1.   Cruise folders
          2.   Bulletins and cruise tips
          3.   Deck plans
       b.   Passenger–cargo liners/freighters
       c.   Yacht charters: Caribbean, Mediterranean, others
       d.   Cruises, by ports of call
          1.   Caribbean
          2.   Mediterranean
          3.   Scandinavian
          4.   South American
          5.   Orient/South Pacific
          6.   Round the world
          7.   Windjammer
  10.   Hotel representatives and hotel chains
  11.   Tour operators
       a.   Bulletins, general correspondence
       b.   File copies of their brochures
  12.   Customer document applications/travel tips
       a.   Passport applications
       b.   Visa applications (by country)
       c.   Tourist card applications
       d.   Health certificates/public health department bulletins
       e.   Custom tips
       f.   Travel tips: United States, Europe, others
       g.   Currency converters
       h.   Immigration forms
       i.   Travel advisories
  13.   Advertising and promotional aids
  14.   Travel agents' fam trips, trade discounts

QUESTIONS AND PROBLEMS

1. What are the two methods of making more money in a business?
2. Give examples of each method.
3. What are the assets in a business? The liabilities?
4. Give a sample transaction in a travel agency.
5. Describe the two forms used in the basic bookkeeping system.
6. List three or more form letters that you would use in a travel agency.
7. How long should agents' copies of airline tickets be held?
8. What type of agency would benefit most from the suggested literature filing system?

chapter 6

Marketing Versus Selling

OBJECTIVES

When you have finished this chapter you should be able to:

1. Give a definition of marketing.
2. Describe the difference between selling skills and marketing skills.
3. Discuss the abilities needed for a good salesperson and a good marketing person.
4. List some examples of sales promotions for a travel agency.
5. Prepare an advertising campaign.
6. Research travel markets.

INTRODUCTION

The key word in today's discussions concerning the travel agent is marketing. *Webster's New World Dictionary* says: "marketing—all business activity involved in the moving of goods from the producer to the consumer, including selling, advertising, packaging, etc." Marketing basically is observing the forest instead of the trees. Most agents are so involved in day-to-day routines that they do not or cannot find time to observe and plan the direction of their business. Most agencies have grown large through the normal growth pattern without much effort from the agent. Many agents were content to sit and wait for business to come to them, but the first three years of the 1980s shocked a lot of agents out of their complacency. The recession and the Persian Gulf War in 1990 reminded them again that the travel market cannot be taken for granted. The slowdown in the economy and the consumers' fear of travel forced the travel industry to take a new look at marketing strategies.

Getting and keeping customers depends on doing the right thing in terms of what the customer thinks, values, and does, but it also depends on what the competition does. The agency's entire operation should be geared toward discovering the customer's total needs and attempting to satisfy them.

Selling is generally concerned with the plans and tactics of trying to get customers to exchange what they have (money) for what you have (services). *Marketing* is concerned primarily with the much more sophisticated strategy of trying to have what the customer will want. Selling focuses on the needs of the seller, marketing on the needs of the buyer. Selling is preoccupied with the sellers' need to convert their product (travel) into cash, marketing with the idea of satisfying the needs of the customer by means of services rendered as well as the other customer value satisfactions associated with planning, preparing, and experiencing his travels.

Marketing, then, is something more than a business function. It is a view of the entire business process. It affects everything an agency does, how it is organized, how it allocates its money between its salespeople, advertising, accounting, and so on. But marketing is concerned with more than the matter of overall business strategy and keeping up with the competition. It is concerned with insights or research into customer behavior, with speculations, hunches, and solidly documented facts about *what* customers want, need, prefer, fear, and value—*who* the prospects are and *where* they live, *how* they make their travel decisions and how they react to various promotional stimuli, various price levels, fashion trends, various tour attributes, different types of salespeople, and different combinations of all of these. Finally, research is done to find out *why* customers are traveling: for business, pleasure, a combination of both, or for personal reasons? Each agency can start research with their own client list by sending clients either a written questionnaire to complete at the end of their trips, or informally by phone, to welcome them back and ask how they enjoyed their trips and what they liked or disliked during their travels.

Research, the tool for marketing, has been used successfully by airlines, hotels, tour operators, and tourist boards, but few individual travel agents have used this tool. Research can be conducted informally with the agents' regular clients, but with the increasing competition (not only from other agents, but also from other competition for clients' money), agents should be looking for new markets and new clients. Professional help is available at a reasonable fee. The Travel and Tourism Research Association (TTRA) has compiled a directory of member companies that offer specialized research services for the travel and tourism industry. The directory is available to nonmembers. TTRA is an independent organization of travel research and marketing professionals. Its nearly 700 members include representatives of airlines, accommodations, attractions, transportation companies, media, advertising and consulting firms, public relations, government tourism agencies (foreign and domestic), convention and visitors' bureaus, universities, and other organizations interested in travel research and marketing. Membership categories are: *basic* for organizations and individuals, *educational* for schools, and *student* (nonvoting) to encourage student participation in TTRA. Membership benefits include the subscription to the *Journal of Travel Research* and other publications and reduced registration fees for their annual conference and seminars.

Marketing is concerned with agency policy. First, an agent must decide what kind of agent she wants to be and what kind of markets she wants to go after. What price tours should be offered: low-, medium-, or high-priced luxury tours? Should they concentrate on the few tour operators who specialize in tours their clientele seems to prefer, or should they stock all the brochures available? Should they make up their own tours or block space on advertised tours? Should their agency insist on cash or allow the customer time payments? Should the agency forward deposits and payments before receiving a customer's money? What about the policy on bon voyage gifts: When is the customer entitled to a free gift from the agent, and how much should be spent on a gift and what form should it take— flowers, champagne, fruit, books, bar credits, a sightseeing trip?

Marketing is concerned with salespeople and sales compensation. How does the agent find, select and train salespeople? Should they be paid commission on sales, straight salary, or a combination of both? Should the agent encourage outside salespeople? How much commission should be paid for simple referrals? Should the tour conductor who is not an employee be paid commission in addition to receiving the free trip?

Marketing is concerned with advertising and sales promotions. Should the agent advertise on television, radio, newspapers, direct mail, or not at all? If so, what days, for how long, at what expense? If direct mail, should it be brochure, newsletter or newspaper, and how often and to whom should it be sent? How should the advertising budget be determined: by a percentage of sales or by a percentage of profits? Should he use the hard-sell; the repetitious, drum-beat approach; or the soft-sell, the quietly intimate conversational approach? Should newspaper ads have lots of picture and little copy, or lots of copy and smaller pictures? Should the ads be humorous or serious? Should they promote the high-priced tour or quote the lowest possible one? Should they sell a specific tour or sell the destination? These are questions that must be asked and answered according to each agent's needs and desires in order to set up an effective marketing program.

Marketing is also concerned with effective organizing. Ads in newspapers and on radio or television, as well as mailing pieces, window displays, and even the decor of the office should be coordinated toward the image the agent wants to place before the public.

A travel agency's survival depends on how effectively individual agents make the decisions involved in formulating a marketing program that will enable them to compete not only with other travel agents but also with the many other industries that are competing for consumer dollars. Domestic airlines in the United States reluctantly increased agents' commissions on airline ticket sales and since then have been directing many pointed questions at the agents' ability to generate new business.

Personal selling procedures and sales promotional efforts will become more and more important. The ultimate success or failure of any marketing effort will be determined by the competence of the people who generate that effort.

SELLING FUNCTIONS

Travel is a business, and like any other business, it must make money for its owners and/or its investors or it will not exist for long. It is a business managed and sold by professionals. Travel is not a can of beans on a grocer's shelf that can be sold by anyone who can read the price tag.

More than one franchise operation has burst on the scene with the grandiose statement that the independent travel agent will disappear the same way that the mom-and-pop grocery disappeared when faced with competition from the chain supermarkets. They claim that eventually the chain operation is going to take over the industry. But as time goes by it is the franchisers who fall by the wayside—simply because they overlook the very important and very obvious fact that you cannot franchise a *personal service*.

Travel agents cannot be compared to grocers who must join a chain or coop in order to exist. As long as appointed agents can sell a ticket for every flight listed in the OAGs or the computer, and as long as they can book any advertised tour or hotel, they have no need to buy a franchise or to join a co-op or any other organization unless they wish to do so for personal reasons. It is ironic that during the past few years a number of chain supermarkets and department stores have gone out of business and the mom-and-pops are coming back and doing very well as epicure shops or boutiques.

The very first conclusion arrived at by Touche, Ross, Bailey, and Smart when they did their first cost study of travel agencies and city airline ticket offices was that travel agents perform 18 different functions in ticketing a domestic airline passenger. Even with automation the list of time-consuming functions is the same:

1. Public relations activities
2. Preparation of advertising
3. Telephone solicitation
4. Face-to-face talks with customers
5. Letters to customers and prospects
6. Checking for availability for reservations
7. Direct access to reservations
8. Letters regarding reservations
9. Furnishing fare data
10. Documentation of tickets
11. Other required documentation
12. Correspondence with carriers
13. Clerical work
14. Ticket billing
15. General accounting
16. Selection of personnel
17. Training personnel
18. Personal time

These 18 diverse functions were listed for domestic sales (air travel in the United States and Canada) and for an airline ticket only. The list of time-consuming functions is greatly increased as soon as the customer adds a request for hotels, car rentals, or other ground arrangements. The list also expands when an international destination is requested and the customer requires assistance with passport applications, visa or tourist card applications, customs rules, and health regulations. Questions must be answered on weather, currency, baggage, and clothing.

Travel consultants must be professional and skilled craftspeople who first sell themselves, then endeavor to fulfill their obligations to contribute productively to company sales efforts to justify and ensure their salaries. Nonproductive employees can bring about business failures and unemployment.

The travel consultant basically is the salesperson for the agency. As the direct link between the agency and its customers, salespeople *are* the agency. It is their responsibility to carry out all the objectives and functions assigned to them by management and to show imagination and flexibility in handling situations that have not been anticipated.

In discharging these general responsibilities, the sales staff has many things to do. They may discuss travel arrangements with customers, make the reservations, issue the tickets, and collect money. They may assist the manager in writing and advertising campaigns. They may help train new employees, arrange window displays, and help stuff envelopes for a direct mailing. They may also serve as a source of market information, keeping management up to date on competitive activities, customer attitudes, and the characteristics and plans of individual customers. They must upgrade their knowledge of the travel products, especially destinations, at every opportunity. Finally, together with these and many other activities, they may prepare the airline sales reports and assist with bookkeeping entries.

RECRUITMENT AND SELECTION OF EMPLOYEES

Recruiting, selecting, and training new employees is a facet of good marketing and one of the very important duties of the manager. Hiring the right person for the job can sometimes be quite costly. Not only is the cost of advertising and payment of an employment agency's fee involved, but there are the unknown costs that result from customer dissatisfaction and reduced morale among the sales force if the new employee is unsuited for the job. Every few years there is a scarcity of qualified personnel caused by people leaving the industry for higher-paying jobs or an increase of new agencies that need experienced personnel immediately. Quite often, desperate managers will hire people without even asking for references. They will accept the fact that applicants are, or have been, employed as travel consultants as a sufficient basis for hiring them. This method of hiring may be the most costly of all.

Experience is the most important qualification that agents look for when hiring new people. Most agents will not even take time to interview an applicant who is not familiar with the travel industry. Experience is important, of course, but enthusiasm and a genuine desire to work and learn should not be discounted.

One solution to the problem of recruiting and training is to hire graduates of reputable travel training schools. There is no denying that it is difficult to train new employees during the hustle and bustle of a busy office. Graduates can be trained more easily in the agent's office procedures and policies than having to retrain those already in the work force. Not all schools are alike, however, and employers should check the credentials of the school as well as those of its students.

Figure 6-2 The challenging Princess golf courses.

Schools that emphasize selling techniques as well as computer training and are taught by people who have also held positions in the travel industry are more likely to turn out students with the qualifications sought by employers.

Another solution is part-time help recruited through high schools and colleges in their work/study programs. By starting their training by filing brochures, answering phones, and doing routine typing tasks, they will at least know the general procedures and office routine when they graduate from school and are ready for full-time employment.

Some travel and tourism schools and colleges offer their students internships in cooperation with local travel agencies, tourist boards, and tour operators. Although usually not paid by the companies they work for, most interns receive college credit. This may be a valuable experience for the student in learning how to function in a real-life business environment and in making valuable contacts within the industry, but it has been my experience that unpaid employees can often be more of a distraction than a help in a busy office. Trainees who are paid at least the minimum wage are more productive and eager to advance.

THE OUTSIDE SALESPERSON

The third possibility is outside salespeople. *Outside salesperson* is a term generally used for commission salespeople, those who do not receive a salary and may or may not be listed on the payroll, but who are paid a specific percentage of sales brought into the office. There usually are three categories of commission salespeople: inside salespeople, outside salespeople, and the referral agent. The first two categories are recognized by the airline conferences if employed full-time or a minimum of 35 hours a week and earn the equivalent of 50 weeks at minimum wage. These salespeople will be eligible for reduced-rate travel privileges. If they are steady contributors to the agent's business, regardless of whether they are listed on the payroll records or paid as an independent contractor and have no other gainful employment, there should be no concern about their legal status. However, the agent should protect himself from ARC or IATAN investigations and the IRS (Internal Revenue Service) by placing all salespeople on their payroll records even though it may mean paying higher payroll taxes. Also, some airlines are now asking for a copy of the outside salesperson's W2 or W9 (payroll tax forms) before granting a request for reduced-rate transportation.

According to a survey taken by *Travel Weekly* on commission salespeople, there are a wide variety of individual pay arrangements and many conflicting opinions on the value of using outside salespeople. The majority of agents use outside salespeople to bring in group business. They will seldom get involved with the paperwork, but may supervise overall planning of a tour and go along with an important group as tour conductor (*tour manager* and *tour escort* are interchangeable terms). Promotional costs for their groups are shared by the agency and the salesperson in the same proportion of commissions earned.

Inside salespeople, as the name implies, may work full-time on the premises of the agent on a commission basis instead of a salary. They cannot be classified as independent contractors, as they are under the management of the owner/manager and are included in the payroll records. They are provided office space and training, observe office hours, and are included in employee benefits. A contract or agreement should be in effect between the salesperson and the agency, spelling out their duties and rate of commission. Some agencies will provide them with sales leads, while others will expect the inside salesperson to bring in their own customers.

The *outside salespeople* are expected to handle all of their own paperwork and follow through on their sales from start to finish, on their own time and usually on their own premises. This requires someone with experience or training; otherwise, the time spent by the regular staff in following up on the commission salesperson's leads would result in less profits rather than more. However, this can be a good way to break in new employees. They would usually start as *referral agents* (at a lower rate of commission); that is, they would refer customers to the agency but would not get involved in the travel arrangements except as an interested bystander. As time goes by, and if the agency and its staff take the time to explain what was done for their referrals and how it was done, a referral agent would gradually develop into an outside salesperson.

How much outside salespeople should be paid is a thorny question. Some agents pay a combination of salary plus commission; others set a pay scale dependent on how much work the person does which could be from 10 percent to as much as 60 percent of the commission earned.

Commercial accounts brought in by outside salespeople may earn 20 percent of the commission earned during the first year and 5 percent on continuing years, again dependent on how much work the salesperson puts into it. Or they may simply be paid a *finder's fee* for the account. Commercial account selling takes more salesmanship, a lot more time, and lots of perserverance. Commercial account salespeople may have to be subsidized for six months or so, until they build a client list.

Careful records should be kept on the business brought in or generated by outside salespeople. It would also be advisable to have a signed sales contract from each that would spell out their responsibilities, limitations, compensation, and what (if any) travel privileges they would be entitled to after a specific period of employment. (Due to scrutiny of independent contractors by the IRS, it would be wise to have the contract drawn up or reviewed by an attorney familiar with labor laws.) They should also receive a copy of the office manual on policy and procedures.

After a trial period of perhaps three to six months, their work and earnings record should be reviewed by the owner and/or manager. If the earnings are less than the minimum requirement set by the office, there should be no hesitation in letting them go. However, if the commission salespeople are capable of processing their own orders at little or no additional expense to the agency, they should, by all means, be encouraged. Some agencies refuse to use anyone other than commission employees.

Rent a Desk

A growing trend among travel agencies is the rent-a-desk option for outside salespeople. The independent contractors rent office space and equipment from the agency and they keep all or most of the commissions earned on their sales, depending on the agreement made with the landlord agency. They pay their own office expenses and may share in the overrides earned by their productivity. They usually receive office support in the form of bookkeeping, automation enhancements, telephone-answering service, participation in health insurance plans, and inclusion in the errors and omissions policy.

They keep their own clientele, set their own hours (within the framework of the agency's hours), pay their own assistants, and must assume all responsibility for their receivables. This option is not for everyone; it takes people who have large personal followings and who are good with customers but don't like to be managed. It may also be difficult for agency owners to cope with the fact that the renters are really their customers who bring in other customers. There may also be resentment from the full-time employees, who see the independent contractors free to service their own clients in their own way and to make more money. Some agencies have set up separate areas for their desk tenants.

Chap. 6 / Marketing Versus Selling

Contracts that clearly spell out the terms of the desk renter and agency landlord agreement are very important. Since the renters are using the agency's name and ARC number in their transactions, they must agree to take responsibility for airline debit memos, credit card chargebacks, and contracts that the renter signed in the agency's name. The contract should describe what the agency will provide the renter and a clear-cut outline of the commission split. In case of termination, the agency should be able to hold back payments of commissions until all of the receivables are collected, and a limited noncompete clause preventing renters from soliciting accounts of the agency and giving the renters the undisputed right to their own client list must be included.

SALES PROMOTIONS

Every customer has a reason for selecting a particular travel agency. The reasons are many and varied. He or she may have heard of the agent from a friend or relative, may belong to the same clubs or organizations, may have heard that it is a long-established and reputable company, may have seen an ad or received a direct mailing piece, or may simply have seen the outdoor sign and stopped in because it was convenient to home or office. Once the customer steps inside the door, it is up to one of the sales staff to do some *personal selling*, to develop that special reason why the customer should use this agency instead of that of a competitor.

Personal selling and *sales promotion*, along with advertising, are the major components of the overall promotional programs of most agencies. The most effective promotional programs are carefully integrated. Each type of promotional activity will bring maximum effectiveness only if it is coordinated with others. Sales promotion activities in particular should be regarded by management as supplementary devices designed to complement and accentuate, but seldom to replace, personal selling and advertising.

Sales promotion devices play an important role in introducing a new agency. The airlines, tour operators, hotels, and other principals in the travel industry are generous in providing the agent with sales promotion materials and window displays, but few have actually attempted to train agents in the sales promotion strategies and techniques needed to develop the potential business in their area. Since this is a specialized field in itself, we do not attempt here to do other than briefly mention ideas and suggestions gathered from personal experience, from other agents, and from the educational seminars sponsored by ICTA, ARTA, ASTA, and the trade papers.

In addition to helping introduce a new agency, sales promotional programs often are used to:

1. Attract new customers and emphasize the complete-service agency.
2. Assist others in the travel industry in developing interest in a new area or destination.
3. Publicize the agency's own escorted tours.
4. Counter a competitor's sales promotions.
5. Reduce the extent of a seasonal decline in travel.
6. Upgrade the business.

Sales promotional activities aimed directly at prospective customers can be divided into those that reach the customer either (1) in the home (or place of business)—direct mail; (2) at travel shows, fashion shows, film shows or lectures to clubs, schools, churches, or other groups; or (3) in the travel agency itself.

Mailings sent directly to the customer's home or business are one of the most effective means of promoting travel agents, their services, and their product. It can be a relatively inexpensive and flexible medium that even the smallest agency can afford. However, direct mail can be a double-edged sword if it is not carefully supervised in both the content material and the market (mailing list) to which it is sent.

The mailing piece itself could be in a variety of forms. It is generally an $8\frac{1}{2}$-by 11-inch sheet of paper with or without a return coupon in the body of the letter. It could be folded and sent as a self-mailer (saving on the envelope costs); it could be a two-part business reply card (postage prepaid cards bring a better return than nonpaid cards); it can be in the form of a novelty item (calendars, pens, scratch pads, sewing kits, etc.), which usually are sent at Christmas time; or it could be a miniature (or even a full-sized) newspaper sent out at regular intervals: monthly, quarterly, semiannually, or annually.

The newsletter that is the most effective is not the stock newsletter or newspaper that the agent sends out with his imprint, but a more personal letter reporting on the agent's own travels, news items about their clients' travels (be sure to get the clients' permission), and plans for the coming months. A good newsletter should be entertaining as well as informative. Articles should be brief—too much information may get boring. Tease the reader to call and ask for more details. Feature stories on destinations are always popular. Travel tips sent in by clients provide human interest stories as well as current information.

However, if the staff has neither the time nor the writing ability to prepare such a newsletter, the stock newsletter should, by all means, be used. These can be ordered from various companies that prepare a shell with photographs and feature articles that can be filled in with the agency's add-ons—an employee profile, special tour offers or destination reports from employees returning from fam trips, or customer reports.

There is no question that the more frequently that customers receive mailings, the more likely they are to call your office when they are ready to travel; but due to increased postage and labor costs, frequent mailings may not be within an agent's budget. Next to a monthly newsletter, a quarterly mailing is the most rewarding. If a quarterly mailing is not possible, semiannual promotional letters should be sent in August, featuring fall and winter tours and cruises, and in early February with spring and summer offerings.

Some agents do not have a set time for their mailings. They send out a mailing only when they wish to announce a special tour. A special mailing of this type is usually sent to a selected list of prospects. For example, a gourmet tour announcement would be sent to a mailing list of restaurant owners, both professional and amateur chefs, and cooking schools.

Timing is an important factor when aiming for the best response. It would be a waste of money to send a mailing to accountants in January or March and April when they are bogged down with end-of-year closings and income tax reports. School teachers and families with school-aged children should be approached with tours that depart during school vacation periods. Professional people and business executives are good prospects for weekend and eight-day holidays. As senior citizens can travel anytime and stay longer, the leisurely cruises, motorcoach, and rail tours appeal to this group.

Most agents cut down on advertising during holidays. But agents who limit their direct mail to once-a-year efforts might consider the Christmas season. A mailing in early December before the post office becomes jammed and before gift lists are completed would be a good time to thank clients for their past patronage and remind them that " a gift of travel can be used any time during the year." Or consider a thank-you card at Thanksgiving and really beat the Christmas rush!

The size of the mailing list varies among agents. Some limit the list to a few hundred; others may run into the thousands. An important point to remember is that it is not the number of *pieces* that go out but the number of *responses* that determines the effectiveness of the mailing. It has been noted that a response of half of 1 percent is considered a good return. However, there are so many reasons why a mailing can fail that it is difficult to judge direct mail efforts on just one or two mailings. This is a medium that must be used consistently for at least two years before management can decide if it is a benefit or an expense that can be eliminated.

The late Richard Revnes (president of Royal Cruise Lines) was well known for his lectures, tapes, and videos on marketing and selling. He had some very good suggestions on direct mail. He recommended using good stationery, first-class postage, personally addressed envelopes (do not use labels unless it is an extremely large mailing), and most important, for a couple, address the envelope to the woman, using her first name. He guaranteed that the response to this type of mailing will be much greater than the minimum response usually predicted.

The best mailing list is drawn from completed and current customer files and inquiries received through newspaper ads and previous mailings. The response from this list should be good since everyone on it already has expressed an interest in travel. Mailing lists obtained from your church or temple, golf clubs, racquet clubs, bowling leagues, rod and gun clubs, and other social or civic groups that may have the agent or one of his employees on its membership roster should also bring in a good response. The general public is more inclined to visit an agency where they know someone.

Mailing lists also can be purchased from firms that specialize in this type of business. Lists can be compiled in whatever category the agent desires: high income, selected streets and neighborhoods, or by profession, religious, or ethnic background. Agents can create this type of list themselves simply by going through telephone books or crisscross directories in their area; however, this is a time-consuming job and may not be as accurate as a purchased list.

The mailing list should be revised and updated continually. Simple errors such as incorrect spelling of names or transposed numbers in the address will hurt the image of an efficient business office. Zip codes should always be used. Regardless of the form in which the mailing list is kept (card file, Addressograph plates, computer list, etc.), corrections or changes should be made as soon as they occur. Since first-class mail is returned to the sender, use the post office to update your list (my apologies to the hard-working postal employees). It is cheaper to send out a letter that may be returned with "nondelivery" stamped on it than to spend hours or days in checking all the names on the mailing list.

The contents of the mailing piece should be checked carefully for grammar, spelling, and punctuation, as well as for accuracy in dates and prices. Clever, catchy phrases may be used in the heading or on the envelope itself to draw the recipient's attention, but the body of the letter should be written in simple, easy-to-understand terms. Avoid big words, foreign phrases, and trade jargon. Even though the letter is sent out to promote a specific tour or cruise, the agency should emphasize the advantages and benefits gained by using a travel agent. If a business reply card is enclosed, it too, should be kept simple and easy to use.

Contests such as "Name the Agency," "Most Interesting Travel Experience," or for best photo taken on a trip; drawings for a free trip or travel accessories; or the latest technique of an "everybody wins" sweepstakes are variations of direct-mail selling that create interest and goodwill by offering free prizes to customers. The prizes can be as simple or as expensive as the budget can stand. Contact airlines and cruise lines for donations of travel bags, books, or other novelties. Hotels (especially the newer ones that need the exposure) will donate a room for two for a weekend or longer. If the advertising budget permits, include the transportation cost in the prize.

We all know that products such as vacuum cleaners, cosmetics, office machines, and tractors can be demonstrated in the homes, offices, and farms of the prospective customers. Now, with the use of videocassettes, travel can be promoted in the same way.

Travel is a product that has to be experienced to be appreciated. Next to offering free trips to prospects, the best method of demonstrating the travel product is with a film, videotape, or slide. Not even lectures by experienced travelers can equal the effect of actually seeing and vicariously enjoying the experience of visiting faraway places.

Film shows for large groups provide a very effective way to promote travel and the travel agency. If the agent has a large enough office or conference room to seat between 10 to 30 people comfortably, it is best to hold the film shows on the premises. This gives the public the opportunity to see and inspect the office, to pick up additional brochures and information from the consultants in attendance, and to meet the airline sales representatives or other travel celebrities invited to the film show. Churches, banks, and private clubs in the immediate vicinity of the office often have meeting rooms for rent at a nominal fee. Banquet rooms in the better restaurants and hotels can also be used, especially for larger audiences.

Film shows should be scheduled from 3 to 6 months in advance. Just as in most other travel arrangements, films have to be reserved in advance for specific dates. Some films are so popular that waiting lists are made up for their use. Films may be borrowed directly from the airlines or cruise lines, but the trend now is to go through a film service company. These companies receive films from airlines, tourist boards, and others and loan them out free of charge to agents. Their only stipulations are that the films be returned promptly and a report given to them of the number of people in the audience. The film service companies are usually listed as motion picture film libraries in the Yellow Pages of phone books. Projectors and screens can also be rented from most film libraries or from photographic supply stores. For a small additional fee they will also deliver and pick up equipment for a show.

The increasing number of videocassette recorder (VCR) owners has stimulated the market for videocassette tapes on all subjects. Tapes on travel are available from many sources. Tapes may be borrowed or purchased from all facets of the travel industry: cruise lines, Amtrak, Eurailpass, airlines, tourist boards, tour operators, and hotels, as well as from the many commercial companies who sell tapes.

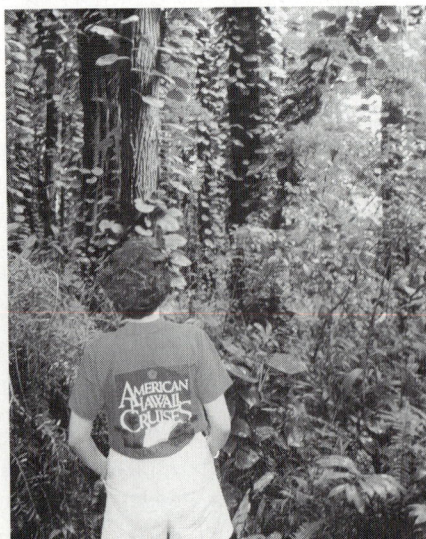

Figure 6-3 Offering more than 45 shore excursions, *American Hawaii* provides something for everyone. This passenger takes in the beauty of Maui.

Vacations on Video in Phoenix, Arizona, one of the best known companies, is a one-stop clearinghouse for many supplier-produced tapes. Their supply of cruise tapes is very good and they are all very reasonably priced.

Most videotapes are inexpensive to own (compared to films) and an agency could easily afford a television set, VCR, and a library of travel destination tapes and travel training tapes to be shown on their own premises or at film shows. Videos can also be borrowed from film libraries or rented from a local video store, but observe the copyright laws and don't copy borrowed or rented tapes unless you have written permission to do so. It is also illegal to copy travel programs off TV or cable for the purpose of using them as business sales tools. These destination tapes are not only a valuable selling tool, they are an education tool for the staff—a fam trip without leaving home.

Agents can now further personalize their film shows by making their own videotapes during their travels with the use of videocameras or camcorders (a camera and recorder together in one unit). It may take a lot of practice to make your tapes as interesting as the professionals do, but it would be well worth the effort. Most audiences appreciate viewing real-life experiences of people they know, or perhaps, seeing themselves on one of your group tours. There are facilities available to help you edit your tapes and add titles, narration, and so on.

The films/tapes used may tie in with a specific tour or cruise offering the agent would like to promote, or they may be a promotion for a destination that is currently popular or appealing to the public. Whatever the theme, the newspaper advertising, the window displays, and the decor of the office should follow suit. For example, if Hawaii is the theme, use films featuring Hawaii and possibly the west coast of the United States or even the Orient. The window display and the office decor should feature Hawaii for at least three weeks before the show. A special brochure rack should be displayed prominently and should contain only information on Hawaii. All newspaper or radio advertising during the three-week period before the show should feature tours to Hawaii and include an additional line to announce the film show, date, and time. A mailing should be sent to prospective customers no later than one week in advance. Be sure to invite clients who have already visited Hawaii. Most people enjoy talking about their travels, and a satisfied customer is the best encouragement and inducement to the prospects.

Some refreshments served to the guests will give the agency and its staff a chance to mingle with the crowd, to introduce themselves, and to answer questions. Refreshments do not have to be elaborate or expensive; in fact, too elaborate a spread may discourage the audience from helping themselves because they do not want to feel obligated to the agency. For large crowds, when the film show is held at a hotel or restaurant, arrange to have a cash bar set up. If the cash bar sells enough drinks, the fee for the meeting room or banquet hall will usually be waived.

Guest speakers can be introduced during the intermission, but it is better to save their speeches for the end. Introductions made before or during the film show will not be heard by latecomers (and sometimes this may be half of the audience). Advise the sales representatives to go easy on the sales pitch for their companies. The audience is usually more interested in hearing about the destination, although advance announcements about special fares and schedules will give the audience the feeling of being part of a select group.

Preparing for a film/video show requires a few hours' work at least 6 months in advance. Call or write to film libraries; request all appropriate brochures, donations, and a guest speaker from the airlines, cruise lines, or tour operators. Quite often, this amount of time is spent on just one booking that may or may not materialize. This, of course, is for the small, informal film shows.

As audiences increase in size and more carriers express an interest in participating, it may be necessary to go into larger quarters and have a combined trade show along with the film. This naturally involves more work and expense. Some agents set up booths and charge each participating carrier a fee to help cover expenses. An admission fee may also be charged to the public.

Many agents prefer to limit the film shows to select groups either before or after a group tour departure. A show taking place after a tour might include a film, tape, or slides taken of the group during their travels. Other agents show films at various club meetings or at church benefit dinners or luncheons. These can be fund-raising events for the organizations by charging an admission fee, which is then turned over to the organization after expenses are covered. Films could also be shown in conjunction with fashion shows held by local department stores or specialty shops, bridal shops, or sportsmen's stores. The procedures described above would be followed for these events as well. The decor of the room (posters and/or window displays), brochures, door prizes, or other giveaways should all follow the general theme of the film showing.

A drawing for door prizes at the conclusion will accomplish two things—it provides names for your mailing list and it increases the goodwill and friendship of the audience. The door prizes could be travel bags or other novelties, or it could even be a fresh pineapple or a dozen oranges—which were once used in an emergency when the sales rep forgot to bring in the flight bags. The entry blank for the drawing also could be utilized for research into the audience's future travel plans. In addition to the space provided for name, address, and telephone number, allow a few lines to ask the audience if they would like to receive brochures or other information for future travel. A follow-up should be made immediately after the film show on any request made on the entry blank or made in person during the discussion periods.

After a year and a half of monthly film shows held on the premises of a travel agency I managed, it was definitely proven that film shows not only bring in immediate bookings from the audience, but also increase the prestige and overall business of the agency.

Travel shows or travel bazaars held by local merchant's associations and local chambers of commerce are also excellent methods of introducing and promoting a travel agency. Even if the agent does nothing more than stand in front of a booth and pass out brochures with the agency's name and address stamped on it, potential customers who may never have thought of contacting a travel agent for their travel plans are being reached.

Figure 6-4 American Hawaii Cruises' SS Constitution approaches Diamond Head and Waikiki Beach after completing her seven-day cruise among the Hawaiian Islands. Ports of call include Honolulu, Oahu; Kahului, Maui; Hilo and Kona, Hawaii; and Nawiliwili, Kauai.

A drawing for free travel prizes will attract crowds to your booth, and written entries will again provide leads for future customers. Arrangements can be made to have the mayor of your city or another community leader draw the winning names. If a photographer from one of the newpapers cannot be present to take pictures of the event, arrange for a professional photographer to take the pictures and send copies to all the newspapers.

As mentioned earlier, sales promotions should be closely coordinated with advertising and personal selling efforts to achieve maximum results. In contrast with personal selling, which is normally directed at individuals, sales promotion is aimed at groups of individuals. A successful sales promotion may bring prospective customers into the office, but it is still the responsibility of the agent and the staff to follow up and finalize the sales.

ADVERTISING

Advertising can be defined in many ways. It is communication between the seller and the buyer. Its main objective is selling to a mass market. There are two types of advertising that concern the travel agent: *primary demand* advertising—ads that stimulate an interest in travel in general and an agency in specific, and *selective demand* advertising, which will publicize a specific tour and departure date but additionally, will stimulate and increase the overall travel sales.

Ads can be further subdivided by *direct* or *indirect* action desired from the prospective customer. The coupon ad is designed for direct action. From the number of coupons received in the office, an agent can get a fairly good idea of the success of the ad. However, with the increase in advertising rates, a coupon may be just so much wasted space because few people will take the time to fill it out and mail it. They are more likely to pick up the phone and call. There is usually a better response to a coupon included with a direct-mailing piece. The effects of an ad for the travel business are extremely difficult to judge. Customers have been known to inquire about a tour that was advertised a year before, or to request brochures for a trip they do not plan to take for several years.

The Advertising Message

The content of an ad—the *message* as the term is used here—includes all the words, pictures, symbols, colors, and other features. The preparation of effective copy takes creative skill, imagination, experience, and lots of hard work. An extensive advertising campaign should be put in the hands of specialists in advertising agencies; this is especially important for new agencies.

The general public is becoming more and more sophisticated about travel. Double-page magazine ads, news stories, and spot announcements on television and radio usually have customers presold on a destination. All customers want from the agent is the price, availability, and departure dates. For this reason, most travel agency ads resemble supermarket grocery ads. The most successful ads (in terms of response) ever written were short, simple, and believable.

Because of the high cost of advertising (even local weekly newspapers now charge as much as dailies' Sunday editions), most agents now use tie-in ads (signature ads) for most of their advertising and reserve special ads for specific tours or cruises that their office may be promoting. Tie-in ads are small box ads added to a large ad placed by a tour operator, airline, cruise line, and so on. The box will contain simply the name, address, and phone numbers of the travel agents who are "tieing in." There may be as many as 20 travel agents included in the listing, but they are very effective and the rate is reasonable. The cost for four tie-ins may cost as much as one 2- by 2-inch ad, but the agency is reaching four different markets and is reaping the benefit of the large, colorful, and descriptive ad paid

Advertising

for by the principals. Many trips are presold to the customer by these ads and agents can profit by advising the public that these tours/cruises are available in their office. The public will search through the list and call the agency most convenient to them.

Travel appeals to everyone; even those who cannot afford it will study the travel pages to see what is being offered. An ad written for a specific tour, cruise, or destination can be brief and still be effective. Good copy is readable and to the point. Where explanatory material is necessary, it should be in smaller type and as direct as possible. Save the clever words, flowery speech, attractive pictures, color, and symbols for your brochure or promotional letter used to follow up inquiries from the advertisement. The headline is the most important part of the travel advertisement; what follows are the basic facts, price, length of tour, dates, and highlights of the tour or cruise. Effective headlines can be made simply by taking key phrases from the brochure that will be sent to the inquiries.

Most travel ads are written under the assumption that the travel public wants the lowest price; however, a worthwhile percentage of those who read the ads would like something better. Allow people to upgrade if they want to, by mentioning options or alternates. If you use a coupon in the ad or promotional material, provide a check box with a short rider that offers a similar offer at deluxe rates or a more extensive itinerary. (*Note*: Make sure the company name appears in the body of the ad or flyer so that when the coupon is clipped, prospects do not forget to whom they sent it.)

From a copy standpoint, always remember that even though a newspaper may have thousands of readers, your ad is talking to only one person at a time. Anticipate the questions most commonly asked about a tour or cruise, give the most important answers in the ad, and suggest that readers call the office for further details. This will reduce time spent on the phones answering shoppers' questions.

Timing and Follow-up

Timing is very important in advertising. Experience has shown that the five most effective months for good reader response are January, February, September, October, and November. April and May are usually the poorest. Therefore, consider concentrating more of your advertising during months when publications are best read.

January and February are the months when most business organizations start making up vacation schedules and people start shopping for summer tours, resorts, and cruises. September and October are good months to promote fall and winter cruises. Also, travel trade publications normally publish lists of special promotion dates of newspapers in the United States. Mark the dates of any local promotions on your calendar and make sure that your ads are included in those issues.

Keep abreast of current events and tie in with special-interest tours. Although the travel pages of the local papers are usually the best place for travel ads, do not be timid about placing your ad on other pages. A Rose Bowl tour, for example, may draw a bigger response if placed in the sports pages; a trade fair or business convention will draw from the financial pages; fashion shows or gourmet tours do well in the women's pages.

When inquiries start coming into the office, keep a record of which ad and which publication drew the most inquiries. This will help you plan future advertising campaigns and will cut down on costly mistakes. At the same time, keep in mind that there can be many outside factors that can cause an ad to be a failure. Weather, news events, strikes, or political upsets can destroy the effects of the best planned advertising campaign. Occasionally, outside events have the opposite effect. A favorable news story about an area or destination you are featuring can increase the number of inquiries tremendously.

The follow-up material sent in response to the inquiries is the time and place for the copywriters to display their talents. A well-written and attractive brochure or letter quite often will be the deciding factor in making the sale. This is the area where the fundamental rules of copywriting can be used to good advantage: (1) get attention, (2) show people an advantage, (3) prove it, (4) persuade people to grasp this advantage, and (5) ask for action.

THE MARKETING BUDGET

One of the stickiest problems that marketing management decision makers face is deciding how much money will be spent on advertising, how much on personal selling (sales staff's salaries and fringe benefits), and how much on various sales promotion devices. There is no firm set of rules that an agent can apply. Only experience and research develop good judgment in the decision process.

Agents must first consider whether they will sell their own tours or will concentrate on selling tours that already are heavily advertised by both the tour operators and carriers. In the latter case, agents can save money by adding their own tie-in ad to the ads ordered by the principals. The display advertising departments of local newspapers will cooperate by notifying the agent when these ads will appear.

A higher percentage of the advertising budget must be allocated when agents market their own tours, and more emphasis must be placed on the personal selling by the agents' staff to direct customers' attention to the agencys' own tours. The popularity of the destination also affects the advertising budget. Selling a new area requires more advertising and more personal selling than does selling an area that is so popular that it is simply a matter of order taking for the flights and hotels.

A final consideration is the price and length of the tours (both time and miles). The more expensive, longer tours require a higher degree of personal selling. The more important the trip is to the client, the more time and advice he will require from the agent.

Advertising is perhaps the most difficult and ambiguous area for which budgeting and results can be measured. Many agents use *percentage of sales* as a guideline for the amount to be spent for advertising, but this method ignores the basic question: What is the real nature of the advertising job to be done? Advertising benefits are cumulative. How can it be pinpointed that this year's ads were more effective than last year's when it is quite possible that the ads were more effective this year because recognition of the agency's name was built up by repeated advertising?

Competition is a yardstick. Using this approach, some agents budget their advertising to match the amount of advertising the competition is doing. This is a defensive approach. It encourages a follow-the-leader policy and ignores the possibility of other and better strategies. It assumes that competitors know what they are doing, but they may be just as much in the dark as you are.

Spending only what you can afford does not solve the problem of how much to spend, and again ignores the requirements of the advertising job. Advertising has two effects: increased sales today and improving goodwill that raises future sales. Advertising should be considered an investment, not just an expense. Since there is so much uncertainty about the specific results and effectiveness of advertising, there is no method of determining the size of the advertising budget that will satisfy everyone.

Methods used by other agents may be useful as a point of comparison, but a new location, a different group of prospective customers, or possible changes in the buying habits of the regular customers will dictate that traditional approaches cannot be followed blindly. Another fact involved is that heavy advertising expenses must be made to introduce a new agent or new service.

TRAVEL MARKETS

Two major markets are the *vacation/leisure* (discretionary) traveler and *commercial* accounts (the business traveler). There are many subdivisions and overlappings between the two. Business people also vacation; business firms can send groups on incentive trips, sales meetings, or conventions.

Vacationers travel by choice and are seeking some kind of dream fulfillment. More time will be needed to probe for their actual needs and desires before an itinerary can be drawn up and reservations made. This may take an hour or several weeks, but the agent will earn from 10 percent to as much as 25 percent commission on this type of booking.

The real growth opportunity for all travel agents is in this market. There is growing affluence in the United States. Not only are leisure travelers increasing, but *luxury* travel is also increasing. Clients are willing to pay for pampering and personal assistance at every step of the way. However, many balk at paying first-class fares when they see the enormous difference between them and the APEX (advanced purchase excursion) fares. The vacation/leisure market requires much more expertise than that needed to service commercial accounts. It means that the staff must be knowledgeable in destination geography, must have good working relationships with the tour operators, must be capable of handling independent arrangements as well as package tours, and must have the tact and patience to research and answer all questions.

At the lower end of the scale, the so-called *mass market*—those interested only in discounted fares and last-minute specials—is turning to travel clubs instead of the travel agent. The irony is that in most cases the travel agent can equal, and often better, the offers and the customer does not have to pay the annual membership fees. There are also a number of clubs and tour operators who will work through travel agents on last-minute offers. The commissions may be low on these discounted fares, but even those on a limited budget require hotels, sightseeing, and/or car rentals at their destinations. This is true also of the many travelers who prefer the family car for their transportation. Hotel/resort commissions for one or two weeks can be well worth the time spent in making the reservations.

The student, black traveler, and woman traveler markets have grown the most in the past 15 years. *Students* eventually graduate, and although the travel industry may lose them for a few years when they marry and while the family is growing, eventually they return as their incomes increase and their taste for travel develops. Work through local boards of education and local teachers to promote travel for continuing education or just-fun trips. Start with motorcoach tours to local points of interest and expand with the use of group air fares to greater distances.

There are a number of tour operators that specialize in the 18 to 35 age group. Contrary to the popular belief that this age group is only interested in singles travel, 20 percent of this age group are couples, and the singles usually travel with a friend.

Then we have the *yuppies* (young urban professionals). Those over 35 are often married and live more affluent lifestyles; most are two-income families. They know the value of organized tours, but they also want the flexibility of independent travel and pay more attention to receiving value for their money.

Blacks are now welcomed almost everywhere around the globe as restrictions are eased or erased. Affluent blacks will travel more and the younger generation is less reluctant to leave home than their elders were. The book and television presentation of *Roots* in the United States has stimulated a great interest in tracing backgrounds and visiting homelands, not only for blacks but also in all Americans.

In this age of women's liberation, the *women's business travel market* is also expanding. According to the U.S. Travel Data Center, in 1989, 39 percent of all business travelers were female. Predictions are that women will account for half of all business travelers by the end of the century. Women travelers are more likely than men to use a travel agent for their business trips as well as for vacation trips.

Hotel chains in the United States are realizing the importance of catering to the growing number of women business travelers and will provide rooms especially decorated and equipped for feminine needs. Many hotels now feature an *executive floor*, which provides added security, as well as lounges and small meeting rooms for the use of their guests. The *concierge*, a well-known feature of European hotels is now installed in many U.S. hotels. The concierge assists with airline reservations, dinner and theater reservations, secretarial services, and any other special services the guests may require. Another new trend is to hire women as concierges or hall porters. Hotels feel that it takes a woman to understand a woman.

Some hotels have experimented with woman-only floors but have discovered that women do not like being segregated in that way. The needs of the woman business traveler are very similar to the needs of the male business traveler. The Marriott hotels discovered that in addition to greater security, such features as full-length mirrors and bathroom amenities are appreciated by men as well as women. Men are using more skin care products than women are, and they take the sewing kits that are put in the rooms—today's man does sew on buttons.

Encourage the single woman vacationing in the United States to travel alone despite the higher cost of accommodations. She may be pleasantly surprised to find that she will have a more enjoyable time alone than when traveling with someone who may not have the same interests or who may not want to do the same thing at the same time. Joining a group tour might be more advisable than independent arrangements when recommending foreign travel, unless the woman knows the language of the country, is an experienced traveler, and/or plans to join friends or relatives at her destination. It is also wise to recommend leaving copies of her itinerary with friends, relatives, or co-workers before departure.

Senior citizens represent an ever-increasing market, although, ironically, as this market increases, the discounts may decrease. Also, a lot of people who qualify for age-based discounts do not like to advertise their eligibility as senior citizens. The American Association of Retired Persons (AARP) accepts anyone over the age of 50. The travel agent must use more tact and diplomacy in servicing this group, while making sure they check the availability of age-related discounts. Most mature travelers prefer using travel agents. They like the convenience of one-stop shopping and a supply of good travel literature before starting their travels.

Special fares and sales promotions have been introduced by a number of domestic airlines, railroads, tour operators and hotels. Most of these discounts apply to people aged 62 and over. These fares will enable even those on a limited budget to travel more frequently. Careful examination of the tour offerings must be made before recommending them to the more mature traveler. Tours should be slower paced, with more free time between side trips. Visits to countries of doubtful sanitation should be avoided if at all possible. More personal attention is required. Even the experienced travelers will need assistance with baggage limits, baggage handling throughout the tour (many may have physical problems and be unable to lift heavy bags), special diets, availability of medical attention if needed, instructions on clothing, and detailed descriptions on day-to-day activities. Travelers' insurance should be a requisite for this group.

The new mature market (people between 50 and 65) travels more often and is interested in more active, adventurous, and intellectually challenging types of trips. Although travel by car and recreational vehicle is popular, interest in cruises, tours with more active as opposed to passive sightseeing, and international travel is increasing.

The mature traveler usually prefers group travel for the comfort, convenience, and social features. Travel agents can tap into this market by contacting local senior centers or leaders of senior organizations. Contrary to popular opinion, seniors are not always interested in the lowest price; they now want to spend money on all those trips they dreamed about when they were 25. They are better educated and more active, physically and socially, than were the seniors of years past. A safari to Kenya or a tour of the Great Wall of China may be more attractive than a tour to a local attraction.

Special-interest travel—programs blending clients' personal interests, hobbies, or avocations with the travel experience—are now available in every category: arts and music festivals, adventure tours for hunters and fishermen, gold mining, water sports, mountain climbing, heli hiking on the Canadian glaciers, river rafting, gourmet and wine country tours, ski tours, Holy Land tours, cruises with special-interest themes, and so on. Churches, private clubs, organizations, and commercial accounts are good sources for special-interest tours. *Jaxfax Travel Marketing* magazine and the *Official Tour Directory* include separate sections on special-interest tour operators/activities that give tour operator name, address, fax numbers, and toll-free numbers.

Spa vacations is one of the fastest-growing segments of the travel industry. According to an article in *Time* magazine, only 500,000 Americans went to spas in 1981, but that number has now swelled to over 5 million. A company called Spa-Finders Travel Arrangements Ltd. was formed in 1987 to cash in on the growing popularity of health and fitness vacations. They have put together a 100-page catalog that describes more than 200 spas, fitness-related resorts, and health vacation packages. Spa-Finders takes bookings for spa stays, spa vacation packages, and all related travel directly from consumers and from travel agents.

The International Gay Travel Association (IGTA), which was established in 1984, now an active organization of over 250 travel agent members across the United States, through its quarterly newsletter helps members learn about destinations and ground services that welcome gay clients. They also offer a marketing mailing service which gives suppliers an opportunity to reach IGTA members directly. Suppliers can send 250 copies of brochures to IGTA, which are distributed to the group. This market is stronger than most people realize, although the fear of AIDS has made some suppliers reluctant to serve the gay traveler.

There is an enormous market in travel for those with special needs (*disabled* or *handicapped*). Some 43 million Americans have one or more physical or mental disabilities, and the number is increasing as the population as a whole is growing older. But only approximately 100 travel agencies handle their travel arrangements. This market requires specialized services from competent as well as compassionate travel counselors. At present there are six tour operators that specialize in travel for the mentally and physically handicapped, working with agents and assisting them in all the necessary details. Evergreen Travel Service, Inc. in Lynnwood, Washington, is probably the largest agency specializing in travel for the disabled in the country, perhaps in the world. Evergreen group programs are commissionable at 10 percent to travel agents and will continue to pay commissions on repeat travel that is booked directly with Evergreen.

Travelers with disabilities are the focus of a law signed in August 1990 that has been called the most sweeping civil-rights statute since the 1964 Civil Rights Act became the law of the land. Starting on January 27, 1992, every business in the United States (except for some exempted private clubs and religious organizations) will become liable for "latent or overt discriminatory practices against disabled people." Essentially, the law guarantees the same rights of access and treatment to people with mental or physical disabilities that nondisabled people enjoy. But now the guarantee is law and Americans engaged in "commerce" (defined in the act as "travel, trade, traffic, commerce, transportation or communication") must fulfill their requirements under penalty of the law.

Enforcement of the law is expected to be primarily complaint driven. Persons with grievances regarding employment practices will have to file complaints with the Equal Employment Opportunity Commission. Public-access complaints will be heard in court, and some proposed rules would allow for jury trials to take place, with the potential of unlimited punitive and compensatory damages. Some of the requirements involve changes that may affect the physical layout of travel agencies.

The U.S. Chamber of Commerce offers a compliance manual, "What Business Must Know About the Americans with Disabilities Act," Publication No 0230. The manual is $20 for chamber members, $33 for nonmembers. Travel assistance for the independent disabled traveler can be found in the brochure "The United States Welcomes Handicapped Visitors," published by the Society for the Advancement of Travel for the Handicapped (SATH). SATH is a nonprofit, tax-exempt educational membership organization dedicated to the promotion and improvement of travel and tourism opportunities for handicapped and elderly persons. The brochure is a good source of advice and guidance for travel to and within the United States.

Honeymooners are good customers. If an agent does a good job on the honeymoon, he or she has won clients for a lifetime as well as additional business from the wedding party and guests. An average summer honeymoon budget is between $2000 and $3000, and the average stay is eight days and seven nights. The traditional wedding and honeymoon is back in style and the travel agent is assuming a more important role in handling honeymoon arrangements. Good sources for the honeymoon business are bridal shops, photography studios, and beauty shops. Keep them supplied with honeymoon package brochures and/or window display material. Join in their bridal shows as an exhibitor or provide films or videos on cruises or the Caribbean (most popular honeymoon choices). Discuss possible co-op advertising.

A growing number of single-parent, two-income families, extended step families, and grandparents treating their grandchildren have created a market that cannot be ignored by the travel industry—*family vacations*. More than 20 percent of airline tickets include at least one child, and 10 percent of business travel involves kids. Families are no longer piling into the family car and heading for the nearest amusement park. Most of these families have more money to spend but less leisure time and are looking for ways to spend quality time with their kids. More than 80 percent of married adults vacation with their children, according to the U.S. Travel Data Center.

Although airline family plan fares have been cut back to the off-seasons and Amtrak has discontinued their family plan fares, the hotels, resorts, cruise lines, and many tour operators are encouraging families with reduced rates and new programs that feature activities in which all can participate. "Kids Stay Free" is advertised in the hotel and motel literature, but the maximum age for free stays varies among the hotels. An increasing number of hotels will offer an adjoining room at half the price of the first room. Most resort hotels will limit the number of guests in a room to four; they will allow five if they use the existing bedding. The rate increases if a crib or cot is ordered for the room.

Tours for grandparents and grandkids were started in 1986 by Helena T. Koenig of Grandtravel of Chevy Chase, Maryland. The itineraries include trips to Kenya for an adventure safari, to Alaska for a wilderness adventure, to Europe, and other trips throughout America. The tours are usually limited to 10 grandparents and 10 grandchildren.

Commercial (corporate) account sales are important to ensure a good "mix" of business in travel agency. When leisure travel is down, the businessperson will, out of necessity, continue to travel. The average agency books 50 percent business travel and 50 percent vacation travel. However, a large number of agencies that specialize in business travel are now looking closer at the leisure market.

Commercial business can be lucrative if the agency exercises control over accounts receivable and frequently evaluates the profitability of its commercial accounts. An agency should enter this market only if it is in a sound cash position, enforces a strict payment policy, and has a good accounting system. Once an agency has to finance a commercial account, it can actually lose money. Wherever possible, agents should try to convince their business accounts to use a credit card.

An agency can increase their income from their commercial account by soliciting the company's sales *meeting and convention planning* business. Since this is a specialized service, the agency must be prepared to designate two or more staff members whose duties will be involved entirely in the preparations and negotiations needed to satisfy the requirements of the corporate account. As with other corporate account business, last-minute changes and additions are quite common and should be supervised by a central department.

The arrangements can be a lot more complex than simply reserving airline flights and hotel rooms. The agent must determine the size of the meeting, number of rooms needed (single or double), meals, beverages, visual/audio aids needed, entertainment, possible sightseeing arrangements for the spouses, and arrangements for transportation between airport and hotel. As this is a lucrative business for all, hotels and airlines are only too willing to assist the meeting planners. Most major airlines have extensive meetings services that include planning theme parties, renting an electronic message center, and multimedia presentations, in addition to providing discounts on group airfares.

Meeting planning as a profession is being recognized by a number of colleges and universities that have installed special courses in their hotel and travel and tourism programs. Eventually, every hotel school will have a program on meeting management. Among the leaders are the University of Massachusetts at Amherst, Metropolitan State College in Denver, Northeastern State University at Tahlequah, Oklahoma, Georgia State University, Washington State University in Seattle, and the University of Central Florida in Orlando.

TELEVISION MARKETING

Travel industry marketing is moving in new directions. There has been much discussion about competition from electronic home shopping services. It worries some agents, and others show no concern; I agree with the latter group. There should be no concern about losing business to these services—in fact, it should bring in new business. Anything that stimulates the public's desire to travel should benefit the entire industry. It must be kept in mind that clients still prefer the human touch when it comes to making travel arrangements.

TOURISM SELF-SCORER

Although this 10-point self-scoring travel marketing test was developed for a special conference of the National Council for Urban Economic Development by Development Counselors International (DCI), it would be worthwhile for agents to test their own marketing programs with these questions. A detailed copy can be obtained by writing to DCI at 733 Third Avenue, New York, NY 10017.

The questions, with a maximum response score of one point for each, include:

1. How well do you really know your product?
2. Do you know exactly what your present and potential markets are?
3. Do you have a U.S.P. (unique selling proposition), and can you back it up?
4. Do you have clear and measurable short- and long-term goals?

5. Is your marketing program fully funded with at least two different funding sources?

6. Have you sold tourism at home first?

7. Do you have a full kit of marketing tools, including advertising, sales promotion, editorial placement, and special events?

8. Are all private, public, and civic tourist interests marching under one banner?

9. Are you particularly emphasizing—in your marketing program—repeat, longer-stay, and year-round business?

10. Have you made a long-term (at least three-year) funding and program commitment?

QUESTIONS AND PROBLEMS

1. Give your definition of marketing and how it would relate to the travel industry.

2. Describe the difference between selling and marketing.

3. How many functions does a travel agent perform in ticketing a domestic airline passenger? Name the most important functions the travel consultant would perform from this list.

4. Which of the two solutions offered to solve the problem of training employees would you select? Why?

5. How would you pay the outside salesperson?

6. What are the three major components of a successful promotional program?

7. What are the objectives of a sales promotional program?

8. Where are the best sources for a mailing list?

9. Make up a sample mailing piece to be sent to a list of professional people.

10. How often should a direct mailing list be revised? Which names would you eliminate?

11. List the procedures you would follow in putting on a travel film show.

12. How much would you budget for advertising in a new office? How much for an established agency?

13. Write a follow-up letter to an inquiry to your ad.

14. List some of the markets that an agency can service.

15. What is your opinion of shopping by cable?

16. How many of the 10 questions in the Tourism Self-Scorer would apply directly to a travel agency?

chapter 7

Airline Sales and Reservations

OBJECTIVES

When you have finished this chapter you should be able to:

1. Determine the best method to service the airline ticket customer.
2. Know when to call on airline sales representatives.
3. List the features that can be found in the North American and worldwide editions of OAGs.
4. Describe the official handbooks that are in every appointed travel agent's office.
5. Ask the right questions to get the information needed before making an airline reservation.
6. Discuss the current controversy regarding airline computer reservation systems.

INTRODUCTION

An airline sales transaction may take as little as 15 minutes or as long as 15 hours from the original request to the issuance of a ticket and collection of payment. Depending on the itinerary, the past experience of the traveler, and the season in which the travel will made, clients will spend an average of three hours or about three office visits for each ticket.

The first contact with the agent, and quite often the entire transaction, is usually by telephone. This first contact, either by telephone or walk-in, is very important to both the client and the agent. Clients usually have a good idea of where they want to go and may have already spent considerable time planning their itinerary. They may ask for brochures and/or information, but it is not at all unusual to have clients walk in and ask for reservations with brochures they had obtained from the airlines, tour operators, or other travel agents. They may even have flight numbers, departure times, and fares. With this type of client, the transaction will be completed in the length of time it takes to make the reservation and issue the ticket. This may sound very simple and uncomplicated; however, these clients can often turn out to be among the most difficult to please. They are presold on a specific airline and find it difficult to believe that another airline may have flight schedules that would fit their purpose better; or because they have flown the route before, they refuse to believe that a scheduled flight has been changed or eliminated. Just as much tact and patience is required with this client as is required with the first-timer.

At the second visit, the client will call or come in to discuss the information received and to plan a specific itinerary. The third visit, if all goes well and there are no changes, is simply to pick up the tickets.

Most businesspeople will make their reservations in one telephone call, or one visit, although they are notorious for making last-minute changes. At the other extreme is the first-timer, who may require as many as 15 hours of consultation, and this does not necessarily include numerous telephone calls for additional information or reassurances that everything has been taken care of.

The impression that agents make on the client at the first contact is quite often the deciding factor when clients are ready to travel. An immediate follow-up for a requested brochure or information is essential. Quite often the brochures can simply be sent with a short message on the agent's business card and the detailed letter can be reserved for confirmation of the arrangements requested. It is during this first contact that agents must sell themselves. Agents must be good listeners and must convince clients that they are talking to knowledgeable and experienced travel consultants.

THE AIRLINE SALES REPRESENTATIVE

The sales representative is the principal sales link between the airline and the travel agent. A good sales representative is the agent's right-hand person, especially today when the complexities of fares and rules need explaining and clarifying. Agents rely on sales representatives to explain new tariffs and keep them up to date on new or improved schedules. During the past few years the changes in fares, schedules, and validity rules have occurred so frequently and so fast that not even the OAG (Official Airline Guides) publishers or airline computer systems were able to keep up. If the sales representatives do not have the answers, they will contact the person or department who can assist the agents.

In addition, agents depend on the sales representatives to keep them informed of new programs or new concepts within existing programs and to assist them with their own group tour programs and sales promotions. They are the liaison between the agents and the reservations department in the event of difficulties or misunderstandings, or in getting seats when they are really needed. And quite often, sales representatives can give them destination information from their own experiences which cannot be found in any reference book.

Due to economic cutbacks, sales representatives are not seen in the agent's office as often as they were in the past. Many airlines have closed down district offices and use "resident" sales representatives (people who actually work out of their homes). Frequent visits are now confined to the most productive travel agencies; small and medium-sized agencies may seldom see the sales representative in person. However, they are still available by phone, and local seminars keep agents current.

Although most agents consider the sales representatives as their own personal representatives, the representatives' duties involve much more than just visiting travel agencies. They are expected to service commercial accounts, military establishments, interline carriers, car rental companies, cruise lines, and hotels. They are also expected to solicit group business from schools, religious organizations, and social clubs.

As far as the agent is concerned, the good sales representative is the one who will come in when needed, listen carefully, be sincerely interested in the agent's problems, and follow up promptly on any request or complaint made to her. Unfortunately, not all representatives follow this ideal, but the majority are hardworking, conscientious people and of real value to the busy agent who may not have the time to read all the bulletins that come into the office.

THE OFFICIAL AIRLINE GUIDES

The format of early aviation guides was based on those used by the railroads. Each airline was requested to submit their time schedules, route maps, and a list of their flying equipment as follows: "number of planes, capacity (state clearly whether this capacity includes pilot and mechanic), type of motor, and number of motors."

The modern *OAG* (*Official Airline Guide*) is designed to permit quick reference to all airline schedules. It is published in two editions. The *North American edition* (also referred to as the domestic edition) combines the flights and fares of all scheduled airlines for the United States, Mexico, Canada, and the Caribbean areas. The *worldwide edition* (international) shows complete city-by-city worldwide scheduled airline flights outside the North American continent. Every travel agent and every airline ticket agent uses the same guides, published by the Official Airline Guides, Inc. in Oakbrook, Illinois. Agents can subscribe to the domestic edition on a monthly or bimonthly basis (with fares or without fares); the worldwide guide is issued on a monthly basis.

Beginning with the May 1991 issues, a number of enhancements were added to the worldwide and North American editions of the OAG. The enhancements were added at no additional cost to subscribers. The first change was the new name, the large guides are now called *OAG Desktop Flight Guide—North American Edition* and *OAG Desktop Flight Guide—Worldwide Edition*.

In addition to listing 240,000 direct and connecting flights, the North American edition was expanded by more than 100 pages to include:

- Aircraft seating charts and seating configurations of 16 airlines
- Mileage between cities
- Diagrams of 43 major airports
- A map with time-zone indicators for the United States, Canada, the Caribbean, and Mexico
- The "How to Use" section appears in English and Spanish

To find flights & fares in the OAG Worldwide Edition...

First locate your **Destination** ("to") city among those listed alphabetically throughout this guide.

Then skim down the listing until you find your **Origin** ("from") city... and see what **Direct Flight Fares** and **Direct** and **Connecting** flights are available.

A **direct flight** is transportation from origin to destination which may be non-stop or have one or more stops. It may, in separate instances, involve a change of plane and/or a change of aircraft. But a change of aircraft and a change of flight number at the same airport constitutes a "connecting flight."

A **connecting flight** is two or more direct flights used in conjunction to provide transportation from origin to destination.

If your **Origin** city is not listed under your **Destination** city, there are no **Direct** or **Connecting** flights and you will have to construct your own connecting flight. (See the end of this section for instructions.)

Under **Destination** cities, you will see data grouped into six categories, as shown in the adjacent "sample listing." The following examples extract from and fully explain each category.

Note: The information in this "Sample listing" is used for example purposes only. It is fictitious and should not be used as actual flight or fare information.

Important—Published connections may not represent the most convenient time, the most direct routing or shortest overall elapsed time from origin to destination. Instructions on how to construct alternate connections are located on the last page of this How To Use Section.

Sample Listing

Category 1	Destination (to) City Data
Category 2	Ground Transportation Data
Category 3	Origin (from) City Data
Category 4	Direct Flight Fares Data
Category 5	Direct Flight Schedule Data
Category 6	Connecting Flight Schedule Data

```
To NEW YORK NY/NEWARK, NJ, USA                          NYC
ALSO SEE LONG ISLAND MACARTHUR, NY, USA
AND WESTCHESTER COUNTY, NY, USA
ARPT EAST 34TH ST HLPT-TSS
ARPT EAST 34TH STREET LANDING SPB-NES
ARPT EAST 60TH ST HLPT-JRE
ARPT JOHN F KENNEDY INTERNATIONAL-JFK-
15.0MI/24.1KM 75MIN'
ARPT LA GUARDIA-LGA-8.0MI/12.8KM 60MIN'
ARPT NEWARK INTERNATIONAL-EWR-
16.0MI/25.7KM 45MIN
ARPT PIER 11/WALL STREET SPB-NWS
ARPT WESTCHESTER COUNTY-HPN
'FOR ALL AIRPORTS USE EAST
SIDE TERMINAL
' BETWEEN 1600 & 2000 90MIN

From AMSTERDAM, NETHERLANDS                    6877 Mi AMS
NLG CO  P        4870       9740  J       2758       5516
                                  Y       2223       4446
        PK  F    4870       9740  C       2758       5516
                                  Y       2223       4446
        TW  F    4870       9740  C       2758       5516
        CO  EX/1006    BH    2007  BL     1250  BO   1562
            EX/1234    HH    2792  HL     2136  HO   2195
            EX/2539    BH    1386  BL     1065  BO   1118
        2    0930       1415     JFK    PK 703   FCY    74M 1
        257  0945       1455     JFK    PA  92   FCYBM  310 1
        16   1115       1520     JFK    PA  35   FCYBM  310 1
                        CONNECTIONS
        0710       0825    FRA    LH 1693  FCMTK  737 0
        1000  FRA  1220    JFK    LH 400   FCBMK  D10 0
    X7  0745       0755    LHR    BA 423   CMSBL  73S 0
        1030  LHR  1320    EWR    BA 185   FJMSB  747 0
        0805       0925    CPH    KL 173   CMBLS  737 0
        1125  CPH  1405    EWR    SK 911   CMBK   763 0
    146 0805       1135    HEL    KL 299   CMB    737 0
        1315  HEL  1500    JFK    AY 101   CMBK   D10 0
```

Category 1 Destination (to) City Data

Provides general information including airport(s) and city code.

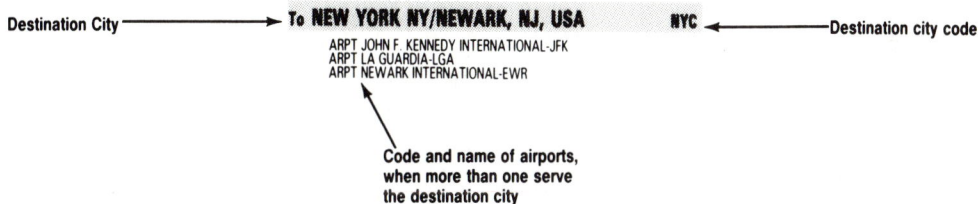

Destination City → **To NEW YORK NY/NEWARK, NJ, USA** NYC ← Destination city code

ARPT JOHN F. KENNEDY INTERNATIONAL-JFK
ARPT LA GUARDIA-LGA
ARPT NEWARK INTERNATIONAL-EWR

↑ Code and name of airports, when more than one serve the destination city

---

Category 2 Ground Transportation Data

Offers airport distance, traveling time and ground transportation information.

Note: Airlines have varying check-in times prior to departure. Please check with your airline to allow adequate time.

Distance from airport to destination city (Miles/kilometers) →
ARPT JOHN F. KENNEDY INTERNATIONAL-JFK-
15.0MI/24.1KM 75MIN
ARPT LA GUARDIA-LGA-8.0MI/12.8KM 60MIN'
ARPT NEWARK INTERNATIONAL-EWR-
16.0MI/25.7KM 45MIN
ARPT PIER 11/WALL STREET SPB-NWS
ARPT WESTCHESTER COUNTY-HPN
'FOR ALL AIRPORTS USE EAST
SIDE TERMINAL

Additional ground transportation information → ' BETWEEN 1600 & 2000 90MIN

← Approximate traveling time from airport to destination city

← Code of airports, when more than one serve destination city

Figure 7-2 "Reprinted by special permission from the September 1991 OAG Desktop Flight Guide-Worldwide Edition. All rights reserved."

More than 160 pages have been added to the worldwide edition, to include:

· Seating charts of 35 carriers' wide-body aircrafts and the Concorde
· Sixty airport diagrams
· World and regional maps, including time zones and major cities
· A monthly listing of movies by airline
· The "How to Use" section appears in English, Spanish, German, French, and Japanese

Category 3 Origin (from) City Data

Provides general information including airport(s) and city code.

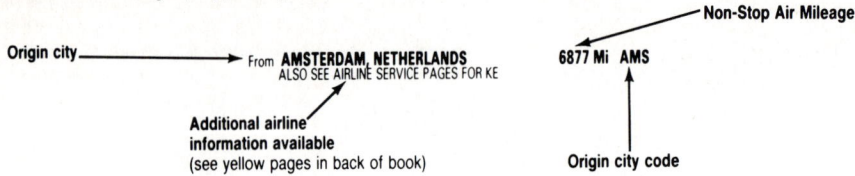

Non-Stop Air Mileage

Origin city

From **AMSTERDAM, NETHERLANDS**
ALSO SEE AIRLINE SERVICE PAGES FOR KE

6877 Mi AMS

Additional airline information available
(see yellow pages in back of book)

Origin city code

Category 4 Direct Flight Fares Data

Fares apply only to direct flights. Do not use direct flight fares for connecting flights as they do not always apply.

Note: Fares within Spain and within Israel already include tax. Refer to Local Tax Section for explanation.

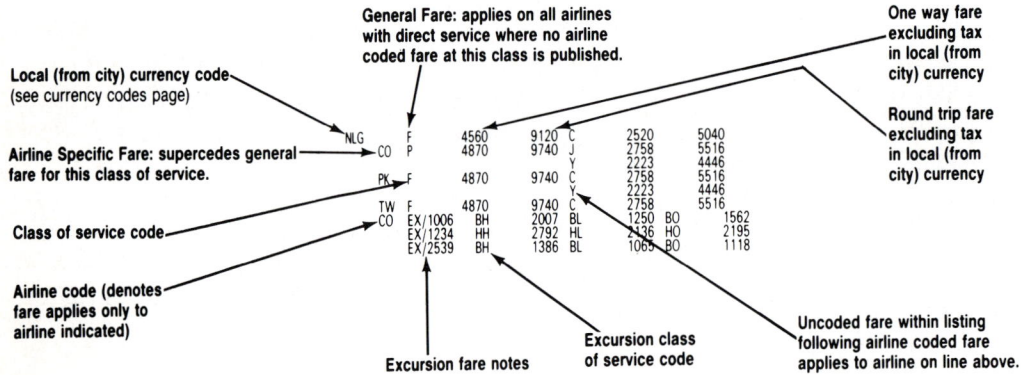

General Fare: applies on all airlines with direct service where no airline coded fare at this class is published.

One way fare excluding tax in local (from city) currency

Local (from city) currency code (see currency codes page)

Round trip fare excluding tax in local (from city) currency

Airline Specific Fare: supercedes general fare for this class of service.

Class of service code

Airline code (denotes fare applies only to airline indicated)

NLG	CO	F	4560	9120	C	2520	5040	
		P	4870	9740	J	2758	5516	
					Y	2223	4446	
PK		F	4870	9740	C	2758	5516	
					Y	2223	4446	
TW		F	4870	9740	C	2758	5516	
CO		EX/1006	BH	2007	BL	1250	BO	1562
		EX/1234	HH	2792	HL	2136	HO	2195
		EX/2539	BH	1386	BL	1065	BO	1118

Excursion fare notes

Excursion class of service code

Uncoded fare within listing following airline coded fare applies to airline on line above.

Category 5 Direct Flights Schedule Data

Direct flights are listed from earliest to latest departure. All times shown are local. Read across the lines — each direct flight is complete on a single line unless an additional information line appears.

The column heading in the upper left hand corner of each listing page indicates in what sequence flight information appears. A ★ symbol, which follows the 2-character airline code on some flights, indicates a code sharing airline, whereby the flight is operated by a different airline than the airline whose code is shown on the flight line.

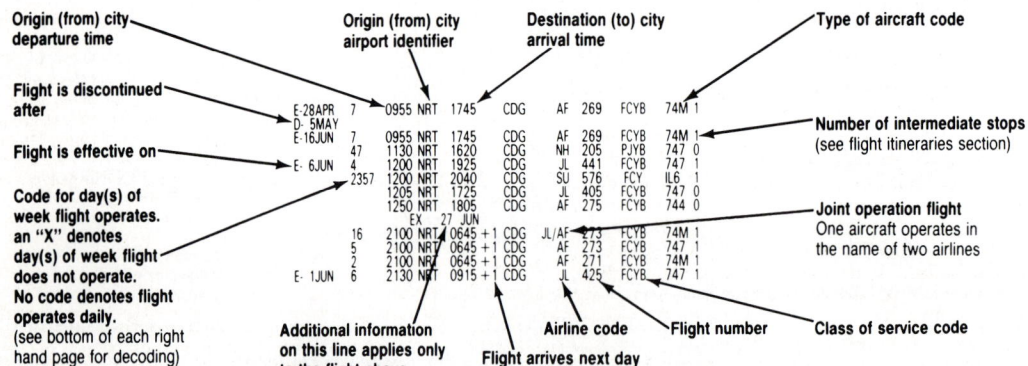

Origin (from) city departure time

Origin (from) city airport identifier

Destination (to) city arrival time

Type of aircraft code

Flight is discontinued after

Flight is effective on

Code for day(s) of week flight operates. an "X" denotes day(s) of week flight does not operate. No code denotes flight operates daily. (see bottom of each right hand page for decoding)

Number of intermediate stops (see flight itineraries section)

Joint operation flight One aircraft operates in the name of two airlines

Additional information on this line applies only to the flight above

Airline code

Flight number

Flight arrives next day

Class of service code

E-28APR	7	0955	NRT	1745	CDG	AF 269	FCYB	74M 1
D- 5MAY								
E-16JUN	7	0955	NRT	1745	CDG	AF 269	FCYB	74M 1
	47	1130	NRT	1620	CDG	NH 205	PJYB	747 0
E- 6JUN	4	1200	NRT	1925	CDG	JL 441	FCYB	747 1
	2357	1200	NRT	2040	CDG	SU 576	FCY	IL6 1
		1205	NRT	1725	CDG	JL 405	FCYB	747 0
		1250	NRT	1805	CDG	AF 275	FCYB	744 0
		EX 27 JUN						
	16	2100	NRT	0645 +1	CDG	JL/AF 273	FCYB	74M 1
	5	2100	NRT	0645 +1	CDG	AF 273	FCYB	747 1
	2	2100	NRT	0645 +1	CDG	AF 271	FCYB	74M 1
E- 1JUN	6	2130	NRT	0915 +1	CDG	JL 425	FCYB	747 1

Figure 7-3 "Reprinted by special permission from the September 1991 OAG Desktop Flight Guide-Worldwide Edition. All rights reserved."

The changes were added to what is already a wealth of information contained in the guides. This includes fares, baggage requirements, excess baggage charges, connecting times, transportation taxes, aircraft performance statistics, frequent flyer/lodger information, and more.

The OAGs are now available in an *electronic edition* (*EEOAG*). The *EEOAG* will also supply current fares on a weekly basis, whereas the printed editions will

Category 6 Connecting Flight Schedule Data

If the direct flights shown are inconvenient for you or unavailable, you may find a connecting flight suits your needs. Connecting flights are two (single connection) or three (double connection) flights strung together to take you to your destination from your origin city. For your convenience, OAG often includes connecting flights from which you may choose. A sample of connecting flights display is shown below. You may also construct your own connections by following the instructions at the end of this section.

Like direct flights, connecting flights are also listed from earliest to latest departure. All times shown are local.

Read across the lines — each connecting flight is displayed as a two-line (single connection) or three-line (double connection) entry unless an additional information line appears.

Single Connections

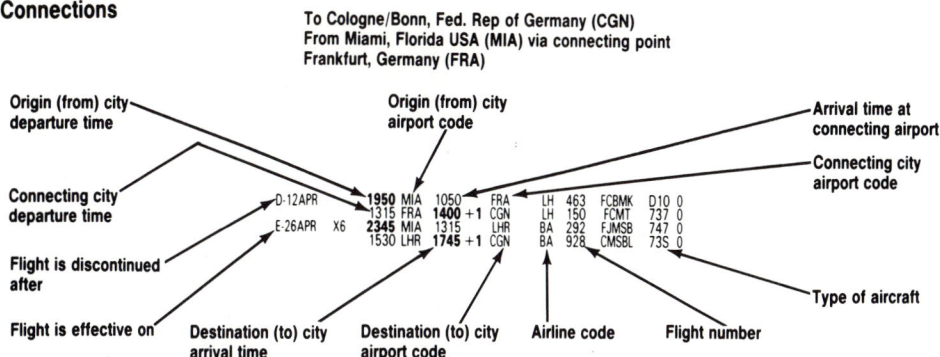

To Cologne/Bonn, Fed. Rep of Germany (CGN)
From Miami, Florida USA (MIA) via connecting point
Frankfurt, Germany (FRA)

Origin (from) city departure time

Origin (from) city airport code

Arrival time at connecting airport

Connecting city departure time

Connecting city airport code

Flight is discontinued after

Flight is effective on

Destination (to) city arrival time

Destination (to) city airport code

Airline code

Flight number

Type of aircraft

```
D-12APR        1950 MIA 1050   FRA    LH  463  FCBMK  D10 0
               1315 FRA 1400 +1 CGN    LH  150  FCMT   737 0
E-26APR   X6   2345 MIA 1315   LHR    BA  292  FJMSB  747 0
               1530 LHR 1745 +1 CGN    BA  928  CMSBL  73S 0
```

In the example of a single connection above, **originating flight** Lufthansa German Airlines (LH) flight 463 departs Miami, Florida USA (MIA) at 1950 hours (the departure time is shown in bold face type) and arrives at the **connecting point**, Frankfurt Fed. Rep. of Germany (FRA) at 1050 hours. Information on the first line regarding equipment, etc., applies to the **originating flight**.

The second line shows the 1315 hours departure time from the **connecting point** (FRA) of **connecting flight** Lufthansa German Airlines (LH) flight 150, arriving at **destination**, Cologne/Bonn, Fed. Rep. of Germany (CGN) at 1400 hours (arrival time is shown in boldface type). The other information on the second line regarding equipment, etc., applies to the **connecting flight**.

Double Connections

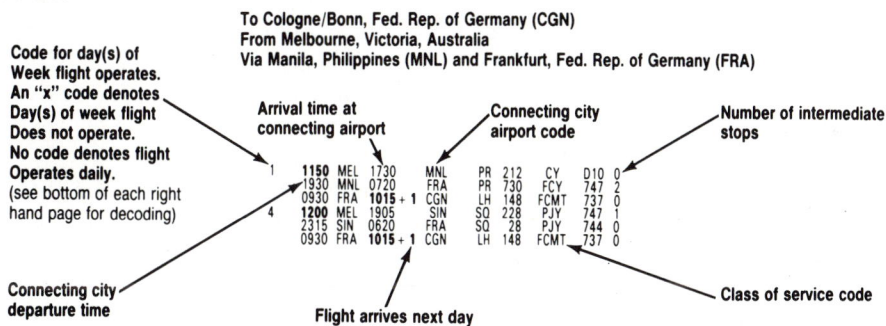

To Cologne/Bonn, Fed. Rep. of Germany (CGN)
From Melbourne, Victoria, Australia
Via Manila, Philippines (MNL) and Frankfurt, Fed. Rep. of Germany (FRA)

Code for day(s) of Week flight operates. An "x" code denotes Day(s) of week flight Does not operate. No code denotes flight Operates daily. (see bottom of each right hand page for decoding)

Arrival time at connecting airport

Connecting city airport code

Number of intermediate stops

Connecting city departure time

Flight arrives next day

Class of service code

```
1    1150 MEL 1730   MNL    PR  212  CY    D10 0
     1930 MNL 0720   FRA    PR  730  FCY   747 2
     0930 FRA 1015 +1 CGN    LH  148  FCMT  737 0
4    1200 MEL 1905   SIN    SQ  228  PJY   747 1
     2315 SIN 0620   FRA    SQ   28  PJY   744 0
     0930 FRA 1015 +1 CGN    LH  148  FCMT  737 0
```

In the example above of a double connection, two connecting cities are shown. on the first line **originating flight**, Philippine Airlines (PR) 212 departs Melbourne at 1150 hours (the departure time is shown in boldface type) and arrives at the **first connecting point**, Manila, Philippines (MNL) 1730 hours. The other information on the first line regarding equipment, etc. applies to the **originating flight**.

The second line shows the **first connecting flight**, Philippine Airlines (PR) 730 departing the **first connecting point** (MNL) at 1930 hours and arriving at the **second connecting point**, Frankfurt, Fed. Rep. of Germany (FRA) at 0720 hours. The other information on the second line regarding equipment, etc., applies to the **first connecting flight**.

The third line shows the **second connecting flight** Lufthansa German Airlines (LH) 148 departing the **second connecting point** (FRA) at 0930 hours and arriving at the **destination** Cologne/Bonn, Fed. Rep. of Germany (CGN) at 1015 hours. (The arrival time is shown in boldface type.) The other information on the third line regarding equipment, etc., applies to the **second connecting flight**.

Figure 7-4 "Reprinted by special permission from the September 1991 OAG Desktop Flight Guide-Worldwide Edition. All rights reserved."

only give a fare range. Any terminal—computer terminal, word-processing system or personal computer—that can be used to send or receive data over telephone lines can be used to reach airline fare and schedule information in the *EEOAG*. After a one-time new subscriber fee is paid, the user is billed monthly based on how much the system is used. Because of the relatively high cost, few small or medium-sized agencies subscribe to the *EEOAG*; its users are mainly business travelers.

The Official Airline Guides, Inc. and Thomas Cook U.S.A. (tour operator and retail travel agency chain), both subsidiary companies of Dun & Bradstreet, announced in October 1986 that the *EEOAG* will begin posting leisure products on the information and reservations system in 1987. The first leisure travel listings will be of a limited number of Thomas Cook's tour products. EEOAG also takes paid listings from suppliers of distress merchandise, such as cruise lines with unsold cabins the week before departure. *EEOAG* users will be able to send an electronic message to Thomas Cook Travel saying that they wish to make a reservation and one of Cook's leisure agents will contact them.

OAG, Inc. receives schedule information from approximately 650 airlines worldwide; this information goes in the printed issues. The airlines use a variety of methods for notifying the OAG of schedules, including letters, telexes, tapes, or even data transmission over telephone lines. The airlines that provide computer reservation systems in travel agencies use an electronic method for data transmission called the Remote On-Line Services System (ROSS). It permits the carriers to update schedules on a live basis, using a CRT connected to the OAG computer. The data are then taped by OAG and distributed to the subscribers of this system. The tapes can be ready in two days, but not all carriers want them that fast since they need time to enter the information into their own computers. Deliveries are twice a week or weekly.

READING THE OAG

The schedules in the printed editions are shown in the same format on the computer screen. It is therefore important that new employees learn to read the OAG before they can learn the computer. Instruction booklets in the use of the guides are available from OAG. The booklets are completely self-explanatory; the user actually tests himself on what he is learning. Travel agents and schools can order supplies at a minimal charge.

Both editions of the OAG show all airline schedules from each city in one listing (see illustrations). Pairs of cities (to and from) are listed in alphabetical order, and flight departures in chronological order. Arrival times, class of service, airline and flight number, type of equipment used, and food service available are all found in the OAG. Ground transportation information is also shown (i.e., availability of limousine service or car rentals). In the worldwide edition the fare information is shown in both U.S. dollars and the local currency of the city of origin.

Because it contains the complete schedule of each airline, it has been condensed by using a number of codes. Explanations of these codes may be found inside the front cover and on the first few pages in the section "Abbreviations and Reference Marks." Separate sections list the airport/city codes and flight itineraries. The flight itineraries section list the flights alphabetically by airline—numerically by flight number—and shows the origin, termination, and enroute cities for each flight number.

The main body of the OAG is devoted to the schedules themselves, listed alphabetically by city. These schedules include all direct flights between any pair of cities and many connecting flights as well. All times shown are local times—the local time at the departure city and local time at the arrival city. The time-zone codes are shown in the headings. From these codes the time difference between cities can be determined.

Practice is essential in learning to read the OAG. Have friends and relatives give you sample itineraries to work on. If you are not yet employed in the industry and do not have access to an OAG, ask your travel agent or call the sales department of almost any airline and ask for an outdated issue.

MD	Air Madagascar
ME	Middle East Airlines/Airliban
MF	Xiamen Airlines
MG	MGM Grand Air, Inc.
MH	Malaysia Airlines
MI	Tradewinds Pte. Ltd.
MJ	Lineas Aereas Privadas Argentinas S.A. (LAPA)
MK	Air Mauritius
ML	Midway Airlines, Inc.
ML★	The Midway Connection (Flight numbers 1600-1999 ■ Midway Commuter)
MM	Sociedad Aeronautica Medellin
MN	Commercial Airways (Pty.) Ltd. (COMAIR)
MO	Calm Air International Ltd.
MQ	Simmons Airlines
MR	Air Mauritanie
MS	Egyptair
MT	Macknight Airlines
MU	China Eastern Airlines
MV	Ansett W.A.
MW	Maya Airways
MX	Mexicana de Aviacion
MX★	Mexicana de Aviacion (Flight numbers 4002-4011, 4014-4019 and 4776-4779 Aeromonterrey, S.A. de C.V. (7M); 7100-7113, 7302-7303, 7401-7406, 7502, 7511, 7600-7601, 7801-7802, 7804, 7901-7902 and 7911-7912 Aero Caribe (QA); 8609-8610, 8615-8616 and 8618-8619 Aviacion del Noroeste (5T))
MY	Helifrance - Compagnie Aerienne d'Helicopteres
MZ	Merpati Nusantara Airlines
NA	Executive Air Charter
NB	Sterling Airways A/S
NC	Norskair
ND	Intair
ND★	Intair (Flight numbers 240-259 Air Satellite, Inc. (QR) #; 940-959 Alexandair, Inc.)
NF	Air Vanuatu (Operations) Limited
NF★	Air Vanuatu (Operations) Limited (Flight numbers 105 and 108 Solomon Airlines (IE); 230, 233-235 and 240-243 Air Caledonie International (SB))
NG	Lauda Air
NH	All Nippon Airways Co., Ltd.
NI	Portugalia
NJ	Namakwaland Lugdiens
NK	Charter One
NM	Mount Cook Airlines
NN	C.A.A.A.—Air Martinique
NO	Aus-Air
NP	Piccolo Airlines
NR	Norontair
NS	NFD Luftverkehrs AG
NT	Norcanair
NU	Southwest Airlines Co., Inc.
NV	Northwest Territorial Airways Ltd.
NW	Northwest Airlines, Inc.
NW★	Northwest Airlines, Inc. (Flight numbers 55-56 KLM-Royal Dutch Airlines (KL); 2000-2499 Horizon Air (QX); 4000-4699 USAir (US) 4700-4799 Stateswest Airlines, Inc. (YW))
NW★	Northwest Airlink (Flight numbers 2500-2999 ■ Express Airlines I, Inc. (9E); 3000-3399 ■ Mesaba Aviation (XJ); 3500-3699 ■ Precision Airlines (RP); 3700-3899 ■ Northeast Express Regional Airlines (2V) ◀)
NX	Nationair
NZ	Air New Zealand
NZ★	Air New Zealand (Flight numbers 320-339 Canadian Airlines International Ltd. (CP); 340-369 Qantas Airways Ltd. (QF); 2000-2999 and 8000-8999 Air New Zealand Link)
OA	Olympic Airways
OC	Sunshine Aviation
OE	Westair Airlines
OF	Sunstate Airlines
OG	Air Guadeloupe
OH	Comair, Inc. ◀
OI	Heli-Transport
OJ	Air St.-Barthelemy
OK	Czechoslovak Airlines
OL	OLT— Ostfriesische Lufttransport GMBH
OM	MIAT-Mongolian Airlines
ON	Air Nauru
OO	Sky West Airlines
OP	Chalk's International Airlines
OR	Air Comores
OS	Austrian Airlines
OT	Evergreen Alaska
OV	Aeromaritime International
OW	Metavia Aidines (Pty) Ltd.
OX	Air Hudik
OY	Sunaire
OZ	Asiana Airlines
PA	Pan American World Airways, Inc.
PA★	Pan Am Express, Inc. (Flight numbers 4070-4071 and 4500-4999 ■ Pan Am Express, Inc. (RZ))
PA★	Pan American World Airways, Inc./Adria Airways (Flight numbers 4036-4037 and 4076-4077 Adria Airways (JP))
PA★	Pan American World Airways, Inc./Malev-Hungarian Airlines (Flight numbers 4072-4073 Malev-Hungarian Airlines (MA))
PA★	Pan American World Airways, Inc./United Airlines (Flight numbers 370-399 United Airlines (UA))
PB	Air Burundi
PC	Fiji Air
PD	Pem Air Limited
PE	Provincial Air Services
PF	Vayudoot
PH	Polynesian Airlines, Ltd.
PI	Sunflower Airlines Limited
PK	Pakistan International Airlines
PL	Aeroperu
PM	Tropic Air
PO	Aeropelican Air Services, Pty. Ltd.
PQ	Pacific Coast Airlines
PR	Philippine Airlines, Inc.
PR★	Philippine Airlines, Inc. (Flight numbers 100-103 Trans World Airlines, Inc. (TW))
PU	Pluna
PV	Panorama Air
PX	Air Niugini
PY	Surinam Airways Ltd.

PZ	LAP— Lineas Aereas Paraguayas (Air Paraguay)
QC	Air Zaire
QD	Grand Airways, Inc.
QE	Air Moorea
QF	Qantas Airways Ltd.
QF★	Qantas Airways Ltd. (Flight numbers 100-101, 333-338, 340, 343-344, 349, 355-358, 367-368, 373-376, 383-384, 403-404 and 461-468 Air New Zealand (NZ); 110-151 and 150-151 Air Caledonie International (SB); 301-308 American Airlines, Inc. (AA); 325-328 Canadian Airlines International Ltd. (CP); 452-453 Lauda Air (NG); 471-472 Ansett Australia (AN); 481-482 Air Niugini (PX); 491-498 Air Pacific Limited (FJ); 880-881 Aerolineas Argentinas (AR); 930-931 Ansett W.A. (MV))
QG	Dynamic Air
QH	Qwestair
QI	Cimber Air
QK★	Air Nova Inc. (Flight numbers 803-804 Newfoundland Labrador Air Transport, Ltd.)
QL	Lesotho Airways Corp.
QM	Air Malawi
QN	Air Outre Mer
QP	Airkenya Aviation Limited
QQ■	Allied Airlines, Inc.
QR	Air Satellite, Inc.
QS	Tatra Air
QT	S.A.R. Avions Taxis
QU	Uganda Airlines
QV	Lao Aviation
QW	Turks and Caicos National Airline
QX	Horizon Air
QZ	Zambia Airways
RA	Royal Nepal Airlines Corporation
RB	Syrian Arab Airlines
RC	Atlantic Airways Faroe Islands
RD	Avianova
RE	Aer Arann
RF	Travelair Goteborg AB
RG	Varig, S.A.
RH	Meridiana
RI	P.T. Mandala Airlines
RJ	Royal Jordanian
RK	Air Afrique
RL	Aerolineas Nicaraguenses A.S. (AERONICA)
RM	Wings West Airlines, Inc.
RO	Tarom-Romanian Air Transport
RP	Precision Airlines
RQ	Air Engiadina
RR	Royal Air Force-38 Transport Group
RS	Intercontinental de Aviacion
RU	Northern Commuter Airlines
RV	Reeve Aleutian Airways, Inc.
RV★	Reeve Aleutian Airways, Inc. (Flight numbers 621-622, 625-626 and 659-660 Peninsula Airways, Inc. (KS))
RW	Seair Pacific Pty. Ltd.
RY	Air Rwanda
SA	South African Airways
SB	Air Caledonie International
SC	Cruzeiro do Sul S.A. - Servicos Aereos
SD	Sudan Airways
SE	Wings of Alaska
SG	Sempati Air
SH	SAHSA— Servicio Aereo de Honduras, S.A.
SJ	Southern Air Limited
SK	SAS— Scandinavian Airlines System
SL	Rio-Sul - Servicos Aereos Regionais
SM	Aberdeen Airways Ltd.
SN	Sabena World Airlines
SO	Austrian Air Services Oesterreichischer Inlands Flugdienst Ges.M.B.H.
SP	SATA Air Acores
SQ	Singapore Airlines
SQ★	Singapore Airlines (Flight numbers 11-12 and 711-712 Delta Air Lines, Inc. (DL))
SR	Swissair
ST	Yanda Airlines
SU	Aeroflot-Soviet Airlines
SV	Saudi Arabian Airlines
SW	Namib Air Ltd.
SX	Christman Air System
SZ	China Southwest Airlines
TA	Taca International Airlines, S.A.
TA★	Taca International Airlines, S.A. (Flight numbers 215-216 and 405-406 Islena Airlines (WC))
TB	Trump Shuttle, Inc.
TC	Air Tanzania Corporation
TD	Transavio
TF	Air Transport Pyrenees
TG	Thai Airways International, I.td.
TH	Lar Transregional - Linhas Aereas Regionais S.A.
TJ	TAS Airways S.P.A.
TK	Turk Hava Yollari
TL	Skyport
TM	LAM— Linhas Aereas de Mocambique
TN	Australian Airlines
TN★	Australian Airlines (Flight numbers 1400-1549 Australian Regional Airline Queensland; 1600-1699 Eastern Australia Airlines (UN))
TO	Alkan Air Ltd.
TP	TAP Air Portugal
TP★	TAP Air Portugal (Flight numbers 147-148 Air Atlantis; 800-823 LAR Transregional-Linhas Aereas Regionais S.A. (TH))
TQ	Transwede Airways AB
TR	Transbrasil S/A Linhas Aereas
TS	Samoa Air
TT	Tunisavia
TU	Tunis Air
TV	Haiti Trans Air S.A.
TW	Trans World Airlines, Inc.
TW★	Trans World Airlines, Inc. (Flight numbers 8150-8155 ■ USAir Express; 8156-8199 USAir (US))
TW★	Trans World Express (Flight numbers 7000-7549 Trans States Airlines, Inc. (9N); 7550-7629 Jet Express (JI))
TX	Transportes Aereos Nacionales
TY	Air Caledonie
TZ	American Trans Air
UA	United Airlines

UA★	United Express (Flight numbers 2100-2349 ■ Mesa Airlines (YV); 2375-2624 and 3100-3569 Westair Airlines (OE); 2640-3099 and 3740-3899 Air Wisconsin (ZW); 3570-3739 Atlantic Coast)
UB	Myanma Airways
UC	LADECO — Linea Aerea del Cobre
UD	Hex'Air
UE	Air LA
UH	Transport Air Centre
UI	Norlandair
UJ	Air Sedona
UK	Air UK
UL	Airlanka Ltd.
UM	Air Zimbabwe
UN	Eastern Australia Airlines
UO	Direct Air, Inc. ◀
UP	Bahamasair
UR	British International Helicopters
US	USAir
US★	USAir Express (Flight numbers 3000-4999 ■ USAir Express)
UT	UTA— Union de Transports Aeriens
UU	Air Austral
UV	Air Kangaroo Island
UW	Perimeter Airlines (Inland) Ltd.
UY	Cameroon Airlines
VA	Viasa
VB	Birmingham European Airways
VC	Servivensa
VD	Air Liberte
VE	Avensa
VG	RFG Regionalflug GMBH
VH	Air Burkina
VI	Vieques Air Link, Inc.
VJ	Air Exel
VK	Air Tungaru Corporation
VM	Air Vendee
VN	Hang Khong Vietnam
VO	Tyrolean Airways
VP	VASP
VQ	Oxley Airlines Ltd.
VR	TACV-Cabo Verde Airlines
VS	Virgin Atlantic Airways Ltd.
VT	Air Tahiti
VV	Air Ivoire
VV	Flexair
VW	Transportes Aeromar, S.A. de C.V.
VX	Aces
VZ	Aquatic Airways Pty. Ltd.
WA	Newair
WB	SAN (Servicios Aereos Nacionales)
WC	Islena Airlines
WE	Rheintalflug Seewald GMBH
WF	Wideroes Flyveselskap
WG	Taiwan Airlines Company Ltd.
WH	China Northwest Airlines
WI	Rottnest Airbus
WJ	Labrador Airways, Ltd.
WL	Aeroperlas
WN	Windward Island Airways International N.V.
WN	Southwest Airlines
WO	Polarwing OY
WP	Aloha Islandair, Inc.
WR	Royal Tongan Airlines
WS	Westates Airlines
WT	Nigeria Airways Ltd.
WV	Maval Aviation
WX	Ansett Express
WY	Oman Aviation (SAO)
WZ	B.A.S.E. Business Airlines
XE	Southcentral Air, Inc.
XF	Skybus Express
XJ	Mesaba Aviation
XO	Xinjiang Airlines
XP	Drakk'air Lines
XQ	Action Airlines
XT	Air Exel NL
XU	Aerovias, S.A.
XV	Nature Island Express
XW	Walker's International
XY	Ryan Air, Inc.
XZ	Flugfelag Austurlands HF
YB	Air Aquitaine
YC	Flight West Airlines
YC★	Flight West Airlines (Flight numbers 610-611 and 635-636 Kingair)
YD	Salair AB
YE	Grand Canyon Airlines, Inc.
YH	Air-Jet
YI	Air Sunshine Inc.◀
YJ	National Airlines (Pty) Ltd.
YK	Cyprus Turkish Airlines Ltd. Co.
YL	Long Island Airlines
YM	Compass Airlines
YN	Air Creebec Inc.
YO	Heli-Air Monaco
YP	Aero Lloyd
YQ	Helikopterservice AB, Euro Air
YR	Scenic Airlines, Inc.
YT	Skywest Airlines
YU	Aerolineas Dominicanas S.A. - Dominair
YV	Mesa Airlines
YW	Stateswest Airlines, Inc.
YX	Midwest Express Airlines, Inc.
YX★	Midwest Express Connection (Flight numbers 1000-1999 Skyway Airlines, Inc.; 8000-8999 International Cargo Inc.)
YZ	Transportes Aereos ɗa Guine-Bissau
ZA	ZAS Airline of Egypt
ZB	Monarch Airlines
ZC	Royal Swazi National Airways Corp.
ZD	Ross Aviation, Inc. ◀
ZF	Airborne of Sweden AB
ZG	Sabair Airlines Pty. Ltd.
ZI	Aigle Azur
ZJ	Teddy Air A/S
ZK	Great Lakes Aviation, Ltd.
ZL	Hazelton Airlines
ZM	Scibe-Airlift

Figure 7-5 ''Reprinted by special permission from the September 1991 OAG Desktop Flight Guide-Worldwide Edition. All rights reserved.''

#	ZN	Compagnie Corse Mediterranee
■	ZO	Mohawk Airlines
■	ZP	Virgin Air, Inc.
	ZQ	Ansett New Zealand
	ZQ★	Ansett New Zealand (Flight numbers 100-399 Tranzair)
	ZR	Muk Air
#	ZS	Hispaniola Airways C. por A.
	ZT	SATENA
■	ZU	Freedom Air
	ZV	Air Midwest
	ZW	Air Wisconsin
	ZX	AirBC, Ltd.
■	2D	Dawn Air, Inc.
	2E	Hermens/Markair Express
	2F	Frontier Flying Service
	2F★	Frontier Flying Service (Flight number 528 Tatonduk Flying Service (3K))
	2P	Prairie Flying Service (1976) Ltd.
	2S	Island Express
■	2V	Northeast Express Regional Airlines ◄
	2W	Wairarapa Airlines, Ltd.
	2Y	Koyukon Air, Inc.
	2Z	Aerolitoral - Servicios Aereos Litoral S.A. de C.V.
■	3A	Alliance Airlines
	3C	Camai Air
	3E	Northwestern Air Lease
	3G■	Virgin Island Seaplane Shuttle
	3H	Air Inuit (1985) Ltd.
	3K	Tatonduk Flying Service
■	3M	Gulfstream International Airlines, Inc.
	3P	Equator Airlines Ltd.
	3Q	Aerochasqui S.A.
	3R	MacAir
	3S	Shuswap Air
	3T	Contact Air
	3V	Waglisla Air Inc.
	4A	Canadian Eagle Airlines Ltd.
	4B	Olson Air Service, Inc.
	4C	Aires
	4D	Air Sinai
	4E	Tanana Air Service
	4F	Frontier Air
	4K	Kenn Borek Air Ltd.
×	4L	Air Alma Inc.
	4M	Island Air
	4N	Air North
×	4V	Voyageur Airways, Ltd.
	4W	Warbelow's Air Ventures, Inc.
■	4X	L'Express Airlines
	4Y	Yute Air Alaska, Inc.
■	5A	Alpine Aviation, Inc.
	5B	Bellair, Inc.

■	5C	Conquest Airlines Corp.
	5H	Odinair
	5K	Kenmore Air
	5P	Ptarmigan Airways Ltd.
	5S	Airspeed Aviation Inc.
	5T	Aviacion del Noroeste
	5U	Skagway Air Service, Inc.
	5V	Aviair Aviation (1984) Ltd.
■	5W	Air San Juan/Chartair, Inc.
	6A	Aviacsa - Consorcio Aviaxsa, S.A. de C.V.
	6B	Baxter Aviation
	6C	Cape Smythe Air Service, Inc.
	6D	Alaska Island Air, Inc.
	6E	Malmo Aviation AB
■	6G	Las Vegas Airlines
×	6H	Canadian Helicopters Limited
	6K	Keewatin Air Limited
	6L	Aklak Air Ltd.
	6M	40-Mile Air, Ltd.
	6M★	40-Mile Air, Ltd. (Flight numbers 620-854 and 856-857 Warbelow's Air Ventures, Inc. (4W))
	6Q	Barrow Air, Inc.
	6S	Ketchikan Air Service, Inc.
	6T	Tyee Airways Limited
■	6V	Air Vegas, Inc.
	6W	Wilderness Airline (1975) Ltd.
	7A	Haines Airways, Inc.
	7B	Simpson Air Ltd.
	7C	Columbia Pacific Airlines
	7F	First Air
	7H	ERA Aviation
	7J	L.A.P.S.A. Inc.
	7K	Larry's Flying Service, Inc.
■	7L	Lake Union Air Service
	7M	Aeromonterrey, S.A. de C.V.
	7N	Air Manitoba
	7R	Redwing Airways, Inc.
	7T	Trans Cote Inc.
■	7V	Alpha Air
	7W	Air Sask Aviation
	8B	Baker Aviation, Inc.
	8D	Dulles Express
	8E	Bering Air, Inc.
	8F	Wilbur's Inc.
■	8G	GP Express Airlines, Inc.
	8H	Harbor Air Service
	8K	Air Vitkovice
	8L	Servicio Aereo Leo Lopez
■	8M	Skymaster
■	8N	Nashville Eagle, Inc.
	8P	Pacific Coastal Airlines Limited
■	8R	WRA, Inc.

	8V	Wright Air Service, Inc.
	9A	Air Atlantic Ltd.
	9C	Icarus Flying Service, Inc.
	9D	Delta Air Charters, Ltd.
■	9E	Express Airlines I, Inc.
	9F	Skycraft Air Transport Inc.
■	9K	Cape Air
	9M	Central Mountain Air Ltd.
	9N	Trans States Airlines, Inc.
	9P	Pelangi Air
	9Q	Taquan Air Service, Inc.
	9R	Flagship Express Services, Inc.
	9S	Sabourin Lake Airways Ltd.
	9T	Athabaska Airways Ltd.
§	9V	Air Schefferville
	9W	Northwinds Northern, Inc.
	9Y	Yutana Airlines

Scheduled Intra-State Air Carriers

	3D	Edgartown Air, Inc.
§	4Q	Trans North Aviation, Ltd.
	4R	Raven Air, Inc.

★ — (Following 2 character airline code) Code sharing carrier—indicates a flight operated by a different air carrier from the air carrier whose code is shown on the flight line.
EXAMPLE: DL Delta Air Lines, Inc. (Flight numbers 1-1299 & 1400-1949)
DL★ Delta Connection (Flight numbers 3000-3499 Comair, Inc. (OH))

■ — Indicates Part 204 commuter air carrier: A part 298 commuter air carrier which has been found fit pursuant to part 204 of the Economic Regulations of the United States Department of Transportation. Flight schedule listings for part 204 commuter air carriers are published in the Official Airline Guide chronologically with those of certificated air carriers.

× — Service temporarily suspended
◄ — National Air Transportation Association, Inc.
§ — Carrier performs seasonal service only
# — Duplicated IATA two-letter airline code. For other (non-scheduled) carrier (not shown in OAG) refer to IATA traffic guide.

Figure 7-6 "Reprinted by special permission from the September 1991 OAG Desktop Flight Guide-Worldwide Edition. All rights reserved."

Remarks

Airline codes and flight numbers are used for examples only.

Equipment L10-JFK-747	Change of equipment at designated airport.
BA904-HKG-BA905	Change of flight number at designated airport.
AZ576 Y-FCO-FY	Change of class of service at designated airport.
Conditional Stopover Traffic	Airline may only carry passengers making a stopover or connection. Passengers may continue on the same or another airline at a later date. Contact airline for specific restrictions.
No Local Traffic	Airline may only carry passengers making a direct connection on the same or another airline. Contact airline for specific restrictions.
Request All Reservations	All reservations must be requested from the operating airline in advance.
Subj Govt Approval	Service subject to receipt of government operating authority
#	(In number of stops column) indicates over 9 stops
Chg Plane	Change of aircraft required at designated airport
EX	Except on
Night Stop	(Airport code) overnight stop paid for by carrier
OP	Operates on
REQ	Appears in place of departure and arrival times and indicates a flag stop
+1	Next day
+2	Second day
+3	Third day
−1	Previous day
•	(In class of service column) indicates change in class of service en route. (In equipment column) indicates change of aircraft occurs en route. Specific information follows flight listing

Equipment Codes

Code	
	Jet Aircraft
AB3	Airbus Industrie A300 (All Series)
B11	British Aerospace (BAC) One-Eleven (All Series)
CNJ	Cessna Citation
CRV	Aerospatiale Caravelle (All Series)
DAM	Dassault-Breguet Mercure
DC8	McDonnell Douglas DC8 Passenger (All 50 Series)
DC9	McDonnell Douglas DC9 (All 10 & 20 Series)
DFL	Dassault-Breguet Mystere-Falcon 10/100/20/200
D1M	McDonnell Douglas DC10 Mixed Configuration
D10	McDonnell Douglas DC10 (All Series)
D8S	McDonnell Douglas DC8 (All 60/70 Series)
D9S	McDonnell Douglas DC9 (All 30/40 & 50 Series)
F28	Fokker F28 Fellowship (All Series)
ILW	Ilyushin IL86
IL6	Ilyushin IL62/62M
L10	Lockheed L1011 (All Series)
L15	Lockheed L1011-500 TriStar
M11	McDonnell Douglas MD-11
M80	McDonnell Douglas (MD-80 Series)
M87	McDonnell Douglas MD-87
SSC	Aerospatiale/British Aerospace (BAC) Concorde
TRD	British Aerospace (Hawker Siddeley) Trident (All Series)
TU3	Tupolev Tu-134
TU5	Tupolev Tu-154
WWP	Israel Aircraft Industries 1124 Westwind Passenger
YK2	Yakovlev Yak-42
YK4	Yakovlev Yak-40
100	Fokker 100
146	British Aerospace 146 (All Series)
310	Airbus Industrie A310 (All Series)
320	Airbus Industrie A320 (All Series)
707	Boeing 707 Passenger
72M	Boeing 727-100C/100QC Mixed Configuration
72S	Boeing 727-200 (All Series)
727	Boeing 727 Passenger
73M	Boeing 737-200C/200QC Mixed Configuration
73S	Boeing 737 Passenger (All 200/200C Series)
733	Boeing 737-300
734	Boeing 737-400
735	Boeing 737-500
737	Boeing 737 Passenger (All Series)
74D	Boeing 747-300 Mixed Configuration
74E	Boeing 747-400 Mixed Configuration
74L	Boeing 747SP
74M	Boeing 747 Mixed Configuration (All Series)
743	Boeing 747-300 Passenger
744	Boeing 747-400 Passenger
747	Boeing 747 Passenger (All Series)
757	Boeing 757-200 Passenger
763	Boeing 767-300/300ER
767	Boeing 767 (All Series)
	Propeller Aircraft Turboprop — Single Engine
BH2	Bell (All Series)
CNA	Cessna (All Series)
NDE	Aerospatiale AS 350 Ecureuil/AS 355 Ecureuil 2
PL6	Pilatus PC-6 Turbo-Porter
	Turboprop — Multi-Engine
AN4	Antonov An24
ATP	British Aerospace ATP
ATR	Aerospatiale/Aeritalia (All Series)
AT7	Aerospatiale/Aeritalia ATR72
BEC	Beechcraft (All Series)
BE1	Beechcraft 1900
BE9	Beechcraft C99 Airliner
BH2	Bell (All Series)
BNI	Pilatus Britten-Norman BN-2A/B Islander/BN-2T Turbine Islander
CD2	Government Aircraft Factories N22B/N24A Nomad
CNA	Cessna (All Series)
CS2	CASA C-212/Nusantara NC-212 Aviocar
CS5	CASA/Nusantara CN-235
CVR	Convair (All Series)
DHT	Boeing Canada DHC-6 Twin Otter
DH7	Boeing Canada DHC-7 Dash 7 Passenger
DH8	Boeing Canada DHC-8 Dash 8 (All Series)
DO8	Dornier 228
EMB	Embraer EMB-110 Bandeirante
EM2	Embraer EMB-120 Brasilia
FK7	Fairchild Industries FH-227
F27	Fokker F27 Friendship/Fairchild (All Series)
F50	Fokker 50
GRM	Grumman G-73 Mallard

GRS	Gulfstream Aerospace (Grumman) Gulfstream I/I-C
HPH	British Aerospace (Handley Page) Herald
HS7	British Aerospace (Hawker Siddeley) 748 Passenger
IL8	Ilyushin IL18
J31	British Aerospace Jetstream 31
LOE	Lockheed L188 Electra Passenger
LOH	Lockheed L100 Hercules
L4T	LET L410 Turbolet
MIH	Mil Mi-8
ND2	Aerospatiale N 262/Frakes Mohawk 298
SF3	Saab SF 340
SH3	Shorts 330 Passenger
SH6	Shorts 360
SWM	Fairchild (Swearingen) Metro/Merlin
S61	Sikorsky S61
VCV	British Aerospace (BAC Vickers) Viscount (All Series)
WLH	Westland 30
YN7	Yunshuji-7
YS1	NAMC YS-11
	Piston Single-Engine
CNA	Cessna (All Series)
DHP	Boeing Canada DHC-2 Beaver
PAG	Piper (All Series)
	Piston Multi-Engine
ACD	Rockwell Commander
BEC	Beechcraft (All Series)
BNI	Pilatus Britten-Norman BN-2A/B Islander/BN-2T Turbine Islander
BNT	Pilatus Britten-Norman BN-2A Mk III Trislander
CNA	Cessna (All Series)
CVR	Convair (All Series)
DC3	Douglas DC3/C-47 Dakota Passenger
DHH	British Aerospace (Hawker Siddeley) Heron
IL4	Ilyushin IL14
PAG	Piper (All Series)
PN6	Partenavia P.68 Victor
YN5	Yunshuji-5
	Ground Transportation Equipment
BUS	Bus
HOV	Hovercraft
LCH	Launch
LMO	Limousine
TRN	Train

Frequency Codes

1 — Monday	5 — Friday
2 — Tuesday	6 — Saturday
3 — Wednesday	7 — Sunday
4 — Thursday	X — Except

"Spec" in a frequency column indicates the flight will operate on the dates specified on the following line.

Effective Range Code

E — Effective on
D — Discontinued after

Fare/Class of Service Hierarchy

R	Supersonic Aircraft
P	First Class Premium
F	First Class
A	First Class Discounted
J	Business Class Premium
C	Business Class
D	Business Class Discounted
S	Standard Class
W	Coach Economy Class Premium
Fn	First Class Night Service
Y	Coach Economy Class
Cn	Business Class Night Service
Yn	Coach Economy Class Night Service
B	Coach Economy Class Discounted
H	Coach Economy Class Discounted
Q	Coach Economy Class Discounted
M	Coach Economy Class Discounted
T	Coach Economy Class Discounted
K	Thrift Economy Class
L	Thrift Economy Class Discounted
V	Thrift Economy Class Discounted
Bn	Coach Economy Class Discounted Night Service
Qn	Coach Economy Class Discounted Night Service
Kn	Thrift Economy Class Discounted Night Service
Vn	Thrift Economy Class Discounted Night Service
U	Shuttle Service (No reservation needed - seat guaranteed)
E	Shuttle Service (No reservation allowed - seat to be confirmed at check-in)

Qualifying Fare Codes

H	Highest level of a fare having more than one seasonal level
K/O	Second level of a fare having more than two seasonal levels
J	Third level of a fare having more than three seasonal levels
F/Z	Fourth level of a fare having more than four seasonal levels
T	Fifth level of a fare having more than five seasonal levels
Q	Sixth level of a fare having more than six seasonal levels
L	Lowest level of a fare having more than one seasonal level
W	Weekend application. Exceptions may apply.
X	Midweek application. Exceptions may apply.
N	Night service

EX/9999 Excursion Fare - Number refers to provisions applicable to fare, see Application of Fares and Fare Notes.

Figure 7-7 "Reprinted by special permission from the September 1991 OAG Desktop Flight Guide-Worldwide Edition. All rights reserved."

Airline Codes & Abbreviations

Airline Codes

	AA	American Airlines, Inc.
	AA★	American Airlines, Inc. (Flight numbers 2961, 2963, 2978 and 2980 Malev-Hungarian Airlines (MA); 6000-6001 Cathay Pacific Airways Ltd. (CX); 6007 and 6009-6010 Air New Zealand (NZ); 6032-6033 Lufthansa German Airlines (LH))
■	AA★	American Eagle (Flight numbers 3000-5799)
#	AB	Aaron Airlines Pty. Ltd.
	AC	Air Canada
	AC★	Air Canada (Flight numbers 1001-1006 Royal Jordanian (RJ); 1007-1012 Viasa (VA); 1013-1018 LOT-Polish Airlines (LO); 1019-1024 Finnair (AY); 1025-1030 Czechoslovak Airlines (OK); 1031-1036 Sabena World Airlines (SN); 1100-1199 Air Toronto (CS); 1200-1409 and 1425-1499 Air Ontario (GX); 1410-1424, 1900-1949, 1977-1981 and 1990-1999 Air Alliance (3J); 1500-1799 AirBC, Ltd. (ZX); 1800-1899 Air Nova Inc. (QK); 1950-1976 and 1982-1989 Northwest Territorial Airways, Ltd. (NV)#)
■	AD	Lone Star Airlines
	AF	Air France
	AF★	Air France (Flight numbers 036-039 Canadian Airlines International Ltd. (CP))
	AG	Provincial Airlines
	AH	Air Algerie
	AI	Air India
#	AK	Island Air
	AL	Alsair S.A.
	AM	Aeromexico - Aerovias de Mexico S.A. de C.V.
	AM★	Aeromexico - Aerovias de Mexico S.A. de C.V. (Flight numbers 2300-2799 Aerolitoral - Servicios Aereos Litoral S.A. de C.V. (2Z))
	AN	Ansett Australia
	AO	Aviaco
	AQ	Aloha Airlines Inc.
	AQ★	Aloha Airlines Inc. (Flight numbers 1000-1999 ■ Aloha Islandair, Inc. (WP))
	AR	Aerolineas Argentinas
	AS	Alaska Airlines
	AS★	Alaska Airlines Commuter Service (Flight numbers 2000-2849 and 2900-2949 Horizon Air (QX); 2850-2899 Hut Airport Limousine, Inc.; 4000-4199 Markair, Inc. (BF); 4400-4499 L.A.B. Flying Service, Inc. (JF)#; 4500-4599 Temsco Airlines (KN); 4600-4699 Bering Air, Inc. (8E); 4800-4899 ERA Aviation (7H))
	AT	Royal Air Maroc
	AU	Austral Lineas Aereas S.A.
	AV	Avianca
#	AW	Aeroquetzal
	AY	Finnair
	AZ	Alitalia
	AZ★	Alitalia (Flight numbers 1612-1617 USAir (US))
	BA	British Airways
	BA★	British Airways (Flight numbers 8001-8100 Euroworld)
	BB	Servicios Aereos Nacionales SA (SANSA)
	BC	Brymon Airways
	BD	British Midland
	BE	Braniff International Airlines, Inc.
	BF	Markair, Inc.
	BF★	Markair, Inc. (Flight numbers 1000-1899 Markair Express, Inc. (2E))
	BG	Biman Bangladesh
#	BH	Augusta Airways Pty. Ltd.
	BI	Royal Brunei Airlines
■	BK	Paradise Island Airlines
	BL	Air BVI, Ltd.
	BM	Aero Trasporti Italiani
#	BO	Bouraq Indonesia Airlines
	BP	Air Botswana Pty. Ltd.
	BR	EVA Airways Corporation
	BS	Gamair, Ltd.
	BT	Baltia Air Lines, Inc.
	BU	Braathens S.A.F.E. Airtransport
#	BV	Bop Air
	BW	BWIA International
	BX	Coast Air K/S
	BZ	Keystone Air Service Ltd.
	CA	Air China
#	CB	Suckling Airways
#	CD	Trans-Provincial Airlines Ltd.
×	CE	Aircity
	CF	Compania de Aviacion Faucett
	CG	Avaiki Air
■#	CH	Bemidji Airlines
	CI	China Airlines
	CI★	China Airlines (Flight numbers 001-002 Canadian Airlines International Ltd. (CP); 003-006 Trans World Airlines, Inc. (TW))
	CJ	China Northern Airlines
	CM	Copa
	CN	Helijet
	CO	Continental Airlines
	CO	Continental Airlines/Air Micronesia (Flight numbers 910-999)
	CO★	Continental Airlines (Flight numbers 2800-2999 Resort Express; 3026-3099 Home James Transportation Services; 3100-3199 Colorado Mountain Express)
	CO★	Continental Airlines/Ansett New Zealand (Flight numbers 4395-4399 Ansett New Zealand (ZQ))
	CO★	Continental Airlines/SAS-Scandinavian Airlines System (Flight numbers 8900-8949 and 9000-9450 SAS-Scandinavian Airlines System (SK))
	CO★	Continental Express (Flight numbers 2000-2799, 3200-3999 and 4400-4999 Continental Express)
	CP	Canadian Airlines International Ltd.
	CP★	Canadian Airlines International Ltd. Canadian Partners (Flight numbers 1001-1008 Air St. Pierre (PJ); 1040-1041 and 1043 Air New Zealand (NZ); 1050-1051 Qantas Airways Ltd. (QF); 1058-1059 Air France (AF); 1068-1069 SAS-Scandinavian Airlines System (SK); 1072 and 1075 Lufthansa German Airlines (LH); 1100-1379 Time Air (1982) Ltd. (KI); 1400-1499 Air Atlantic Ltd. (9A); 1550-1599 Calm Air International Ltd. (MO); 1600-1714 Inter-Canadien; 1730-1739 Air Alma Inc. (4L); 1750-1768 and 1779-1783 Canadian Frontier (4F); 1769-1778 and 1784-1999 Ontario Express Ltd. (9X))
	CQ	Air Normandie - Normandie Locavion S.A.R.L.
	CS	Air Toronto
	CT	Compania Aerea de Viaje Expresos, C.A. (C.A.V.E.)
	CU	Cubana Airlines
	CV	Air Chathams
	CW	Air Marshall Islands
	CX	Cathay Pacific Airways Ltd.
	CX★	Cathay Pacific Airways Ltd. (Flight numbers 882-883 American Airlines, Inc. (AA))
	CY	Cyprus Airways, Ltd.
	CZ	China Southern Airlines
	DA	Dan-Air Services Ltd.
	DB	Brit Air
	DC	Golden Air Commuter AB
	DE	Condor Flugdienst GmbH
■	DF	Aero Coach Aviation International, Inc.
	DI	Delta Air (Germany)
	DJ	North Cross Airways AB
	DL	Delta Air Lines, Inc.
	DL★	Delta Connection (Flight numbers 2000-2999 ■ Atlantic Southeast Airlines, Inc. (EV); 3000-3699 Comair, Inc. (OH)◄; 4300-4999 ■ Business Express (HQ); 5200-5999 Sky West Airlines (OO))
	DM	Maersk Air
	DN	Air Exel (Belgique)
	DO	Dominicana de Aviacion
■	DQ	Coastal Air Transport
	DS	Air Senegal
	DT	TAAG-Angola Airlines
■#	DV	Nantucket Airlines
	DW	Dlt Deutsche Luftverkehrsgsellschaft MBH German Commuter Airlines
#	DX	Danair
	DY	Alyemda - Democratic Yemen Airlines
■	ED	CCAir Inc.
	EE	Euroberlin France
#	EF	Far Eastern Air Transport Corp.
	EG	Japan Asia Airways Co. Ltd.
	EH	SAETA - Sociedad Ecuatoriana de Transportes Aereos Ltda.
	EI	Aer Lingus P.L.C.
■#	EJ	New England Airlines, Inc.
	EK	Emirates Airlines
#	EL	Air Nippon Co., Ltd.
■	EM	Empire Airlines
	EN	Air Dolomiti S.P.A.
#	EO	Air Nordic Sweden
#	EQ	TAME C.A.
	ET	Ethiopian Airlines
	EU	Empresa Ecuatoriana de Aviacion
■	EV	Atlantic Southeast Airlines, Inc.
	EW	Eastwest Airlines
	EY	Europe Aero Service
#	EZ	Sun-Air of Scandinavia A/S
	FA	Finnaviation
	FB	Promair Australia Pty. Ltd.
	FC	Berliner Spezial Flug
	FF	Tower Air, Inc.
	FG	Ariana Afghan Airlines
	FI	Icelandair
	FJ	Air Pacific Limited
■#	FK	Flamenco Airways, Inc.
#	FL	Airlec
#	FN	Niue Airlines Ltd.
#	FO	Western New South Wales Airlines Pty. Ltd.
	FQ	Air Aruba
	FR	Ryanair
#	FS	Missionary Aviation Fellowship
	FU	Air Littoral
	FV	Viva Air
■#	FX	Express Air, Inc.
■	FY	Metroflight Airlines
	GA	Garuda Indonesia
	GC	Lina-Congo
	GD	TAESA - Transportes Aereos Ejecutivos, S.A. de C.V.
	GE	Foshing Airlines
	GF	Gulf Air Company
	GH	Ghana Airways
	GI	Air Guinee
	GJ	Equatorial-International Airlines of Sao Tome
	GL	Greenlandair Inc.
	GN	Air Gabon
#	GP	China General Aviation Corp.
	GQ	Big Sky Airlines
#	GR	Aurigny Air Services Ltd.
	GR★	Aurigny Air Services Ltd. (Flight numbers 713-714 and 717-718 Air Atlantique (KI) #)
	GS	Makung Airlines
	GT	GB Airways Ltd.
	GU	Aviateca S.A.
	GV	Talair Pty. Ltd.
	GW	Central American Airlines
#	GX	Gill Aviation Ltd.
	GY	Guyana Airways
#	GZ	Air Rarotonga
	HA	Hawaiian Airlines
	HA★	Hawaiian Airlines (Flight numbers 1101-1110 Air Marshall Islands (CW))
	HB	Malitas-Mali Tinbouctou Air Service
	HC	Naske-Air
■	HD	New York Helicopter Corporation
#	HE	Trans European Airways
■	HG	Harbor Airlines, Inc.
■	HI	Papillon Airways, Inc.
	HJ	Holmstroem Flyg AB
	HK	Noble Air
	HM	Air Seychelles Ltd.
■	HO	Airways International, Inc.
	HP	America West Airlines, Inc.
■	HQ	Business Express
#	HR	Southern Pacific Regional Airlines
#	HS	Air North International Ltd.
	HV	Transavia Airlines
	HW	North-Wright Air Ltd.
	HX	Hamburg Airlines GMBH & Co.
■	HY	Metro Airlines
#	HZ	Agderfly A/S
×	IA	Iraqi Airways
	IB	Iberia
	IC	Indian Airlines
	ID	Air Guyane
	IE	Solomon Airlines
	IG	Alisarda S.P.A.
■	IH	Loken Aviation, Inc.
	II	Business Air Limited
	IJ	Transport Aerien Transregional
	IL	Istanbul Airlines
■	IN	Adirondack Airlines
	IO	•T.A.T. Export
#	IP	Airlines of Tasmania
#	IQ	Interot Airways
	IR	Iran Air-The Airline of the Islamic Republic of Iran
	IS	Eagle Air Ltd. (ARNARFLUG)
	IT	Air Inter
■	IU	Helitrans Air Service, Inc.
	IV	Air Gambia
	IW	Minerve
#	IX	Flandre Air Airline
	IY	Yemenia Yemen Airways
	IZ	Arkia Israeli Airlines Ltd.
	JA	Norway Airlines
	JB	Helijet Airways
	JC	Rocky Mountain Airways
#	JD	Japan Air System
	JE	Manx Airlines
#	JF	L.A.B. Flying Service, Inc.
	JG	Swedair AB
	JH	Nordeste-Linhas Aereas Regionais S.A.
	JI	Jet Express
#	JJ	Brasil Central Linha Aerea Regional S.A.
#	JK	Link Airways
	JL	Japan Airlines
	JM	Air Jamaica Limited
	JM★	Air Jamaica Limited (Flight numbers 982-986 and 989-991 Air Canada (AC))
#	JN	Japan Air Commuter Co., Ltd.
	JO	Twente Airlines
	JP	Adria Airways
	JQ	Trans-Jamaican Airlines, Ltd.
	JR	Aero California
×■#	JT	Iowa Airways, Inc.
	JU	Yugoslav Airlines— JAT
	JV	Bearskin Lake Air Service Limited
	JX	Jes Air
	JY	Jersey European Airways Ltd.
#	JZ	Avia AB
	KA	Dragonair - Hong Kong Dragon Airlines Ltd.
	KB	Druk-Air
#	KD	Kendell Airlines
	KE	Korean Air
	KF	OY Air Botnia AB
#	KG	King Island Airlines
#	KI	Air Atlantique
	KK	Transportes Aereo Regionais S.A. (T.A.M.)
	KL	KLM— Royal Dutch Airlines
	KL★	KLM— Royal Dutch Airlines (Flight numbers 517-518, 531-532 and 537-538 Cyprus Airways, Ltd. (CY); 2787-2788 and 2790 Air UK (UK))
	KM	Air Malta Company, Ltd.— Air Malta
#	KO	Cook Strait Skyferry Ltd.
	KP	Safair Lines (Pty) Limited
	KQ	Kenya Airways
	KR	Kar-Air
	KS	Peninsula Airways, Inc.
#	KT	Turtle Airways Ltd.
	KU	Kuwait Airways
	KV	Transkei Airways Corporation
	KW	Carnival Air Lines
	KX	Cayman Airways Ltd.
#	KY	Waterwings Airways (Te Anau) Ltd.
	LA	Lan Chile S.A.
	LB	Lloyd Aereo Boliviano
	LC	Loganair, Ltd.
#	LD	Lineas Aereas del Estado (LADE)
#	LE	Link Airways
#	LF	Linjeflyg
	LG	Luxair— Luxembourg Airlines
	LH	Lufthansa German Airlines
	LH★	Lufthansa German Airlines (Flight numbers 502-503 Vasp (VP); 1290 and 4706-4707 Finnair (AY); 4512-4513 and 4708 Aeroflot-Soviet Airlines (SU); 4526-4529 and 9878-9881 Lloyd Aereo Boliviano (LB); 4628-4629, 5050-5055, 5360-5999 and 9972-9989 Cimber Air (QI) or Contact Air or Delta Air (Germany) (DI) or Dlt Deutsche Luftverkehrsgsellschaft MBH German Commuter Airlines (DW) or Maersk Air (DM) or NFD Luftverkehrs AG (NS) or Tyrolean Airways (VO) or Westkustenflug (WK); 4702 Cyprus Airways, Ltd. (CY); 4716 El Al Israel Airlines Ltd. (LY); 4722-4723 Japan Airlines (JL); 4728-4729 Korean Air (KE); 4736-4739 Cathay Pacific Airways Ltd. (CX); 4760-4764 and 4766 Air China (CA); 4770 South African Airways (SA); 6100-6299 Euroberlin France (EE); 6450-6459 Canadian Airlines International Ltd. (CP); 6472-6479 Air Mauritius (MK); 6490-6491 Namib Air (Pty) Ltd. (SW); 6520-6521 American Airlines, Inc. (AA))
	LI	Liat (1974) Ltd.
×	LJ	Sierra National Airlines
	LK	Goldfields Air Services
	LL	Bell-Air
	LM	ALM— Antillean Airlines
	LN	Jamahiriya Libyan Arab Airlines
	LO	LOT— Polish Airlines
#	LP	Nyge-Aero
	LR	LACSA
	LS	Iliamna Air Taxi, Inc.
	LT	LTU International Airways
#	LU	Theron Airways
	LV	LAV - Linea Aeropostal Venezolana
	LW	Air Nevada
	LX	Crossair A.G.
	LY	El Al Israel Airlines Ltd.
	LZ	Balkan— Bulgarian Airlines
	MA	Malev— Hungarian Airlines
	MA★	Malev— Hungarian Airlines (Flight numbers 82-83, 90-91 and 2026-2027 Pan American World Airways, Inc. (PA))
#	MB	Western Airlines

Figure 7-8 "Reprinted by special permission from the September 1991 OAG Desktop Flight Guide-Worldwide Edition. All rights reserved."

Airline tickets must be issued at the fare quoted by the carrier. Travel agents are held responsible and charged for undercollections but can apply for refunds if it is discovered that a ticket was issued, in error, at a higher level. Fares are quoted through the airline reservations department, the computer, bulletins from the carriers, or in the airline tariff books. It must be kept in mind that fares are not guaranteed unless a ticket is issued as soon as a fare quote is received (usually within 24 hours).

The automated agent will search for fares through the computer; the non-automated agent will usually subscribe to the ATPCO (Airline Tariff Publishing Company) passenger tariffs. The (paid) subscription includes eight books: (1) United States Passenger Fares Tariff, (2) Canadian Passenger Fares Tariff, (3) North American Routing Guide, (4) Domestic General Rules, (5) Canadian General Rules, (6) Joint Passenger Fares Tariff–EJ (Canada), (7) Visit Another Country Tariff, and (8) Canadian Domestic General Rules. Most domestic tariffs are revised every two weeks, others every four weeks. International carriers (members of IATA) are governed (and quite often, owned) by the country of origin. Fare changes are not as frequent as for U.S. carriers (since deregulation), which can change at a moment's notice if they want to. IATA carriers will usually have two changes during the year. Many carriers will publish their own tariff bulletins and distribute them to the agents—one in the spring for the summer rates and one in the early fall for the fall, winter, and spring rates.

The *Air Tariff*, a paid subscription, publishes the tariffs and general rules for IATA carriers. *Book 1* is published in three volumes and includes selected European normal fares/rules, selected Western Hemisphere fares/rules, and selected domestic fares: Worldwide Fares Book; Worldwide Rules, Routings and Ticketed Point Mileages; and Worldwide Maximum Permitted Mileages. Book 2 is also published in three volumes and contains a much broader range of Western Hemisphere fares/rules (but not within or between the United States and Canada) than shown in Book 1: Western Hemisphere Fares; Western Hemisphere Rules; Routings and Ticketed Point Mileages; and Western Hemisphere Maximum Permitted Mileages. *Book 3*—Europe Fares, Rules, Routings and Mileages—contains a much broader range of European fares/rules, including UKK domestics, than those shown in Book 1.

The tariff books are used by both airlines and travel agents and are usually the last word in settling questions or disagreements regarding passenger rules and fares. The OAG is the bible of the industry as far as schedules are concerned, but the tariffs are relied upon for accurate fares and rules used in constructing fares. The airline rate desks use these tariffs to compute fares for a complicated routing.

The tariffs' format is similar to that of the OAG, substituting columns of fares for schedule times and flight numbers. The important difference between the domestic tariff and the international tariff is in observing the maximum mileage allowed for the listed fares. If the stopovers selected by the client exceed the mileage permitted, the fare is then increased proportionately. Long and detailed itineraries for international travel should always be computed on the mileage system to give clients the best possible fare for their routing.

TRAVEL AGENTS' HANDBOOKS

The Airlines Reporting Corporation (ARC) distributes the *Industry Agents' Handbook* to all appointed agents. This official handbook was developed by the certificated carriers that are members of the Air Traffic Conference. This handbook is written in a very clear and simplified form and is an invaluable aid for both the newcomer and the experienced agent. It covers all facets of airline sales, reservations, and ticketing, as well as sales reports and agency resolutions. It is revised twice a year, or more frequently as the need arises.

IATAN publishes their handbook in two volumes. The *Travel Agents' Handbook* includes the sales agency rules and resolutions governing the operation of the approved agency. The second volume is the *Ticketing Handbook*, which is revised on a yearly basis. These ticketing handbooks are used by both airlines and travel agents and contain the official airline ticketing requirements.

THE RESERVATION

Although this chapter is devoted to airline sales, the same procedures for making an airline reservation are used for most other travel arrangements, substituting flight numbers and name of airlines for tour numbers, tour operator's name, steamship line, railroad, hotel name, and so on.

The automated agent will check the CRT instead of picking up the phone, but the basic principles remain the same. The first step in making any type of reservation is obtaining all the pertinent information from the client. A preprinted form helps to remind the agent to ask for all the details needed. It is most important to get the full name, address, and telephone numbers of the passenger. Double-check dates and days of the week—this can be vital when using excursion, discounted, or tour-basing fares.

The airlines use the same procedures, and the information that a reservations clerk or computer system requires is the same regardless of the carrier used. Many airlines have separate departments or *agency desks*, which handle only calls from travel agents. Special numbers are assigned to these departments. These telephone numbers are to be used only by employees of the travel agency; they are not to be given to the general public.

An important factor to keep in mind is that airlines are *common carriers* and are obligated to accept passengers regardless of race, color, or creed on a first-come, first-served basis. Except for restricted passengers—the physically handicapped or those persons whose behavior might be hazardous to other passengers—the airlines are not allowed to take passengers off a flight or cancel their reservations in favor of someone else. It is wise, therefore, to make reservations as far in advance as possible and advise the passengers to check in as early as possible. A confirmed reservation, or a ticket in hand, will not guarantee a seat if the passenger checks in less than 20 minutes before flight time.

Under normal conditions and for normal fares, a week or 10 days is sufficient time to place a reservation and obtain the flight the passenger desires. *Normal fares* are first class and coach. They have no advance reservation requirements and no minimum-stay requirements and the ticket is good for one year. (This can be extended as long as the passenger notifies the airline and asks for an extension before the expiration date.)

With deregulation and the increased competition among airlines, a steady stream of *excursion* and *discounted fares* have been introduced. The majority of these special fares have restrictions. Make sure that you, as the travel consultant, and the passenger read all the fine print in connection with these fares. Most are based on the ticket being used for a round trip even though the newspaper ads will headline "$99 One-Way." Most will have advance reservation requirements— 3 days, 7 days, 14 days, 21 days—as well as *minimum-stay* requirements. Other considerations, even for normal fares, are the time needed for an advance reservation (which might vary at different times of the year, time of the week, time of the flight itself, popularity of the route, etc.) Keep in mind that space is usually heavily booked well in advance for holidays and special events. Also keep in mind that space is usually more in demand in the *high season* for a particular area than in the *low* or *off-season*. It is not at all unusual to book space for a popular resort area as much as one year in advance.

If all flights are sold out, the airlines encourage passengers to go to the airport and take their chances of getting a seat on a *standby* basis. An *open ticket* can be issued, but there is no way of assuring passengers of a definite seat with this arrangement. Experience has shown that airlines can accommodate many of the standby passengers because of late cancellations and *no-show* passengers. Many airlines encourage this procedure by paying for the ground transportation of passengers who go to the airport and fail to secure space on a standby basis if they are paying normal fares. Check each airline for details on this subject.

After passengers give you all the pertinent facts, the next step involves locating the information needed in the computer, OAG, steamship guide, or railway guide, as the case may be. If possible, conduct this search for availability while the client is in the office or on the other telephone line so that alternative arrangements can be offered and decided upon without delay.

The following information is needed whether you are calling the carriers or using the CRT in building a PNR (passenger name record). Some of the information is preprogrammed in your CRT, but for the benefit of those without automation, we will use the standard format in calling in a reservation:

1. Identify your agency and yourself. At this point you may be asked for the agency's ARC or IATAN ID number (it is actually the same). More and more principals are listing agents by this ID number. When they enter it in their computer, your record is displayed and will give your agency's name, address, and phone number, which eliminates asking for this information.

2. Request the number of seats needed for the flight number, date, and class of service for the city pairs (city of origin/city of destination). Use the word *need*—this identifies the request as a new booking.

3. Be prepared with alternate flights and dates—especially during busy seasons or when requesting special fares. If space is not available, immediately place your client's name on the *waitlist* and take the alternate flight that is acceptable to the customer. Travel agents' requests are put on a *priority waitlist* that is worked before the waitlist from the public.

4. Give the passenger's family name and initials (title, if applicable, i.e., Mrs., Captain, Father, Reverend) and the names and ages of children in the party.

5. Give the passenger's home telephone number (hotel room number, if applicable). Give the passenger's business telephone number if he or she is leaving from the office. This is important in case of flight changes or delays, because if it is too late or too early to call the travel agent, the airline will call the passenger.

6. Request special requirements: for example, special meals (Kosher, vegetarian, etc.); passenger needs wheelchair or medical assistance; passenger speaks only Spanish.

7. Obtain an option date or time by which passengers must secure their confirmed tickets or else risk losing the reservation or special fare. Naturally, this information is not necessary if the ticket will be issued as soon as the reservation is confirmed. [*Note*: When issuing tickets for passengers who made their own reservations, call the airline that confirmed the space and advise the reservationist that you are ticketing and to remove the time limit (if there is one). This call should also be made if a ticket is issued weeks or months after a reservation was made, to verify the flight schedules and fares. When making the call, advise that you are ticketing.]

8. Ask for the reservationist *sine* (name) and show this on your itinerary along with the date of request. This can be very important at times. Occasionally, you may have booked the reservation with a new employee

who pushes the wrong button on the computer and the reservation you thought was confirmed is lost. By giving the supervisor of the airline the name and date, it will be possible to get the reservation reinstated. Most airlines will also give you a *record locator number*. The use of this number will bring up a record much more quickly when changes or cancellations are made. (Your CRT will also end with a record locator number in the PNR.)

Occasionally, passengers will request a reservation within 24 hours of departure and there is no time for pickup or delivery of their tickets, which means that they will have to pick them up at the airport; or a client may request a ticket for a relative, friend, or business associate who will pick up the ticket at the airport in another city. This will necessitate use of the PTA (prepaid ticket advance). The reservation is made as usual, but the airline is notified that this is a PTA. A nonrefundable service charge is collected for a PTA. Occasionally, a travel agent may absorb this fee rather than lose a good client.

In addition to the reservation information above, the airline will ask for the PTA number. The ticket will not be issued unless this number is in the record. The PTA reservation record can be entered in the agent's own computer; however, this is one of the documents that must be written manually.

The passenger or sponsor will send payment to the agency, and this PTA is included on the ARC sales report in the same manner as an actual ticket. In the event that the passenger does not pick up and/or use the ticket issued against the PTA, no refund can be made until the airline is notified and a written authority to refund is sent to the agency. The airline has to verify that the ticket was not used, and this takes time.

When making an airline reservation there are two standard rules. A *domestic reservation* is booked with the originating carrier even if there is more than one airline involved in the itinerary. For example, if a Cleveland passenger goes to Chicago on United Airlines, continues to Las Vegas on American, and returns on TWA, the entire space is requested through United and the ticket is validated on United. *International* travel is booked through the first carrier crossing water. For example: Departing from a gateway city to a point outside the United States and Canada, a passenger may request a seat on TWA from New York to Athens, and a domestic flight from his or her home city to New York will be booked on American

Figure 7-9 International Flagship Service, first class—B767.

Airlines. The entire itinerary will be placed with the TWA reservations department and the ticket will be validated on TWA.

Requesting the entire reservation through the originating carrier will simplify the handling when more than one airline is involved and will protect the passenger traveling via connecting flights by providing the receiving carrier with proper arrival information. This will also ensure proper execution of reconfirmation rules because each airline gets complete itinerary information from the originating carrier.

Occasionally, when there is a long and/or complicated itinerary and time is vital, the agent may obtain confirmations directly from each connecting carrier. If so, the agent must be sure to give the originating carrier as well as each connecting carrier the passenger's complete itinerary, including the current reservation status of each flight.

When agents prepare a complicated itinerary that does not use established connections, it is their responsibility to determine and adhere to the airline's minimum connecting times. It is important, as a service to the passenger and a requirement of the airlines, that sufficient time be allowed for the passenger and his baggage to move from one airplane to the other.

RECONFIRMATION

Reconfirmation may be defined as a specified time prior to scheduled departure time of the flight concerned by which a passenger must have restated her intention to use space that was booked at a station other than her boarding station. If the passenger has not so advised the office at the boarding point, the space concerned will be released for resale, including the entire remaining itinerary.

In some cities in the United States where airline traffic is heavy, passengers are required to reconfirm their return or continuing reservations. In Canada, reconfirmation is requested after a stopover of six or more hours between flights. (*Note*: Stopovers between flights of less than 4 hours domestic or 12 hours international are called *connections*; such passengers need not reconfirm.) Passengers whose trips originate at a point other than at the one where they booked their reservations also need not reconfirm.

American Airlines Reservations

When booked in North America, reconfirmation is required at least 72 hours prior to departure from European points for westbound Atlantic flights. This rule applies to most international destinations, including the Caribbean. In the event that a passenger arrives and departs from a city within the 72-hour time limit, reconfirmation is not required, as this is classified as a connection. Passengers are not required to reconfirm space out of the city where they book their reservations or start their journey; however, since deregulation, airlines can change or cancel flights without advance notice. To protect your passengers, verify the flight schedules with the airline or through your CRT at least 24 hours before their departure.

It is essential that passengers be advised whenever the reconfirmation rule is applicable to any portion or portions of their itinerary and that they be warned of the consequences of failure to reconfirm. Reconfirmation may be accomplished in the following ways:

1. At the airport ticket office immediately upon arrival at the destination.
2. At the city ticket office.
3. By telephoning the airline reservations office.
4. By telegram or mail if the other methods are not convenient.

The preferred method is to take the ticket to the city or airport ticket office, as that would enable the airline passenger agent to examine the ticket to see that it is in order.

Reconfirmation rules have been set up for cities where airline traffic is heavy and to help solve the problem of no-shows. It has been found that passengers who restate their intention of using flights booked in advance are more likely to use their reservations. Passengers should also be instructed to cancel their space, at least 24 hours in advance if possible, if they find that they are unable to travel as planned. This will release the space for someone else. If passengers are on a waitlist for a return or connecting flight, advise them to notify the airline where they may be reached in the event the waitlist clears.

Reservation Ethics

Both ARC and IATAN have a code of reservation ethics and they are quite similar. The following code is taken from the IATAN handbook:

Smooth handling of reservations is the efficient way to operate. Properly followed procedures mean productivity and fast, effective customer service.

Keep accurate and complete records covering all reservations transactions. Include flight numbers, class of service, date of travel, departure and arrival times, status of segments, names and initials of passengers with their correct contact address/telephone number and ticket status.

Conduct each transaction in a businesslike and efficient way. Keep in mind at all times the need for correct and efficient handling of each transaction.

Reserving Space

- Always adhere to standard reservations procedures.
- Never deliberately make duplicate reservations for the same passenger.
- When a request for a party or group is not confirmed, do not attempt to secure the space by requesting the required number of seats in several individual transactions.
- Do your best to establish a positive contact address and telephone number for every passenger and advise the airline accordingly. This is important as it helps airlines to serve your customer properly when your office is closed.

- Always request or process all reservations for a specific itinerary, and advise subsequent changes through one airline. Where this cannot be done, each airline with which reservations have been made must be informed of reservations made with other airlines.

Canceling Space

- Whenever a passenger cancels his reservation, the canceled space must be immediately released. Normally, this is done in the same manner as that in which the original space was obtained. When a passenger changes a travel itinerary, ensure that all space and supplementary services that are no longer required are canceled at the time that new reservations are made.

Ticketing

- Issue tickets in accordance with the status of each flight segment involved (i.e., open, confirmed, waitlisted). Never issue a ticket showing "space confirmed" unless confirmation has been received from the airline concerned.
- Never ticket a passenger for multiple reservations when it is evident that only one of them will be used.
- When required to do so, report in the prescribed manner all deposits collected.
- Strictly adhere to all ticketing time limits established by the airlines.

COMPUTERIZED RESERVATION SYSTEMS

The airlines started working on automation for their reservation systems soon after World War II, but the first type of automation offered to the travel agents was teleticketing in the 1960s. Subscribers would call in the reservations and request the airlines to drive (print) the ticket on a machine located in the agency's office. These machines are still available, but less than 1 percent of ticket stock issued to travel agents is used for teleticketing.

The airlines continued to upgrade their own automated systems but it was not until the late 1960s and mid-1970s that they started offering CRSs (computer reservation systems) to travel agents. Contrary to general opinion, the CRS is not free to travel agents. Even the high producers of airline sales may pay a fee to have a CRS installed in their offices. Hardware (consisting of the computer, monitor, and keyboard) is leased or purchased from the host airline; and a monthly fee is charged, per unit, to access the data from the airline's system. In addition, a fee is charged for each printer. Most agents have two printers, one for printing the ticket and itinerary, and the second to print invoices and statements.

American Airlines (SABRE) first installed reservation units on an experimental basis in 1968, and TWA (PARS) and United Airlines (Apollo) tried a few installations in 1972. The early systems were not successful until they added the direct-access feature. This feature allows subscribers to access other airline computers directly, depending on how many are participating in the host airline's system. Several other airlines started marketing their systems to travel agents and by mid-1980, five systems dominated the market: American Airlines' SABRE, United's Apollo, TWA's (merged with Northwest Airlines) PARS, Eastern's System One (now owned by Continental Airlines), and Delta's DATAS II.

February 1990 brought the formation of Worldspan, a linkage of TWA's and Northwest's PARS' subscribers with Delta Air Linc's DATAS II travel agencies that included part-ownership by Abacus, a Far East airline consortium. A possible linkup with System One is expected.

Numerous complaints from nonvendor airlines and travel agents caused the government to step in through the Civil Aeronautics Board (CAB) to investigate vendor practices. The major complaint concerned biased flight listings that favored the vendor's own service; agents were concerned about contracts that could go on forever and restrictions on the use of more than one system in their offices.

In late 1984, the CAB issued rules governing the use of reservation systems. They ordered an end to bias, but the vendors were permitted to charge fees for the listings from other airlines and could bias listings from the airlines unwilling to pay the fees. Agents' contracts were held at the maximum five-year term and contained heavy liquidated damage clauses if the agent tried to change vendors before the contract expired. In addition, *rollover* clauses were added so that when an agent added a new piece of equipment, the contract started another five-year term. These rules expired November 30, 1991.

The Department of Transportation (DOT), which replaced CAB, proposed a number of changes that have not yet been agreed upon: (1) agents' contract terms would be reduced from five years to three years; (2) "rollover" clauses would be prohibited; (3) "minimum use" and "parity" clauses requiring agents to book a high percentage of their clients through a vendor's CRS will be prohibited; (4) vendors will be barred from requiring use of their systems as a condition for special commission payments; (5) agents should be allowed to access all systems from a single terminal; and (6) airlines that object to vendor booking fees should be able to request arbitration procedures.

Canada's CRS Operations

Transport Canada (Canada's version of DOT) is in the process of replacing regulations that became effective in 1989 when Air Canada and Canadian Airlines International merged and formed *Gemini*, the only Canada-based CRS. Gemini controls the vast bulk of the Canadian market, but American Airlines SABRE reservation system has made significant gains among automated retailers in Canada. Covia's Apollo system purchased one-third of Gemini in mid-1989 and is in the process of developing a Canadianized version of Apollo that will become the common system for all Reservec (Air Canada) and Pegasus (Canadian Airlines Intl.) retailers.

The proposed CRS rules will be binding on any CRS in Canada. After receiving comments from the vendors and travel agents, Transport Canada will issue another draft policy and permit all interested parties another chance to comment. This will result in a final policy that will provide the basis for a specific set of regulations to be prepared by the National Transportation Agency (NTA). The NTA, which will be responsible for enforcement, will then provide one more chance for all parties to make comments before issuing a final version of the rules.

The proposed regulations, announced in April 1991, are as follows:

- Forbid minimum-use, rollover, and unreasonably punitive liquidated damage clauses in agency contracts and forbid tying the choice of CRS to commissions or other considerations.
- Forbid vendors to make it difficult for agents to select equipment from a source other than the vendors.
- In a reciprocity provision, permit the vendors to discriminate against any foreign airline that discriminates against the Canadian CRS owner in its system.
- Require that vendors charge nondiscriminatory fees for bookings and all other services provided to participating airlines.

- Forbid the use of commercially sensitive PNR and other data generated by a CRS in an anticompetitive or predatory manner.
- Require that vendor-carriers not refuse to participate, "on a commercially reasonable basis," in any CRS operating in Canada and that they participate fully so as not to undermine a competitor's viability.

The computer reservation systems provided by the airlines help the agents do their job easier and more efficiently, but they are only *tools* for getting the information needed to service the clients. Quite often, a telephone call to the airline is still needed to verify the information received from the computer.

QUESTIONS AND PROBLEMS

1. What is the average time taken to reserve a flight and issue a ticket?
2. In your estimation, which type of client is easiest to serve?
3. Describe the duties of the airline sales representative.
4. What is the main purpose of the *Official Airline Guides*?
5. In which section of the OAG would you find the two-letter airline codes? The three-letter city codes?
6. Where would you find in what time zone a city is located?
7. What do you find in the tariff books?
8. What is the first step before making a reservation?
9. Describe a PTA and explain when it is used.
10. List all of the items of information needed when calling in a flight reservation.

chapter 8

Airline Ticketing

OBJECTIVES

When you have finished this chapter you should be able to:

1. Discuss the standard ticket and how and when it is used.
2. Describe the difference between accountable documents and nonaccountable documents.
3. Recognize when a ticket imprinter is needed.
4. Give your opinion of debit memos on nonrefundable tickets.
5. Discuss security rules and how to keep track of airline ticket inventory.

The agents' *standard ticket plan* was started in 1965 by ATC and has gradually expanded to include IATA and non-IATA airlines and Amtrak tickets. The plan is administered by the Airlines Reporting Corporation (ARC). The essential elements of the standard ticket plan are as follows:

1. A single standard ticket stock, instead of separate stocks for each appointing airline
2. One-step imprinting on the ticket of the name of the issuing airline and the agent's validation at the time the ticket is issued
3. A consolidated sales report and single-sum remittance for all airlines to a designated bank
4. An area bank, acting as a clearinghouse, to break down and send the amount due each airline
5. Computer-generated sales summaries to each agent and carrier for their respective sales activity

There were originally six accountable forms used by travel agents: the four standard tickets (printed in one-through-four-flight coupon books), the MCO (miscellaneous charges order), and the tour order. The continuous-roll machinable (transitional) ticket and the teletype ticket were added for the use of agents who use the teletype or computer printers. During the past years other forms were added, and in 1983, several were discarded. One- and three-flight coupon books are no longer printed. Agents were permitted to continue using stock on hand but could no longer reorder these forms. Group tickets and tour tickets were discontinued and stock on hand was returned to ATC's ticket division in Chicago. The PTA (prepaid ticket advice) was added to the plan to be used in place of the MCO when remitting payment for prepaid tickets. The MCO is now used to supplement air transportation special charges and for deposits or payments on ground orders (tours). Boarding pass stock and automated ticket boarding pass stock have been added. There are other forms used that are not accountable, such as the unnumbered forms, which are described later in this chapter.

The *standard ticket* is the most important single element of the plan. A complete understanding of how and when it is used is essential. The ticket is in booklet form and is composed of several detachable parts called *coupons*. It is designed and carbonized so that the entries will imprint on the auditor's coupon and on each succeeding coupon. Each ticket consists of:

1. *Front cover*—the presence of the front cover is required during travel.
2. *Auditor's coupon*—green (sent with the weekly sales report).
3. *Agent's coupon*—pink (kept by the agency).
4. *Flight coupon(s)*—retained by the passenger until flight boarding time. A separate flight coupon is required for each change of carrier and for each portion of the journey where a change of flight, change in class of service, or a stopover is involved.
5. *Passenger coupon*—the presence of the passenger coupon is required during travel. It is then kept by the passenger for his or her personal records.

The standard ticket is the only type of air ticket that ARC-appointed agents are authorized to report through area banks on behalf of the participating carriers.

Figure 8-2 Nashville Airport—American Airlines Hub.

The ticket is actually a contract between the carrier(s) indicated in the itinerary of the ticket and the passenger. Each valid flight coupon:

1. Authorizes passage between the points and via the routing indicated.
2. Serves as evidence of payment of the fare shown on the ticket.
3. Serves as evidence that an interline agreement exists between the carrier named in the routing and the ticketing carrier.
4. Indicates the class of service, flight number, and date of travel.
5. Contains all information necessary to ensure expeditious and proper handling of the online and interline customer and his baggage via the routing shown.
6. Contains a record of all conditions that must be known at time of reissuance or refund.
7. Contains all information necessary for billing purposes between issuing and carrying airlines' revenue accounting departments. The value of flight coupon(s) is based on the entry in the fare basis box and the fare construction/routing information applicable to transportation covered by the ticket.

While the specific use of each of the accountable forms differs, several things are common to all. First, they must all be ordered from ARC on the prescribed ticket requisition form, accompanied by a check in the required amount. Next, manual (handwritten) tickets must be validated using an airline's identification plate on a validator (imprinter) that imprints the date of issue, the identification of the issuing agent, and the name of the carrier for which the ticket is issued. When completed and validated with the imprinter, the ticket becomes a valid contract of carriage between the carrier and the customer. Finally, and most important, these forms are *accountable* (the agency must keep track of every numbered ticket that has been issued to it).

NONACCOUNTABLE/ADMINISTRATIVE DOCUMENTS

Certain nonaccountable documents are required for processing sales, refunds, or adjustments through the area banks. Some are issued to the agent directly by the airlines; other forms must be ordered from ARC on the ticket requisition form.

Ticketing Forms

Universal credit card charge form **(also in automated form):**   Used for credit card sales.

Cash refund notice **(also in automated form):**   Used to return for voluntary refund partially or wholly unused cash tickets. This form is completed and attached to the ticket.

Crredit card refund notice **(also in automated form):**   Used to return for voluntary refunds on partially or wholly unused credit card sales tickets.

*Ticket exchange notice***:**   Used when taking in a ticket for exchange. Enter exchanged ticket number, new ticket number, and type of transaction (even exchange, additional amount collected, or refund due on the original ticket).

*Ticket transmission recap***:**   Used to report a group of tickets.

*Sales report settlement authorization***:**   Used to record and report all ticketing transactions and authorizes the area bank to draft the agent's bank for the amount shown for the weekly sales. This form is completed and a copy attached to the auditors' coupons and all are sent to the area settlement bank each week.

*Extended routing slip***:**   Must be used to supply complete fare calculation when there is insufficient space on the ticket fare calculation box.

*Revalidation stickers***:**   A small sticker that is placed over the flight information line on the flight coupon when there has been a change in the date of transportation or a change in the carrier. Originally, all carriers issued their own revalidation stickers to the agents; however, in February 1987 ARC required the agents to use a standard sticker with the preprinted agency code number on each sticker. The preprinted code number is intended to make it easier for carriers to trace revalidated tickets back to the agency. Because the agent's identification number is preprinted, the revalidation stickers are shipped separately and may arrive a week later.

Adjustment Forms

Agent automated deduction form **(AAD):**   Used to claim up to $25.00 on the sales report for sales listed incorrectly on a previous weekly sales report. Used most often to claim a commission when the commission code was omitted in error on the auditor's coupon.

*Sales summary adjustment request***:**   Used to correct errors that occurred on recent sales summaries.

*Central collection request***:**   Used for submitting outstanding uncontested credit memos (money due from the airlines) through the central collection service.

Notices

*Special fare notice***:**   Used for fares involving travel restrictions; are stapled to the cover of the ticket.

*Reissue notice***:**   Used on an optional basis, for the purpose of protecting the agent's commission. This notice is attached to the front cover of the ticket to request airline ticket agents to reissue tickets (rather than refund and issue new tickets) for passengers who wish to make changes.

*ATB (automated ticket/boarding pass) notice set***:**   Used to alert passengers that a boarding pass is included with the ticket.

*Passenger notice***:**   Used in connection with fares involving administrative service charges (cancellation fees). This is stapled to the cover of the ticket to alert passengers that if changes are made in the itinerary, they will bc liable for these fees.

CARRIER-GENERATED FORMS

The following forms have been developed for use by individual participating carriers:

Debit memo: Used to reflect monies due the airline that should be included (paid) in the next report.

Credit memo: Used to reflect overpayment to an airline that may be deducted from your next report.

Recall commission: Used to reflect debits arising from commission claims not properly supported, or a recall (lost) commission when passengers return their ticket to the airline for a refund.

Authority to refund: Used to permit agents to refund previously paid PTA (prepaid ticket advice). May be deducted from the next report.

Carrier central collection request: Used by carriers to collect unpaid debit memos or recall commissions from an agent.

Each of these forms has a detachable stub that must be mailed with the next sales report to support the deduction or adjustment. Always check your ticket inventory records and the agent's coupons of the tickets mentioned in these forms to verify the debit or credit. Airline audit department employees are only human—they, too, have been known to make errors. Quite often a transposition or just one incorrect digit in the ticket number or the agent's ID number will cause them to debit the wrong agency. Agents have reported receiving three and four debit memos for the same ticket. They are also billed for recall commissions when the carriers' counter agents refuse to reissue a ticket as an "exchange" and will issue a new ticket and tell the passenger to ask their travel agent for a refund on the original issue.

Recent years have brought forth such a proliferation of debit memos that individual agents, as well as ARTA, are trying to stem the flow with suggestions to agents as well as carriers to reduce the time spent in researching debit memos. It would be a big help if carriers would attach a copy of the ticket with the debit memo. This would enable the carrier and the agent to determine immediately if the correct agency is debited (by checking the agent's ID number) and the agency would not have to search reports to locate the passenger's name.

The complaint voiced by most agents concerns the debit memos for recall commission on nonrefundable tickets that were refunded by the carriers. Since the airlines are willing to break their own rules and issue refunds, the refund should be in the form of an MCO to be used at a later date. This protects the airlines' income and there would be no need for debiting the agent for a recall commission. This rule should also apply when a carrier reissues an agent's ticket at a lower fare. Continental Airlines was the first airline to announce in the fall of 1990 that they will protect the travel agent's commissions when they refund nonrefundable fare tickets or when they exchange agency-written tickets for a lower fare. The ideal solution would be to eliminate debit memos for amounts less than $25; this would be most cost-effective for both partners.

Credit memos for your overpayments on the sales reports are very rarely initiated by the airlines. If you discover an overpayment due to incorrect addition on the ticket or sales report, use the AAD form if it is less than $25 or send a letter immediately (with a photocopy of the ticket and report) to the individual carrier and request a refund. Also, do not hesitate to write and state your case if, for example, an error of omission in the fare basis box brings forth a debit memo for a higher fare. Airlines are usually very prompt in settling a legitimate claim; if not, use the central collection request form.

All ticketing supplies are obtained from the ARC ticket division in Chicago using their form 1190—the ticket requisition. The initial form is included with the application for a new agency. Thereafter, an additional copy is sent automatically with each ticket shipment. It takes a minimum of 3 weeks to receive a shipment of ticket stock, so it is necessary to have a good internal control of supplies. Agents are permitted to maintain supplies on a basis of 3 months' consumption.

Upon completing the ticket requisition order, remove and keep the agent's copy for the office records. The original copy of the requisition is to be sent to ARC in the self-addressed envelope provided with each requisition. A check in the amount prescribed by ARC must accompany each order. (They will not process the order until payment is received.) Tickets and deliveries were once free, but since June 1, 1981, ARC requires payment with each order to cover their costs of handling.

On July 1, 1991, ARC eliminated a flat $20 ticket requisition fee and replaced it with a four-tiered fee schedule based on the weight of any automated tickets ordered. New fees, depending on the desired type and amount of automated ticket stock, are $15, $25, $45, or the actual cost for extremely large orders. ARC estimates that 40 to 50 percent of all orders will cost $15, and less than 1 percent will fall in the top category. The requisition form was changed to conform to the new fee schedule.

Therefore, it is imperative to check the ticket inventory before completing the order to avoid an additional payment for a few items that were omitted from the order. (The ticket requisition is used to order both accountable and nonaccountable documents.) Agents have the option of ordering tickets via facsimile machine to ARC's special fax requisition service at (708) 677-1154. ARC accepts payment for ticket requisition fees by four corporate credit cards: American Express, Diner's Club, Master Card, and Visa. Although agents who fax their orders must pay by credit card, agents who mail orders can pay by credit card or check.

The shipment of stock will include a ticketing shipping order in duplicate, listing all the items ordered (shows beginning and ending numbers of each item). Check this list against the shipment, sign the *agent acknowledgment* copy, and return immediately to ARC. Unless the signed acknowledgment is received by ARC, they will not honor any future ticket orders. On the rare occasions when items are needed on short notice, the agent can call the ticket division directly in Washington, D.C., where to meet such needs, an emergency supply of various forms is maintained at headquarters.

Figure 8-3 Raleigh Durham Airport—American Airlines Hub.

A ticket imprinter is required to validate a manual ticket by imprinting the date of issue, the identification of the issuing agent, and the name of the airline for which the ticket is issued. When completed and validated with the imprinter, the ticket becomes a valid contract of carriage between the airline and the passenger. Neglecting to validate passengers' documents will cause embarrassment and possible additional costs if airport ticket agents refuse to accept them. It is a good idea to develop the habit of validating tickets before making any entries on them. The validator is also used to imprint the information contained on the credit card on the credit card charge form.

Ticket imprinters are designed to make clear impressions precisely placed in the appropriate boxes on the standard ticket forms. Such impressions provide for input to automated accounting systems and make the ticket compatible with optical character recognition equipment. Each accredited agency location on the ARC agency list must purchase at least one imprinter. There is no limit on additional machines if the agent feels that more can be utilized. An extra imprinter is an asset as a backup unit in the event that the first imprinter needs repair or replacement. However, the quality and sturdiness of imprinters makes servicing requirements infrequent. If the imprinter fails to operate, telephone ARC (202) 626-8085 for hand-validation authorization. ARC will send a letter authorizing the agency to handwrite or typewrite the validation for a specified time. This procedure should also be followed if the machine or the ARC agent identification plate is broken or stolen.

For inclusion on the ARC agency list, the applicant submits a check (made out to the manufacturer) and an order for the validator at the time he or she completes the initial order for tickets. As soon as the application is approved, the validator is shipped collect by whatever method is requested.

AIRLINE AND AGENT'S IDENTIFICATION PLATES

The third and last items necessary to complete an air ticketing transaction are the airline identification plates and the agent's identification plate. As soon as an agency is approved by ARC, it is assigned an identifying number and issued a small metal engraved plate that contains the agent's name, city and state, and an eight-digit code number [the first two numbers indicate the location (state), the next five are the agent's code number, and the last is the check digit]. Additional plates may be purchased from ARC. The extra plate may be used if the first becomes misplaced, broken, or if there is a second validator.

Each airline that participates in the standard plan will be notified of an applicant's approval and will then issue a certificate of appointment and provide the agent with its identification plate. (Even though an agent may be approved by ARC and IATAN, the final decision to issue the plate rests solely with the individual airlines.) Should an airline identification plate become worn or damaged, contact the airline or its local sales office for a replacement and hand authorization. The plates are provided without cost but remain the property of the airlines.

As is the case with the accountable ticketing forms, extreme care should be taken in maintaining and controlling the identification plates. A list of airlines that have issued you plates should be kept in a safe place, separate from the plates themselves. In the event of theft or fire damage, the airlines must be notified immediately.

AREA BANK FUNCTIONS

Area banks have been designated throughout the United States to receive and process the single consolidated sales reports that agents submit each week on all sales made on standard ticket stock. They will then generate and present drafts to the agent's bank for the amount due. The geographical location of an agency determines to which area bank it will report. This determination is made by ARC and each agency location is duly notified of the correct area bank and is provided with proper mailing or delivery instructions.

The area bank receives the report and remittance and serves only as a clearinghouse to sort the auditor's coupons (and other documentation) by airline, compile the amount due each, and remit to the appropriate airline. The auditor's coupons (and other documentation) are forwarded to each issuing airline.

The area banks will notify ARC about such matters as late remittances, financial irregularities, and an agent's failure to submit a report within the prescribed time. However, area banks do not audit the reports. They do check the accuracy of computations and the numerical sequence of tickets on each report. Questions related to fares, commissions claimed, and unearned commissions are handled by the individual airlines.

SECURITY RULES FOR TICKET STOCK

Stolen ticket stock from travel agency offices and airline ticket counters has been a serious problem to all concerned. The IATA security section calculated in March 1984 that fraudulent use of stolen airline tickets was costing the industry over $200 million every year. The actual figure was probably much higher, but carriers have been secretive about fraud-related losses and have traditionally been reluctant to prosecute passengers who have been caught with suspicious tickets. However, ticket thefts dropped considerably in 1990, even over the previous year. Early in 1990, ARC hired a Los Angeles–based investigator to work with local police on robbery and fraud investigations and set up a special hot line for agents to phone in robbery reports. Agencies are also reportedly taking additional precautions, such as locking doors and screening customers.

With the introduction of standard ticketing, stolen tickets are not traceable. A supply of ticket stock and validation plates could be validated by anyone having access to the type of machine used by travel agents, department stores, gas stations, and other businesses. The airlines and agency organizations have been working on short- and long-term solutions to the entire ticket theft and fraud problem—including a recent decision to phase in, over the next six years, a new generation of automated ticket/boarding passes. The ATB2, with a machine-scannable strip, will make it easier for airlines to scan for lost, stolen, and fraudulent tickets at check-in, thus removing a major incentive for the theft of tickets. Until this is in effect, it is the agent's responsibility to take steps to protect stock from thefts. Agents are liable for stolen ticket usage indefinitely if they violate the ARC's ticket security rules at the time of the theft.

The ticket security rules are as follows:

When attended by agency personnel, an agent may maintain at each authorized agency location a working supply of traffic documents sufficient to meet operational requirements.

When the agency location is not attended by agency personnel, all unused ARC traffic documents, except automated ARC traffic documents in use as a feed roll, must be kept in a locked steel container. The maximum number of ARC traffic documents the agency may maintain on the unattended premises is 80 manual ARC traffic documents, or the average weekly number of manual ARC traffic documents issued at the location during the preceding calendar year (i.e., total number sold in the previous year, divided by 52).

An agent that uses automated ARC tickets may, in addition to the working supply of manual tickets described above, keep up to 200 tickets in each printer at any time that the printer is unattended. An agent may also store

Figure 8-4 United Airlines Business Class 747.

an additional 600 ARC transitional automated tickets, or 200 per ticket printer, whichever is greater, or up to 6000 ARC automated ticket/boarding pass forms, in a locked steel container that is protected by an electronic alarm system.

The reserve supply of traffic documents (i.e., all in excess of the working supply permitted) must be kept in one of the following off-premise storage facilities: (1) a safe deposit box in a bank or savings and loan association; or (2) hotel safe; or (3) furrier's vault; or (4) jeweler's vault; or (5) commercial storage facilities providing storage and retrieval service for high value and sensitive materials such as furs, artworks, computer data files, or corporate records; or (6) the facilities of armored carrier and storage companies that are in the business of storing and/or transporting money, jewelry, precious metals, and other high-value items; or (7) any other equivalent off-premises storage facility that the agent describes to ARC and which ARC approves in writing.

The agent may store the total supply of traffic documents on the premises when the location is unattended if prior written notice is given to ARC and the documents are secured in (1) a walk-in steel vault; or (2) a windowless concrete-walled storage room equipped with burglar-resistive laminated or solid steel door; or (3) a safe, from which all wheels and casters have been removed, which is bolted, cemented, or otherwise secured to the floor or wall and which is "burglary resistant," bearing an Underwriters' Laboratories classification of TL-15, TRTL-15 X 6, TL-30, TRTL-30, TRTL-30 X 6, TRTL-60, TXTL-60, or a classification equivalent thereto.

The notice to ARC should describe the on-premises storage facility in sufficient detail to show that it meets one of the foregoing requirements, and must be approved by ARC in writing. In addition, lock up validators and plates when not in use, preferably in separate steel containers from the ticket stock. Install dead-bolt locks on all doors and put safety latches and bars on all windows and wire mesh on skylights and basement windows. These features can be designed and installed in a way that will not detract from your office decor.

Install an adequate alarm system. There are relatively inexpensive alarm systems that more than pay for themselves in loss prevention from theft and damage. Makeup a security checklist for your employees to use before closing up. Example: Have all the tickets and validation plates been locked up? Are the doors, the safe, and the windows locked? Is the alarm turned on?

Keep the ticket stock and plates out of sight and out of reach. Make sure that there are at least two employees in the office at all times. It has happened (to me personally) that a group of people will enter the office and will split up; one person will involve the lone employee in a complicated itinerary while the others walk around the office and pick up any valuables in sight. I lost a billfold with all my personal credit cards and $90 from petty cash. Fortunately, they were not interested in the ticket stock.

If your agency is burglarized, make certain that nothing is touched unless absolutely necessary. Go to another phone and call the police. Give police officers complete information, including descriptions of any curious strangers who have been in your agency asking questions prior to the burglary.

Give police a complete description of all stolen property, including the serial numbers of any ARC traffic documents that are missing. (Use your copies of the ticket acknowledgment orders and current sales reports to determine the missing numbers.) Ask police to list these numbers in the stolen articles' file of the National Crime Information Center (NCIC), Washington, D.C.

Immediately report the burglary—by phone—to ARC's Fraud Prevention Office, at (202) 626-5786 or (202) 626-8047 after 5:00 P.M. Eastern time. This is an important first step in advising all airlines of the numbers of the stolen tickets. Complete a copy of the Confirmation Report, Form A, in the *Industry Agents' Handbook* and forward it promptly to the ATC Fraud Prevention Office along with a copy of the police report.

BASIC TICKETING PROCEDURES

Even though an agency may be automated and its printer issues the tickets, errors can occur if the proper information is not entered in the passenger name record (PNR). Coding errors can be very costly. It is important that consultants maintain a thorough knowledge of tariffs, routings, and fares. They must keep current on special excursion fares, their validity dates, and restrictions; they must keep abreast of weekend and midweek fares and the expiration dates of high-, low-, and inter-mediate-season fares. It should become a matter of routine to check for the best possible fare or to construct routings that will be most advantageous for the client. It is the responsibility of the agent to use carriers that will provide the best service for the client's needs.

1. Confirm the seats through either the computer or the airline reservation office.
2. Do not make duplicate reservations.
3. Cancel reserved space immediately upon receiving such notice from a customer.
4. Traffic documents must be used and reported in strict numeric sequence and validated on the date entries are made. In the event that a ticket or other document is withdrawn from stock for any reason, such ticket must be invalidated by stamping or writing void across the face. Retain the agent coupon for audit or record purposes; all other copies must be destroyed. Completely voided ticket sets should not be submitted with the report.
5. Select the form of passenger ticket in accordance with the number of flight coupons required when issuing a manual ticket. (Automated tickets are printed in four flight booklets.) Where because of the number of coupons required, it is necessary to issue conjunction tickets, select the form of ticket that will result in the least number of booklets and the least number of voided coupons for the itinerary. For example, if

five coupons are required, select three two-flight booklets; if 26 coupons are required, select seven four-flight booklets.

6. All tickets issued initially in conjunction with one another shall have consecutive numbers and be completed in numeric sequence.

7. Use the ticketing identification plate of an area bank settlement plan (ABSP) carrier scheduled to participate in the transportation. In the event ticketing identification of a carrier scheduled to participate in the transportation is not available, use the identification plate of any other ABSP carrier who has provided authorization (either verbal or written) for such use.

8. When preparing an automated ticket using a travel agent's stand-alone computer system, ticketing identification is determined on the same basis as manual ticket issuance. (In other words, if the agent does not have the airline validation plate, she cannot ticket on that carrier.)

9. Before delivering a completed ticket to the passenger, the agent must detach the auditor's and agent's coupons, together with the voided coupons (if any). Voided coupons are usually stapled to the auditor's coupon and submitted with the appropriate sales report. Most carriers have determined that they no longer need the void coupons. Void coupons from an otherwise valid ticket set may be destroyed from tickets issued on all carriers except those listed in the *ARC Industry Agents' Handbook*; however, many agents prefer to staple them to the agent's coupon rather than destroy them.

10. If the customer requests changes after the ticket has been issued and reported, a revalidation sticker may be used. For domestic transportation the sticker may be used to change the reservation status and/or carrier when there is no change in routing, class of service, or fare. For international transportation the sticker cannot be used if there is a change of carrier unless permission is received from the original carrier.

11. A separate ticket is issued for each passenger. The only exception is for a child under 2 years of age traveling with an adult using domestic transportation. The adult's ticket would then show "Mrs. (Mr.) John Smith and infant." International transportation requires payment and individual tickets for infants.

12. Adhere strictly to all ticket-time-limit requirements established by the carrier. If these rules are not followed, the reserved space might be allocated to another passenger.

13. To avoid unnecessary reissuance by a carrier, an air transportation exchange order (envelope type) or miscellaneous charges order (MCO) should not be issued when a regular ticket can be issued.

14. When completing any ticketing document, use a typewriter, or write firmly in order to get legibility down to the passenger's coupon. All entries must be in block letters.

15. Do not erase or strikeover, as this invalidates the ticket. If an error is made, void all coupons and issue a new ticket.

16. Never use ditto marks (″) in any of the boxes. Each coupon must have all the pertinent information written in full.

17. Spell out the full name of each city in the itinerary. Do not use codes. Whenever duplicate city names exist, include the state abbreviation to avoid misunderstanding.

18. Be sure to enter the stopover codes in the area preceding the name of the city. An X indicates that stopover is not permitted with the fare used on the ticket; an O indicates that stopover is permitted. The omis-

sion of these codes will affect the fare structure and may affect the passenger if he decides to change his itinerary while traveling. The agent risks being charged a higher fare when the airline auditing department catches the error.

19. Determine all factors that affect the fare applicable to the passenger's travel and make sure that the appropriate entries are shown on the ticket. The fare basis box must have the correct code or the passenger may have to pay a higher fare at the gate if an alert ticket agent discovers a discrepancy. If an incorrectly written ticket is not caught at the airport, the agent will receive a debit memo from the carrier for the undercollection when the ticket coupons reach the audit department.

20. All special fares have restrictions, usually on the minimum and maximum time permitted for travel. This means that the "not valid before" and "not valid after" boxes on the ticket must be filled in with the appropriate dates.

The ARC *Industry Agents' Handbook* and IATA's *Ticketing Handbook* are complete, concise, and very instructive. Every document used by the travel agent can be found in these handbooks with full explanations and illustrations. They are invaluable quick references and should be in constant use in every agency. The handbooks eliminate the necessity of calling individual airlines for information.

MOST COMMON TICKET-WRITING ERRORS

At one time, ARC estimated that the average travel agency sales report contained 125 transactions, multiply that by 39,000 travel agencies, and you come up with the staggering figure of 4,875,000 transactions per week. Although there are no statistics available on ticket errors, my personal survey of a number of agents revealed that the most common errors involved omitting the commission codes on the auditor's coupons (the agency is not credited with commission earned unless the commission code box has been completed), incorrect codes in the fare basis box, omitting the dates in the "not valid before" and "not valid after" boxes, and omitting the X's and O's (which designate if a stopover is permitted on the fare).

Another common error involves neglecting to observe minimum connecting times when arranging independent trips that require one or more connections. A recent survey at a major international airport showed that 47 percent of all misconnected luggage was the result of someone failing to observe the minimum connecting times. What might have been intended to provide a faster connection actually caused a major inconvenience.

ARC also reported that 3000 charge forms a week are returned to travel agents by area banks due to an incorrect account number. This means that the customer must be called to verify the credit card number and the charge must be resubmitted. This causes at least a week's delay in the agent's receipt of commission and in processing the charge.

Not as many errors as might be expected involve fares, possibly because customers will check their tickets and make sure that the agent gave them the fare quoted. The major error involving fares occurs when the advance purchase (or ticketing) date was ignored or forgotten. This usually means that a higher fare is now in effect for that particular ticket. Unless the date was missed because the customer neglected to make payment, the agency can be held liable for payment of the increase in fare. A tickler file on ticketing dates should be set up by non-automated agents and checked daily. Automated agents have their queues, but if these are not checked on a daily basis, the reminders will be useless.

A more serious result of travel agency errors costs their clients money when agents do not take the time to check on all possibilities for lower fares or convenient routes. A simple question put to the client: "How flexible are your plans?" will enable the travel agent to determine if checking the discounted fares would benefit their clients or be a waste of time. Most businesspeople are forced to use the higher fares due to their rigidly fixed schedules. Meetings cannot be changed or postponed, and their own out-of-the-country clients cannot alter their appointments. Specific airlines are used to gain frequent flyer discounts; route selections are made with the expressed purpose of meeting business associates at connecting cities.

A survey of airline bookings during the third quarter of 1989 by Topaz Enterprises, Inc. of Portland, Oregon, showed that travel agents cost their clients more money by selecting high-cost routes than by any other type of error. The next two costly errors (for the client) resulted in higher fares when an alternative airport or airline was not offered. Failure to offer advance purchase discounts, capacity-controlled discounts, and failure to waitlist for lower fares also cost their clients money.

Travel Industry Taxes

Until mid-1986, air ticket taxes were simple to compute—8 percent U.S. domestic tax, 4 percent on Canadian tickets, and a $3 U.S. federal departure tax. On July 7, 1986 a $5 customs user fee went into effect. Agents were notified that this fee was to be collected on "any traffic document issued on or after July 7, having an itinerary with transportation into the United States, including Puerto Rico, from a point outside the U.S."

By January 1991 additional taxes were imposed on the travel industry and new bills are being considered by Congress. IATA reports that the situation is so bad that their directory of airport and ticket taxes and charges on international air transport now fills two volumes; with over 600 different taxes around the world. As in many areas of business, other countries follow the U.S. example. If countries that depend heavily on tourism followed the United States Travel and Tourism Administration's (USTTA) fee of $1 for incoming visitors, the travel industry could be stuck with dozens of new taxes, possibly defeating the whole purpose of taxation to pay for tourism development.

The eight taxes currently imposed on the travel industry in the United States are as follows:

1. A 10 percent airline domestic ticket tax
2. A $6 international departure tax
3. Up to $12 per trip for passenger facility charges
4. A $5 customs' user fee on international passengers
5. A $5 immigration user fee on international passengers
6. A $2 agriculture plant/health inspection service user fee on international passengers, with the exception of Canada, by the Agriculture Department of Animal and Plant Health Inspection Service (APHIS)
7. A $1 United States Travel and Tourism fee
8. A 6.25 percent cargo waybill tax

Airline association officials of both the International Air Transport Association (IATA) and the Air Transport Association of America (ATA) are concerned that these taxes and fees are threatening the transportation industry. At a press conference in New York, May 1991, suggestions were made to rollback or eliminate some of these taxes to reduce air travel cost and improve financial stability.

All of these surcharges and taxes add to the agents' responsibility for collecting fares, plus the added time needed to explain the additional taxes and fees. The tax barrage has been making headline news. According to an article in the *Wall Street Journal*, "this year [1991] alone they [travelers] will pay an additional $2.5

billion in airline ticket taxes and fees. Hotel room taxes have jumped $500 million in three years. And car renters and cruise-line customers are paying taxes that didn't exist a few years ago."

QUESTIONS AND PROBLEMS

1. Name the essential elements of the standard ticket plan.
2. List the accountable forms used in the standard ticket plan.
3. Describe the ticket booklet and the purpose of each coupon.
4. List the security measures required by ARC.
5. What equipment is needed to issue a ticket?
6. What is the purpose of the area bank?
7. In your opinion, which seven of the basic ticketing rules are most important?
8. List some of the most common ticket-writing errors.
9. Describe the new taxes that now have to be collected with the airline fare.

chapter 9

Tours

OBJECTIVES

When you have finished this chapter you should be able to:

1. List variations of a tour.
2. Differentiate between group tours and group departures.
3. Define wholesalers and retailers.
4. List the advantages of taking an escorted tour.
5. Suggest popular destinations for domestic travel.
6. Write the copy for a tour brochure.
7. Read a published tour brochure.
8. Sell and book a tour from the brochure.

What is a tour? Quite often the word itself will frighten or alienate some clients, who visualize a group of people being shepherded from place to place—the "if it's Tuesday, this must be Belgium" picture. They are of course, thinking of the escorted group tour, which is only one of many variations of a tour. To a travel agent, a tour is a prearranged itinerary to a place, or places, of interest, planned and operated for either independent travelers or for groups. A tour may consist simply of hotel accommodations and airport-to-hotel transfers such as the Miami Beach tour packages or Las Vegas tours, which consist of hotel accommodations and a midnight show and cocktail; or it may be an extensive round-the-world itinerary.

An air tour uses air transportation exclusively; a rail tour will use trains for the major portion of the tour, although passengers may fly or bus to the originating point; a bus or motorcoach tour will use buses for the transportation. The air/sea tour uses air one way and ship one way or the combination of air to the embarkation point and then cruise. Tours may combine two or more methods of transportation in combination with ground or land arrangements. Ground (or land) arrangements are literally just that: arrangements made for accommodations, travel, and other services "on the ground" as compared to air or sea arrangements.

Tour is defined by the *American College Dictionary* as "to travel from place to place, a long journey including the visiting of a number of places in sequence. SYN: Excursion, jaunt, junket." Tours are trips made for pleasure. An *excursion* is a short trip, often no more than a day's outing, made usually by a number of people, as a result of special inducements (low fare, a special event, etc.). *Jaunt* is a familiar word for a short, agreeable trip, especially by auto (take a little jaunt to the country). *Junket*, with a still stronger suggestion of pleasure seeking, is frequently applied to a trip made ostensibly on official business, enjoyed at public expense (a congressional committee goes on a junket). Junkets have come to mean tours offered free to customers of casinos in Las Vegas and the Bahamas. A *tour* is a planned trip to celebrated places, to see interesting scenery, and so on. Most people take tours whether they realize it or not. When they buy transportation, transfers (or car rentals), hotel accommodations, meals, and sightseeing, they are purchasing the ingredients of a tour. Never settle for just selling an airline ticket without first trying to sell your clients a tour. Even business travelers could be sold a *package tour* that includes all the foregoing ingredients accommodated to their time schedules.

The terms *package* or *package tour* also may make a prospective customer shy away from the travel agent. They visualize a plan where they have to pay for services they neither need nor want. A tour package can be many things, but basically it is a program for a set number of days, with a set number of features for a set price. It is a program with a goal. It may be for a particular area, such as Bermuda, Mexico, or New York. It may be for a specific market—week-end holidays, eight-day holidays, or two- or three-week vacations. The program must be carefully planned and arranged to provide the features that past experience has shown are the features that are most often requested for that area or for that period of time. Needless to say, tour operators cannot afford to put their time and money into planning, advertising, and selling a package that will not be salable.

A package tour generally includes just the basics—hotel accommodations, transfers (transportation between airport and hotel), and/or car rental and one sightseeing tour. The package is put together by the tour operator (wholesaler) and sold through the travel agent (retailer). It is a convenience for both the travel agents and their clients. Clients know the cost of their vacation before they leave home and will get the benefit of *group rates* even though they are traveling independently. The travel agent can confirm the arrangements with one call to the tour operator rather than many calls to a number of places for rates and reservations.

A tour may also be a program of transportation and ground arrangements specifically tailored to the individual's preferences and not advertised in a tour folder. This type of tour is referred to as the FIT, foreign independent tour (or travel), and the DIT, domestic independent tour (or travel). These codes are working terms for the agent to describe an itinerary in which the agent puts the components of the tour together, working directly with the suppliers: hotel, sightseeing services, steamship lines, nightclubs, bus and taxi services, and of course, the airlines. The suppliers will usually quote a *net* figure to the agent and allow him to *mark up* the price to the client to cover time and expenses. If net rates are not used, the suppliers have to quote normal or rack rates for individual reservations, which makes FITs or DITs more expensive than package tours.

The amount of the markup is left to the agent's discretion. It can vary from 10 percent to as much as 40 percent, depending on the amount of time spent with the client in putting together the itinerary and the number of telephone calls, cables, and letters written to the suppliers. It is also based on whatever the market will bear. The add-on charge will also depend on how much advance notice the agent is given to prepare the itinerary and confirm all the reservations. Cables and long-distance telephone calls for last-minute trips will naturally increase the cost. The average markup is between 10 and 15 percent, the amount of commission normally received from a tour sold through a tour operator (wholesaler).

In the 1930s and from 1946 through the early 1960s, the emphasis was on vacation and leisure travel and a travel agent's business consisted mostly of FITs or ethnic visits to the "old country." As tour operators expanded and more and more group tours and packages became available for the agent's customers, the FIT market dwindled. It became strong again in the 1980s. Most FITs can now be accommodated by combining packaged tours. If this is not possible, the agent can send the itinerary to a tour operator, who will use her resources and contacts to make the necessary arrangements. This eliminates much of the agent's paperwork but still gives clients the customized service they want.

Do not discount the FIT market entirely. There are still buyers who can afford and prefer the more personalized services that were sold in the past. The market for FITs and DITs will be among veteran travelers who are not only looking for new worlds to discover, but will demand and expect a higher quality of service not only from the agent but also from hotels and carriers.

Agents who keep up to date with the many new hotels, new areas of interest, new attractions, and can tie them in with the excursion and discounted fares offered by carriers will increase their earnings and actively demonstrate that they are the experts the ads proclaim them to be.

TOUR OPERATORS/WHOLESALERS

Tour operators who do not deal directly with the public are generally known as *wholesalers*, although they can be both wholesalers and retailers. The wholesaler will put together all the components of the tour package. They reserve space with the carriers for specific dates, they reserve rooms at the hotels in each city in the itinerary, they request meals for the group, and they contract for the sightseeing and transfer services in each area. They then have brochures printed and distributed to all the travel agencies. Wholesalers depend entirely on retail travel agents to sell their tours.

Naturally, wholesalers must mark up the tour arrangements to cover their cost and the commission they pay the agents as well as earn a profit for themselves. But even with this markup, clients benefit because of the group rates used throughout the tour. The contractor, who is assured of a full bus load for the transfers to the hotels and the sightseeing trips, will charge less per person than if it were necessary to use private cars or limousines to transport a small number of passengers. Therefore, the wholesaler must have a minimum of 15 (some require 35) for each tour departure. The luxury or higher-priced tour wholesalers can meet their expenses with groups of 10 or more.

These groups are formed by clients who purchased the tour from travel agencies all over the United States. The members of the group will assemble at the gateway city, usually New York (JFK), Toronto, or Montreal if it is a European tour; Los Angeles, San Francisco, or Seattle for Hawaii, the Orient, and the Pacific; New York or Miami for the Caribbean or South American tours; New York, Chicago, New Orleans, San Antonio, or Los Angeles for Mexico; and New York or Chicago for the majority of domestic tours going east or west. These are the major gateway cities, although Chicago, Boston, Philadelphia, Miami, Houston, and Washington, D.C. are now used more frequently for international travel. Tours can also originate anywhere in the United States or Canada if the retail travel agent has formed a group with the minimum number of participants required by the wholesaler. Charter tour operators will send a plane to the agent's home city if they know they will fill all the seats there.

GROUP TOURS

Years ago, both clients and agents shied away from group tours and preferred the independent itineraries: clients, because of the freedom of choice, and agents, because it not only gave them the opportunity to use their knowledge and expertise as a travel consultant but also because of the higher revenue from the more expensive arrangements.

Although clients may still shy away from group tours as such, they now seek out *group departures*, which give them the benefit of the lower group fares along with freedom of choice in the ground arrangements. There are many categories of group tours and there are variations within each category. *Escorted* tours can be fully escorted, partially escorted, or hosted. Tours are arranged for affinity groups and nonaffinity groups. *Affinity groups* (those whose members belong to the same social, fraternal, professional, religious, or charitable organization) will often charter an airplane for their own use if the group is large enough, or will use group fares provided by the airlines. *Nonaffinity group* tours are actually what the travel agent sells.

Fly/drive package tours are popular in both the domestic and international markets. The package consists simply of a car rental and hotel/motel accommodations in the city or number of cities the client selects. The fly/drives are not recommended for international travel unless the client knows the language of the country(s) or is revisiting an area well known to him or her.

Next in line are *charter tours*. In 1978, the CAB approved the public charter, which eliminated the old alphabet charter types. Until then we had OTC (one-stop inclusive tour charter), ITC (inclusive tour charter), and the ABC (advance booking charter) as well as the affinity charter. The old charters had strict rules that were constantly ignored and abused, and since the CAB did not have the personnel to supervise each charter, they approved the public charter. Public charters must be arranged and sold through independent charter tour operators. They cannot be sold by the airline. The operator is free to promote and sell the charter to the general public through the travel agents and is not required to include accommodations or ground features, but they may add these to the air fare and sell it as a package.

Charter packages offer bargain fares, but the customers must be warned that since charters are not scheduled airlines and their equipment is limited to one or two aircraft, delays and changes often occur, and usually at the last minute. It is not unusual to hear of charter passengers spending from 4 to 24 hours at the airport waiting for their airplane to arrive.

All of the above are technically group tours—not because the groups stay together during the entire stay, but because the tour operator has blocked (reserved) a specific number of seats and/or rooms and other features at a group rate that enables him to offer the packages at a lower price than if they were arranged at the individual rate. In fact, the tour operator has to guarantee that those seats, rooms, and so on, will be sold in order to get the group rate. If they are not sold, the tour operator absorbs the loss.

ESCORTED TOURS

Escorted or conducted tours provide an escort from a starting point back to the starting point and include transportation necessary to reach the areas of principal interest. There are many terms used for this escort: group leader, tour director, tour manager, tour conductor, or tour escort. The terms are used synonymously, but there can be a great degree of difference in the experience and knowledgeability of handling a group in each designation.

Group leader or *tour director* are terms most often used for one of the members of the group who has been so designated to qualify for the free pass given by the airlines when there are 15 paid passengers using a fare that provides this free pass. The tour conductor pass may also be used by the travel agency to send one of their staff with the group. The tour conductor, who is a member of the group, may not have any experience in conducting or escorting tours but is given the pass as a reward or inducement to help the agent form the group. This type of tour conductor also is called a *tour organizer*. *Tour director*, *tour manager*, or *tour escort* are the terms used for the professional person who is escorting the group.

A *fully escorted tour* will have an escort from the home city, throughout the tour, and back to the home city. This type of tour is usually arranged by local travel agents, who will send one or more of their staff with the group, or it may be an affinity group that will have their own tour leaders as escorts.

Some tours will have both a local group leader and a professional escort sharing the responsibilities involved throughout the entire itinerary. Some tours will have the escort join them at the domestic gateway, others will have an escort meet them at the first stopover and continue with them until they board their return flight back to the domestic gateway. Most of the lower-priced tours will use the services of a different escort in each city visited, whose principal duties will be to meet them at the airport and assist them through customs and then perform the same service at the time of departure. This is also referred to as the *hosted tour*—the local host escorts the group. During their stay in each city, travelers often will have the choice of taking their sightseeing trips as a group or individually. The sightseeing motorcoaches each have their own local guide. This is especially true of tours that use air transportation between the cities visited. If the tour utilizes a motorcoach throughout the itinerary, the group will do all sightseeing as a group in their own bus. Quite often, the local sightseeing will be combined with transportation between stopovers.

Escorted tours, prepared by reputable tour wholesalers, are one of the most important travel products sold by the travel agent. The professionally planned and escorted tour should always be recommended to the first-time traveler. They also are preferred by the more sophisticated travelers, who know from past experience that the tour manager will not only handle all the usual details of baggage handling, tipping, reconfirmations, and getting them through customs, but is also well prepared to handle unexpected delays or difficulties. A tour manager is also familiar with the customs of each country visited and can advise travelers as to what to do and how to do it properly.

When selling a tour, escorted or not, it is psychologically important to brief prospective clients on every detail. Even the most experienced travelers will feel

Figure 9-2 Tauck Tours.

like a "fish out of water" when visiting an unfamiliar area. People dislike to show their inexperience and hesitate to ask questions. Many astute businesspeople back away from tours simply because they do not want to lose face with the wife and family by revealing their ignorance of foreign travel. With these types of clients, a supply of general information brochures, business customs, and hotel brochures on each country visited will do wonders in overcoming their resistance to buying tour packages. The assurance that the tour operator has a local representative in each city to assist with the unexpected will do much to ease their minds and help them relax and enjoy their travels. Agents should also assure the clients that in the event of emergencies or illness, the airline office personnel will do everything possible to assist them. In many cases the airline teletype messages between their offices will be faster than by most other means.

By giving clients an unbiased and professional evaluation of the tour packages available, agents are truly counseling and aiding clients in their decisions. Quite often, agents can upgrade the package by providing a better class of hotel and more extensive sightseeing arrangements.

DOMESTIC TRAVEL

Until the 1950s, when the number of airlines increased and more and more passenger seats became available, domestic travel in the United States was centered on the railroads. Rail tours to the West Coast and Canada and south to Florida were the mainstay of the retail travel agents. Air travel was expensive, but the timesaving factor stimulated new business. Selling domestic travel by air was a simple, uncomplicated matter until the early 1960s. There were only two classes of service: first class and tourist (coach) class. There were no special or excursion fares until the "Discover America" fare began in 1965. This fare was simple to use, as it could be used every day of the week except Friday and Sunday and had few restrictions.

This fare was the forerunner of many other discounted fares: family plan, youth fares, and tour-basing fares. The CAB outlawed family plan and youth fares as discriminatory in 1974. Increased fuel costs in the 1970s caused the cancellation of many of the discounted fares. However, during the years these fares were in effect, domestic travel was greatly stimulated and brought many new customers to the travel agents' offices.

Domestic Travel

153

After deregulation and the seesaw of fares, domestic travel had suffered. Although motorcoach tours of the United States now offer a greater variety of destinations and are growing in popularity, not all vacationers have the time to spend on crossing the country by bus. During this period, airlines offered tour-basing fares to resort areas. (Tour-basing fares are discounted fares offered to passengers who must book a package tour in order to receive this fare.) These fares were replaced by domestic advance-purchase fares, which can be sold with or without a tour package.

Domestic travel used to be considered the poor relation of the travel industry. International travel was more glamorous, more expensive, and brought in higher commissions, but political problems in so many countries, the currency fluctuations, the Persian Gulf war, and the recession of 1990–1991 have turned the tables. Domestic leisure tour sales were the first to rebound at war's end, but travelers have grown increasingly price sensitive and value conscious. Surveys have shown that safety measures are also important to both corporate and leisure travelers.

Now more than ever, travel agents are actively selling and promoting domestic travel and are always searching for new tours and destinations that can provide security, value, companionship, and educational opportunities to offer their clients. Theme park vacations, such as Disneyland in California and Disneyworld and Epcot in Florida, are drawing not only Americans but tourists from all over the globe. In a 1991 survey commissioned by the National Tour Association (NTA), travelers indicated that they wanted to see natural wonders, such as the Grand Canyon and national parks; visit warm-weather beaches; view fall foliage; and attend special events and festivals.

State tourist boards are most anxious to assist the travel agent with promotional material to stimulate travel in the United States, as are the hotels, tour operators, and the government. The states have such a wealth of natural and humanmade attractions that agents tend to take them for granted. The United States has facilities for every type of tour imaginable, from archaeology to zoology. Domestic travel, properly handled and promoted, can be the bread and butter of the travel agent's business.

PROMOTIONAL AIR FARES

In the travel industry, excursion fares are *special fares*. Special fares are always round-trip fares, which in accordance with the rules set for each fare, apply only for travel during a specified application period and are subject to the conditions decided upon by the airlines. Special, tour-basing, and promotional fares are discounted fares and designed to increase business, especially during low or off season. Family plans and special rates for accompanying children (in some plans, children up to age 17 qualify for a lower rate) are often offered during the off or low seasons. To some extent they do succeed in bringing in customers who would not normally have traveled until they saw an airline ad featuring extremely low fares. However, the fare wars we have seen in the past few years only succeeded in diluting a market that was already there.

The traveling public is now very price conscious. Even affluent travelers will ask for the lowest available fare even though they have selected a luxury tour. The standard comment is: "All the seats are on the same plane, so we might as well use the lower fare and have some extra shopping money."

Because of the fluctuations in air fares, most tour operators will no longer include the fare in the cost of the tour (unless it is a charter operation). They may show the fares in effect at the time the brochure was printed, with the qualifying remark "subject to change." The majority of fares used with both domestic and international tours is the APEX (advance purchase excursion) fare. As the name implies, the ticket must be issued in advance of travel. APEX fares impose penalties when there are changes or cancellations after the ticket is issued. In 1987 an APEX fare was introduced in the domestic market that is nonrefundable.

International APEX fares are lower than other excursion fares and usually have three fare levels: peak (high season), shoulder, and low season. APEX fares do not permit stopovers on the routing; however, they can be combined (e.g., a tour that starts in London and ends in Paris can use half of the round-trip London fare and half of the round-trip Paris fare with travel between points on other methods of transportation, usually a motorcoach).

The second most commonly used fare for international travel is the GIT (group inclusive tour). This fare can be more flexible than the APEX fare as far as stopovers are concerned, but it is dependent on a specific number of passengers traveling together throughout the tour. This fare also requires advance payment and penalizes the passenger if changes or cancellations are made after the ticket is issued.

Agents must keep up to date on all of these promotional fares to give their clients the best possible combination of tours and fares. It is their responsibility to advise their clients of the various restrictions and the advantages and disadvantages of each fare. The individual airlines do all they can to inform and instruct travel agents in these special fares. Bulletins are sent out and seminars are held in major cities as soon as new tariffs are approved. The travel trade publications are also very helpful in reporting new fares and new rules. Quite often the trade papers will publish the news before the airlines have had time to issue their bulletins.

THE APPROVED AIR TOUR

To encourage the promotion and sale of air transportation through the development and promotion of inclusive tours, international carriers pay an added commission on the air ticket for each *qualified* sale (also known as an *override*). The domestic carriers dropped this override when they decided on an across-the-board flat rate of 10 percent commission on all air tickets.

Inclusive tours are advertised journeys, including specific features, arranged and promoted with tour literature by a tour operator, and paid for in full by the purchaser before starting on the tour. To qualify for the tour commission, the advertised air tour must consist of round- or circle-trip air transportation, travel to and from a point, by a routing that may include some surface transportation, sleeping accommodations, and one or more other facilities or attractions, such as transfers, sightseeing motorcoach trip or car rentals (but not including purchase of cars), meals, tickets for the theater or sports events, or other arrangements.

The tour operator prepares sample brochures for specific tours and submits this to one of the IATA member carriers (usually, the carrier that will be used for the international route) for approval. If approved, the carrier assigns an IT (inclusive tour) code number. To qualify for the tour commission, the IT number must appear on the air ticket. The tour code helps to identify both the main IATA carrier involved in the tour and the specific tour (and, where applicable, supports the use of special fares that may be used only in conjunction with the sale of a tour).

The following is an explanation from the IATA *Ticketing Handbook* of the inclusive tour code which is entered in the tour code box of a ticket:

Characters 1 and 2: IT (inclusive tour).
Character 3: last digit of year of approval of tour.
Characters 4 and 5: two-character code of sponsoring airline that has approved the tour.
Character 6: digit 1, 2, or 3 to indicate the IATA conference area in which the tour approval has been given.

Characters 7 to 14: to identify the specific tour, an airline may use fewer than the eight characters allocated.

TOUR LITERATURE REQUIREMENTS

Tour literature must be produced by the tour operator at his own expense. In recent years IATA has relaxed its rules regarding financial support of inclusive tours provided that the tour operator has met the requirements mentioned previously. IATA's Resolution 870a also stated:

The value of any support given by the Member (Carrier) shall not exceed the costs to be incurred by the Tour Operator in developing, advertising and promoting the Inclusive Tour with the proviso that such support will not be used to provide the air transportation of the Inclusive Tour at a lower level than that set forth in the Member's tariffs.

When Inclusive Tour support is given by a Member, the Tour Operator shall produce tour literature which shall contain:

(1) the Tour Operator's name;
(2) a description of the Inclusive Tour;
(3) the price of the Inclusive Tour;
(4) the Inclusive Tour Code;
(5) a clause limiting and qualifying the degree of responsibility of the Member.

Although it is not stated in the IATA requirements, the tour folder should not only be attractive in appearance but should be written in easily understood terms and show an itinerary that is clear and explicit as to what features are included in the tour price and, more important, what is not included. Specific details accompanied by pictures do the best-selling job. The average client is not interested in artwork when shopping for a tour. A brochure with actual photographs of the areas they will visit will most often influence the customer's final decision. Remember, when clients ask for a brochure, they may have already decided where to go; now they are looking for facts and figures that will either confirm their decision or alter it.

The tour brochure is in essence the travel contract between the tour operator, the retail travel agent, and the traveler. The tour operator lists the services the traveler agrees to purchase. A contract is defined as an agreement between two or more persons that is enforceable at law. Substitution of inferior accommodations, for example, could be considered a breach of contract. The tour operator, the principal, appoints the travel agent to negotiate a contract (order/reservation) with the prospective traveler. Ordinarily, agents bind the tour operator to the contract when they accept the payment from the client; however, if agents do not disclose the name of the tour operator, they become liable to the same extent as though they are the principal.

HOW TO READ A TOUR BROCHURE

Although tour folders and/or brochures may vary in size and format, they all must conform to the rules mentioned in the preceding section. The important information agents must look for is as follows:

1. Validity dates. Dates of departure from the gateway city for international or charter tours, and/or the period in which the price shown is valid. With

the many fare choices now available, it is especially important to check the validity dates in order to quote the correct total price of the tour. It is also very important to check the validity dates on brochures for areas such as Florida, Mexico, and the Caribbean that have seasonal changes in hotel rates.

The validity date is not always found in the same place on each brochure. It may be on the front cover, it may be included with the rate chart, it may be in a box in the itinerary, or it may be found on the back cover under the responsibility clause.

2. Gateway city. The city from which the flight will leave the area and/or the city where the client can join the tour. The majority of brochures will clearly state where the tour will originate and it is the agent's responsibility to make arrangements for clients from their home city to this point of departure.

Brochures seldom state the actual hour of departure for charter tours or GITs (group inclusive tours). Tour operators may not know the departure time until almost the last minute. Sometimes even the gateway city is not known until just before departure. This is usually caused by the shuffling of smaller groups to join others in order to comply with the number of passengers required to use the group or charter fare. This situation naturally makes it difficult to reserve connecting flights for the clients. Quite often, the agent just has to make an educated guess as to when the group will leave and make the connections accordingly.

3. Name of the tour operator and/or wholesaler is always given in the responsibility clause. It may or may not be found in the body of the brochure, although the large well-established tour operators such as American Express, Cartan, Cook's, Bennetts, and Olson's will feature their name prominently, as it will encourage repeat business from their previous customers.

4. What the tour includes. Most tour brochures will include a general conditions or general information column or page (depending on the size of brochure), which will list exactly what is or is not included in the price. Some brochures still make it a guessing game where agents must examine the itinerary day by day to discover what their clients will receive for their money. Where the itinerary lists a sightseeing tour as suggested or optional, this is not included in the price of the tour. If the itinerary says "see" instead of "visit" an attraction, you will view it from the motorcoach window. Some brochures also are very ambiguous about the meals included in the tour.

Figure 9-3 Zeus Tours, Yacht Cruises, Inc., 366 Seventh Ave., New York, NY 10018 212-0006, (800) 447-5657.

There again, agents must read all the fine print to determine whether or not, and how many, meals are included in the tour price.

5.   Tour price. This is another area where the agent must read all the fine print. Most brochures quote the total cost, but many feature a base price for the low season, while additional costs, such as the tax, service charges, and surcharges for high season, are buried somewhere in the body of the text.

Another important cost the agent must determine is whether or not the transportation between sightseeing attractions is included. For example, some Hawaii tours will include the air fare between the islands, while others will note that this must be added to the passenger's round-trip transportation from his home city. In Mexico, some tours will provide only one-way transportation between Mexico City and Acapulco since many tourists may prefer to terminate their tour in Acapulco. Also check whether or not admission charges are included in the sightseeing tour or if transportation only is provided to the attractions listed.

6.   Hotels. Luxury tours will list the names and locations of the hotels used in the tour, but the majority of low-cost, budget tours will often state "Hotel . . . or similar" or may omit names entirely. This can be a very touchy subject and may cause lost sales unless the agent is perfectly honest and advises clients in advance that low-cost tours do not use the best hotels, which is one reason why they are low in cost.

The hotel selection does make a big difference in the cost of the tour. The higher-priced tours will use hotels that are conveniently located, have a good restaurant on the premises, and whose rooms are large and attractively furnished.

The desire for an honest opinion and advance notice of what to expect from their tour are the main reasons that tour customers consult an agent. Agents who neglect to point out the disadvantages of a specific tour are not doing themselves or their clients any favors. Clients may still take the tour, and they may come back with complaints about the tour, but the point is that they will come back to an agent who did not hesitate to point out the bad features as well as the good.

Most tour operators will ask the tour members to complete a questionnaire at the end of the tour stating their likes and dislikes regarding the tour arrangements. From these answers they can determine what features should be changed or omitted from future tours. Most complaints reported on these questionnaires concern the hotel selection, usually because it was too far from shops and other attractions. Other complaints are about side trips that were omitted, or limited sightseeing time at the site. Tour guides seem to receive equal numbers of complaints and compliments. The main reason for the complaints was that the tour did not come up to the client's expectations based on the information given in the tour literature.

For this reason it is essential that agents read and examine the tour brochure thoroughly and not hesitate to request additional information from the tour operator/wholesaler, when necessary, then give their clients full details.

CLOSING THE SALE

Selling a tour can be as simple and straightforward as selling straight transportation or hotel rooms. The key to unlocking tour sales is the same. The travel consultant tries to fulfill the client's needs and likes and, perhaps, a lifelong dream. This is where it is so important to ask the right questions in the right manner and to listen carefully to the answers. Clients who are going to spend several thousands of dollars for a tour or cruise should not be rushed into a decision, but at the same time, do not let them walk out of your office without making a commitment—collect the deposit.

As always, the first step is determining the destination(s) desired, the dates and the length of time they have at their disposal, the number of people traveling, and the type of tour: independent, group escorted, group hosted, or group departures with independent land arrangements upon arrival at the destination. Ask how flexible they can be and get alternate dates in the event the tour they request is not available. As tactfully as possible, ask for a price range. Don't try to judge a client's financial position by their appearance. A man in jeans or coveralls might be the owner of the shopping center down the street.

With all the misconceptions that prevail about tours, it is very important that the agent ask enough questions to find out exactly what customers have in mind. Someone may walk in and say that she is planning a tour to Italy when all she really wants is a ticket to Milan to visit relatives.

The next step involves the selection of brochures that would most closely fit your customer's request. This is the area where most agents err. Many tend to select tours that would fit their own personal budget and sell down rather than up, making price their final consideration. Even though customers may give you a price range, first try to find the itinerary that fits their specifications, regardless of price. If the tour you have selected appeals to them, they will pay the price. Another error made is loading the customer with too many brochures. A happy medium appears to be a selection of three or four brochures containing the itinerary requested.

As soon as your customer indicates a preference, immediately get name(s), address(es), and phone number(s) and call the tour operator to check for availability. Do this while the customer is at your desk and can make an immediate decision if changes must be made. At times, this action will disturb the customer who is not quite certain that this is the tour for him. Agents can allay their doubts by assuring the customer that he will have an option period (usually a week) in which to make a definite decision and make a deposit. Most tour operators do not consider it a confirmed reservation until they have received a deposit.

BOOKING THE TOUR

Nine of 10 tour sales require only the following steps:

1. A telephone call to the tour operator or tour desk of the carrier to inquire about the availability for the departure date requested. Provide the tour number from the brochure, and advise if there are any special requests or upgrades in hotels.

2. If the tour is available, provide the client's name. In turn, you will be told the option date by which the deposit must be made in order to confirm the reservation. (If the tour is not available for the date requested, ask that your client be placed on the waitlist and ask for the first available date.)

3. Deposits are collected and forwarded to the tour operator and/or carrier. (The procedure varies according to the type of fare used for the tour package.)

4. When the written confirmation is received, the client is notified of when the balance of payment is due. You should also note this date in a tickler file or calendar so that you can remind the client several days before the due date. Now that most tour operators are computerized, it is important to observe deposit and payment dates, as reservations are cancelled automatically unless the tour operator has been advised that the payment is in the mail and/or given the agent's check number.

5. Final payments are collected and forwarded to the principals.

6. Tour documents are issued by the tour operator and sent to your agency. Agents usually issue the round-trip air ticket based on the reservation information given to them by the tour operator and add on the fare from home cities to the gateway city. On some tours, the tour operator also issues the air tickets.

7. The final step involves double-checking the tour documents and air tickets to make sure that all is in order (errors can creep in at the last minute) and verifying that your clients have their passports, visas, and health certificates (where necessary).

Occasionally, some sales may require more than one telephone call to locate an available tour for the date your client desires. Complications may also arise if a tour is canceled because the tour operator did not receive the necessary number of participants for that departure. As mentioned earlier, the GIT fare can be used only when the minimum number of passengers has been reached. This means that if an alternate tour cannot be found (or an alternate date is not acceptable to your client), there will be a substantial increase in the airfare.

As long as your client has been advised in advance that this possibility exists, it is surprising how few will object or cancel their arrangements.

THE FOLLOW-UP

Following up through personal contact with the customers after they return can be just as important as the first contact. This provides agents with the opportunity to keep abreast of developments in the areas his customers have visited and encourages repeat business. When customers know that you are sincerely interested in hearing about their experiences and, more important, are willing to listen to their complaints with a sympathetic ear, they are more likely to return to your agency with their future business.

Some agents, such as myself, take the easy way and ask the customers to call or stop in upon their return. It is amazing the number of people who will do this and will even consider it an honor that the agent wants to hear their opinions. Other agents use a preprinted and predated letter that is mailed when the customer returns. Others will send a questionnaire called a *trip evaluation*. The disadvantage of preprinted forms and questionnaires is that the personal touch is lost, and customers who make frequent trips will receive the same letter or card after each trip. A personal call or handwritten note is a better way of maintaining a close relationship.

TRAVELERS' TEN COMMANDMENTS*

· Thou shalt not expect to find things as thou hast at home, for thou hast left home to find things different.
· Thou shalt not take anything too seriously, for a carefree mind is the start of a good holiday.
· Thou shalt not let the other travelers get on thy nerves, for thou has paid good money to enjoy thyself.
· Remember to take half as many clothes as thou thinkest and twice the money.

*From the lounge of the Lake Eacham Hotel, Yungaburra, Queensland.

- Know at all times where thy passport is, for a person without a passport is a person without a country.
- Remember that if we had been expected to stay in one place, we would have been created with roots.
- Thou shalt not worry, for he that worrieth hath no pleasure and few things are that fatal.
- When in Australia be prepared to do somewhat as the Australians do.
- Thou shalt not judge the people of the country by the person who hath given the trouble.
- Remember that thou art a guest in other lands, and he that treats his host with respect shall be honored.

QUESTIONS AND PROBLEMS

1. What is a tour?
2. What are the basic ingredients of a tour?
3. What are the advantages of a prepaid package tour from the client's viewpoint?
4. Describe an FIT and a DIT.
5. What is a GIT?
6. What are the basic requirements for a GIT tour package?
7. List some special fares used with tours.
8. In your opinion, which domestic destinations are the most popular?
9. Plan an advertising or promotional program featuring a domestic tour.
10. What is an approved air tour?
11. How can you claim additional commission on an international ticket?
12. What is the difference between an escorted tour and a hosted tour?
13. Where would you look for the tour operator's name on the brochure?
14. How many brochures would you give a prospective client?
15. What information do you need from a client before you can recommend a specific tour?
16. Which is the most important document a client needs before taking a tour to Europe?
17. What are the selling points of an escorted tour?
18. Make up a follow-up letter to send to a returning client.

chapter 10

Tour Operators

OBJECTIVES

When you have finished this chapter you should be able to:

1. Give a brief history of tour operators.
2. Describe the various categories of tour operators.
3. List the major components of a package tour.
4. Discuss the key people in the tour operators' organization.
5. Describe the importance of tour guides.
6. Suggest methods to improve agent/tour operator relationships.

A great amount of time, effort, and money go into creating a tour. Planning, packaging, pricing, and marketing the final product takes skill, knowledge, experience, and foresight. Tour operators are the *tour manufacturers*. Tours are a creation of their imagination, ideas, initiative, and industry. Established and reputable operators have a large, experienced staff to process the many time-consuming operational details and to handle any emergency situation. They must market their product well and operate it successfully.

Tour operators can be wholesalers and retailers. Thomas Cook, Inc. and American Express are good examples of a dual organization. Retail travel agents can also be their own tour operators and wholesale their tours to other travel agents. In fact, most tour operators are the outgrowth of successful retailers in their own group tour operations.

The travel agency business originated on a group tour basis rather than a retail basis. In 1841, Thomas Cook, a printer and temperance worker in England, chartered a train and sold tickets at 25 cents each for a round trip to a temperance convention. This was the first round-trip ticket and the first special train in history. It launched a travel bureau that is still one of the leading tour operators and travel agencies in existence today. Until 1907, when Cook's started handling individual arrangements, a Cook's tour was an organized, escorted tour.

It also was in the early 1800s that steamer cruises became popular on both the rivers and the oceans. In 1840 the Lansing Travel Bureau opened in Albany, New York near the eastern end of the Erie Canal and specialized in river cruises. This agency is considered to be the first travel agency in the United States.

The expansion of the railroads on both sides of the Atlantic brought about an increase in travel for pleasure. Again, Thomas Cook led the way when he decided to organize his tours on a profit-making basis. On his first organized tour from Leicester to Liverpool on August 4, 1845, he supplied each member of the tour with a printed itinerary—the birth of the first tour folder. The individual traveler started receiving special attention from Thomas Bennett in 1850, the originator of Bennett's Tours, still a large and powerful wholesale company in Europe and the United States. Bennett started in Oslo as an arranger of special tours of Norway for visiting dignitaries from Britain. His arrangements were the birth of the FIT (foreign independent tour) or ITT, as the British call it. Bennett's opened their first U.S. office in Boston in 1919.

Both Cook's and Bennett's firms pioneered in blocking a number of hotel rooms for clients and in the prepayment of hotel accommodations which form the basis of an independent or a group tour. In the early days of innkeeping, reservations were unheard of: Rooms were sold on a first-come, first-served basis. In 1867, Cook's introduced the hotel coupon, the forerunner of today's hotel voucher.

Brownell Tours of Alabama started business in 1887 when W. A. Brownell escorted the first American tour of Europe on a prearranged basis. His son continued it (as a college professor) at the University of Alabama. During this period, they operated private tours only. His grandson, George, moved the main office to Birmingham (the present location) and branched out into regular escorted tours that were sold primarily through travel agents. (Incidentally, in 1970, Brownell Tours announced that beginning in 1971, they were withdrawing their regular scheduled escorted tour program from the nationwide travel market and returning to the promotion of private tours.)

The American Express Company was formed in 1850 and, in 1858 entered the travel business as a steamship agent for the Atlantic Royal Mail Steam Navigation Co., but this did not last and it was 50 years later that they reentered the travel business. Today they are one of the largest tour operators/retailers in the world and operate hundreds of tours each year which are sold through their own branches and are also available to other retailers (travel agents).

Ask Mr. Foster and Cartan Travel Bureau are two other top tour operators who started in the United States in the 1800s. Ask Mr. Foster is also a retailer and has numerous branches nationwide. Cartan wholesales only.

It was only between the Civil War and World War I that the travel business really started flourishing. Travel by steamship expanded everywhere around the world. Americans were discovering Europe and immigrants were pouring into the United States. Business was booming in both directions. Steamship cruises flourished on the Great Lakes and along the coast from New York to New Orleans.

In those early years, travel agents specialized in groups and were mainly steamship and railroad agents and escorted tour operators. This may be why the notion still exists that the travel agent is interested only in groups. It was in the post–World War I period that agents started to diversify and tour operators began to sell their tours through other agents. Exprinter Tour Operators, said to be the first pure travel wholesale operator in the United States, started in 1928.

It was in 1919 that the first commercial airline flights started in Europe. That same year also saw the formation of IATA (at that time known as the International Air Traffic Association) by six European air companies, and the opening of the first American air ticket office at the old Waldorf–Astoria Hotel in New York City. April 10, 1941 was the date CAB (Civil Aeronautics Board) approved the first domestic airlines agreement covering the appointment, retention, and remuneration of travel agents. At that time, sponsorship by one of the airlines and approval by a majority of the airlines were the only requirements for ATC accreditation.

The post–World War I period also brought a great increase in the number of travel agencies, but it was the post–World War II period that brought on the spectacular development of the commercial airlines and the beginning of a new era in the travel industry. In 1928 and 1929, records were set for steamship travel that have never been equaled. Steamship travel steadily declined while air traffic increased, but it was not until the early 1950s that air dominated all phases of travel. Both the business traveler and the pleasure traveler preferred planes to ships or trains. Today, however, the trend is back to cruises for pleasure travel, and transatlantic and transpacific transportation by ship has dwindled down to a few major steamship lines (and these are usually on round-the-world cruises).

All through the ages, from the first caravans across the deserts to Christopher Columbus's search for a better route to the Indies, businesspeople were the travel industry's major customers. Today, pleasure travelers equal the business travelers and are steadily increasing in numbers. With the inventions of the wireless, telephones, television, and now computers, businesspeople can conduct most of their affairs without leaving their offices, thus eliminating much of their traveling for purely business reasons. However, sales meetings, conventions, and incentive travel can be very profitable for agents specializing in commercial accounts.

TOUR RELATIONS

Today, thanks to the miracle of modern air transportation, 90 percent of our world can be reached by anyone. We have eliminated distance. With the combined efforts of airlines, steamship lines, tour operators, and travel agents, still-developing areas of the world will blossom into major tour destinations. Diversification and new programs are becoming ever more important. Approximately 50 percent of the key income group ($40,000 and over, ages 25–54) in the United States is looking for the more novel and adventurous vacations, and the availability of a good tour at a good price will entice first-time travelers to visit areas they had never considered before. There is, however, an increased necessity for closer cooperation among all the components of the travel industry. A tour operator may put together an outstanding tour only to see it jeopardized by the airlines' decision to eliminate or cut back on flights, or announce new fares and new validity periods that will make the tour program obsolete. Agents will convince their clients to take a particular tour only to discover that the tour was cancelled because of poor response or because the hotels requested were not available.

The success of charter tours (tours based on the use of charter flights) should prove the point that good organization and cooperation can benefit everyone involved in the operation. The disadvantages of a charter package should also be noted; the low cost may attract first-timers to air travel, but by the time all the taxes and extras are added to the base price, the customers soon discover that the bargain tour is no bargain. Repeat business from charter clients will usually bring requests for individual arrangements or escorted tours with more features included and a willingness to pay more for these benefits.

The market for pleasure travel has been steadily increasing during the past 40 years. Vacations have become a high priority for affluent, middle-aged Americans, even those who are home-centered, and travel agents do exert a major force in planning and booking trips. But unless the travel industry puts a more concentrated effort in producing and promoting tours that will appeal to the entire family, there is more competition now from campers and vans, video games, private swimming pools, and time-share condominiums.

Tour wholesalers and carriers need the many retail outlets provided by the travel agent and the travel agent needs principals he can rely on to provide clients with the vacation of their dreams. The travel industry no longer just provides transportation. Planes must arrive and depart on time, baggage must be handled promptly and efficiently, hotels must provide clean, comfortable, and attractively furnished rooms (size and location are not always the first consideration), meals must not only be varied but well prepared and well served. All these services are the responsibilities of the principals, but it is the travel agent who must shoulder the blame in the eyes of the client when any one of these services is found lacking.

The travel industry is there for the convenience of the client, but too often, this fact is overlooked or ignored. Carriers want to sell seats, but the complexity of fares and validity periods, too-frequent schedule changes, and a display of indifference to individual needs discourages a borderline customer from leaving the car in the garage and flying to his chosen destination. Horror stories from returning passengers on poor service and lost baggage have been increasing in the same proportion as the increases in discounted fares.

Tour operators cancel tours at the last minute or will send inexperienced tour managers to escort the group. They insist on full payment at least 30 days in advance and then send the travel documents the day before the departure. There even have been cases where clients left home with only a receipt from the agent to show that they were indeed booked on the tour.

Hotels overbook and then refuse to honor an agent's reservation even though the client may present a confirmation slip from the hotel itself. To make matters worse, they will often refuse to assist the client in finding other accommodations.

These are not extreme examples; unfortunately, they happen almost every day. The principals involved forget that vacation plans are not that flexible. Businesspeople may accept a cancelled flight or schedule change and change their schedules accordingly; but most employees, even the executives, must vacation on a set schedule. Baby-sitters must be hired; work loads must be adjusted; temporary replacements must be hired; wedding and honeymoon arrangements cannot be changed at the last minute. Clients are not interested in the industry's problems, and rightly so. When they buy a new car or color TV set they are concerned only that these items operate smoothly and trouble-free. Once clients are convinced that the travel agent's services will not increase the price of the trip; they are not interested or concerned that the agent may be overworked and underpaid, or that the carriers and tour operators may be losing money on their reservations.

Much work has to be done to improve tour relations among all the components of the travel industry, and it is encouraging to note that improvements have been made during the past 10 years. The airlines, tour operator organizations, cruise lines, hotel associations, and travel agent organizations are taking long and careful examinations of their own and each others' operations. Airline sales representatives are encouraged to take the ICTA (Institute of Travel Agents) program and work for their CTC (Certified Travel Counselor) rating so that they can better understand the travel agent. More tour operators are becoming members of the United States Tour Operators Association (USTOA), an organization that provides bonding and travel agent/tour operator liability insurance. This eliminates some of the guesswork involved in selecting a tour operator.

DEFINING THE TOUR OPERATOR

Tour ingredients consist of transportation, transfers or car rentals, hotels, meals, and sightseeing. The tour operator is the architect or master chef who assembles the ingredients and creates travel, creates a market, creates leads, and creates an annuity by having satisfied clients who return year after year. They are principals who sublet to other principals and agents and pay a contract price or a commission. In their relationship with retail agents, the wholesale tour operators, like their chosen carriers, share dual and common obligations, responsibilities, and problems. Each is a principal, but in the sale and operation of the tour, the tour operator is the principal, the airlines are selected contractors, and the retail travel agents are the vendors. This is a delicate relationship and it must be understood and properly maintained.

In the complex and intricate business of travel, tour operators are as necessary in their field as an attorney, doctor, or any other professional. The tour that is planned and managed by a reputable tour operator contains hidden and priceless ingredients: the experience, integrity, and reputation of the producer. Intelligent and experienced travelers have learned that it pays to have a travel consultant, a reputable agent, and an experienced tour operator. They understand and are prepared to pay for their services, as they know that in the long run the preplanned trips will not only save time enroute but will give them more value for their money.

A lot of the confusion at the present time arises from the complexity of tour-producing outlets. As the saying goes, "everybody wants to get into the act." The lines of demarcation are getting more and more blurred as time goes on. In recent years the airlines have been expanding their tour departments, purchasing hotels, and (in Europe) buying out tour operator firms. Franchisers and travel agent cooperatives are also going into the operation and promotion of their own tours. Escorted tours are offered by newspaper editors, radio and TV stations, schools, and colleges. Everybody from YMCA secretaries to cultural society directors are operating group tours. Many hotels, carriers, and government tourist offices are competing with each other for package, sales incentive, and convention tours.

Many of these nonprofessional tour operators do create the desire for travel and through their initiative and promotional efforts often create a large volume of business that might not otherwise move. However, the majority of them will bypass the travel agent because they have not been educated in the fact that their tours could be handled more efficiently and, in the long run, more economically by professional travel agents in cooperation with professional tour operators and they will still get their free trips as tour conductors.

To summarize briefly, the following are the various categories of tour operators:

1. *Retail operators*: tour operators who deal directly with the public. They design, operate, advertise, and sell almost exclusively to their own clientele.

Figure 10-2 Tauck Tours.

The retailer may be a small travel agency or a multibranch organization that markets hundreds of tours. Larger firms may offer their tours to other travel agents and pay them commission. Smaller firms may accept bookings from other travel agents at their own discretion. Even though there is an unwritten rule that an agent can book her clients on any advertised tour, there are several reasons why this is not a general practice. In the first place, the retail operator may already have the nucleus of a group and is only advertising to pick up additional business. Second, most agents hesitate to book their clients with another retail agent because they fear the loss of repeat business since the retail operators will automatically add the client's name and address to their own mailing list. Third, the retail operator may not have included a commission in the price structure of his tours and cannot afford to accept bookings from other travel agents except when they are falling below their quota and are in danger of cancelling their tour or taking a loss on the group. At this point they would welcome bookings from other agents, even though they sacrifice their own commissions on the sale. Approximately 22 percent of all retailers also operate as wholesalers.

2. *Wholesale operators*: tour operators who do not deal directly with the public. (They are also known as pure wholesalers.) These firms design and operate tours exclusively for sale through travel agents. They do not accept direct bookings and avoid direct sales contacts with the public. Those operators who specialize in GITs (group inclusive tours) select the supporting carriers. Those who contract land arrangements only may suggest a carrier, but the final decision is up to the client and her agent. A "straight wholesaler" operates the tours at the source—through his own offices or through local contractors. A "retailer/wholesaler" packages and promotes tours through both his own outlets and those of other travel agents.

3. *General tour contractors*: tour operators who do not package and promote their own tours. They forward reservations to wholesalers or local contractors. The carriers' tour departments, cooperatives, affinity groups, and nonprofit organizations would fall under this category.

4. *Local tour contractors*: local tour operators who provide the services required by all other categories where they do not have a local office or are not dealing at the source with the hotels. Local contractors secure, book, coordinate, supervise, and handle payments of all services in their territory. Their services are invaluable for an efficient and successful group or FIT operation.

Defining the Tour Operator

Organized in 1972, USTOA has achieved wide industry official and public recognition as a symbol of financial stability, reliability, and integrity in the operations of its members. At present they have 41 members. Membership in USTOA is expensive and their requirements are the most stringent in the industry. There are many good tour operators who are not members, but the USTOA logo on the brochure assures the travel agent that this is a tour operator that can be trusted to perform as advertised.

To qualify for membership in the association, no fewer than 18 airlines, hotels, financial institutions, retail travel agencies, and other organizations must give references vouching for an applicant's reliability and financial stability. The prospective member must have been in business for at least three years, must meet or exceed minimum tour sales volume requirements, must carry at least $1 million of professional liability/errors and omissions insurance policy with worldwide coverage, and must participate in the USTOA's Consumer Protection Plan.

The plan began in 1976 and has been modified several times since. The most recent and most significant change took effect on April 1, 1990, when each participating operator was required to supplement its bond, letter of credit, or other surety to provide additional coverage, up to a maximum of $5 million. USTOA stipulated that the plan would be triggered by an operator's insolvency or failure, even if it is not immediately involved in a formal declaration of bankruptcy. Operators have two options for coming up with the additional protection. They can put up a $5 million surety or participate in a USTOA insurance program that provides an aggregate annual coverage of $5 million in default protection.

Thirty-five members use the insurance option, whereas six large tour operators elected to provide their own $5 million surety: American Express, Classic Hawaii, MTI, Pleasant Hawaiian, Tauck Tours, and Super Cities/Great Escape Vacations.

In 1978, the Civil Aeronautics Board was considering implementing rules and regulations for scheduled-service tours. In comments filed with the CAB, USTOA stated that "substantial need does not exist for any such regulation by the Board," and suggested instead that both the government and the industry should encourage adherence to an industry-developed program of performance standards for operators and other suppliers. USTOA believes that industry self-regulation is a more acceptable alternative than government-imposed rules. A special committee was appointed in November 1978 that worked out a definitive industry-developed, realistically practicable "Ethics in U.S. Tour Operations/Standards for Integrity." The active members of USTOA have pledged to adhere to these ethics and standards and have made it a requirement for continuous membership in the organization.

The key role of USTOA is to educate the public and the travel agents in the value of package tours. To that end, they have published a brochure, "How to Select a Package Tour." The brochure is sent to those who respond to their ads.

TOUR OPERATORS' CODE
Principles of Professional Conduct and Ethics

1. It is the responsibility of active and affiliated active tour operator members of the United States Tour Operators Association (USTOA) to conduct their business affairs forthrightly, with professional competence and factual accuracy.

2. Representations to the public and retailers shall be truthful, explicit, intelligible and avoid deception, concealment or obscuring of material facts, conditions or requirements.

3. In advertising and quoting of prices for tours, the total deliverable price, including service charges and special charges, shall be stated or clearly and readily determinable; and the pendency of any known condition or contingency, such as fares subject to conference and/or government approval, shall be openly and noticeably disclosed.

4. Advertising and explanation of tour features shall clearly state and identify the facilities, accommodations, and services included; any substitutions of features or deviation from the advertised tour shall be communicated expeditiously and the cause thereof be explained to agents and/or clients involved.

5. Each active and affiliated active tour operator member of USTOA shall so arrange and conduct its business as to instill retailer, consumer and public confidence in such member's financial stability, reliability and integrity, and shall avoid any conduct or action conducive to discrediting membership in USTOA as signifying allegiance to professional and financial integrity in tourism.*

THE WHOLESALE OPERATION

Wholesalers must start their programs at least one year before the first tour departure date. Some programs are planned years ahead, such as tours involving special events: World Expositions, the Olympic games, and the Passion Play at Oberammergau, which occurs every 10 years. They can spend from four to six months developing a salable package, then from three to four months laying out and printing their promotional material. They spend an average of four to five months traveling to discover new and interesting places and checking on hotel operations and their foreign representatives.

The first step in planning the program involves a review of the tours offered during the past year. This review is based on the reports from the tour escorts, comments received from the passengers, and discussions with the airlines serving the area.

The mechanics of designing the tour depend greatly on tour testing. From surveys taken by trade publications, both wholesalers and airline tour departments emphasize the importance of sampling the tours before the package is made available to the traveling public. Most operators will sample more than once to make sure that noted corrections had been made, or will send a staff member to act as tour leader to see firsthand how a tour is running. Airline tour departments also keep a close tabulation of passenger reports. Passengers are requested to fill out a questionnaire and as many as 18 percent usually do so. In addition, airline salespersons will go on tours anonymously as paying passengers and report on the tours. This flow of information is fed into computers and enables tour departments to gain an excellent picture of the strengths and weaknesses of tour programs as well as the preferences of the public.

The most vital ingredient in the composition of the tour package is the hotel. Most tour problems concern the quality of hotels. If a tour participant can retire to a comfortable bed in a clean and attractive room, he or she will be more tolerant of bad weather, dusty roads, and uncongenial tour partners. Hotels are selected according to type, service, location, facilities, convenience, and price. Inspections are made of the sizes of rooms, availability of air-conditioning, adequacy of public rooms, elevator service, and last but not least, the food. Tour managers must make sure that meals are not duplicated along the route; and where meals are included in the price, he must see that all tour members are served the same food in equal

*USTOA, "How to Select a Package Tour."

The Wholesale Operation

portions. Adults can be amazingly immature at times, especially if they see a tour member eating steak while they are eating fish or chicken.

The location of the hotel is a very important consideration. It should be in the center of town, especially in the larger cities, and within walking distance of shops, theaters, and nightclubs. There are exceptions, of course; in some cities the best hotels are on the outskirts of the city.

Official hotel ratings can be both misleading and inconsistent, which is why on-the-spot testing is so important. It is a well-known fact that a first-class hotel in one country may be rated as second-class in another country; or a second-class hotel may actually be superior to an officially rated first-class.

When the hotels are selected, tour operators purchase bedspace or guarantees to purchase a specific number of rooms from the hotel management. By guaranteeing rooms, they are obligated to pay for those rooms, whether used or not. From start to finish, a tour program is a gamble. Many factors can affect sales. Weather, floods, politics, local strikes, or uprisings are just a few of the events that may affect a tour that was a "sure thing" in other years.

The next most vital ingredient in the tour package is the local sightseeing at each stopover in the itinerary. Except for the larger companies, such as Cook's and American Express, which use their own equipment, most wholesalers contract local tour operators to provide the motor coaches and guides. In selecting local contractors, the decision should be based on their reputation, how long they have been in business, type of equipment used, type of office, and size of local operations. Some testing should also be done on the sightseeing itinerary to check mileages and time allowed.

Most complaints from returning clients are centered on the fact that they were rushed through the sightseeing tours and did not have enough time at each attraction to enjoy and appreciate it. Travelers prefer fewer stops with a longer interval at each attraction. Except for the one- or two-hour city sightseeing tour run purposely to familiarize the tour members with the area, more time should be provided for individual enjoyment.

The next step in preparing an itinerary is to check restaurants, recreational facilities, special features, and transportation to special events to determine what to include in the tour price. Pricing a tour and preparing the brochure for the printer are very important steps. This material must be checked and double-checked to eliminate misleading statements and to ensure that the facts are accurate and up-to-date and that all costs have been included in the price quoted.

The price tag on a tour folder has been a source of controversy not only with the public but also between the retailer and the wholesaler. Much of the controversy is caused by the fact that tour costs are not itemized, and wholesalers have been accused of an unreasonable markup. In a few instances, the accusation is justified; however, most wholesalers offer a good product at a fair cost. If retailers would take the time to list the cost of each item in the itinerary, they would find that the wholesaler's expense, which is built into the cost, is not out of line and usually includes extras that clients could not duplicate on their own.

Wholesalers must prepare a salable package, estimate their costs, and provide for a true profit. If the product is inferior or the price too high for his market, it will not sell. If the price is too low, the wholesaler will go broke sooner or later. Their estimates must include their investments in preparation, promotion, and marketing. On top of all this, they must also be prepared to pay a minimum of 10 percent commission to their retail agents. (Many wholesalers have a sliding scale of commissions payable to retail agents based on either the number of bookings received or the dollar amount of sales accumulated over a year's time.)

Most major tour wholesalers will print from 3 to 5 million brochures a year. With continual increases in postage, printing, and paper, these costs are considerably higher today than ever before. For this reason, their mailings now consist of one sample copy and a reorder card. Added to the cost of printing and postage are mailing house handling fees, staff and accounting costs, trade advertising, agent familiarization tours, and direct mailings.

With increasing competition from the airlines, conglomerates, and hotel chains (who prepare their own tour packages), and with today's modern marketing and merchandising methods, major tour operators are required to maintain a much larger cash fund than in the past. Many airlines require advance deposits to hold seats, and more and more hotels are insisting on advance payments. Wholesalers are now forced into taking business risks never before necessary.

This places a greater responsibility on the travel agent in selecting a tour operator/wholesaler. There have been many incidents of tour groups stranded because the wholesaler went into bankruptcy after the groups left the United States. Most of these incidents involved charter tour operators, but the public is unaware of the distinctions between wholesalers and retailers and will immediately blame all travel agents for these mishaps.

THE TOUR ESCORT OR TOUR MANAGER

Key people in the tour operator's organization are the tour escorts. They are not just sightseeing guides; their judgment, integrity, and personality can make or break a tour. The best tour escorts are those with the most experience, those who have traveled extensively in the areas to which they lead the groups. Escorts should be fluent in at least one foreign language if they are leading tours to foreign countries. They must be professionals dedicated to their jobs.

The majority of employment inquiries the travel agent receives are applications for the job of tour escort. There seems to be just as many, if not more, misconceptions about the tour escort's duties as there are about the travel agent. Most people think the tour escort just goes along for the ride and their duties consist of holding lectures or group discussions about places to be visited. This may be true of a tour conductor who qualifies for a free ticket in return for forming a group of at least 15 paid passengers, but it is not true of the professional tour escort.

There is a worldwide shortage of good, trained tour managers, and many tour operators, especially those who operate the economy or thrift tours, are recruiting college students to work full time during the summer seasons. This, of course, means that inexperienced tour escorts are learning their job at the expense of the group members. Tour operators who specialize in higher-quality tours have stricter standards for their tour managers. Several insist on rigorous training programs held in their own offices, some as long as 18 months, plus a period of apprenticeship under an experienced tour manager.

The office training consists of familiarizing the prospective tour manager with the actual procedures of creating and preparing the tour program, as well as the two areas of tour managing: operations and group relations. The operational phase of the training concerns itself with the following duties:

1. Meeting the group at airports, rail depots, or steamship piers to begin their assigned tour
2. Making announcements and giving instructions
3. Checking the passenger list and reviewing the documents, vouchers, and tickets needed for each passenger
4. Exchanging, reevaluating, and picking up transportation tickets on certain tours
5. Counting and transferring baggage at airports, depots, etc.

6. Getting the group on and off planes, trains, boats, or buses with baggage
7. Checking tour members in and out of hotels
8. Paying hotel bills, charges, admissions, and issuing vouchers covering items on the tours
9. Seeing tour members off on sightseeing trips and accompanying those that do not provide a local sightseeing guide
10. Arranging extra sightseeing or evening tours for members of their group
11. Reconfirming airline flights, hotel rooms, and/or special arrangements
12. Preparing and forwarding daily reports to the home office

A most important aspect of the escort's job is maintaining good group relations. They must be experienced in dealing with people and have a sense of public relations. It is vital that they have a mature attitude in the performance of their duties and possess the ability to relate well to people with varying demands. Tour escorts assume the role of father, mother, nurse, companion, travel agent, accountant, quality control supervisor, guide, disciplinarian, and friend.

Tour operators have developed standards of procedure for escorts based on past experience. Reports received from tour managers on actual problems and how they were solved are used as training material. How to cope with the passenger who suddenly becomes ill, the heavy drinker, the late riser, the chronic complainer, and other individual behavior problems are a few of the situations the tour manager must handle. Bad weather, cancelled or delayed flights, a bus breakdown or traffic congestion, strikes, or demonstrations may also keep him busy looking for alternate travel arrangements or searching for unexpected overnight accommodations and meal arrangements.

A willingness to work for a low starting salary for a week that often extends beyond 100 hours is another requirement. However, daily spending allowances for meals not included in the tour, laundry, and other expenses are added to the salary. Some tour operators, usually the budget tours, do not pay escorts at all. They give them a free trip and that's all. The pay scale depends on the escort's experience and on the tour's length, destination, and composition. Some operators also offer a different pay scale to Americans than to foreign nationals. There is a wide agreement among operators that former travel agents make the best escorts. Although teachers and students are adequate as escorts, they cannot compare with the ex-travel agent for full knowledge and know-how when it comes to traveling.

From a *Travel Weekly* poll of tour operators, 85 said they insist on hiring college graduates, and 65 percent said that all, or almost all, their escorts are age 30 or older. Half the operators hire both men and women as escorts (although several said that they prefer men), 40 percent hire only men, and one hires women exclusively. Among reasons given for not hiring women was that the pace is a bit too strenuous for a woman. "Often a situation calls for muscle power that women just don't have." Also: "We cater to women primarily; therefore, men are most appealing [as escorts]." At the other extreme was the operator who preferred women, noting: "We find that, on the average, women make the best escorts because they're more patient, understanding, and better at human relations."

TOUR GUIDES

With rising cultural and educational levels, the traveling public is becoming more and more demanding as regards the professional qualifications of tour escorts and guide services. With the exception of the United States, the National Tourist Offices (NTO) of all major countries establish and regulate standards for every facet of the tourism industry. Tourism is the major industry not only in Europe but also in most countries around the world. Specific regulations govern hotels, tour operators, travel agents, motorcoach services, and the reception and information staff of each NTO.

Guide/interpreters occupy a particularly important place among the reception and information staff of every national tourist office. The term covers persons responsible for guiding tourists within a town or specified tourist zone and furnishing them with all necessary information. The NTO maintains a register of experienced and certified guides available to tour operators. Tour operators notify the NTO of their needs and the dates needed, and unless they specify the guides by name, NTO will assign the guides to the groups as they arrive.

To safeguard against malpractices and poor service on the part of unqualified persons, a number of laws give broad definitions of the term *guide/interpreter*. The main requirements for admission to the profession of guide/interpreter relate to the following points:

1. *Minimum age*. The minimum age is fixed in the regulations of several countries (i.e., Greece, on attaining majority; Israel, 21).
2. *Nationality*. Some countries (i.e., France, Italy, U.A.R.) require that the guide/interpreter be a national of the country.
3. *Good conduct and behavior*. Some regulations include this point (i.e., France, UAR).
4. *Educational qualifications*. The majority of countries require a baccalaureate (bachelor's degree) or equivalent (i.e., Spain, Italy, Portugal); some countries require a university degree; Greece requires at least two years of archaeological studies; other countries accept several years' experience in the tourist field.
5. *Training courses*. The candidates selected have to take courses organized by the competent national, provincial, and local authorities. They then have to pass an examination. In countries where there are no official regulations in this field, it is the local tourist associations or professional organizations that look after training.
6. *Proficiency in languages*. Most countries require candidates to be proficient in at least one or more foreign languages; Greece requires a proficiency in five: Greek, French, German, English, and Japanese.

One of the major problems is that concerning the system of remuneration. Details relating to remuneration are fixed by the public authorities or other competent bodies. The pay scales generally provide for remuneration on an hourly, half-day basis, fixed rates for guiding groups, and specific extras for overtime. In some countries, guide/interpreters are expressly forbidden to accept gratuities or to receive commissions from shopkeepers.

According to a law passed by the Mexican government, tourist guides are classified in three categories:

- *Local guides*: whose activity is circumscribed to certain towns, zones, museums, and monuments
- *General guides*: are authorized to guide tourists all over the country
- *Specialized guides*: who possess, apart from basic training in tourism, specialized knowledge in certain fields (flora, fauna, minerals)

A deposit or other security is asked from the guides to cover any possible damage they may cause to tourists. Mexican law also expressly forbids guides (1) to ask tourists directly or indirectly for rates higher than those fixed by government; and (2) to encourage tourists to buy or accept services from shopkeepers and thus receive unjustified commissions.

The travel agent is the middleman—and quite often the man or woman in the middle. In the past 10 years there has been a growing tendency in small-claims courts to rule in favor of the client and not the travel agent, possibly because of the influence of Ralph Nader and consumerism. The agent frequently is considered to be responsible even in cases where it is quite obvious that he could not control the circumstances (i.e., the plane is late and a client missed connections; a steamship line cancels a port stop because of bad weather or political problems on the island; or a tour bus driver gets into trouble with local police and cannot complete the sightseeing tour).

The current trend in the courts leaves the agent even more vulnerable and even more at the mercy of her suppliers. There have been many discussions in government circles on protecting the consumer from fraudulent practices, but how do agents protect themselves? At this time there is no way they can screen a tour operator or wholesaler except through past experience or recommendations from fellow agents. The airlines will lend their support and sponsorship to all manners of tour programs with little more than superficial investigation into the stability or efficiency of the organization concerned. Clients will often select a tour brochure simply because a well-known airline's name is featured on the cover, and the agent is compelled to book a tour with an unknown supplier.

The major complaints against tour operators center on glowing descriptions in the tour folders that cannot possibly be lived up to; delayed or nonexistent transfer services; meals or other special services that are omitted without explanation; pertinent information concerning shopping hours or local holidays not mentioned in the brochure or final itineraries. Other typical complaints are late arrival of vouchers, or vouchers sent with incorrect spelling of the client names and inaccurate dates, hotel substitutions without advance notice, and tour guides who disappear after meeting the clients and leave them at the mercy of bus drivers who can speak only the local language.

Of course, tour operators have complaints too: airlines that do not live up to their promises; hotels that overbook and shift groups to other, often less good, hotels; agents who do not forward the information needed to preregister passengers.

Many of the complaints on both sides are based on poor communication, but it is the agent's responsibility to make sure that the client is informed of all the disadvantages as well as the advantages of any particular tour the client requests. If possible, agents should put all their comments in writing at the time they confirm the reservations so that there can be no misunderstanding as to what is and what is not included in the tour package. Most important, agents must make sure that they have disclosed the name of the tour operator who is providing the service.

Most tour bookings are made by phone, but when payment is sent to the tour operator, it would be advisable to put all agreements and instructions in writing. Too often, tour operators will shrug off their responsibilities by claiming that they were not informed in time of special requests or that the travel agent should have known what to do without being advised by the operator—based on the agent's past experience. This argument does not hold, considering that each booking is different and that each operator follows different procedures. It is in this area where standard terminology and standard procedures would be most helpful to the industry.

Many tour operators and airlines ask their passengers to complete a questionnaire reporting their experiences and the treatment received. This should be carried one step further; agents should also report their opinions and experiences with tour operators. However, at the present time, there is no place where they could register their complaints except, perhaps, to trade publications.

QUESTIONS AND PROBLEMS

1. In what year was the first group tour organized?
2. When did the CAB approve the first airline agreement with travel agents?
3. What were the principal sales made by the early travel agents?
4. Describe the tour operator and his or her duties.
5. List the categories of tour operators.
6. What are the principal duties of the tour guide/escort?
7. Suggest methods for selecting a tour operator.
8. How can travel agents protect themselves against law suits from clients based on their experiences at the destination?
9. Select a destination and put together the components of a group tour.

chapter 11

Hotels and Resorts

OBJECTIVES

When you have finished this chapter you will be able to:

1. Describe the difference between hotels and resorts.
2. Discuss hotel ratings and how they could improve.
3. List the hotel reference books.
4. Determine when to use hotel representatives.
5. Select a hotel for a sales meeting.
6. Describe some new services offered by hotels.
7. Discuss training methods for hotel staff.
8. Suggest methods to improve agent/hotel relations.

Selecting the right hotel or resort for the right person at the right time and place is one of the most important decisions to be made by the agent. Location of the property is the prime factor in almost all requests, whether it is the businessperson who does not want to waste time getting to his or her appointments, vacation travelers who want to "get away from it all," or at the other extreme, the person who wants to go where "all the action is."

It is at this time that agents must exercise their ability to listen carefully and to read between the lines. Although price is often mentioned as the first criterion, it is surprising how often the cost consideration is tossed aside when a client is presented with something that is really appealing. Too many agents book a client in just any hotel rather than sometimes suggesting a more expensive hotel, and sometimes even a less expensive one, more suited to the client's actual needs.

Hotel selection is so important, whether it is for a simple booking for one night or included in a tour. Unfortunately, hotels can be one of the most difficult areas in travel counseling because of the limited number of hotel listings with good, factual material about the hotels, and the lack of hotel ratings that can be depended on for unbiased opinions. Unless agents have personal knowledge of a hotel, they must rely on the claims in the brochure and the hotel rating lists now available. Naturally, each hotel brochure presents the most attractive pictures and the most glowing descriptions. Hotel ratings vary according to the system used and almost every one of 53 countries that do classify their accommodations use a different system.

Resorts far outperform standard hotels in terms of occupancy levels, room rates, and operating profits. In recent years, Americans are confirming that they like their vactions in one-stop packages. They are taking shorter vacations and

Figure 11-2 Jenny Lake Lodge dining room in Wyoming's Grand Teton National Park. Photo courtesy of the Grand Teton Lodge Company.

more vacations. A trend has developed away from the traditional two-week vacation in favor of two or more one-week holidays and/or long-weekend breaks. Discount airfares requiring a Saturday night stayover have had a dramatic effect on the hotel industry. Saturday night was the hotel industry's slowest night of the week in 1975. Now it is the busiest, partly because businesspeople stay over a weekend to qualify for lower fares and partly because weekend vacationers can take advantage of lower rates also offered by car rental companies and hotels.

Most resort brochures give more facts and general information than do most hotel brochures. The resort brochure usually has a map and provides information on how to get there by plane, rail, bus, or private car, and gives the mileage from the major cities in the area. This can be most helpful to both agents and clients, especially since many resort hotels in the United States were built years ago in areas convenient for rail passengers but not for most air routes. Resort brochures will also mention the checkin and checkout times, which are so important in making up a client's itinerary.

Children's rates and children's facilities, appropriate clothing needed, rental rates (if any) for sports equipment, dining room hours, and evening entertainment facilities are the questions most frequently asked by the clients. Unless agents have made personal visits to the resorts or hotels, they are most likely to recommend the ones that have supplied them with the most complete information.

HOTEL RATINGS

A uniform system of rating hotels would benefit the entire travel industry and would simplify the agent's job of selecting a hotel. The traveling public attaches much importance to advance information about the hotel or resort they will visit.

The Association of Official Tourist Offices (AOTO), formerly known as the International Union of Official Travel Organizations (IUOTO), has for many years been recommending the adoption of an international system of classification of hotels. It has drawn up a set of standards that it has been recommending to its member national tourist organizations as a basis for working out official classification systems in their respective countries. National tourist organizations are ordinarily the sole authority in any country empowered to publish official hotel guides for distribution both inside the country and abroad.

During the late 1960s and early 1970s, IUOTO worked on a standard rating plan, and it is encouraging to note that many countries have either adopted the plan or are drawing from it. The following is a draft of the rating plan:

Luxury Class

Luxury class hotels include those of great luxury, comprising arrangements provided for the first class (noted below) and also:

1. Luxurious public rooms; very large hall, reception, and reading rooms
2. A number of apartments with private sitting rooms (suites)
3. Spacious rooms furnished with studied perfection
4. At least 75 of the suites or rooms with completely private bathrooms (bath and shower combined) and 25 percent with washrooms with shower and WC (water closet—toilet)
5. Equipment and general appointment of most modern standards
6. Open-air or indoor swimming pools, according to the climatic conditions

First Class

First-class hotels include those of very great comfort comprising the installations provided for the second class and also:

1. Spacious common rooms
2. Apartments with private sitting room
3. Spacious rooms appointed with high-class furniture of good taste
4. At least 60 percent of the apartments or rooms with completely private bathrooms (bath and shower combined)
5. The remaining 40 percent of the rooms with washrooms with shower and WC
6. Adequate reception service, cashier, doorkeeper, and restaurant facilities

Second Class

Second-class hotels include those of great comfort, comprising the arrangements provided for the third class and also:

1. Reception hall and reading room (the reading room should be separate from the bar and users should not be obliged to buy a drink)
2. Private apartments, if possible
3. Spacious rooms appointed with items of comfort and furniture of high quality
4. At least 25 percent of the rooms with complete private bathrooms (bath and shower combined)
5. At least 75 percent of the rooms with washroom with WC (i.e., washbasin, bidet, toilet)
6. Telephone with outside connection in 50 percent of the rooms
7. High-class general appointments, especially sanitary fixtures
8. Qualified staff

Third Class

Third class hotels include those of good comfort, comprising the arrangements provided for the fourth class and also:

1. A lift (elevator) for three floors
2. Carpets in the common rooms
3. Forty percent of rooms with washrooms with WC (i.e., washbasin, bidet, toilet)
4. All remaining rooms with bidets with running water
5. House switchboard with internal telephone in rooms
6. Telephones with outside connection in some rooms and at least one such telephone per floor
7. A common bathroom or shower for every 10 rooms and at least one per floor
8. Sanitary fittings of high quality
9. Reception service

Fourth Class

Fourth-class hotels include those of average comfort, with at least 10 rooms comprising the following arrangements:

1. Common premises, including a lounge or sitting room available to guests or lobby with necessary appointments
2. Central heating or automatic heating appliance
3. Telephone cabin at the disposal of the guests
4. Bright and well-appointed rooms, which should have a window with either shutters or thick double curtains, fitted with furniture of good quality and carpets or bedside rugs (the latter necessary where the climate permits); complete and modern electrical equipment consisting of three lights with separate switches for the ceiling, bed, and washbasin
5. Hot and cold running water in all rooms, the fixture to be located behind a screen or a semipartition
6. At least 50 percent of the rooms with a bidet with running water
7. Twenty-five percent of the rooms with washrooms made up of fixed installations or private shower (these rooms should be rooms adjoining the bedrooms but quite distinct from them)
8. A common bathroom or shower for 15 rooms in transient hotels; in residential hotels there should be a common bathroom or shower for seven rooms
9. A common WC for five rooms: at least 2 on each floor, one for women and the other for men
10. Sanitary fittings of good quality and in a perfect state
11. Breakfast service in rooms
12. Independent hotel entrance in case the premises include a restaurant and a public house

There are generally 4 to 6 main categories in what may be termed tourist hotels. The categories are designated in three principal ways: letters (class A, B, etc.), figures (1, 2, etc.), and star symbols (*, **, ***). Most U.S. and Canadian hotels and motels would easily be rated as luxury or first-class by the standards above, but ratings on domestic hotels and resorts would be most helpful to travel agents and tour operators in other countries as well as the local travel industry in arranging that individual's or group's "Visit the U.S.A."

THE EVOLUTION OF HOTELS

Once hotels were free. According to Ludy's *Historic Hotels of the World*, centuries before the birth of Christ the inn was nothing more than a plot of ground, staked out near a spring, which was sometimes walled in or had a crude fence built around it. Later, flimsy shelters were built over such camping grounds. Travelers came to use the plot and no payment was expected.

The true inns of antiquity were born out of strange combination of trade, travel, sex, and religion. In ancient times the Greek city states included in their trade treaties the provision that itinerant merchants should be given free accommodations. State inns were built near the large temples, where pilgrims received free room and board. Certain wealthy families in a community were assigned to receive all strangers entering its gates. As time went on they began to exact a specific payment, and an industry was born.

In the middle of the seventeenth century, the stage coach appeared on the roads of England, France, and most of the European continent, and with them came the growth of the coaching inn. As a middle class began to emerge and travel began to expand, these inns served as junction stations, with their own booking offices, waiting rooms, and ticket services for extensive networks of routes.

By the early eighteenth century, inns of considerable size and some luxury began to spring up in France. About this time the word *hotel* replaced *inn* as an indicator of a more luxurious and ostentatious type of lodging house.

With the coming of the railroad early in the nineteenth century, the coaching inns were replaced by the railway hotels. The first major railway hotel was built at Euston Station, London, in 1838. The great international fairs of that time further expanded travel in Europe and brought about a hotel building boom. The Swiss invented the idea of the resort hotel and it became the model for many countries.

Across the Atlantic, meanwhile, inns and hotels were playing their part in the Revolution and the early years of the new republic. The first hotel to be built for that purpose in the United States was the City Hotel, opened in 1794 with 70 rooms on the Bowery, New York City. This was followed by the Tremont House in Boston in 1829 with 170 rooms and rates of $2 a day, including four meals. Its major appeal was that for the first time in this country a guest could rent a single room with private key exclusively for himself and go to bed with the knowledge that he would not be sharing it with strangers before the sun rose. Other hotels and resorts were also built in that era, such as the Parker House in Boston in 1855 and the Waldorf in New York in 1893, and the Statlers and Hiltons began their empires.

But it was the "horseless carriage" in the late 1800s and Ford's Model T, first built in 1908, that, directly and indirectly, helped to open up travel in many countries and continents and, in time, modified the way of life of millions. With the increase in family travel in their own personal cars came the development of motels (motor hotels). Many motels in the United States today are comparable to luxury hotels in other countries. In fact, in many areas in the United States there is no longer much difference between the motel and the hotel. They all cater to the car trade, since even the air traveler quite often checks in with a rented car.

REFERENCE MATERIAL

The *Hotel & Travel Index*, published quarterly by the Reed Travel Group, is the closest to a worldwide hotel directory in one volume that is available to the travel agent. Elwood P. Ingledue, founder of the index and a pioneer in building closer ties between agents and hoteliers, was inducted into the ASTA Travel Hall of Fame on September 26, 1986. In a career spanning half a century, Ingledue innovated many of the basic tools of the trade and concepts that travel agents use today. In 1939, when he published a slim 32-page directory called *Index to the Informant*, the forerunner of today's *Hotel & Travel Index*, the travel industry was just starting. There were 250 agencies in the United States selling mainly steamship tickets.

Elwood's directory listed reputable hotels in 11 western states and paved the way for agents to market hotels. Through the years he published the first assured rates and lobbied hard for hotels to honor agent commissions. In 1947 he included a symbol in the index indicating those hotels that did. In the same year he authored the *Code of Fair Play*, the basic ground rules through which agents and hoteliers work with each other. ASTA adopted the code in 1956, and the American Hotel Association followed suit in 1958. The *Code of Fair Play* is still in existence.

The index is not a complete listing since it includes only the larger and better-known hotels and resorts. It does not provide descriptions or ratings. Its value to the agent is in the information supplied regarding the hotel representatives, city maps that show the hotels' exact locations, and codes indicating whether or not each establishment pays a commission to the agent (and the percentage of commission).

OAG BUSINESS TRAVEL PLANNER guides you through the lodging selection and travel planning process from start to finish. Use the companion publication to the OAG BUSINESS TRAVEL PLANNER, the OAG Desktop Flight Guide - North American Edition, to make flight schedule arrangements.

Unique business travel planning features make the OAG BUSINESS TRAVEL PLANNER the only hotel & travel directory ideally suited for planning business trips within North America.

An all-in-one travel planning source, its largest section covers destinations in the United States (Hawaii is displayed separately), listed alphabetically by city name. Separate sections immediately follow for destinations in the Bahamas, Bermuda, Canada, Caribbean, Hawaii and Mexico. Information for countries in Central and South America precede the individual sections for U.S. Military Installations and Colleges/Universities.

HOTELS

To find a list of available hotels, just turn to your destination city. For convenient usage, hotel entries are presented by location. . . Near Airport, City and, for major business destinations, Suburban.

How To Read A Hotel Listing

OAG BUSINESS TRAVEL PLANNER hotel listings give you everything you need to compare your options and choose accommodations.

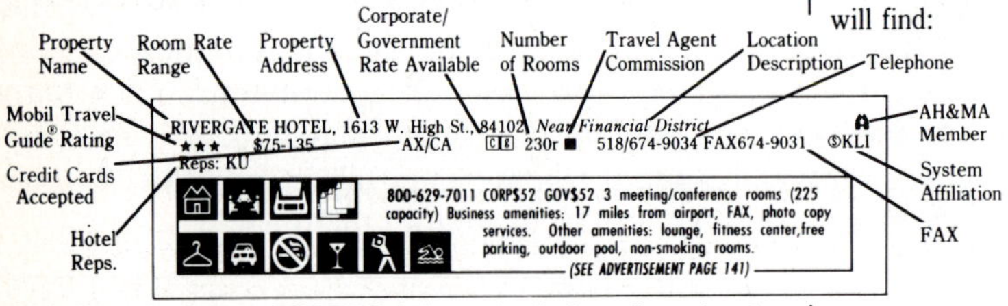

As indicated above, a BIZ BOX follows the listing of any hotel with an advertisement of 1/8 page or more. The BIZ BOX provides additional information regarding the business services and other amenities offered by the hotel.

Refer to page 10 or the inside back cover for a complete decode of symbols and abbreviations. For decoding of hotel systems, representatives and reservation services and toll free numbers for booking reservations, see the Hotel Reservations Directory.

Unless otherwise indicated adjacent to the rate range, rates are based on the European Plan (no meals). Most listings include an approximate room rate range (low single to high double). When a rate range is not supplied, the minimum single, low double or weekly rate will be presented. State and city taxes are **not** included in the listed rates. All rates are displayed in U.S. dollars.

Keep in mind that room rates displayed are for guideline purposes only. Always confirm rates prior to booking reservations.

Up to a maximum of three specific credit card codes may be included in a hotel entry. If a property accepts four of the five credit cards listed on page 10, the remark, *CC:Most* will be displayed; *CC:All* will appear if all five cards are accepted. Please note that additional credit cards may be accepted at many properties.

Only hotels/motels in the 48 contiguous states, certain cities in Canada and cities in Mexico near the U.S./Mexican border are rated by the **Mobil Travel Guide ®**. For properties located within these areas which do not include a MOBIL rating, no adverse criticism is implied or should be inferred. Motels, lodges, motor hotels, hotels, inns, resorts, and guest ranches containing star ratings or NR designators, **copyright © 1991 by Mobil Oil Corporation**, New York, N.Y. For additional information regarding Mobil ratings see page 10.

DESTINATION FACTS

The OAG BUSINESS TRAVEL PLANNER features individual entries for more than 14,500 destinations throughout North America. You will find destination entries for all cities receiving scheduled airline service as well as all cities and towns with a population of 2,000 or more. Also qualifying are resort/ski areas, national parks, military installations and colleges/universities.

Destination information is categorized into three sections, Getting There, Getting Around and City Basics. Depending on the size of the destination, some or all of the following may be included in its listing:

Getting There

AIRPORTS, AIRLINES & CHARTER AIR TAXI
If a city has its own airport(s) and receives scheduled air service, you will find this symbol (✈) adjacent to the city name. Also, you will find:

- airport name(s) and code(s)
- mileage and direction FROM the city TO the airport
- a list of airlines serving the city

For destinations without scheduled air service, you will find a reference to the nearest airport and any additional points of air service nearby, accompanied by the mileage and direction FROM the airport TO the destination.

Charter Air Taxi references, which feature operator name and phone number, may be displayed under any city entry.

Getting Around

CAR RENTAL & AIRPORT GROUND TRANSPORTATION
To help you get from the airport to your destination you will find a full variety of available ground transportation options. If you want to rent a car, references include all major car rental companies operating at/in the vicinity of the airport and in the city. Available airport ground transportation services including travel times, fares and operator names, as well as public transportation alternatives, are also provided.

For your quick reference, a list of airport ground transportation operators with phone numbers, area served and symbols denoting availability of scheduled service is also included. For a decode of symbols, see page 10 or the inside back cover. Operators displayed without a symbol provide non-scheduled service only.

If scheduled airport ground transporation service is available to a destination not receiving airline service, the operator name will immediately follow the mileage reference.

Figure 11-3 "Reprinted by special permission from the (September-November, 1991) *OAG Business Travel Planner*. All rights reserved."

ABOUT THE MOBIL TRAVEL GUIDES® (Cont.)

Ratings are based upon the inspection reports, written evaluations of staff members who stay anonymously at establishments throughout the year, and an extensive review of guest comments received by **Mobil Travel Guide**.

The rating for each establishment — motel, lodge, motor hotel, hotel, inn, resort, guest ranch — is measured against others of the same type. The criteria for rating accommodations are related to the number and quality of facilities, guest services, luxury of appointments and attitude and professionalism of staff and management.

Because each type of establishment is viewed also in terms of its own style, unique characteristics, decor and ambience, these additional qualities are also considered in determining a rating.

The following symbols are used in rating motels, lodges, motor hotels, hotels, inns, resorts and guest ranches:

★	Good, better than average
★★	Very Good
★★★	Excellent
★★★★	Outstanding — worth a special trip
★★★★★	One of the best in the country

A further rating designation exists and that is Unrated. When major changes have occurred during the one-year period prior to publication, there will be no star rating. These changes may be in management, ownership and/or general manager. If an establishment is undergoing major renovation, refurbishment or has been in operation less than one year, it will be unrated. Properties listed in the Business Travel Planner but unrated in the **Mobil Travel Guides** are denoted by the code NR.

Motel, Lodge, Motor Hotel, Hotel, Inn, Resort and Guest Ranch listings containing starred ratings

© Copyright 1991 by **Mobil** Oil Corporation, New York, N.Y.

ABOUT RUNZHEIMER

For over 21 years, Runzheimer International has reported travel expense guidelines in **Runzheimer Meal - Lodging Cost Index.** These surveys of moderate business travel costs assist corporations and governments with a defensible standard for employee reimbursement.

Starting in 1990, Runzheimer provides data from the Index in cooperation with **OAG's Business Travel Planner.**

WHO IS RUNZHEIMER INTERNATIONAL? — Founded in 1933, this international management consulting firm services over 2,000 businesses and government agencies, worldwide. In addition to its Wisconsin headquarters, the company has offices in Chicago and Toronto.

Runzheimer International's business is dedicated to research, analysis, and reporting of business auto, travel and living costs. These unique standard cost reimbursement systems are the basis of over $1 billion in direct reimbursements annually, to employees numbering in the hundreds of thousands.

Runzheimer has been consistently recognized for its expertise in consulting. More than one half of Fortune 500 firms as well as government agencies such as the I.R.S. and G.S.A. are active clients.

HOW ARE COSTS SURVEYED? — Runzheimer International has determined that it is not necessary to price all lodging and restaurant properties in a city in order to create reasonable reimbursement figures. The criteria for inclusion of a property into the database include: "first class" rating, frequented by business travelers, convenient to business centers, and "moderate" costs for the location.

Restaurants designed primarily for take out food or without table service are not included in the survey of business travel expenses.

The actual collection of data is done first-hand and in-house by trained Runzheimer personnel. All data are collected for the sole purpose of determining meal and lodging reimbursements.

HOW IS THE DAILY BUSINESS EXPENSE DETERMINED? — Once data for a location have been collected, Runzheimer selects information from this database representative of moderate business travel costs to this area.

Runzheimer Daily Business Travel Expense represents the average cost of purchasing one night's single occupancy lodging at a standard corporate rate, and the average of three meals: breakfast, lunch, and dinner.

For example, Runzheimer Daily Business Travel Expense for Anytown, USA, is $97. This means that a business traveler on a "moderate budget" would have a 50% probability of spending not more than $97 in Anytown.

WHAT ABOUT TAXES, SEASONALITY, AND FOREIGN EXCHANGE? — Runzheimer Daily Business Travel Expense includes all applicable taxes and service charges for both meals and lodging. A 15% gratuity has been added to meal costs and is included in the daily figure.

Data for locations outside the U.S. are reported in U.S. dollars. The data are collected by Runzheimer International in the local currency and then recalculated with valid exchange rates prior to publishing.

The expense data reflect year-round costs unless otherwise indicated. Those locations which experience seasonal variations in lodging costs are indicated along with appropriate effective dates.

Travel expense data are collected throughout the year and each Runzheimer Daily Business Travel Expense is updated yearly.

HOW DO I USE IT? — Runzheimer Daily Business Travel Expense assists corporations and governments in many ways. Some uses include:

- Budgeting - Determining costs for frequently traveled locations.
- Auditing - Establishing realistic expense guidelines.
- Travel Policy - Creating defensible and uniform guidelines for a variety of locations in a standardized format.

ADDITIONAL INFORMATION — Cost guidelines found in Runzheimer Daily Business Travel Expense are published in **Runzheimer Meal - Lodging Cost Index.** Additional information on lodging, meals, and local ground transportation is researched for over 750 locations, worldwide by Runzheimer International. This information is available in print or electronic media. For additional information, please contact:

Runzheimer International
555 Skokie Blvd., Suite 340
Northbrook, IL 60062
(708) 291-9011

Figure 11-4 "Reprinted by special permission from the (September-November, 1991) *OAG Business Travel Planner.* All rights reserved."

City Basics

For major business destinations, OAG BUSINESS TRAVEL PLANNER gives a wealth of pertinent travel facts including the following:

- Runzheimer Daily Business Travel Expense*
  For information pertaining to this cost, see page 11
- Government Per Diem* - the maximum rate reimbursed to government employees traveling on official business. The rate encompasses lodging, lodging taxes, meal and incidental expenses related to subsistence.
- attractions
- climate chart*
- convention/exhibition facilities, with addresses and phone/fax numbers
- calendar of events
- for additional information. . .; addresses and phone/fax numbers for the Chamber of Commerce, Visitors & Convention Bureaus, etc.*

* Travel facts noted with an * above may also appear for other selected destinations.

MAPS & DIAGRAMS

You'll easily pinpoint important locations with the help of over 200 detailed maps and diagrams. From country, island, metropolitan and area maps to airport diagrams, city center maps and resort area maps, these detailed visuals put everything in perspective for you.

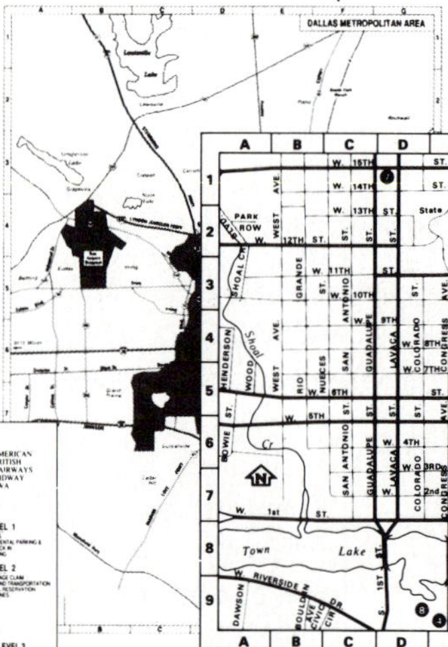

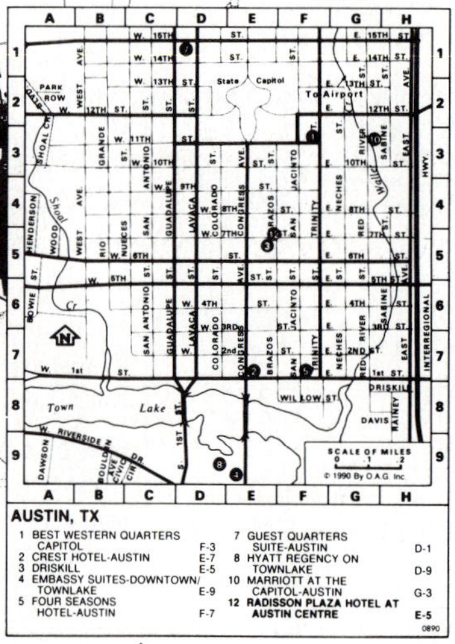

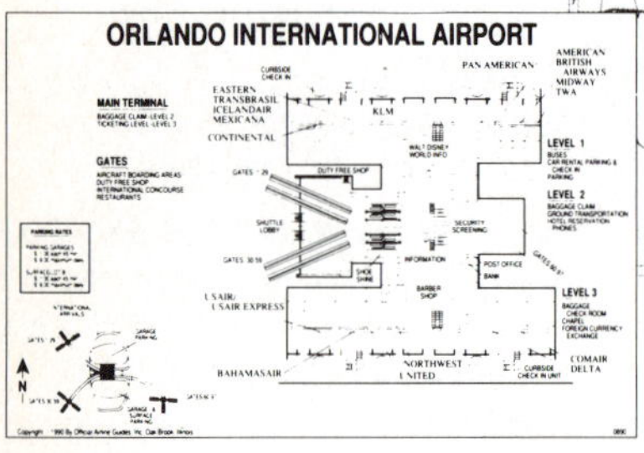

DIRECTORIES

To help you in booking reservations, OAG BUSINESS TRAVEL PLANNER provides a Hotel Reservations Directory and a Dial 800 Directory.

The headquarter office locations and toll free numbers of hotel systems, hotel reps and reservation services referenced within individual hotel entries are featured in the Hotel Reservations Directory.

The Dial 800 Directory features toll-free numbers for 13 categories of other travel related services, including airlines, airport ground transportation operators, car rental companies and charter air taxi operators.

COUNTRY BASICS

"The Basics" are featured for all countries in the Americas. Under "The Basics" heading you will find a variety of country-specific travel details:

- attractions
- climate
- communications
- consulate offices
- currency
- documentary requirements
- electric current
- for additional information (tourist board locations worldwide)
- import allowances (tobacco/liquor)
- languages spoken
- public holidays/calendar of events
- state hotel & motel associations
- taxes (airport departure/arrival)
- time (including banking, business & shopping hours)
- tipping
- U.S. chamber of commerce office locations
- U.S. foreign service office locations

And More. . .

If you're planning a trip outside the United States, refer to General Travel Information Section for an explanation of the various terms featured within Documentary Requirements as well as these travel facts:

- how to obtain a passport
- U.S. customs
- Visa service office locations
- Medical assistance

BUSINESS TRAVEL REPORT

A quarterly newsletter contains items of interest to the business travel planner and individual business traveler.

AMERICAN HOTEL & MOTEL ASSOCIATION

This section provides a description of AH&MA activities, services and publications along with general information about the lodging industry.

FREQUENT FLYER/GUEST PROGRAMS AND AIRLINE CLUBS

The programs include an up-to-date summary of the many features of Frequent Flyer and Frequent Guest programs offered by airlines and hotels listed within the OAG BUSINESS TRAVEL PLANNER.

In addition to membership fees, the Airline Clubs section will provide you with a list of club locations as well as special features. Club locations are also displayed on airport diagrams.

Figure 11-5 "Reprinted by special permission from the (September-November, 1991) *OAG Business Travel Planner*. All rights reserved."

ABBREVIATIONS

AC	Telephone area code	R	Number of rooms
AX	American Express	REPS	Hotel representatives
CA	MasterCard		and reservation services
CC	Credit Cards	RP	Renovated property
DC	Diners Club	S	Number of suites
DS	Discover Card	SR	Scheduled for Mobil
DWB	Double with bath		Travel Guide®
NP	New property		reinspection
NR	Listed in Mobil	VI	Visa
	Travel Guide®,	WK	Weekly
	but not rated		

GENERAL SYMBOLS

AIR INFORMATION

✈ Receives scheduled air service

AIRPORT GROUND TRANSPORTATION INFORMATION

◆ Scheduled service   ◆ Scheduled and non-scheduled service

HOTEL LISTING INFORMATION

Mobil Travel Guide® Ratings

★ Good, better than average
★★ Very good
★★★ Excellent
★★★★ Outstanding-worth a special trip
★★★★★ One of the best in the country

Rate Plans

Ⓐ	American Plan (breakfast, lunch and dinner)	Ⓒ	Continental Plan (light breakfast)
Ⓑ	Full breakfast	Ⓜ	Modified American Plan (breakfast and lunch or dinner)

Commissions Paid to Travel Agents

◄	7% agency commission	►	12% agency commission
▼	8% agency commission	✦	15% agency commission
■	10% agency commission	●	20% agency commission

Other Hotel Listing Symbols

Ⓐ	American Hotel & Motel Association Member	Ⓔ	Government rate
		Ⓟ	Free airport pick-up service provided
Ⓒ	Corporate rate	Ⓢ	System Affiliation

BIZ BOX SYMBOLS — BUSINESS AMENITIES

✈	Near Airport		In-room work area
	City		PC's available
	Suburban		In-room modems
	Resort		Secretarial services
	Beach		Photo copy services
	Casino		Airport pick-up
	Meeting/Conference rooms		Courtesy van
	Business center		Local calls free
	FAX		

BIZ BOX SYMBOLS — OTHER AMENITIES AND FACILITIES

	Room service		Restaurant
	Airport pick-up		Lounge
	Courtesy van		Entertainment
	Concierge		Fitness center
	Valet services		Pool
	Free parking		Indoor pool
	Local calls free		Outdoor pool
	Non-smoking rooms		Golf
	In-room beverage maker		Tennis
	Handicapped facilities		Jogging trail

ABOUT THE MOBIL TRAVEL GUIDES®

The **Mobil Travel Guide** has been rating motels, lodges, motor hotels, hotels, inns, resorts and restaurants since the first edition was published in 1958.

In 1970, Official Airline Guides entered into an agreement with the sponsors of the **Mobil Travel Guide** which enables us to use selected portions of their motel, lodge, motor hotel, hotel, inn, resort and guest ranch information and their Mobil quality ratings.

THE LISTINGS — **Mobil Travel Guide** selects a representative cross section of accommodations which give the traveler a wide range of choice at all levels of luxury, type and price. There is no charge to an establishment for inclusion in the **Mobil Travel Guide**.

Space limitations necessitate the omission of many fine places; however, no adverse criticism is implied or should be inferred.

Neither Prentice Hall nor Mobil Oil Corporation can be held responsible for changes in prices, name, management, or deterioration in services. There is no contractual agreement between management and **Mobil Travel Guide** to guarantee prices or services.

THE RATINGS — The rating categories, ★ through ★★★★★, apply nationally. The principal areas of evaluation are quality of physical structure, furnishings, maintenance, housekeeping and overall service. Climate, historic, cultural and artistic variations representative of regional differences are major factors in each rating.

No rating is ever final, since each is subject to annual review; hence each establishment must continue to earn its rating and has a chance to improve it as well. Every effort is made to assure that ratings are fair and accurate; the designated ratings are published to serve as an aid to travelers and should not be used for any other purpose.

Every establishment listed is inspected by experienced field representatives who submit detailed reports to the editorial offices. From these reports, the editors extract factual information for listings and ascertain that establishments to be recommended are clean, well maintained, well managed and above average.

Figure 11-6   ''Reprinted by special permission from the (September-November, 1991) *OAG Business Travel Planner*. All rights reserved.''

The book contains listings of all hotel/motel systems and management companies throughout the world, as well as individual hotels. Properties are organized geographically and alphabetically by country, state, and city.

All major hotel representatives and reservation services are listed alphabetically by letter code (rep code) as used in the listings. More detailed listings and advertisements are also contained in the book. The detailed listing will show the number of rooms in a hotel, current rates, manager's name, hotel rep's code, credit card acceptance, local phone number, 800 number for reservations, code denoting automated airline reservation system, and symbol for amount of commission paid to agents.

Other important facts in this book are the mention of scheduled flight times (number of hours) to the city (or the nearest airport), mileages from airport to city centers, and daily average temperatures. Airport information and a separate listing of hotels and motels located convenient to airports are also shown. However, it does not provide information on railroad depots, piers, bus stations, or the availability of hotels in these areas. The travel industry is so air oriented that other methods of transportation are being neglected. However, travel agents must know about all methods of travel and are frequently asked for a hotel near these other terminals. In these cases city maps are very useful.

Reed International, a major publisher of travel information in Europe and the Far East, purchased News Corporation's Travel Information Group from Rupert Murdoch in 1989. This acquisition, which includes the *Hotel & Travel Index*, the *Official Hotel & Resort Guide*, *Travel Weekly*, and several other well-known U.S. travel industry publications, as well as Utell International, the hotel reservation and representation firm, makes the British-based firm the leading information and publishing company for the travel industry. The Travel Information Group combined with Reed's existing business, ABC International, became the Reed Travel Group. The *Hotel & Travel Index/ABC International Edition* was added for travel agents working in foreign countries. Features of the enhanced international edition include instructions in four languages on how to use the directory.

The *Hotel & Motel Redbook* is the official directory of the American Hotel and Motel Association (AH&MA). Founded in 1910, AH&MA is the trade association that represents the lodging industry in the United States. As a federation, the AH&MA represents nearly 50 percent of the total rooms in the United States, accounting for close to 85 percent of the $57 billion in total revenues generated by the industry in 1989. Its members include hotels, motels, and resorts in the 50 States, District of Columbia, Puerto Rico, and U.S. Virgin Islands. Approximately 9000 establishments within the United States and approximately 1500 hotels abroad are members of AH&MA.

To qualify for membership, hotels and motels are required to meet the highest standards of hospitality. This serves as a reliable guide to travel agents in selecting a hotel, as only hotels, motels, and resorts that have been accepted as members of the AH&MA can use the AH&MA logo in their advertising.

In the fall of 1987, the OAGs (*Official Airline Guides*) announced the merger of *RedBook* with their *Travel Planners* as a result of a lease agreement with AH&MA. The title of the North American edition was changed with the March–May 1991 issue to *OAG Business Travel Planner, North American Edition* and was greatly expanded. New features include a business travel report, and sections on frequent flyer programs, frequent guest programs, medical assistance, and Runzheimer's daily business travel expense (included under the "city basics" section for major cities).

Hotel/motel listings, when applicable, are broken down into two or three categories: (A) near airport, (B) downtown and other, and (C) suburban (properties located in suburbs within an established radius of the city). The AH&MA symbol identifies all members of the American Hotel & Motel Association. Individual listings may include a cross-reference to a hotel system and/or hotel representative/reservation service toll-free reservation number. It is strongly recommended that when making reservations either through a hotel system, hotel representative, a reservation service, or directly with the individual hotel, rates be agreed upon in advance.

Information in the *OAG Business Travel Planner, North American Edition*, includes the *Mobil Travel Guide* quality ratings. Ratings are based on the inspection reports, written evaluations of staff members who stay anonymously at establishments throughout the year, and an extensive review of guest comments received by *Mobil Travel Guide*.

AH&MA also publishes two other directories that may be useful in the agency's meeting planners department: the *Directory of Hotel & Motel Systems*, a comprehensive annual reference source listing more than 800 hotel/motel chains, management companies, and referral groups; and *Who's Who in the Lodging Industry*, an annual publication with 40,000 key lodging industry executives, consultants, and suppliers.

The *Official Hotel Guide* (*OHG*) (formerly the *OHRG Official Hotel & Resort Guide*) was relaunched in March 1991 by the Reed Travel Group with a new name and new format. The new format replaced the four volumes of four-ring binders with loose-leaf inserts. The *OHG* is now published in a more streamlined, ready-to-use form of three perfect-bound volumes and will be published once a year to replace the five annual updates that had been necessary to keep it current. The first two volumes focus on all 50 states, the Carribean, Mexico, and Central and South America. The third volume contains listings from Europe, the Middle East, Africa, Asia, and the Pacific.

OHG is one of the best sources available for in-depth information (also one of the more expensive). It contains objective evaluations of over 30,000 properties worldwide. Included are detailed property descriptions, full tariff data, complete commission information (including slow-pay and no-pay advice), and hotel reps (with toll-free telephone numbers.) Features include facilities locators that pinpoint recreational activities (golf, tennis, skiing, health spas, dude ranches, marinas, national parks, etc.) for the hotels and resorts in given geographical areas. Comprehensive maps showing all the hotels for a particular area, international telephone codes, and more detailed reservation information provide more data for the users. It also includes editorial commentary on attractions of interest to tourists.

STAR (*Sloane Travel Agency Reports*) Service began as a newsletter in late 1960 and soon converted to an organized reference manual and has become one of the leading primary sources of unbiased, comprehensive hotel information for the travel industry. *STAR* was purchased by ABC International in 1987 and is now called the *STAR Service*.

Major improvements over the years include a periodically revised listing of hotel chains and representatives with their toll-free telephone numbers, addition of a section evaluating cruise ships, and institution of a free personal advisory service for subscribers on hotels not listed.

Reports are submitted by a large staff of hand-picked travel writers and travel agents. Reports are based on firsthand studies of facilities, service, management, cuisine, location, atmosphere, reputation, type of clientele, maintenance quality, and value offered. Reports also provide all necessary technical information: street address, number of rooms and baths, rates, manager's name, commission policy, and North American representatives. Revisions are published every quarter.

Many of the ARC airlines publish their own tour hotel books, that include their package tours, but of course, each airline will feature the destinations that are on their routes.

Pan American Airways and Trans World Airlines publish a virtual library of travel books. Pan Am's *New Horizons World Guide* and the *U.S.A. Guide* are valued reference books for facts on climate, customs, documentary requirements, calendar of holidays, restaurants, and night life as well as hotel recommendations. These books are not only good reference books in the agency, but they may be ordered for resale to the general public, as both Pan Am and TWA will give agents the retailer's discount. Since they are relatively inexpensive, they also make good bon voyage gifts.

The hotel representatives issue lists of the hotels they represent with descriptive material as well as rates. All of the large hotel chains publish directories of their properties. These can be quite useful, especially when a client tells you that he wants only Ramada Inns, for example, throughout his itinerary. It is quicker to check the directory than to look up each city in one of the hotel reference books.

Occasionally, one of the travel trade publications will coduct a survey on hotels or publish hotel ratings from the major cities or resorts around the world. The articles are worth clipping and saving for future use.

Firsthand knowledge is, of course, best in giving an agent more self-confidence and persuasiveness in selling a hotel or resort. Even though their personal rating may not agree with the experts, the fact that they have been there adds to their stature as an expert in travel. Some agents take notes on each hotel visited; others rely on their memory. It is better to put it in writing. The main purpose of travel agents' familiarization tours is to visit the hotels in any given area. After going in and out of a dozen hotels, details become blurred. A checklist should be prepared in advance covering the features that each agent and customer would like to know about. A personal file of this nature would be most helpful in refreshing the agent's memory on the individual hotels that have been inspected or visited.

The tourist or visitor's information boards of individual countries, states, or resort areas (i.e., Caribbean Tourist Board) are also good sources of information on the hotels and resorts in their jurisdiction. These offices will furnish lists of the major hotels and resorts, and many will also publish lists of other accommodations, such as pensions (boarding houses), small inns, bed and breakfast homes, chateaux-hotels, and condominiums. Many of the national tourist offices publish excellent reference books on their countries; Australia, France, Germany, Greece, and South Africa are among those that are really outstanding.

Most of the hotel reference books mentioned here, plus many other selections, can be ordered from the Forsyth Travel Library. Stephen F. Forsyth started this service in 1976 with a whole range of travel-related publications that have interest both within and outside agents' offices. Reference books that are difficult to obtain can be ordered from Forsyth's, such as the *Thomas Cook Timetable* (published in Britain, a comprehensive schedule of British and European Passenger rail and local shipping service), the *ABC Shipping Guide* (also published in Britain), and *Ford's Freighter Travel Guide*. They carry a number of books on country inns, bed and breakfasts, and castle-hotels of Europe. Display models of airplanes and cruise ships are also available from Forsyth's.

HOTEL REPRESENTATIVES

Hotel representation was born in the early 1930s. The late Edith Turner is generally credited with being the first hotel rep, although she did not own her own firm but worked first for the Savoy Company of London and later for a cooperative that eventually became Hotel Representative, Inc. (HRI). Prior to the emergence of representatives, travel agents went to steamship lines for foreign hotel space because many shiplines owned or had a strong financial interest in hotels.

The role of the hotel representative is often confused even in the minds of professionals. Most major hotel representatives regard themselves as management and marketing consultants first and foremost, and booking agents second. They act as an employee of the hotels in generating sales, building good public relations, advising on management problems, and cooperating with local tourist development boards in promoting business to the entire area. They also assist the hotels with direct mailing programs and the solicitation of group business.

Travel agents play a very important part in the success of the hotel rep organization. It has been estimated that agents account for over 80 percent of the individual bookings and a substantial percentage of all group bookings. The hotel representative is also an important ally for the travel agent. Some hotel representatives will refuse to accept accounts that do not pay commissions to agents, and they will assist the agent in collecting late commissions from hotels. Many of the larger hotel representative organizations will send staff personnel to make sales calls on agents and assist them with special bookings.

Although there are dozens of small, one- to three-person operators in the hotel representation field, approximately 15 companies account for the bulk of the sales volume. Utell International (UI) is one of the giants, with 6500 members. HRI—The Leading Hotels of the World (LHW) is one of the largest luxury hotel representative companies. The association of luxury properties was founded in 1928 by a group of marketing-minded European hoteliers. It began with 38 properties. Since then it has grown to 245 members. Among the members are such legendary names as the Oriental in Bangkok, the Mandarin in Hong Kong, and the Hotel Okura in Tokyo (These three are ranked 1, 2, and 3, respectively, in a leading list of the 50 best hotels in the world.)

In an interview with *Travel Agent*, Joe Giacoponello, president of The Leading Hotels of the World, said that many travel agents eager to book clients into the best-known resorts in an area still do not appreciate the fact that these are international resorts, pressured for space from other parts of the world and fill up early. "What we want to do is to familiarize agents more with our alternative destinations and resorts—excellent luxury properties, but ones which may not be as well known to agents as some of our others, and where they may have less trouble finding space."

An excellent sales tool for the agents and the hotels is a descriptive directory that is revised annually. The organization supports agents with an industry depository program to handle its overseas members' commission and to refund payments through the New York office. By accepting the accounts for its hotels, payments are expedited and additional costs resulting from bank currency conversion charges are avoided.

The firm does not solicit new members; hotels must apply. Applications are screened by a committee of hoteliers and properties are then inspected by members of the executive board's admissions. Only an average of 12 applications a year are accepted. The standards are very strict. If the association gets complaints from guests about a particular hotel, the manager is advised and has a period of six months to rectify the problem.

In the past the hotel representative's major efforts were aimed at the individual leisure travel market. This situation is changing. Today, many hotel representatives report that corporate travelers and incentive groups account for as much as 50 percent of their business and this percentage is growing. Over the past decade, corporate and incentive travel have become increasingly important to many of the hotel representation services. Small groups are naturally a good market for resorts in their off-seasons and also for newer city hotels which have the space and the facilities to accommodate this segment of the market. There is, too, a monetary significance in meeting, group, and incentive business: Food and beverage consumption quite frequently provides more revenue than bednight accommodations, since group guests tend to hold their meetings and banquets in the hotel itself.

Representatives are reimbursed in various ways by their principals. They may charge a monthly or annual retainer, a fee based on gross volume of business done by the hotel, or an override on sales booked for a property. Quite often it may be a combination of all three. The usual override consists of half the commission percentage that goes to travel agents (normally, 10 percent).

COMPUTERS IN THE HOTEL INDUSTRY

Automation is helping hotels provide even more personalized services and amenities than it used to. For example, the time-consuming job of maintaining guest history files is now easily managed with the computer. Reservations from around the world can be confirmed in half the time. Agents' records (name, address, phone number) are stored in the computers by their ARC (IATA) ID numbers, which eliminates asking for all this information when an agent calls to make a reservation. Many hotel chains will automatically print the confirmation (in duplicate) and mail it to the agent immediately after the call is completed.

While all the representation firms have geared up electronically, not all expect automated bookings to become the major source of business. Most services are online with the major airline systems and can confirm bookings within seconds, but automation does not totally replace the need for agents to call for a room on a sold-out night or other special service. Personalization will never be totally eliminated, especially in booking the luxury hotels. Enhanced technology, however, will help deal with two perennial problems: collection of commissions and consistency of rates, both in computers and at the hotels themselves, although these problems are not as great with representation services as they are with the chain hotels and independent hotels. Contractual obligations require all members of a service to pay commissions and hold to rates provided to the central reservation system.

Commissions to travel agents are paid much more promptly than they ever have been. In fact, some hotel chains boast that the agent's commision check is in the mail as soon as the guest checks out, thanks to their computer system. Also thanks to computers, many hotels are installing self-service computer terminals for express checkin and checkout service. All that is required is a reservation and a credit card. Computerized records are also enabling hotels to establish their own "frequent traveler" clubs, where members earn credits or, sometimes, cash for merchandise or free or discounted trips in cooperation with an airline mileage plan.

MAKING THE RESERVATION

The most important items of information needed for a hotel request are the number of *nights* required and the *dates* of arrival and departure. Next in importance are the *time* of arrival and *method of transportation* (air, rail, bus, or private car). Names in full, ages of children (if any), the number of people in the party, and the type of room requested (single, double, twin, triple, family, etc.) complete the information needed.

Special instructions should also be noted, such as adjoining rooms—first floor only—poolside, and so on. The hotels want to know if the client wants a non-smokers' room, a nonallergenic foam pillow, or extra towels. The hotels also need to know the business traveler's company name, address, telephone number, and title in order to give appropriate recognition to a VIP client. This also enables the hotel to extend their corporate rates to clients.

Hotels charge by the number of nights the guest will be occupying the room, although most advertisements and brochures on package plans stress the number of days—"eight days, seven nights." This invariably brings on questions and complaints if the clients are arriving late afternoon or evening, especially if they are paying for meals. The solution to this particular problem is to request room only for the first night and the meal plan for the remaining nights.

Hotel reservation records are filed according to date of arrival. Changes or cancellations must always show this date. It is only after guests have departed that their registration card is filed alphabetically in the hotel's guest history.

The time of arrival is important to the hotel reservationist in deciding on the room to be assigned to the guests. The hotel day starts at 6:00 A.M.; however, occupancy of rooms by arriving guests may not be possible until after the established checkout time. Most hotels' checkout time is 12 noon or 1:00 P.M. If the room is required beyond the hotel's posted checkout time, the hotel management must approve it. During slack periods most hotels are lenient about enforcing the checkout rule, but if the lobby is filled with new arrivals, they will not hesitate to speed a departing guest.

If clients have made late afternoon or evening reservations for their departure and do not wish to spend the waiting time at the airport, they can ask the porter or head bellman to store their bags until they are ready to leave. Most hotels and resorts will accommodate the guests, usually for a small fee per bag. Depending on availability, hotels will also provide a *hospitality room* for groups who arrive early in the morning and need a room to use for freshening up until their rooms are ready. They will also provide the hospitality room for groups who must check out early but have several hours to wait for their departing flight. Often, the room will be charged to the group on a day rate, or it may be gratis, depending on the availability and the size of the group.

The ages of the children are important in determining the rate to be charged. Many hotels and resorts will permit children under 12 (some hotels use the age limit of 18), to occupy the same room with their parents at no extra charge or will provide an adjoining room at no extra charge. (Meal plans, of course, are charged separately, but there is usually a discount for children.) Bassinets or cribs must be ordered for infants and cots for the older children.

GLOSSARY OF HOTEL/MOTEL TERMS

The use of the correct terminology when requesting rooms is very important. From the "Glossary of Hotel/Motel Terms" prepared by the Hotel Sales Management Association, the following terms should be used:

Adjoining Rooms: Two or more rooms side by side without a connecting door between them. In other words, rooms can be adjoining without being connected.

Cabana: A room adjacent to pool area, with or without sleeping facilities, usually separate from the hotel's main building.

Connecting Rooms: Two or more rooms with private connecting doors permitting access between rooms without going into the corridor.

Double: A room with one large bed for two persons. (More and more hotels are now using double beds in every room.)

Duplex: A two-story suite (parlor and bedroom) connected by a stairway.

Efficiency: An accommodation containing some type of kitchen facility.

Hospitality: A room used for entertaining (cocktail party, etc.).

Hospitality Suite: A parlor with connecting bedrooms to be used for entertaining.

Junior Suite: A large room with a partition separating the bedroom furnishings from the sitting area.

Lanai: A room overlooking water or a garden with a balcony or patio. (Resort hotels primarily.)

Parlor: A living or sitting room not used as a bedroom. (Called a salon in some parts of Europe.)

Resort Hotels: A hotel with recreational facilities such as swimming pools, tennis courts, golf course on the premises or nearby, one or more restaurants, a private beach or access to one, nightclubs or bars with entertainment and dancing, and other activities geared especially for the enjoyment of the guests.

Sample: A display room for showing merchandise, with or without sleeping facilities.

Service Charges/Gratuities (Tips): Amount added to your bill, usually 15 percent, to cover the tips to the hotel personnel.

Single: A room to be occupied by one person.

Studio: A one-room parlor setup having one or two couches that convert to a bed, or a bed that folds up against the wall. (Sometimes called an executive room.)

Suite: A parlor connected to one or more bedrooms. When requesting a suite, always designate the number of bedrooms needed.

Tourist Hotels: This classification, used most often for international hotels, simply means that amenities are scarce, rates are therefore lower, and the hotel is usually located in a undesirable area for most vacation travelers.

Twin: A room with two single beds for two persons. (Beds can be adjoining with one common headboard.)

Twin Double: A room with two double beds for two, three, or four persons; sometimes called a family room or double-double. (Also called a quad room.)

Rollaway beds are available in most hotels at a nominal charge (added to the room rate). They can be installed in bedrooms or parlors for extra persons occupying the room. Unless it is a family with several small children, few hotels can accommodate more than four in a room. In fact, many hotels in resort areas will limit occupancy to no more than three in a room.

To prevent misunderstanding with both the clients and the reservation desk, it is important to specify in detail the requirements needed. For example, if a couple asks for a hotel room, find out in advance if they prefer a double bed or twin beds. The request should then be worded: I need one room for two people with one bed for one night.

Specific location requirements can be made at the time the reservation is made; however, the clients must be advised that not even the hotel can guarantee that the requests will be honored; it all depends on the availability of rooms at the time of check-in. The clients should be advised that they have the right to ask for a change if they find the room to be completely unsuitable. If the desk clerk is uncooperative, they should ask for the sales manager. Every hotel sales office also handles public relations, and that is the office most interested in maintaining the goodwill of the guests.

MEAL PLANS

AP (American Plan):   The rate includes three full meals and room. Also known as full board or full pension.

B and B (Bed and Breakfast):   A privately owned home that offers rooms for rent and will include a breakfast in the rate. Very popular in Great Britain and now available in most states in the United States. Also known as pensions.

CP (Continental Plan):   The rate includes breakfast and room. In most countries the continental breakfast consists only of coffee, tea, or chocolate and toast or roll.

EP (European Plan):   No meals included in the room rate.

MAP (Modified American Plan):   The rate includes breakfast, dinner, and room. Also referred to as half-board or demipension.

HOTEL RESERVATION FORMS AND PROCEDURES

The hotel request for either foreign independent itineraries or group tours should be in writing, either by letter or by a preprinted reservation form and sent as far in advance as possible. For individual domestic hotel reservations, the telephone is the quickest and most efficient method of making the request. The most commonly used forms are those that can be ordered from Willow Press. Some agents have devised their own hotel request form and have it printed locally.

These forms are usually in three parts (Willow Press also prints them in five parts). The original and duplicate copy are sent to the hotel. The hotel will then return the duplicate with either their confirmation or refusal. The triplicate is the file copy, usually placed in the client's file. There may be some value to the fourth or fifth copies where clients are leaving before confirmation is received and they are given a copy of the request to present to the hotel. Extra copies may be placed in the commissions due file or used for bookkeeping purposes.

When agents do not use the preprinted hotel request forms, the preprinted reservation form included with the rate sheet from the hotel should be used rather than a short note or postal card. In fact, using the hotel's reservation form, when available, is recommended over all others. Mail sorters in each hotel are constantly on the lookout for their own reservation cards, which are immediately turned over to the reservation manager. Quite often, a postal card or agent's letter will be put aside and not be acted upon until the second or third request.

To summarize, the procedure usually followed in making the hotel or resort reservation is as follows:

1. Select the hotel, either from personal knowledge or from the reference books and manuals previously mentioned, or the client's specific request.
2. If the clients are flying to their destination, check brochures for a package

rate and book the package either through the airline or directly with the tour operator. If the hotel or resort preferred is not included in the tour brochures, or the client objects to the package, then

3. Check the reference books or hotel directories for a toll-free phone number for the hotel or for the hotel representative that has that account.

4. If none of these are available, call the hotel direct. Most hotels will accept collect calls for reservations. If time is limited and the hotel refuses to accept a collect call and the commission on the booking is not worth the effort, ask the client if he is willing to pay for the call. If the answer is yes, the simplest method of handling the charge is to ask the operator to charge the call to the client's home or business phone number (with the client's permission, of course).

5. If time permits, put the request in writing directly to the hotel. Allow two or three weeks for a reply from an international location.

6. When the confirmation is received, collect and forward the deposits required. Although some hotels do not ask for a deposit, it is in the best interest of the client and the agency to forward at least one night's payment. Clients are then protected in the event of a late arrival. Commissions are not usually deducted from a deposit unless the deposit is also the full payment.

Occasionally, a hotel will ask for a *guarantee* in lieu of a deposit. A guarantee is a promise to pay for the room whether or not it is occupied. Clients must be made fully aware of this and cautioned to make changes or cancellations as far in advance as possible. Guarantees should always be made in the client's name; otherwise, he will not be as conscientious about the cancellation if he thinks the agency will be held responsible. Most hotels will now guarantee rooms upon receiving a guest's credit card number.

Impress on the client the importance of advance notice in the event of a delayed arrival or cancellation. Where deposits or guarantees have been given, the hotel will hold the room for late arrivals; otherwise, they usually hold them until 6:00 P.M. (4:00 P.M. at resorts). In the event of no-shows, hotels have the right to withhold a desposit refund or charge a cancellation fee since they lost revenue for the room that night.

GROUP RESERVATIONS

Group reservations (10 or more) must be made through the group desk of the hotel chain, hotel representative, or the individual hotel. In many cases, the initial request can be made by phone, but it should be followed up with a written request confirming the details arranged by phone in order to avoid any confusion or misunderstandings that may arise later. Note the date, time of day, and the name of person who took the call. Unless hotel management issues a formal contract, add a paragraph to your letter stating: "Unless we hear from you to the contrary within 10 days, this will constitute our agreement on the above requests and rates."

The contract or confirming letter from the hotel should specify dates and number of nights; the number of doubles and singles being held; rates per night; whether the rates quoted are gross (commissionable) or net (noncommissionable) group rates; taxes; service charges to cover gratuities; policy on accrued complimentaries; and any special service included, such as meeting rooms or welcome drinks.

The hotel should also specify dates that must be observed: the dates when deposits and final payments are due, the last date the tour may be cancelled without penalty, the date when you must reduce booked space or risk paying a penalty, and the date by which final names must be submitted. These dates must be strictly observed to avoid losing the space.

If the guests' names are known at the time of request, a rooming list (list of prospective guests in the order in which they will share rooms) should accompany the letter; otherwise, the rooming list should be sent at least two weeks before the group arrives. The information needed for individual bookings is even more important when booking a group. Special instructions should be spelled out in detail and the hotel should be advised of the name of the group (if any) and the type of group (i.e., social organization, business conference, convention, etc.).

The hotel should also be advised in advance if there will be a required registration room, meeting room, or other special facility. Menus must be decided upon for special luncheons, dinners, or banquets. If exhibits will be displayed, the hotel must know how many, how they will arrive, what equipment is needed (tables, chairs, visual/audio equipment, electrical current, etc.), and whether a watchman will be needed when the exhibits will be unattended.

Group rates are usually quoted at the net price (does not include provision for the agent's commision). The agent adds on his markup. A deposit is required at the time of confirmation from the hotel. Some hotels will bill agents after the guests depart, but the majority require full payment in advance. Care must be taken to maintain the status quo after the payment has been sent. Cancellations or changes must be forwarded to the hotel immediately. The group must be advised that rates are charged according to the number of people occupying the room. If four people in a room decide that it is too crowded and request two double rooms, the rate will go up for each person; or if there is a last-minute cancellation and a double becomes a single, there will also be an increase in rate. The group must also be told that each person must pay for personal charges, such as room service or phone calls, at the time of checkout.

If the group is not escorted by a member of the travel agent's staff, it would be advisable to select a member of the group to act as liaison between the hotel management and the group members. It should be this person's responsibility to check the rooming list with the registration desk and note the group's room numbers. At the time of departure, this list should be checked with the cashier to make sure that individual charges have been collected from each person, and a personal inspection of each room should be made to be sure that no personal belongings have been left behind.

In recent years, hotels have started adding a baggage handling charge for groups, paid in advance. In theory, this is a good idea. It eliminates some of the confusion upon arrival and departure. However, there have been many occasions where the bellhops still insist on their tips—claiming that the hotel management does not pay them. In the event that a special meal or banquet is paid in advance, the catering department will also add in 15 percent for tips, plus the local tax.

NEW SERVICES

Competition for the business traveler is stimulating hotels into new and creative ideas to attract a larger share of this market. Major hotels around the world have outfitted themselves with executive business centers where guests have ready access to fax, telex, copy machines, and secretarial services. They usually have staff members available to assist in making appointments, deal with language difficulties, and help with other problems. Many hotels are offering special services as standards, such as guaranteed reservations, express check-in, video checkout, VCRs in the room, telephone jacks for personal computers, and complimentary newspapers and coffee delivered to wake-up calls.

AT&T introduced an interpreter service called the *Language Hospitality Plan* in 1991 for hotels and motels nationwide. The service brings an interpreter on the phone to help hotel staff with non-English-speaking guests with such services as check-in, reservations, and room service. Guests can call a toll-free number from their rooms for their interpretation needs, paying by credit card. AT&T is providing the service through its own Language Line Services, which provide a range of 24-hour interpretation and translation facilities in more than 140 languages. Calls made by guests to Language Line Services are commissionable to hotels.

Eight-panel Point Talk Translators will be placed in guests' rooms. The cards explain the Language Line services and have lists translating commonly used words and requests by guests from English into Spanish, Japanese, Italian, German, and French. Travel agents can purchase these cards in volume to give to clients going overseas. The cards can be custom designed to include agency logos.

Another growing trend is the *all-suite hotel*. Geared originally for business-people who prefer the comfort and convenience of entertaining people in a sitting room separate from the bedroom, these properties also attract families in the summer months and weekend vacation travelers. One of the pioneers in the all-suite market is the Guest Quarters, based in Washington, D.C. They now have nine all-suite properties and are planning on adding three more in the near future. A typical Guest Quarters suite is roughly double the size of a regular hotel room and includes a living room, dining area, separate bedroom, and fully equipped kitchen.

All of the Guest Quarters properties feature a special suite service in which hotel staff will not only deliver the meal, but set the dining table (with real china) and lay out the meal. There's also a grocery service, in which attendants shop for, deliver, and put away grocery orders in the kitchen.

After seeing the success of the all-suite properties, many traditional middle-market and economy chains are getting into the act. Holiday Inns has its Embassy Suites, and Quality Inns and Marriott have started on the same type of promotion. Pickett Hotel Co. develops and manages hotels offering only suites. It was selected the leading all-suites hotel company in 1988 by *Business Travel News* magazine. Pickett began in 1983 and has since opened 12 Pickett Suite resorts, hotels, and inns east of the Mississippi. He hopes to add 30 more by 1992, mainly by acquiring old hotels and improving them. In 1989, the surprise winner in the first-place category was the three-property Pointe Resorts chain, which was included in the suite segment for the first time.

Women travelers are also receiving special attention. An "amenities basket" in the bathroom containing shampoo, cosmetics, shower cap, and sewing kit is becoming standard practice in many first-class hotels. Full-length mirrors and skirt hangers in the closets, good lighting, and a large mirror with several electrical outlets in the bathroom for hair dryers and other appliances, and even a telephone and a speaker in the bathroom, are now provided. Many hotels also make sure that their female guests are placed in rooms near the elevators and in well-lit corridors to ensure their personal security. Most women business travelers prefer meals in their room or in the hotel dining room. Hotel employees are trained to provide equal facilities for the solo women diner as for male guests. The Embassy Row Hotel in Washington D.C. created an *ambassador's table* in its Lucie Restaurant, modeled after the captain's table on cruise ships. Individual guests may join the hotel's social staff and other unaccompanied diners.

In many major cities around the United States, hotels are creating special floors that provide extra security and *concierge service*. The concierge will make dinner reservations, obtain theater tickets, send out the laundry, and take messages for guests. The floor will usually have a private room that serves continental breakfasts in the morning and drinks throughout the day; spas or saunas and other fitness facilities may also be included.

However, a survey in February 1988 conducted by the new Royce Carlin Hotel–Huntington (New York) of 210 Long Island business executives revealed that the concierge service is seldom used. Business people rarely or never need secretarial help while staying at a hotel. As for amenities, 24-hour room service was in first place; second in importance was a selection of pay TV movies.

These opinions were confirmed by the Swissotel Advisory Council in March 1991. Turn-down service was given low value, especially if the maid comes at a late hour; no in-room safes, but minibars in the rooms are a must; irons and ironing boards as well as hair dryers that are not attached to the wall are appreciated. As a result of business traveler's growing annoyance with hotel dress codes, the board also agreed on the importance of a relaxed dress code throughout the hotels, including fine dining areas.

Stale-smelling rooms top the pet peeve list of business travelers. Nonsmokers can now request rooms that have been set aside especially for them so they will not be bothered by odors left over from smokers. Many hotels are increasing the number of nonsmoking rooms from 10 percent to 25 percent. Inefficient and unfriendly front desk personnel was the second biggest complaint, and late or missed wake-up calls the third.

One of the biggest headaches of business travel—the expensive credit card phone call—may soon be a problem of the past, thanks to efforts being made by AT&T, the Federal Communications Commission (FCC), and Congress. Most calls are made through *alternative operator service* (AOS) firms that lease phone lines from AT&T and pay commissions to the hotels and airports on the calls made from their premises. In some instances, AOS rates have been four times higher than those of AT&T, but because many firms do not identify themselves, the business traveler never learns about the high cost until the phone bill arrives.

Much of that is changing now that AT&T and MCI have signed exclusive agreements with most of the leading hotel chains to provide direct access to their respective systems from hotel systems. In the meantime, Congress is working on a bill that requires AOS firms to identify themselves on the line so that travelers know that they are not using AT&T and prohibits charges for incomplete, unanswered calls. Travelers will have to be told by the hotel that they have the right to use any long-distance carrier they choose, and they will be given the phone number of the FCC's consumer affairs office. If after six years the FCC does not see improvements in the way that hotels and AOS firms handle calls, it will be obligated to regulate the industry.

AGENT/HOTEL RELATIONSHIPS

The basis of good agent/hotel relationships lies in good communication and in understanding each other's problems. It is the agent's responsibility to forward exact details on each booking, and it is the hotel's responsibility to keep the agent informed on current or proposed developments that may affect the decision regarding the hotel selection. It is also the hotel's responsibility to honor confirmed reservations made through the travel agent.

High on the list of improvements that could be made to improve agent/hotel relations are the need for accurate information on rates, facilities, and services, prompt response to inquiries, and professional courteous treatment by all hotel personnel. The Persian Gulf war and the recession in 1990–1991 increased awareness in the hotel industry of the importance of the travel agent industry.

The agent's major complaints about the hotels are:

1. Refusal to honor a reservation made by the agent, and worse, the desk clerk will advise the clients to book their rooms directly with the hotel in the future and bypass the agent.
2. Refusal of the agent's request for rooms but will offer the room to the client who calls direct.
3. Overbooking—this is a problem not only with hotels, but also with airlines, steamship lines, and tour operators. They will take a calculated risk in overselling their space, as they know from past experience that a certain percentage of reservations will cancel out; however, there are times when the expected cancellations do not materialize and the client is embarrassed and inconvenienced.
4. Hotels that announce they pay commissions, yet require one or more reminders to send payment.

Most of these complaints are based on the fact that the agent is made to appear incompetent and unreliable by the hotel management and staff. Undermining the agent with his client does not always benefit the hotel. Most of the agent's clients are loyal and will personally boycott the hotel that attempts to pass the blame to the agent when there are no rooms available even though the client holds a confirmed reservation. Relations between the hotel, agent, and the client would improve considerably if the hotel staff were trained to regard agents as the hotel's outside salespeople, which is what they really are. These salespeople are extensions of hotel sales departments and they get paid only when the hotel gets paid by the clients. Agent's clients should be treated with the same respect and consideration as the guests who book their reservations independently. Improvements have been made in this respect in the past few years, especially with chain hotels, but there is still room for improvements.

It is understandable that the hotel will reserve a few rooms during the busy season to accommodate VIPs and regular guests that are not made available to the travel agent, and it is possible that the client will call the hotel just as they received a cancellation and are now able to accept the request that was originally refused to the agent. But these facts should be explained to both the agents and their clients to prevent loss of respect and goodwill between agents and clients. Protecting an agent's image should be just as important as preserving the hotel's image.

It is also understandable that the hotels, notably Carribean resort hotels, are reluctant to pay commissions to agents for bookings during the busy seasons when there is no problem in filling their rooms. But on the other hand, hotels that cooperate with the agent when she is in desperate need of accommodations for her clients will be the hotel that would receive first consideration during the off-seasons. It has been estimated that travel agents generate as much as 98 percent of the business booked at some of the major resort hotels in America. Louis Harris studies of the travel industry for *Travel Weekly*, held every two years, show that travel agents are constantly increasing their hotel bookings.

The increase maintains a steady progression in the volume of agents' hotel bookings since the first study was conducted in 1970. Since that year, hotel bookings by agents have increased sevenfold. Yet hotel commissions lag behind cruise commissions and barely outstrip the car rental industry as a source of agency revenues. Hoteliers have stepped up their efforts to increase their share of agency business. Programs such as centralized commission payment plans, travel agent guarantees, and preferential treatment for clients who book hotels through agents have been installed by many hotel chains. Large chains are more apt to developing market strategies aimed toward agents, and resort properties are much more dependent on agent bookings than are city-center hotels.

"What is the quality of service at the hotel?" is a question the clients are constantly asking. It is not unusual to find clients returning to the same resort year after year simply because the management and staff are friendly and cooperative even though the premises are lacking the more modern conveniences of newer resorts.

One of the major problems of hoteliers in maintaining good service is the lack of experienced personnel. The rush to build more and bigger hotels to accommodate the increasing number of travelers is going on all over the world, which has resulted in a shortage of trained people to service the hotels. Although there are many fine hotel management schools in Europe and new courses are given in colleges in the United States, the shortage of trained staff will probably affect the hotel industry for a number of years before the supply equals the demand.

Hotel chains across the United States are trying to find ways to improve employees' awareness of the importance to provide better service to guests. Surveys have revealed that the leading complaint received from guests concerns unfriendly, poor service.

The Sonesta International Hotel Corp. has installed a program called Sonesta's Personal Service Employees' Training Program. The program was designed as a board game complete with play money and championship competition among Sonesta properties, with prizes for the best teams. Employees are given hypothetical questions and scenarios to solve. The game has been so successful that the American Hotel & Motel Association is examining the possibility of adopting it.

Other chains are spending more money on internal training programs and also spending more on customer research. Hilton Hotels are now providing multilingual staff members to assist international travelers. Hotel managers are beginning to realize that a return to ways of the old-fashioned innkeeper who was just as concerned about the comfort of his guests as with the profits of the house may be the way to go.

Students at the well-known Cornell University School of Hotel Administration expressed their concerns for the hospitality industry at a lecture series held during 1990. Globalization and how it will affect the hotel industry topped the list of concerns. They agreed that there will be a greater need for multilingual hotel staff to service the global market, which is fast developing, and that this will mean a greater need for service-oriented staff. Environmental concerns and an expected increase in health awareness is expected to lead to new hotel designs, and hotels will also be looking for more unique locations to develop.

The Council on Hotel, Restaurant and Institutional Education (CHRIE) is encouraging travel and tourism schools with hospitality and/or hotel management programs to join their organization. CHRIE was founded in 1946 by educators and industry executives for the purpose of "improving the quality of hospitality education." There are two primary categories of membership in CHRIE: individual and institutional/corporate/organization. CHRIE provides a wide range of member services designed to accomplish the organization's goal. CHRIE's annual conference is the most important event of the year for hospitality and tourism educators. Educators and industry professionals meet for seminars, panel discussions, paper presentations, general sessions, and social functions. Nonmembers may attend at a slightly increased rate.

THE COMMISSION QUESTION

Generally speaking, most hoteliers value the agent's business, but there is some feeling that not all travel agents are worth the 10 percent commission paid for each booking. There may be some merit to this feeling when an agent does no more than pick up a phone and place an order for a room. Yet the agent may have put in a number of hours with that client before he picks up the phone. The agent who truly earns his commissions aggressively promotes and sells not only the established hotels, but also the newer properties that need the support the most during their first season.

Commission policies are the major bone of contention between travel agents and the lodging industry. The most common complaint in recent years is that hotels do not pay commission on all rates. Most hotels say that they pay commission only on published rates (*rack rates*). However, these generally are the highest room rates, usually charged to the "walk-in" customer, and most hotels sell less than 15 percent of their rooms at that rate. Many hotels refuse to pay commission on discounted rates and will refuse commission on rooms sold by agents during peak seasons. Also, very few hotels will pay agent's commission on overstays (when the client stays longer than originally scheduled). Hotel guides fail to note exceptions to hotel policy regarding commission. Agents should inquire about commission policies at the time of booking and note the information and the name of the person who provided it.

Quite often the agent will book clients in a hotel whose policy forbids paying commissions to travel agents. The agent knows in advance that she will not earn any income for the time and effort in securing this reservation but wants to preserve the client's goodwill and future business. However, where the hotel promises to pay commissions and either fails to pay at all or requires several time-consuming reminders, it is definitely a breach of contract and damages the hotel/agent relationship. Unless the commission due was a sizable amount and the agent belonged to an agent association, she usually had no recourse except to forget about it and place the hotel on her personal blacklist and pass the warning to fellow agents. *Travel Trade*'s involvement in assisting agents to collect overdue hotel commissions has made a big difference in the battle to bypass travel agents. Agents use their standard operating procedure (S.O.P.) letter and have received tremendous results. Not only are agents receiving overdue commissions, but hotels are making internal policy adjustments that more equitably compensate agents for their efforts and assure prompt commission payment on future bookings.

COMPLIMENTARY ROOMS

One of the fringe benefits of travel agency employment often used to lure new employees into the business is the complimentary or reduced-rate accommodation offered by hotels to travel agents and their employees. Too many agents forget that these privileges, just as the commission, should be earned and not just taken for granted or exploited for the benefit of friends and relatives.

The original intent of offering complimentary rooms was to encourage agents to make a personal visit and inspection of the property. Personal knowledge is a tremendous aid in selecting the right hotel for the client. It is difficult to recommend a hotel unless the agent has made a personal visit to the property. Other than personal inspections, the agent must depend on returning clients to advise them of current conditions.

Organized familiarization tours, jointly sponsored by the airlines and hotels in a given area, are one of the best methods of becoming acquainted with all the hotels and sightseeing attractions in that area. Agents are given the opportunity to meet the management and staff at each hotel as well as making a personal inspection of a sample room in each price category that the hotel has available.

Many agents will request complimentary accommodations at the finest hotels for themselves and their families and then return home and sell a competing hotel to their clients, usually because of the price factor. It only stands to reason that if agents accept the hospitality of a hotel or resort, they should do their utmost to promote and sell that property to their clients. However, if their clientele are interested only in the low or moderately priced establishments, they should confine their visits to those they can honestly recommend to their customers. Agents should confine their requests for free or discounted rooms to a minimum and for business purposes only. Like the agent, hotels are in operation to make money. Very few agents will pay for a free trip for one of the clients unless it is for a tour organizer who has brought in group business; and then, 9 times out of 10, the agent will ask the hotels to provide the accommodations.

There is also this thought to consider: Agents can give a more completely unbiased recommendation to their clients when they are not obligated to the hotels that have provided them with free or reduced rate rooms for their personal use.

QUESTIONS AND PROBLEMS

1. What are clients usually most interested in when requesting a hotel?
2. How would you determine which hotel is the best selection for a client?
3. What were the important factors that brought about changes in the hotel industry?
4. Which reference book would you use to find a hotel for someone who is driving to his destination and needs only a hotel along the way?
5. Describe the duties of a hotel representative.
6. Make up a sample hotel request listing in order of importance of the information needed by the hotel.
7. What are the usual hotel checkout and checkin times?
8. Describe the food plans available at hotels and resorts.
9. How would you make a reservation for a group of 10 or more?
10. What are agents' complaints with hotels?
11. Can you suggest any ways of improving agent/hotel relationships?
12. How can the agency increase the hotel bookings?

chapter 12

Motorcoach Travel

OBJECTIVES

When you have finished with this chapter you should be able to:

1. Tell the difference between ground arrangements and transfers.
2. Describe meeting services and when they would be used.
3. Discuss when a sightseeing trip differs from a package tour.
4. Compare motorcoach tours in America with those in Europe.
5. Make the arrangements for a group motorcoach tour.

There are many terms in the travel agency's glossary which are confusing and often misunderstood by the new traveler. Ground and/or land arrangements (services performed on the ground as compared to air or sea) is one, and transfers is another.

In the travel industry, *transfer* simply means the transportation of the traveler from one place to another by taxi, limousine, motorcoach, or private car. Transfers are usually performed between airports (or other terminals—bus, rail, or pier) and the hotel and return. Transfers are also used to transport individuals or groups of travelers from their hotel to a specific attraction or performance (i.e., the theater, opera, or a sports event).

Sightseeing stops are not included in the straight transfer, although there may be occasions when the two can be combined. For example, most tours to the "Big Island of Hawaii" will include stopovers at both the Kona Coast and Hilo, and since many of the scenic attractions lie between the two coasts, it is more advantageous and expedient to include sightseeing stops with the transfer from the Kona hotel to the Hilo hotel. There may also be occasions when groups have extra time between checkout and departure to include a sightseeing stop along the way to the airport.

Meeting services are provided for travelers visiting a foreign country to assist them with baggage handling and in going through customs or, as in Hawaii where the *lei greeting* has proved so popular, simply to greet the arrivals and welcome them to the city.

Transfers and meeting services are vital parts of a group tour or FIT. Veteran, independent travelers may omit the request for meeting services, but they too recognize the usefulness of prepaid transfers unless they are being met by personal friends or business associates at their destination. These are services usually provided by the tour operator, depending on the cost of the tour. The low-cost, budget, or do-it-yourself type of tour may omit the transfers entirely or supply only the transfer from the city air terminal to the hotel, in which case passengers use airport buses to get to the city terminals. The higher-priced, luxury tours will provide the transfer direct from airports to the hotel. Again, the conveyance will vary depending on the cost of the tour. The lower-priced tours will use buses and the higher-priced tours will use limousines or private cars.

When the agent is assembling her own group tour, transfer services may be contracted directly with local suppliers. For international travel, names and addresses may be found in the agent's tariff books published by the local tourist boards of the country or city involved. In the United States as well as worldwide, transfers for groups may be arranged through local transit systems or through Gray Line Sightseeing Co., the American Sightseeing International Co., or with the use of the Master-Key from WATA (World Association of Travel Agents).

The most important factor involved in ordering transfer or meeting services is maintaining good communications between the tour operator or the local contractor regarding the passengers' time of arrival and departure and the method of transportation used. When agents neglect to notify the principals involved of flight schedule or itinerary changes, clients complain that "there was no one there to meet them." Naturally, if clients make these changes at the last minute and incur a cable or long-distance call to notify others of the changes, he must bear the cost of these charges or take the responsibility of notifying the principals at his destination.

SIGHTSEEING TRIPS

Even travelers who plan to spend their entire vacation at a resort hotel will usually take one or more sightseeing trips during their visit. The majority of travelers will judge the success of the tour according to the number of sightseeing trips included and the number of famous places visited, even though only briefly. While a smooth flight and comfortable hotel are very necessary ingredients of a good tour, it is the sightseeing trips that provide most of the pleasure. Satisfied clients are those who had a good time on their tour and who saw and learned even more than they expected. A well-chosen and well-planned sightseeing trip with a knowledgeable and pleasant guide will ensure that good time.

There are sightseeing bus companies in every city in the world that has tourist attractions. The two largest companies are Gray Line Sightseeing, Inc. and American Sightseeing International (ASI). Gray Line started in 1910 and now has over 200 affiliated companies around the world. American Sightseeing began in 1947 and has over 100 affiliates. Both companies are well known and have built an excellent reputation not only with the public, but also with tour operators and travel agents.

Each company provides agents with tariff books that are revised annually, a supply of city sightseeing brochures for every city listed in the tariff, and a book of tour orders (vouchers). Unless otherwise specified in the tariff, the tour orders are issued on a *sell and report* basis. Half- or full-day sightseeing tours require no advance reservations. The Gray Line tour order is issued in triplicate; the original goes to the customer to present to the bus driver, the second copy is forwarded with payment to the city office where the tour will originate, and the third copy remains in the book for the agent's record. ASI tour orders have four copies. The last copy is left in the book, which is then returned to ASI for a replacement when the book is completely used; otherwise, the procedure is the same as Gray Lines'.

The tariff book advises the amount of commission to be retained by the agent and the address and telephone number of the originating tour office. Many of these offices now have 800 numbers for direct contact (information or booking).

City sightseeing folders are an invaluable aid in selling independent travel. Even clients who are driving to their destination and come in for only a hotel reservation can be sold a sightseeing tour. The appeal lies in the fact that they can take a rest from driving and have a well-informed guide tell them all about what they are seeing at their destination. If the clients are not interested in prepaying their sightseeing tours because they are not sure they will have time for them, at least they can see from the brochure what the attractions are in the area they are visiting. They can then book the sightseeing tours with the hotel's tour desk or head bellman. Although the agent may lose commissions on these sales, it is better than issuing vouchers that will be returned for refund. Unfortunately, the sightseeing companies take weeks, sometimes months, before they send refunds to the agent.

Almost all sightseeing bus companies will charter their buses for simple transfers or for special sightseeing excursions. The rates are based on time or mileage, whichever is greater, with a usual minimum of 25 passengers. They also provide net rates for smaller groups (6 to 15 persons). The tariff books will quote rates on charter or group fares for most cities; otherwise, the office in the destination city should be contacted directly, preferably in writing.

ASI Headquarters in New York City will accept collect calls for group bookings. They will provide quotes on groups, completely cost out multicity itineraries, and provide personal assistance on specific requests.

BUS/MOTORCOACH TRAVEL

The least expensive domestic public transportation is bus. It also is the least expensive in many areas around the world, although in many countries, without the well-kept roads needed for bus travel, second- and third-class rail tickets provide the cheapest method of transportation. Modern-day coaches are furnished with comfortable reclining seats, foot rests, air-conditioning, public address systems, and modern rest rooms. (Buses for charter use can also be provided with portable bars and game tables.) Greyhound Line's dual-level Super Scenicruiser, built by their own bus-building subsidiary, Motor Coach Industries, Inc., revolutionized bus travel in the mid-1950s. This has been replaced by their new Supercruiser, which represents a new concept in bus design. The new coaches provide more passenger comfort, with wider seats, increased headroom, a wider passenger aisle, large glare-free picture windows, and a turbine engine, said to be safer and much more economical to operate.

New, nonstop, express bus routes on modern highways with a greater frequency of service and new, or remodeled, bus terminals are some of the factors that make bus travel in the United States and Canada appealing to people besides the price conscious. Also, there is no denying that travelers can see more of the attractive parts of the country from the scenic level of a bus than from the window of a train, whose tracks usually run through the poorer or industrial sections of each city; or from an airplane window.

Greyhound Bus Lines and Continental Trailways, the two largest coast-to-coast bus lines in the United States, merged in 1987. Fred G. Currey (chairman and president) headed an investment company that purchased the bus line from Greyhound Corp. in March and acquired Trailways Lines, Inc. in July 1987. The ICC (Interstate Commerce Commission) approved the merger in May 1988.

Currey announced plans for new emphasis on customer services and innovations, such as a new computer-based ticketing system that issues tickets in 20 seconds. The combined Greyhound/Trailway company maintained scheduled service to more than 10,000 communities in 48 states. Currey said that Greyhound would aggressively try to double its market share in the $1.3 billion bus charter industry. Currey's plans were doomed in March 1990 when drivers walked off the job in a contract dispute over wages and benefits. Reorganizing in Chapter 11 bankruptcy, Greyhound cut its driving force from 6000 to 3500 and eliminated its charter business. Nonetheless, the bus line still stops at 95 percent of the cities, towns, country stores and wide spots in the road that it served until 1989. Greyhound emerged from bankruptcy and resumed trading on the American Stock Exchange in November 1991.

Greyhound's withdrawal from the charter business made it easier for hundreds of smaller, local firms to bid on military and athletic team movements, convention shuttles, school groups, seniors, and tour operator contracts. Bus operators did very well with charter and tour business when Greyhound/Trailways were driven back to the basics of scheduled route service.

Doing business with bus lines is a simple process. No formal agreement or contract is required. If the agent holds ARC or IATAN appointments, all she has to do is call for a ticket and send in the payment less commissions. Standard commissions are 10 percent for charters and intercity tickets, and as much as 15 percent on escorted tours. If the agent desires appointment or revenue forms, that can be arranged with the nearest office. Appointed agents would be issued ticket stock, tariffs, schedules, a validator, and other supplies. The main advantage of becoming an appointed ticket agent is that tickets may be issued upon demand, but if the demand is small and infrequent, the additional bookkeeping and security requirements would not be worth the effort.

Requests for straight bus transportation are usually turned away by most travel agents. Because the fares are low and the commissions earned are low, ticketing this kind of travel is not worth their while. However, bus (or motorcoach, as they now wish to be known) tours, especially short weekend tours to nearby scenic places, are increasing in popularity in the United States. There is a new market of motorcoach tour clients: younger, more sophisticated, more affluent. They have learned the ways of motorcoach travel in Europe and they are ready to adopt it in the United States.

For years, bus tours were considered suitable only for the elderly; although the senior citizen and retiree market is still the strongest, the camaraderie of group travel may be one reason more people, and younger people, are turning to motorcoach tours. The younger clientele is more interested in special events, unusual locations, and packages that feature intermodal transportation, as opposed to regional tours entirely by motorcoach. Elderly travelers may feel more secure on a tour that starts from their "own backyard" rather than flying to a distant point to pick up the tour.

There are many tour operators and travel agents who specialize in motorcoach tours and make a good living from them. Bixler Tours in Ohio, Anderson Tours in Pennsylvania, Tauck Tours in New York, and Mayflower Tours in Illinois are good examples. These operators are both wholesalers and retailers. They receive much of their business directly from the public. A few, such as Bixler Tours, will protect the travel agents' commissions on repeat business from agents' referrals. Tauck Tours (which, incidentally, claim to be the first bus tour operator, originating in 1925) have stated that 85 percent of their business comes from travel agents.

Cosmos Tours, which for years operated motorcoach tours in Europe, now offers tours of the United States. These were originally started as a service to their European clients. "Visit U.S.A." air fares are attracting inbound business to the United States. One tour operator estimates that at least 5 percent of his motorcoach tour members are international visitors.

In Europe, motorcoach tours are used quite extensively. The countries are closer together, the roads are good (in most countries), and the convenience of taking the tourist directly to the sightseeing area makes coach travel a pleasant experience for both the tour operator and the client. All the details enroute, including checking into hotels, are handled by the *courier* or tour leader. Hotels in Europe are usually more receptive to groups than they are to the individual American traveler. The staff is more pleasant and more willing to serve.

In 1988, a joint marketing agreement to raise interest in the Canadian tourism product in the American market was signed by Bernard Valcourt, Minister of State (Small Businesses and Tourism) and the American Bus Association (ABA). The government of Canada and the ABA agreed to promote the market tours to Canada. However, major Canadian motorcoach companies have stopped sending buses into the United States, complaining that ICC insurance requirements cost them nearly 10 times what they pay for some Canadian coverage, thus making the trips unprofitable. Some tour operators feel that the consumer will pay the increased cost, while others have reduced or eliminated the U.S. portion of their business. Other tour operators are actively seeking a solution to the dwindling supply of Canadian buses for U.S. travel.

The majority of tours to Europe and the Middle East use buses almost exclusively, especially since the airlines no longer offer fares that permit stopovers at no additional charge. Motorcoach tours are also becoming more frequent in South America. Since most of the European buses are built by the same firms, the equipment is standard on almost all tours. The majority of them are air-conditioned and have receiver headsets at each seat that enable the passengers to hear the tour leader's commentary despite traffic noises. Most European tours also use the same hotels—the room location may vary according to the amount paid for the tour. The itineraries are also very similar. (This is an area in which a creative agent or tour operator could examine and offer something new.)

MOTORCOACH TOUR AND CHARTER INDUSTRY

Chartering a bus for affinity groups or chartering a bus to operate and promote a bus tour is now much simpler than it was before November 1982, when the bus industry was deregulated. Under deregulation, route authority is permissive and tour operators no longer need to get broker licenses from the Interstate Commerce Commission (ICC) nor post a bond. The ICC did retain the authority to require a minimum amount of insurance coverage per motorcoach. Those standards include $5 million in coverage for large buses and $2.5 million for smaller ones.

The ICC no longer monitors the financial condition of a motorcoach operator and relies on the Department of Transportation (DOT) to conduct safety inspections of motorcoaches. As far as the financial fitness of a new entry is concerned, DOT assumes that if someone has the resources to start a business, he should be financially fit, willing, and able to provide the service.

Before deregulation, travel agents could not charter a bus, sell individual seats, and advertise their own bus tours unless they had a bus tour broker's license, which was very expensive and difficult to obtain. However, even though the rules have been liberalized, most agents continue to block group space with tour operators who specialize in motorcoach tours, but now the agents can advertise the tours and sell individual seats in the agency's name.

The following material was excerpted from the booklet *NTA Today* by special permission from National Tour Association, Inc.:

Since the deregulation of the American bus industry in November 1982, the rules of the tour and travel business have changed. The early tour brokers in the 1920's, such as Arthur Tauck, Sr., Tom Parkhill, Floyd Bixler and Mrs. W. M. Moore, assembled groups of people to travel together, sold tickets and chartered buses for transportation.

As roads and equipment improved, so did the demand for more and different tours. But with the growth of the new tour industry, the railroads no longer enjoyed a monopoly over freight and passenger traffic. Raising the cry of "destructive competition" they demanded that Congress step in to protect them. The result was the Motor Carrier Act of 1935, which brought the transportation of passengers and freight by motor vehicle under the jurisdiction of the Interstate Commerce Commission (ICC). The Act also made provision for licensing of passenger brokers.

Following World War II, during which tourist transportation was suspended, Arthur Tauck, who had been granted a passenger broker's license before the war, applied to ICC to enlarge the geographical scope of his license. The legal battle following ICC's refusal and the forming of the National Tour Brokers Association (NTBA) to assist him succeeded in getting the rules

Figure 12-2 Lancaster County, Pennsylvania. Courtesy of the Pennsylvania Dutch Visitors Bureau.

changed to allow tour brokers to use the services of carriers holding charter authority instead of restricting them to use only the carriers holding special operations authority. There were only a few special operators, and since they competed with the tour brokers the lack of adequate equipment could have seriously hurt the industry.

Tour brokers of the 1950s were still industry pioneers in many ways. They were subject to regulations over which they had very little control, and, quite often, did not understand. The large bus companies dominated motorcoach travel. And NTBA had the monumental task of establishing tour brokers as an industry, promoting motorcoach travel, and working with members to help them operate efficiently and profitably.

With deregulation, the National Tour Brokers Association changed its name to the National Tour Association (NTA), reflecting the beginning of a new era. The new name embraces a much broader travel industry association, which includes tour operators, air and cruise lines, bus companies, hotels, restaurants, sightseeing companies and many other related businesses. From the original dozen members who gathered around one small table, to today's conventions which draw more than 2500 delegates each year, NTA's goals have remained the same: to provide better, safer and more innovative choices for the group traveler.

Deregulation has given NTA an even more important role: to act, through its high standards of quality, as an advocate for the consumer, assuring that group travel in North America remains one of the travel industry's greatest products.

GROUP MOTORCOACH SALES

Arranging bus charters for affinity groups has been a profitable sideline for a number of agents. Now that restrictions have been lifted insofar as advertising is concerned, group travel is growing faster than most other segments of the travel industry. If the affinity group cannot fill the bus from its own membership, the tour can be advertised to the public, which eliminates the fear of last-minute cancellation of the tour.

It is now easier than ever for agents to get into the bus charter and tour business. Modern equipment can be leased or rented, liability and other insurance comes with the bus, and the bus company furnishes the driver. Costs are better controlled. Once a contract has been signed with the chartering bus line, rates will not change unless revisions are made in the time or mileage. Convenient pickup points are arranged in advance and the group is taken directly to their destination, without the need for transfers from terminal to hotel. Many bus lines have set up charter departments to assist travel agents and tour operators. Their personnel can help in locating and arranging hotels, meals, sightseeing, entertainment, and special events.

Just as in all other travel arrangements, all vital statistics must be obtained from the group if it is a private charter, or decided upon by the agent before contacting the bus lines for rates:

1. The dates of departure and return to the originating point.
2. The time of day for leaving and the time of day for returning to the starting point.
3. The exact address of the pickup point (if there is more than one, list them all) and the address at the destination or turnaround point.
4. Will there be any overnight stops en route? (The drivers are not permitted to work more than a normal working day unless there is an overnight stop. Otherwise, the bus line must provide two drivers.)

5. Will there be a use for the bus at the destination? (If the bus is used for a transfer from the hotel to a specific address, such as a bowling lane or convention hall, there is usually an additional charge based on time or mileage, whichever is higher. Some states and cities forbid the use of an out-of-state bus for local transfers and sightseeing. This would require the additional charter of a local sightseeing company to take the group about the area.)

6. How many meal stops will be necessary, and what category of restaurant/cafeteria will be used? A private group may ask for low-cost meals, while others may want to stop at the best restaurant in town. The restaurants must be notified in advance. Not many are equipped to serve a busload of people on short notice.

7. If the charter is for an affinity group, the bus line must be advised of the official name of the group, school, business, or other organization and the name of the group leader.

Charter bus prices vary according to the destination, type of equipment used (i.e., 35-, 40-, or 48-passenger bus), and the amount of services required. If both the originating point and destination point is on a scheduled bus line itinerary, the price may be lower than that quoted by a smaller or private bus line. However, the scheduled bus line may not allow the use of the bus at the destination point. If the destination is off the beaten path or the use of the bus at the destination is important, the smaller or private bus lines will be more economical and flexible. If the destination point is within a short distance from the home city but still within the state, a local transit system bus may be the best choice.

When the charter is for an affinity group, the group manager must be advised to collect a deposit as soon as the date and equipment have been confirmed. It is psychologically important that the group start making their payments as soon as possible. The balance should be collected *before* the group departs. There have been many instances (usually with social clubs) where the group takes several months to pay for their charter simply because the group leader or treasurer did not have time to collect and forward the money to the agent. At times, it may be necessary for the agent to send a staff member to collect the money as the group boards the bus.

Arranging, promoting, and selling motorcoach tours can be fun as well as profitable. It allows agents to be as creative and innovative as they wish. Quite often agents can arrange visits to relatively unknown areas that tour operators cannot afford to program since they must, out of necessity, sell their tours to greater numbers. Once agents develop a reputation of well-planned and interesting tours, their success is almost guaranteed. Repeat business for motorcoach tours is almost as great as that for cruises.

An additional line in a Yellow Pages advertisement stating that "bus charters can be arranged" or a listing under "bus charters" will bring in more of this business, if desired. A notation on all promotional mailing pieces to prospective groups that bus charters can be arranged for transfers and sightseeing, as well as for entire journeys, would also stimulate new or additional business.

QUESTIONS AND PROBLEMS

1. What are ground or land arrangements?
2. What is a transfer, and when is it most commonly used?
3. Describe a meeting service.
4. Name the two best-known sightseeing companies.

5. To what type of client would you recommend a bus tour?
6. When was the bus industry deregulated?
7. List some interesting places that you would like to visit by bus.
8. Make a list of prospective customers you could approach to sell a bus tour or charter.

## chapter 13

Rentals

OBJECTIVES

When you have finished this chapter you should be able to:

1. List the major car rental companies in the United States.
2. Discuss the need for collision damage waivers.
3. Advise clients on car rentals abroad.
4. Plan a European auto tour.
5. Discuss the procedures for a camper vacation rental.
6. Describe other rentals that are commissionable to travel agents.

The convenience of driving about in the comfort of a personal or rented car is known to millions of potential clients. It has long been a fact that the automobile is the agent's and airline's biggest competitor. The person who takes his or her family on a trip in their own car, or even a rental car, will seldom consult an agent. If she belongs to AAA (American Automobile Association), she generally asks for a trip ticket and maps; if not, she will stop at the nearest gas station for maps and trust to luck to find suitable accommodations at the end of a day's drive. However, more and more vacationers are taking a plane, bus, boat, or train and then renting a car when they reach their destination.

Excursion (discounted) air fares and a larger selection of fly/drive packages have made traveling by air more attractive for long trips, and clients are more receptive to a car rental at their destination. This gives them the freedom of movement they are accustomed to when they travel with the family car. Lower weekly rates, weekend specials, and unlimited mileage specials have also helped stimulate the car rental bookings. Fly/drive packages give the vacation traveler the assurance of a hotel/motel room each night at reasonable rates. Packages to popular resort areas, such as Disneyworld and Epcot, also include admission tickets.

Car rentals are used not only by travelers, but local residents use them for special occasions (weddings, graduations, etc.) or for temporary use while cars are under repair. Corporations will order them for their clients' use.

Although the big three—Avis, Hertz, and National—are better known to the traveling public, travel agents should not ignore the *discount* car rental firms. Major car rental companies have airport locations, while the discounters are usually off the airport grounds. This inconvenience may discourage some renters from using smaller companies, but the lower rates make up for this. Quite often the free airline terminal and hotel pickup/return service is not as inconvenient as waiting in line at the airport counter. The smaller, regional companies offer everything the majors do, usually at lower rates and often with better service.

The business travelers have long been the mainstay of car rental companies, and most all rentals give a corporate discount to the businesspeople. Travel agents earn 5 percent commission on bookings made for business travelers and they still get the discount. At one time, several car rental companies announced plans to move to a flat fee per transaction and eliminate the travel agents' 5 percent on commercial bookings. Agents objected to the proposal and the car rental companies gave up on the idea.

Commission scales vary from one company to another. Most car rental companies pay 5 percent on businesspeople who also receive a corporate discount. They pay 10 percent on promotional leisure business, but they vary on prepaid vouchers and volume bookings. Many will pay up to 40 percent bonuses on volume bookings. The off-airport companies pay anywhere from 10 to 20 percent. Quite often a new car rental company will entice the travel agents with larger commissions during their beginning years and then drop to the standard 10 percent.

Major car rental companies outlined plans for the future and clarified their feelings and dealings with agents:

Alamo Rent a Car. During the past few years, Alamo's network has expanded from primarily leisure-based locations to 80 percent of the top commercial destinations in the United States. Macdonald Clark, executive vice president and chief operating officer, has said that it is his company's philosophy to provide travel agents with a good product that is easy to sell and to pay their commissions promptly every 10 days. If commission is not received on time, the company guarantees to pay double commission. If the agent sends an automated queue about payment and receives no response within 72 working hours, the usual commission is tripled. Alamo continues to pay travel agents 10 to 15 percent commission on all rates, and 10 percent on Alamo's corporate program, Business Express.

Alamo has also developed an information video for ICTA to promote travel agent training and helped develop the car rental chapter for ICTA's upcoming marketing textbook for agent certification. In addition, Alamo has produced a video guide to the car rental industry. An educational video is shown to new travel agents through travel schools.

American International Rent A Car. This company recognizes that agents have been, and continue to be, the key to American International's growth. "Because some 75 percent of all our reservations are booked through the travel agent distribution system, we continue to fully support their efforts through our commission system that pays off on length of the car-rental as well as mileage accrued." They pay 5 percent for commercial bookings, a minimum of 10 percent on leisure business, and 15 percent on leisure bookings made for Florida, Hawaii, California, or Arizona. Additionally, they offer low, unlimited-mileage corporate account rates nationwide to consortium members.

The recession brought its share of problems to American International. They filed for Chapter 11 Bankruptcy protection in April 1992.

Avis. Having entered the computer age in 1972, Avis is constantly expanding and improving the technology demanded by today's market. The "Shopper's Guide," available only from Avis, lets travel agents quickly find the best available rate for any client through their *SABRE* terminal or by telephone. Fifteen percent commission is paid on most of those transactions.

Thanks to the computer age, Avis provides "rapid return" and "rapid rental" terminals at major airports, and a variety of sophisticated management tools, such as travel patterns, vehicle preference, average mileage per employee or client, reservations changes or last-minute upgrades, commission tracking, and computerized scanning of rate options to provide only the lowest applicable rate at the touch of a computer key.

Because at least 65 percent of its customers are business travelers, Avis also offers Automated Hotel Check-in, Weather Track Phone, Avis Cares, MiniLeases, a convention and meeting services program, and several telecommunications features.

Avis customers in Britain, Belgium, France, West Germany, Holland, Italy, and Switzerland can now locate the nearest English-speaking doctor or dentist by using a special "On Call Europe" toll-free telephone number. The 24-hour, seven-day-a-week number connects travelers with Avis consultants at the company's British databank. In addition to medical help, Avis offers current information on hotels, restaurants, special events, local festivals, museums, historical monuments, shopping, sports, theater, opera, and concerts.

Budget Rent A Car. This company receives over 70 percent of its business from travel agents. As travel agents expand in serving the business traveler, Budget plans to keep its leadership role in emphasizing agency sales. Budget's commitment to helping agents build sales is reflected in its override program that pays up to 50 percent of the base commission to volume producers. They also have a commission tracking group and an improved automation system that permits backward and forward booking search (within a 24-hour period each way). That way, if a client changes travel plans and rents a car a day later or a day earlier, it does not come back as a no-show. They are trying to cut down on the reported no-shows, which have been an issue for some time.

Budget has a number of programs directed to the business community. Their CorpRate program gives unlimited mileage and direct billing. No minimum number of rentals is required for the Budget credit card. In many airports they have a computerized mapping system for multiple destinations: a Metro Map details driving directions block by block. Car phones are offered throughout Budget's fleet; portable cellular phones are four dollars a day plus regular calling charges. The

Lincoln Town Car is Budget's most popular rental. Budget has also joined several frequent flyer programs—renting a car from Budget increases the bonus miles in their accounts.

Budget also serves clients' longer business trips and vacation needs with their worldwide group of "Budget Plan" packages that are guaranteed in U.S. dollars in most countries in which they are offered. Budget pays 5 percent on commercial business, 10 percent on leisure, and up to 40 percent in terms of overrides.

Dollar Rent A Car. Agents are responsible for delivering over 70 percent of Dollar's business. Dollar's policy is to pay 5 percent on contracted business in which Dollar is the primary or co-supplier, 10 percent on any and all discretionary business, and 20 percent on all prepaid business. In addition, Dollar assists agents in expanding their car rental business with an agreement with Maritz Motivational Company to reward a target group of agencies with merchandise earned through booking credits.

Dollar has a three-tiered corporate account program: Silver, Gold, and Gold Plus. The level of discount depends on rental volume and individual negotiations. Some east coast cities levy a surcharge, but mileage is always unlimited. Locations in Phoenix, San Diego, and Las Vegas have car phones; this service is expanding.

Enterprise Rent A Car. Enterprise pays 5 percent on government and corporate business and 15 percent on everything else. They process agent's commissions within four working days. In addition, commission is paid on the damage waiver and personal accident insurance they sell to customers. Enterprise provides pickup and transfer service to airports, bus, and train stations.

The Hertz Corporation. The world's leading vehicle renting organization, Hertz, is represented in over 120 countries, operating a fleet of approximately 400,000 vehicles from over 5000 locations. The founder, Walter L. Jacobs, opened a car-rental operation in Chicago in 1918. Five years later he sold the business to John Hertz, president of Yellow Cab and Yellow Truck and Coach Manufacturing Company. This rental business, called Hertz Drive-Ur-Self System, went through several owners until December 1987, when Hertz was sold to Park Ridge Corporation. The company was formed by Ford Motor Company and certain members of Hertz senior management for the purpose of purchasing Hertz. In June 1988, Volvo North America Corporation joined Ford and Hertz management as an investor in Park Ridge Corporation. Hertz is headquartered in Park Ridge, New Jersey; Oklahoma City, Oklahoma is the site of the Hertz Worldwide Reservation Center and Data Center, established in 1970.

Hertz is firmly ensconced in the business travel market; some 70 to 75 percent of its total business comes from corporate accounts. Hertz boasts a multifaceted program benefiting the business traveler, starting with its corporate rate programs, which provide customized services and discounted rates based on the client's needs and business volume. Hertz has also joined the airlines in the frequent flyer programs.

Figure 13-2 Hertz Instant Return.

Figure 13-3 Hertz Counter.

Mobile cellular phones are installed in their luxury cars and computer-printed driving directions and video mapping are available at larger airports and some downtown locations. The printout instructions—complete with street address, phone number, mileage, and driving time—are available in French, German, Italian, and Spanish, as well as in English. Business centers are also now available at 14 airports. With a credit card, customers can send and receive faxes, voice messages, drop off Federal Express packages, and consult an interactive video services directory.

In an effort to help travel agents encourage their clients to travel, Hertz is offering travel agent clients car rental upgrade and discount coupons. "These coupons are an effective tool for travel agents to use in generating increased business," said William A. Maloney, Hertz Division vice president of travel industry sales and marketing. "To make them easier to use, we designed the coupon so that they could be used as ticket stuffers by the travel agents. There is space on the back of each coupon for the travel agency stamp." Mr. Maloney pointed out that Hertz has responded to the travel agents' needs as a direct result of suggestions by the Hertz Travel Agent Advisory Board.

National Car Rental.   National's weekend special and one-way rates, assured reservations, and emergency road service programs appeal to both the business and leisure markets, although Michael Olsen, vice president of corporate communications for National, maintains that the leisure market is more likely to be affected by an economic downturn than is the corporate client. A substantially large percentage of the car rental business is tied to airline growth. As prices for aviation fuel increase, which in turn drives up the cost of airline tickets, this can affect whether people fly and thus whether they rent a car. Travel agencies provide National with more than 50 percent of their volume. They especially appreciate travel agents' support in the leisure market, where agents typically have a greater chance to make a recommendation on a car rental company.

National has an Expressway Computer System that automatically attaches the reservation to the rental. Since the reservation carries an ARC number, the agent is assured his commission. A new program, "Compliments of. . . ," lets agents refer corporate account to National to receive special low corporate rates, international discounts, and electronic advantage service. The referrals strengthen their partnership with clients, speed up transaction time, and show clients the agents' interest in saving clients' time and money.

National pioneered the field with the 1987 introduction of its Emerald Club, which, among other things, offers bonuses such as free travel based on special promotions and how much the renter spends. The annual membership is $50; the initial joining fee is $60.

Payless Car Rental Systems, Inc. Payless, a 100 percent franchise system owned by the Sampo Group, has created a special department to make certain that agent commissions are protected. At its new international headquarters, the company is upgrading its computer system to track agency commission throughout the Payless system. Payless offers luxury cars at a savings of $10 to $15 a day over competitors.

Thrifty Rent-A-Car System. Thrifty pays agents 10 percent on all direct bookings made and 5 percent on any booking made through the airline reservations system. About 55 percent of their reservations come through travel agents. They have a centralized commission payment program that pays commissions on rentals at every location around the world, both franchised and corporately owned, and helps to eliminate the agent bypass program. Three-tiered corporate programs at all 375 U.S. locations include unlimited mileage, no extra charge for additional driver or drivers between 21 and 25, limited liability, and no surcharges, except at New York/Newark.

Tropical USA Rent a Car. This company is identifiable as a regional off-airport price specialist, and as such, they are the most competitive in each of their markets in 7 western states plus Hawaii. Originally established to serve the leisure market, Tropical is making a concentrated effort to gain a small but reasonable share of the price-oriented business travel segment. Because Tropical is basically a low-overhead operator, it has been able to keep to a competitive pricing level. Tropical is offering basically a unified flat gross and net rate (paying 10 percent to agencies and more to consortiums) throughout its regional system. Seventy-five percent of their business is prebooked through travel agents and tour operators. USA Rent a Car, based in Tampa, Florida, merged with Tropical in April 1992. The new company, Tropical USA Rent a Car will be based in Tampa.

Value Rent-A-Car (formerly Greyhound Rent-A-Car). Value, headquartered in Florida, was purchased in May 1990 by Mitsubishi, the first Japanese car manufacturer to buy into a U.S. car-rental company. The company, which currently operates 25 locations in Florida, Georgia, Colorado, Arizona, and Nevada, is ranked fifth among car rental firms that compete predominantly in the leisure market. They plan to open additional stations in each state. The purchase gave the Japanese company a major new customer in Value, which is stocking 70 percent of its fleet with the highly rated Japanese cars.

Since taking over operation of Value Rent-a-Car, Mitsubishi has "improved and transformed Value's relations with travel agents," according to Jeffrey C. Davis, Value's senior vice president of operations. "We believe the travel agent is the key to the leisure market, which we are targeting. So you're going to see a very heavy, renewed and long commitment to the travel agent community." Value has moved to ensure fast and error-free payment of commissions on a weekly basis. The company has launched a VIP (Value's Important Partner) program, offering agents prizes for their level of bookings with Value. The company is continuing with the "Value Plus" inclusive add-on that encompasses all extras, including maximum CDW coverage, and is fully commissionable to travel agents.

Consumer complaints regarding the exorbitant charges and unnecessary need for CDWs (they release the renter from liability in an accident) brought about legislation in Hawaii and California to abolish CDWs. Other states that get heavy leisure traffic are looking at similar legislation. Most of the major car rental companies support the idea, although they say that the rental prices will go up to absorb the companies' increased liability. So far, the car rental company lobbyists have fought successfully against anti-CDW legislature. Car rental firms in Florida were so anxious to limit their liability in accidents that they floated the idea of not opposing an increase in the present $2 daily surcharge now paid to the state on all rentals.

At least 7 states—Hawaii, Arizona, Illinois, Massachusetts, Minnesota, Nevada, and North Carolina—have already passed or are considering rental surcharge legislation to ease their budget deficits. This could have a devastating impact on the car rental industry according to the American Car Rental Association (ACRA). While some surcharges are on a per-transaction basis, some are on car registrations. From the consumer's point of view, surcharges not only make car rentals more expensive, but few of them realize that it is a tax over which the company has no control. In the meantime, car rental firms around the country said they expect rates to rise in 1991–1992 due to the increase in cost of purchasing their fleets. Because of the competition in the marketplace, some firms may hold to current rates by buying fewer cars and eliminating some pricing discounts.

Car rentals rank as the fourth largest source of business for retail agents. The dollar amount of business could increase enormously if agents would get more involved in generating car rental bookings. Businesspeople should be advised that they will continue to receive their corporate discount even if they book through an agent. Every travel agent should have reminders posted on their desks or computers to ask for the car rental booking from every air, cruise, and rail passenger. (Budget Rent A Car and Amtrak have signed an agreement calling for the establishment of Budget locations in 300 Amtrak stations. Since more and more business travelers and vacationers are traveling by train, the agreement marks a new era of convenience for train passengers.) Predictions are that in the decade ahead there is going to be more emphasis on convenience and service than on price.

Used Car Rentals

Rent-A-Wreck, Rent-A-Heap, Rent-A-Dent—used-car rental companies are expanding all over the United States. They feature low-cost used cars, vans, and pickup trucks for people traveling on a low budget. Rent-A-Wreck has a directory of 300 offices in 42 states (including Hawaii), Australia, and the Dominican Republic. Rent-A-Dent has 50 locations in 15 states and more are in the future plans. Used car rentals feature neighborhood locations with rentals starting at $8.95 per day.

Clients who have used these companies report that cars are clean and well-maintained and seldom more than two or three years old. Attendants are friendly and courteous. Most of these companies pay 10 percent commission to travel agents and have toll-free reservation numbers.

CAR RENTALS ABROAD

During the past few years the proliferation of fly-and-drive and tour packages to Europe have focused attention on car and camper arrangements, which can be made through a travel agent. Fly/drive packages can be sold successfully to various markets other than the vacation traveler. Business travelers appreciate the convenience of a car at their disposal and the timesaving achieved by the elimination of waiting for transfers; students and teachers like the low-cost, individual arrangements, which enable them to come into closer contact with the people of the country; ethnic travelers, whose relatives may live in hard-to-reach cities or villages, are spared the necessity of long layovers to make their onward connections.

Car rentals in Europe can be a lucrative source of income for the U.S. travel agent. Years ago, travel by car on the European continent was considered only by the brave. Even Europeans did not use cars in the same manner as Americans did. Now, however, roads and motel facilities are beginning to rival those in the United States. Major gasoline companies have opened gasoline stations across the entire continent, and international road signs (using pictures and symbols that are universally understood) are seen in more and more countries, including the United States. Even the international driver's license is not a requirement in many countries, although it still is a good suggestion, as not all local policemen read English.

Prior to World War II, automobile renting was a relatively unknown business in Europe. It was after 1947, when the automobile manufacturers in Italy, France, Germany, and Great Britain became productive again, that a steady increase began, and today several hundreds of car hire companies are operating successfully in Europe. The majority of these companies are small, according to American standards, which led to the formation of alliances, unions, or groups. This type of organization is closely controlled by its owners, but through cooperation in operational and marketing procedures and systems, it can offer the touring public more economical services, with greater personal attention to the individual. The Kemwel Group, formed in 1908, is such an organization. They are wholesalers only; they do not compete with the agent by selling direct to the public. Their car rental services can be ordered directly from their Harrison, New York, office or through many international air lines. Kemwel and Air France started a new program in 1991 featuring savings on car rentals in eight European countries. Kemwel Auto Vacancies provides an economical group A car that includes unlimited mileage, all local value-added taxes, and full collision damage waiver charges. To qualify, passengers' round-trip transatlantic flights must be on Air France, and car reservations must be made at least seven days before departure from the United States. Cars must be picked up and returned to a Kemwel station within the same country. Drop-off at other selected Kemwel stations in other countries is allowed for an additional charge.

For a complete vacation package in Europe, the Kemwel Auto Vacancies program also makes available hotel vouchers valid at more than 700 hotels in 20 European countries using the facilities of MinOtels and Holiday Inns. Kemwel offers similar fly/drive packages in conjunction with several other international airlines, such as Iberia in Spain, SAS to Denmark, Norway, and Sweden; and Northwest Airlines in London, Edinburgh, Glasgow, Paris, Amsterdam, Frankfurt, and Munich.

Renting a car for your clients traveling in Europe can be as easy as it is in the United States. Hertz, Avis, National, and Budget have expanded their overseas branches in every major city. (The majority of these branches are franchised.) Auto-Europe, Inc., a pioneer in the car travel business, puts out brochures annually which are complete sales guides for both agent and prospective client. The brochures cover car rentals, campers, and motorhomes. The Cortell Group, Maggiore, Inc., and Europe-by-Car are other well-recommended European car-rental companies. They furnish car rentals or chauffeur-driven cars in any of the major cities of western Europe.

Counseling the client on car rentals abroad requires a complete and up-to-date file consisting of brochures from the car-rental companies, road maps, currency converters, current-events calendars (most shops and gas stations are closed during local holidays), and other general information on the countries to be visited. Clients must be reminded to check their passports for expiration dates and apply for visas

Figure 13-4 Hertz Self Service Return.

if they plan to drive into a country that requires a visa. They must also check their driver's license to make sure that it is valid during the rental period. Some international car rental companies also require that the driver has had a driver's license for at least one year.

BOOKING THE CAR RENTAL

The most important questions to be answered by clients, whether they are booking a fly/drive tour package or a straight car rental, are as follows:

1. How many people will be traveling in the car?

2. How much luggage are you planning to take?

3. What make and model car? (European cars are smaller in size than American cars. The lowest-rate car is not necessarily the most economical if you plan to drive long distances with a substantial amount of luggage and more than two people in the car.)

4. How long a period of time will the car be needed? Rentals are based on a 24-hour day, and overtime is charged on an hourly basis. There are special rates for weekend rentals and discounted rates for weekly or monthly rentals. (If the car will be used for more than three months in Europe, a visa may be required.)

5. Point of pickup and drop-off? Most companies will deliver the car to the airport; however, some will deliver only at their city station or will advise a telephone number to call to have the car sent to the airport upon the customer's arrival. The car may also be delivered to clients at their hotel the following day at a specified time. Many first-time travelers are hesitant about driving themselves from the airport to their hotel and would prefer using the transfers for this purpose and use the rental car strictly for sightseeing. The drop-off point is important in determining the rental charges. In some areas, there is no drop-off charge between key cities. This policy is now also available within Europe.

6. Special equipment needed? Luggage racks, sports equipment racks, automatic shift, or air-conditioning often involve an additional charge. Auto-Europe, Inc. provides free hand controls in rentals for disabled travelers in Britain and on the continent. The firm recommends that disabled drivers pick up cars at downtown city locations rather than at airport stations because mechanics who install the specialized equipment are more readily available at downtown locations. Auto-Europe also offers chauffeur services for the blind or for disabled persons traveling in wheelchairs.

7. Check on insurance coverage provided by the car rental company and consult your own insurance advisor to determine whether additional coverage is needed. In most cases a comprehensive fire and theft insurance is also included in the rental rates. Although this insurance will cover theft of the vehicle, it will not cover personal belongings left in the rented car. Most car rental companies include a $100 to $650 deductible collision insurance. A collision damage waiver (CDW) providing full collision coverage is available for an additional fee collected at the time of pickup.

EUROPEAN CAR PURCHASES

Purchasing a car in the United States and picking it up in Europe is now a very simple operation, but it is no longer the bargain it was years ago unless the purchaser is planning on touring Europe two or three months or longer. The savings would be in the cost of the car rental for that period of time. Buyers of the most expensive cars may receive the biggest savings. Years ago, the American car buyer went through a maze of confusing red tape, delays, and expenses in order to bring his car back to America. Today, the transaction can be completed in the amount of time it takes to fill out the order form and submit the deposit.

Car purchases are now seldom made through the car rental companies and travel agents. The car manufacturers prefer that the purchase arrangement be made through one of their dealers in the United States. They will execute all the documents required in the United States for processing the order, arrange insurance coverage for use of the car abroad, arrange for shipment, and at an optional additional cost will provide U.S. Customs' clearance service in the United States. The new car can be picked up at the factory or, depending on the make and model selected, at a wide variety of European cities. Be sure to select a reputable company and read all the fine print in the order. Although most companies will refund the initial deposit in the event of cancellation, if the client orders special equipment, colors, or custom interiors, they would be liable for the additional charges.

Cars purchased abroad must conform to U.S. emission requirements. The Environmental Protection Agency (EPA) has revised its regulations that govern the manner in which nonconforming vehicles (vehicles not originally manufactured to meet U.S. emission requirements) can be imported. These new rules affect all nonconforming vehicles imported after June 30, 1988. Purchases will have to go through commercial entities that have the responsibility of ensuring that the vehicles are properly modified so as to conform to federal emission requirements. Not all vehicles will be permitted entry into the United States, even if such entry is made through one of the commercial entities; buyers should check first with the EPA.

European governments consider cars delivered to bona fide tourists as personal exports and exempt from payment of local European duties, taxes, and other fees normally levied on sales to resident purchasers. Germany, however, requires payment of their export tax at the time of pickup, which is fully refundable if the vehicle is exported from Germany within six months of delivery. (Depending on the make and model, the export tax will range between $500 and $1000.) The purchaser completes a refund claim at the time the vehicle is turned in for shipment to the United States. Usually, the refund is processed promptly, but there have been occasions when the client has had to wait for several months.

U.S. import duty is levied on all car imports. Years ago the import duty was less if the vehicle was driven in Europe and shipped to the States as a used car. This rule was abolished in the late 1970s, and all cars now pay the same amount, usually 3 percent of the invoice price. The state and local taxes are paid when the car is registered at home.

It may take some searching to find a dealer that specializes in handling overseas deliveries. Reservations must be made from 4 to 16 weeks in advance, and final payment is due no later than 30 days before delivery date. Shipment to the United States takes from 4 to 6 weeks. If the buyer needs the car any sooner, the company can arrange to have it sent by air cargo. This, of course, is much more expensive than having it sent by freighter to the port nearest the customer's home city.

PLANNING A EUROPEAN AUTOMOBILE TOUR

The Kemwel Group makes the following recommendations when planning a customer's tour of Europe by car:

> First of all it is important, as in all other planning considerations, to have the client's personal desires foremost in mind, and then to explain the do's and don'ts of car travel.

Most Americans think they can travel as fast by car in Europe as they can in the United States and Canada. Some think there are no speed limits on most European highways. These conceptions are totally erroneous, and even if they were not, it would not be desirable to plan a fast trip by car because Europe has so much more to offer in the way of close-to-each-other sights and spots of interest than other countries have. You, as a travel advisor, must have a good general knowledge needed to advise a specific customer. Secondly, you must know how long it takes to get from one place to another by car, bearing in mind that road conditions, etc., do not permit equally fast—or slow—driving on all roads.

A good European motoring atlas which shows not only driving distances but also the actual driving time from major points to major points on the most frequented highways of Europe and the inter-European touring routes is invaluable to any itinerary planner.

The itinerary must be *personalized* to meet the wishes and interests of the client. For example, do not bypass Florence if someone wants to see art. Do not send a student of modern architecture to Rothenburg for that purpose, etc. Clients may have ethnic interests, shopping interests, sports interests, social study interests, etc., etc., etc. The professional travel consultant will know where to send them. Maybe they just want to have a good time, enjoy gourmet food, night-life, bikini beaches, and meeting the people. To know where these features exist is the agent's challenge. It may sound a little frightening at first, but it isn't, really. In time, the agent learns a good deal about different countries from experience. Also, a dedicated agent will certainly pick up a good deal of information from literature and by "osmosis" by being in the travel business—and by socializing with seasoned travelers. The main sources will be found in literature, of which there is much, of varied quality and content.

Government Tourist Offices are so helpful; they will even assist you in sketching individual itineraries, if you ask for advice, and they will send it back with accompanying collateral brochures free of charge. Maps are available showing scenic routes and points of special touristic interest. One word of warning: Do not try to do automobile itineraries by copying motorcoach itineraries. It just will not work. Motorcoaches skip through many things that are the exact reason for the client wanting to self-drive. The coaches are driven by expert drivers who drive fast and steadily for hours on end. This is not what the self-drivers want; they want leisure, individuality and no pressure.

ADVISING CLIENTS ABOUT CAR TOURING

1. Do not allow clients to rush. They should not be on the road for more than 6 to 8 hours in any one day. (Consult a motoring atlas for driving times.) Not more than one-half to two-thirds (of the number of days) of the entire itinerary should be on the road. Frequent packing and unpacking becomes a chore that can ruin a trip. One-night stopovers should be avoided as much as possible. It is better to pick night stops strategically so that much can be seen by circling back to the same hotel two or three nights.

    In other words, do not keep clients on the run; let them move logically from sightseeing center to sightseeing center. This makes for much better planning and more pleasurable motoring.

2. Do not recommend city sightseeing by self-drive car. Unless one knows the city thoroughly, it is impossible—and an exhausting and unreasonable strain on the driver. Suggest that clients use conducted sightseeing buses in major cities (it is more commission in the agent's pocket, too) and

they will have much more fun than trying to beat local traffic and parking difficulties. An alternative is, of course, to have a local agent arrange for a chauffeur/guide for a day, but restrictions in some areas do not permit guides to drive the cars.

While the clients are off on a conducted sightseeing tour, this could also be a good opportunity to have the car serviced and checked over by a local garage. (If travelers would have their car rentals serviced as they would their own back home, they would never have the mechanical difficulties that always seem to occur in the most out-of-the-way places.)

3. Avoid delivering car rentals to clients immediately after landing from a transatlantic flight, if at all possible. They are tired then and in no mood to tackle strange cars and traffic. Clients, agents, and car rental companies are better off if clients settle down in their first-night hotel and have the car delivered or picked up when they have time to receive instructions on how to drive it and service it—something that is practically impossible during rush hours at a busy airport. (Imagine what it would be like at JFK, O'Hare, or any other large U.S. airport; and European airports are equally hectic.)

Airport drop-offs at the end of the car tour are simple; all the client does is leave the car at a parking lot (if the agency does not have a special drop-off point at the airport) and take the papers and keys with her when she checks in.

4. Recommend overnight accommodations when at all practical and possible (if they have not purchased the fly/drive package that includes accommodations). The problem of traveling without accommodations is that one spends so much time searching for suitable places to sleep. In the peak season, it is not as easy as it sounds, either. After the first miserable night, many motorists find that they must start thinking of a place to stay overnight around 4:00 P.M. They could drive on until early evening if they were assured of accommodations. Also, it is a loss of commissions to the travel agent if he does not sell as much as possible to each client.

5. Watch out for routing pitfalls. Cars cannot be driven through the Brenner Pass during the winter; certain ferries do not operate at certain times of the year; and so on.

6. Clients should have enough local currency on hand to purchase gasoline. Not all gas stations will accept travelers' checks or credit cards.

With these simple guidelines and common sense, thorough agents can plan a very good itinerary, even though they may never have been to the destination themselves.

CAMPER/MOTOR-HOME RENTALS: UNITED STATES AND EUROPE

Travel by recreation vehicle (RV), auto, and truck increased 2 percent in 1991, up 8 million trips from the same period in 1990. A poll by the U.S. Travel Data Center shows that Americans are tailoring their summer vacations to meet the current economic situation. In addition to economic concerns, a shift in American lifestyles and values appears to be causing some of the rise. An increasing number of people are simplifying their lives to spend more time with loved ones; this results in a higher interest in camping, nature, and vacationing with family and friends. RV vacations also give Americans a chance to combine two of their favorite activities: driving for pleasure and camping.

A study conducted by the University of Michigan Survey Research Center in the fall of 1984 revealed a vast untapped market for travel agents to arrange rentals of recreational vehicles. The study found that over 12 million families or 18 percent of U.S. households are likely to rent or buy an RV in the future.

The Michigan study corroborates findings of previous studies by other sources. For example, in September 1983 the Canadian Recreational Vehicle Association commissioned the research firm of Woods Gordon to conduct a cost-comparison study of a motor-home vacation versus those that combine use of air travel and hotel or private auto and hotel. Costs of the vacation trip in each instance were based on a family of two adults and three children. The results showed that a motor-home vacation costs less than half the amount of a comparable vacation using air travel and hotels.

Other studies found about half of all RV rental clients are in the 25- to 59-year age group. They are an affluent group able to afford longer vacations and more likely to book through a travel agent.

Eastern Airlines and Camp America, Inc. introduced the Fly In/Camp Out vacation program in 1969 in the southern states of Florida and North Carolina. The program proved so successful that it was expanded across the United States and Canada, and Air Canada, Continental Airlines, United, and TWA offer the services also. Campers as well as car rentals are also available in Hawaii. The rental companies will arrange for a camper or car at each island on the client's itinerary.

Campers have sleeping accommodations for four to eight people (depending on the model selected) and come equipped with bedding and cooking equipment. Motor homes have sleeping capacity for four or five. Camper clients are picked up at the airport and taken to the first-night campground, reservation guaranteed (motor-home renters can pick them up at the airport location). They are furnished with maps and telephone numbers for suggested campgrounds, suggested itineraries, and a thorough briefing by experts on all mechanical equipment of the camper vehicle, and they are on their own for as many weeks as they desire. There is no mileage charge, and a discount is given if they rent the vehicles for five weeks or longer. Drop-off privileges for one-way rentals are included if they are arranged in advance.

Camping in Europe has long been a popular pastime with vacationers. There are more campsites, and most are better than any found in the States. Most are clean and spacious, with a wide variety of services—from hot showers to grocery stores to recreation facilities. Some have all the features of major resorts—at campers' prices. Paris has a campsite right in the heart of the city, although the majority of campsites in Europe are on the outskirts of the major cities.

KLM Royal Dutch Airlines and Continental Campers, Inc. introduced the Campmobile GIT package to Europe in 1970. Since that time most major European car rental companies have motor homes and campers available for vacationers. Arrangements can be made in the United States, and delivery is available in most major European cities. The vehicles come completely equipped with bedding, dishes, and so on, for the number of persons in the party. One of the features of the campmobile is the separate tent, which is part of the equipment. It can be set up on the campsite to be used as a living room by day and an extra bedroom at night. Motor homes include sleeping bags in the equipment.

Camper/motor-home tours can be highly recommended for families and for rugged individualists. The cost is low; besides hiking, there is no cheaper way to tour the country. Campground prices range from $7 to $25 a night depending on the number of people in your group and if you need an electrical outlet. Credit cards are accepted throughout Europe, but carry cash for gasoline. Gas stations are numerous and many are associated with reasonable priced restaurants; most do not accept credit cards.

Camper/motor-home tours offer a good opportunity to meet people and get to know them. Even language barriers fall apart when people of mutual interests get together in a campsite. Camper tours also offer the most freedom in travel. There is no need for hotel reservations, although it is recommended that campsite locations be found by 4:00 P.M. each day or reserved ahead by telephone or mail. Meals can be prepared in the camper or at the campsite.

For clients interested in this type of vacation, a membership with the National Campers and Hikers Association in Buffalo, New York is recommended. They will provide an identification card that is accepted everywhere and will also entitle the member to a discount at most campsites. Also, they should purchase an International Camping License from AAA (American Automobile Association) for $25. The card indicates that a premium has been paid (covering up to 15 people) in respect to third-party liability for accidents while camping abroad. Clients should stock up on Michelin maps, sold in bookstores in the United States and they should also double-check the expiration date on their local driver's license. They should check with their insurance company for coverage overseas and while driving a vehicle.

RENT-A-HORSE/DONKEY

There is rent-a-car, rent-a-chalet, rent-a-yacht, and now rent-a-horse—the newest mode of traveling in Italy, where the unknown countryside, Renaissance villages, abbeys, castles, and wineries can be discovered. Daily itineraries are planned as well as overnight trips and cross-country rides for the more experienced riders.

Groups of 20, accompanied by English-speaking guides, grooms, and a minibus for luggage (or for those who may tire enroute), ride from 4 to 5 hours a day. Morning and afternoon periods of instruction and supervised riding are available daily for the beginners and include hotel accommodations based on double occupancy with private bath, all meals, and transfers to riding centers. For the more experienced riders, the price is higher, but offers the foregoing inclusions plus use of horses, guide, and grooms for the longer trips. Nonriders may accompany the riders, but not on horseback, at a reduced daily rate (for hotels, meals, and transport).

This is commissionable to travel agents at 10 percent and arrangements may be made through Rent-a-Horse, Viale Mazzini 4, Rome, Italy.

Horse trips are also available in Ireland, Great Britain, Spain, and Czechoslovakia. Riding safaris are offered in Kenya.

A new mode of transportation—donkeys—has been added by Maduro's Auto Rental and Taxi Service on St. Eustatius in the Netherlands Antilles. They also offer car rentals and taxi service. All rates are commissionable to travel agents.

Donkey rides are also featured in tours to Greece. The island of Santorini and Lindos on the island of Rhodes are famous for donkey hire to the top of the mountains.

Traveling the Holy Land on a donkey was standard for biblical figures. Now clients can do it that way and get a taste of what life was like 2000 years ago at Sataf, an open-air museum in the Judean Hills, 8 miles from Jerusalem. It is one of several ecotours offered by the Society for the Protection of Nature in Israel. This one-day tour departs Jerusalem on Sundays and is recommended for fairly good hikers. Other programs include 1- to 4-day hiking trips and 9- to 12-day tours. The society offers a 10 percent commission to travel agents.

RENT-A-HOUSEBOAT

Something for everyone is available in the travel agency that keeps alert to new tours and possibilities in travel. Houseboats, or aqua-homes as they are sometimes called, can be rented in major tourist areas. At the present time they are available in Florida and the Virgin Islands. Aqua-home rental ports have also been authorized in the Chesapeake Bay area, the Middle Atlantic states, the Midwest, Texas, the Mississippi River, and Europe. Franchises in Mexico, the Bahamas, and other areas in the United States are being established. The United States Travel Service can furnish a list of houseboat rentals in the United States.

Chris-Craft Aqua-Home Rentals, part of the franchising division of Chris-Craft Industries, has established these rental ports. Prices are dependent on boat size and equipment, season, and location of rental port. The boats sleep anywhere from two to eight persons. Each houseboat has a stall shower, wall-to-wall carpeting, and a kitchen (equipped with a large refrigerator, three-burner electric stove, rotisserie oven, double stainless steel sink, and cooking utensils). Also available are television sets, dinghies, barbecues, disposable linens, plates, cups, and so on. Advance ordering of food and other provisions can be arranged. The houseboats are equipped for extended cruising with complete safety equipment.

Renting houseboats is not inexpensive, although when the expenses are divided by four to eight people it can provide for a low-cost vacation for all. Travel agents can make reservations through a local Chris-Craft dealer.

RENT A HORSE-DRAWN CARAVAN IN IRELAND

In 1971, some 13 operators in most Irish counties, from Blarney Romany Caravan Company Ltd. in County Cork to the south, to Gipsy River Tours in County Roscommon to the north, started offering fully equipped covered-wagonlike caravans for four or five persons (each drawn by a horse specially selected for its quiet disposition). For more energetic travelers, a saddle horse can be rented to accompany the caravan.

The caravan season extends from March through October and on a normal day you travel from 12 to 14 miles, which allows ample time for sightseeing, picnic-style meals cooked on the caravan grill, and sociable evenings spent at pubs along the route. The cost is reasonable and includes all the oats the horse can eat but does not include food for the passengers. Travel agents can contact the Irish Tourist Board in New York City for further details.

RENT-A-CAT

Fifteen years ago a lonely guest at the Anderson House Hotel in Wabasha, Minnesota was offered the companionship of the proprietor's cat. When he checked out, he told John Hall that in the 27 years that he had been a traveling salesman, his stay at the Anderson House had been the most memorable because of the cat. That gave Hall the incentive to provide a special service to his guests. Today he has 11 cats, which are booked nearly every weekend, especially Morris, a 30-pound feline.

Guests usually reserve a cat in advance when they book their rooms, and with 51 rooms in the hotel, Hall anticipates getting more cats to meet the demand. In addition to the cat companion service, the inn features hot bricks to warm your feet while in bed during the winter, a shoe shining service, mustard plaster for the skin, and sleigh rides in the winter.

LEASE-A-PLANE

Rental planes are a new way to go. Lease-A-Plane International in Illinois has rental centers across the United States. Rates are similar to car rentals—there is a daily rental fee plus mileage.

PRIVATE JET CHARTERS

Arranging private air charters on business jets (or "bizjets" as the fly persons call them) continues a slow but steady growth. Corporate owners of private jets are increasingly interested in finding other users for the corporate jet when it is not being used by their own executives. Firms that manage and operate the corporate jet, such as Martin Aviation, are looking for charter business for their clients. They have been encouraging travel agents to attend receptions and seminars to learn about charters and the various types of equipment available. Agents earn 5 percent commission on charters that may start at $20,000, round trip, and seat from 8 to 18 passengers.

The National Air Transporation Association, a general aviation trade group, has available a new brochure on choosing an air charter operator. Designed for the consumer, but useful as a starting point for travel agents, the brochure gives a few broad hints about the types of aircraft available and explains how to check out an operator's safety record with the FAA. For a copy call NATA at (703) 845-9000.

MISCELLANEOUS RENTALS

Bermuda is noted for bicycle and motorscooter rentals since car rentals are prohibited.

Deep-sea fishing charters are available at almost every seaside resort. Many of these companies will pay a commission to travel agents if the reservations are prepaid.

Rental of sporting goods such as golf clubs, tennis racquets, scuba diving equipment, fishing rods, and so on, usually are not commissionable to travel agents, but knowledge of whether or not this equipment is available and the rates charged is a necessary part of an agent's consulting service.

Yacht rentals are also increasing in demand. These can be arranged in Greece, with or without a crew, and in the Bahamas and many of the Caribbean Islands. A listing of yacht rental/charter companies can be obtained from local tourist boards.

Vacationers now have several alternatives to hotels in many of the sun areas in Europe, Hawaii, Mexico, and the Caribbean—*villas* and *condominiums*. The accommodations are completely furnished and most include maid service and linen laundry service. Many of these are included in commissionable packages to the travel agents.

QUESTIONS AND PROBLEMS

1. Name some selling points you would use to persuade an air traveler to rent a car at his destination.
2. Why would you recommend the international driver's license to prospective car rental clients who are going to Europe?
3. List the information needed before you can book the car rental.
4. Is there any advantage to buying a car in Europe?
5. Give some of the pointers you would pass on to your clients who are planning on touring Europe by car.
6. Where would you rent a camper or motor-home?
7. List some of the other rental services a travel agent can arrange for her clients.

## chapter 14

Rail Tours
and Transportation

OBJECTIVES

When you have finished with this chapter you should be able to:

1. Give a brief history of Amtrak.
2. List the tour operators and private train tours available.
3. Differentiate between Superliners and Viewliners.
4. Describe the various types of sleeping accommodations on trains.
5. Discuss rail travel in other countries.
6. List the number of Eurailpasses available.
7. Suggest methods of promoting rail tours.

Rail travel was increasing in popularity with American travelers even before the energy crisis in the late 1970s, which really brought on a boom in train transportation. There are still a great number of travelers who refuse to fly and do not want the tiresome responsibility of driving long distances. This segment of the traveling public, along with train buffs, were especially happy when the Rail Passenger Service Act was signed on October 30, 1970. This act authorized the National Railroad Passenger Corporation (Amtrak) to manage the basic national rail network and be responsible for the operation of all intercity passenger trains, excluding commuter trains, under contracts with the railroads.

Although the federal government holds stock in the corporation and supplies an annual appropriation, Amtrak is a private entity and operates as a for-profit corporation. Over the past few years, the U.S. Congress reaffirmed its position on several occasions, stating that a national rail passenger system is an essential part of a balanced national transportation system.

Amtrak operates only passenger rail service and is not affiliated with the Consolidated Rail Corporation (Conrail). It is confusing because Conrail, which is a freight railroad, formerly operated commuter lines in some regions also served by Amtrak, and because Conrail owns some right-of-way over which Amtrak operates.

In 1929, the nation's railroads carried 77 percent of intercity passenger traffic by public mode in the United States. Buses carried 15.4 percent, and the airlines had an immeasurably small amount. By 1950, more than half the passenger trains had disappeared and the railroads' share of intercity passenger traffic had declined to 46.3 percent. In the meantime, traffic on buses increased to 37.7 percent, while the airlines' share had grown to 14.3 percent. By 1970, railroad passenger traffic had dropped to 7.2 percent, and there were fewer than 450 trains still operating. Airlines dominated the public carrier market with 73 percent, while buses, still in second place, held on to barely 16 percent (Amtrak Facts, 1974).

Despite the growth of the airlines and near extinction of the passenger train, the dominant mode of transportation over the last five decades has been and remains the private automobile. It accounts for approximately 86 percent of all intercity transportation. These trends have left the United States with a serious imbalance in its transportation network.

Now, interest in rail travel is increasing. Vacation travelers are rediscovering the train (peak ridership on most runs occurs during vacation and holiday periods and on weekends). In California as well as the corridor between New York City and Washington, D.C., state and local agencies are looking at intercity trains to serve commuters as well as destination travelers. Service is improving. New bilevel Superliner cars with reclining seats and large windows have been added on all western routes out of Chicago. By the end of 1988, Amtrak also upgraded its fleet of 7 Turboliners, used exclusively on its New York State routes. By 1991, Amtrak had 282 Superliners and 6 deluxe sleeping cars, with a special configuration for the Washington–Florida Auto Train. At that time they put through their order for 140 new double-decker Superliner cars for delivery, beginning with 55 in late 1993. The Superliner cars are specifically designed for the routes to the west, where the overloads are larger, with higher inside clearance in tunnels. The Viewliners (new single-level coaches, diners, and sleepers for eastern routes) are scheduled for delivery in 1994.

Route options are increasing. In late 1979, the Desert Wind began service between Los Angeles, Las Vegas, and Salt Lake City. Amtrak is studying the feasibility of adding a half-dozen new major routes. The longest big route that is being considered is the Chicago-to-Florida route. There is an enormous interest in every region for new service.

In May 1991, the Texas High Speed Rail Authority chose Texas TGV, a French–American consortium, to build a 200-mph-plus train that would link Dallas with Houston, Austin, and San Antonio. Scheduled to begin operating in 1998, it will be the first U.S. high-speed train comparable to those in Europe and Japan. Several other states, including Illinois, Wisconsin, and Minnesota, are currently studying similar rail systems, but none are as far along as that in Texas. Previous attempts to introduce bullet trains to this country, in Florida and California, were derailed by financing problems, cost concerns, and ridership questions.

The proposed train is getting strong support from the Texas travel community, whose members foresee it boosting travel in both business and leisure markets. Texas TGV plans to keep fares 20 percent below airline prices. The group plans to make travel agents a key part of its ticket distribution system, giving them easy reservation access and paying a commission comparable to the 10 percent paid on most air bookings.

The key factor is that the traveler needs an alternative to car and air travel. Crowded highways and increased expenses are taking away the pleasure of touring the country by car. Congested airports, ground delays, baggage handling complaints, and the complexity of fares are some of the reasons why some vacationers are turning away from air travel. Trains are making a comeback. In the 1980s, Amtrak experienced a steady growth in passenger numbers, bringing improvements in on-board services and schedules. Predictions are that group travel by rail will see the same increase in the 1990s. A growing number of tour operators and private rail companies are counting on rail to become a significant group travel segment.

Trains are a perfect travel vehicle for groups. On board, they promote a social atmosphere in which people can get up and move around almost like they can on a cruise ship. With popular Amtrak routes, often difficult to book during the peak seasons, private rail companies are making a bid for business in certain markets. One of the most ambitious of the ventures is Transisco Tours, a $12 million investment in bringing private rail travel to northern California and Nevada. The company has a long-term contract with Amtrak to operate the private train on the historic transcontinental route segment between the Bay Area and Reno, using Transisco's own locomotives. They can allocate one rail car exclusively for a group of 40, or cordon off half a car for a group of 24. Maupintour, Connor Tours, and Frontier Tours are among tour operators who are using Transisco. Transisco and Holland America/Westours have formed a partnership to start a private rail enterprise in the Canadian Rockies and Florida in 1992. Westours has been successful with its rail tours in Alaska.

Trans Unlimited Tours couples their two vintage private rail cars, the Virginia City and the Plaza Santa Fe, to the rear of Amtrak trains. The Virginia City offers an experience reminiscent of luxury rail travel for the wealthy. In the 1950s, travel writer and bon vivant Lucius Beebe purchased the car and had it redecorated by a Hollywood designer in an elaborate baroque style. The car is chartered to tour operators and corporations for sightseeing trips or meetings. The Plaza Santa Fe is one of six dome cars built for the Super Chief that ran between Chicago and Los Angeles in the 1950s. It is topped with a dome that affords a 360-degree view from the roof. Downstairs there is a lounge with a sunken bar and dining room.

The American European Express, the luxury rail service that started in 1990 with a run from Chicago to the East Coast, has temporarily ceased operations. They suffered a big setback in June 1991 when a derailment damaged half of the line's 12 cars.

Amtrak launched their own experiment in luxury rail service in August 1991, by adding a private car to weekend trains operating on its route between New York and Pittsburgh. The specially designed dining/lounge car, which Amtrak is leasing from the owner, accommodates 10 passengers and is equipped with its own kitchen, lavatory, dining area, and lounge. Amtrak is marketing this under the Keystone

Classic Club label. Agents will be able to make individual and group bookings through Amtrak's Arrow reservations.

Other luxury, private-car rail tours are available through Finlay Fun Time Tours, Key Tours, Rail Ventures, Princess Railtours, Sentimental Rail Journeys, and Slotsy Tours. Private rail cars let you travel in stylish exclusivity, but generally the cars are linked to the back of a regularly scheduled train and fares are more expensive than Amtrak's.

SELLING POINTS FOR U.S. RAIL TRAVEL

The romance of rail travel is still a powerful stimulator for a great number of Americans. It was the trains that tied the country together—they followed the adventurers' westward trails, originally pioneered by covered wagons and the Pony Express. The most inspiring method for a voyager of today to study his own country and understand its amazing development is to ride one of the fine trains through the west. Riding through old western towns and Indian territories is a lesson in American history that is enjoyable as well as instructive.

Rail travel is a relaxed, gracious way to see America: the only way available to see the countryside from the ground without the stress of driving and to enjoy solid creature comforts. Besides the essentials of clean, spacious cars, on nearly all routes, various types of sleeping accommodations offer outstanding comfort. There are glass-topped, picture-windowed sun lounges, and tavern observation cars. Coach trains have been improved with reclining seats. Most routes are on a reserved-seat basis, where everyone is assured of a seat. Sleeping accommodations should be reserved in advance; however, if a passenger decides to change after she boards the train, the porter can sell any available bedroom.

Another unique feature of rail travel is dining car service. The gleaming silver and linen tablecloths may have been replaced with plastic, but the appetizing menu selections, the pleasant surroundings, and friendly service are all a part of "the Amtrak experience." Dinner is served efficiently but without haste, and eaten leisurely while viewing the scenery. The food is good and the prices are comparable to those in any good restaurant. Children's menus and snacks are available in the cafe and lounge cars.

Years ago, some roads had become famous for their food specialties. Sad to say, they seldom offer them now unless enough passengers start demanding them again: the King's Dinner on the Illinois Central, the Champagne Dinner on the Santa Fe, the steak dinner on the Missouri Pacific, Wenatchee apple pie on the Great Northern, North Carolina ham-and-eggs on the Seaboard-Coast Line, the Bon-Ton salad on the Burlington, the tenderloin steak dinner on the Milwaukee Road, the Alaska black cod on the Union Pacific, cream of chicken à la Reine on the Seaboard-Coast Line, Maryland crab cakes on the Baltimore & Ohio, Colorado mountain trout on the Rock Island, and seafood platters on the Louisville and Nashville. (Amtrak has kept the names on these routes even though the individual railroads are no longer operating them.)

Unexcelled sightseeing is the most outstanding sales advantage in pleasure rail travel, especially on trains going west. There is no better way to see a country than to see it from the ground, see it up close, and see the changes in scenery from state to state.

Amtrak Services

All space is now sold on a coach base fare; sleeping accommodations are computed separately and added to the base fare. A variety of accommodations are available, but they are not all available on all trains. The *Official Railway Guide* or the timetable should be checked to see which are offered on the route chosen by your clients. The Heritage Fleet (HEP), serving the long-distance eastern routes, have the following accommodations:

Slumbercoaches: Single slumbercoaches offer a comfortable seat by day that converts into a foldaway bed at night for one person. A double slumbercoach is equipped with an upper and lower bed that converts into a sitting area for two during the day. These are the most economical sleeping accommodations.

Roomettes: For the individual traveler looking for a private accommodation, the roomette is larger than a slumbercoach and is equipped with a comfortable seat and a fold-down bed.

Bedrooms: More spacious than a roomette or double slumbercoach, the bedroom accommodates two people. In some instances, two adjoining bedrooms have a fold-away wall that can be pulled back to make a bedroom suite for family travel.

All conventional sleeping accommodations have private washing and toilet facilities, reading lights, attendant call systems, and individual climate controls.

The Superliners' coach cars and sleeper cars are in two levels. The lower levels in the coaches have the food and beverage centers that complement the dining car, and the lower levels in the sleeper cars provide the toilet facilities for the economy bedrooms and family bedrooms. The Superliners have four categories of bedrooms:

Economy Bedroom: Comfortable seating for two by day, and comfortable sleeping berths at night.

Family Bedroom: Accommodates two adults and two children; there's plenty of seating for daytime travel, and adult and children's beds at night.

Deluxe Bedroom: Provides passengers with a large sofa and a reclining swivel chair for day use, two beds for sleeping, a coat closet, and private toilet facilities.

Special Bedroom: A lower-level room designed expressly for a handicapped person and traveling companion. It includes two reclining facing seats that convert into a lower berth, an upper berth that folds down from the wall, and a specially equipped rest room with toilet and sink. Because this room is on the lower level and passage between Superliner cars is on the upper level only, car attendants provide meal and beverage service to handicapped passengers.

Rail and motorcoach service is available through Amtrak's agreements with Greyhound and Trailways to provide connections at numerous destinations; for example, to Atlantic City and Cape May from Philadelphia, from Flagstaff to the Grand Canyon or Phoenix. The ticket is written as a through ticket with coupons provided for the bus connections. Motorcoach fares are found in Amtrak's tariff; however, it may be wise to check the current fare with the individual lines before issuing the ticket. Motor homes and car rentals can be reserved and confirmed with the rail arrangements through Amtrak's reservation office.

The Auto Train to Florida, once privately owned, is now operated by Amtrak. This unique service allows rail passengers traveling to Florida to take along their private automobiles on special car carriers at the back of the train. Dinner, a continental breakfast, snacks, and a feature film are included in the ticket price.

It can be reserved in either direction or round trip from Lorton, Virginia (just outside Washington, D.C.) to Sanford, Florida (a half-hour from DisneyWorld and less than an hour from Daytona Beach). Depending on the season, the trains run

Figure 14-2 This Superliner economy bedroom can accommodate two adults and features a full-length closet, a folding table, mirror, and storage space for two suitcases. Photo courtesy of Amtrak.

daily or three times a week. Confirmed space is necessary for both the passengers and the car. Children's rates are available, but no pets are allowed.

Speaking of pets, Amtrak discontinued transporting pets in 1977 when new regulations were issued by the Animal and Plant Health Inspection Service (APHIS) of the Department of Agriculture. In the past, if pets were placed in proper containers, Amtrak would carry them in its baggage cars. The new rules required climate control (air conditioning and heating) in the baggage cars, special holding areas at each station, and that the pets be fed and watered every four hours. Amtrak estimated that it would cost $13.8 million to comply. Rather than spend the money, the company chose to terminate its pet-carrying operations. The only animals they carry now are guide dogs for the blind or deaf.

Group travel is a big part of Amtrak's business. They handle groups of 15 (the minimum) or up to 999. Groups are booked through the Group Department, which is very knowledgeable and cooperative. They will not only book the group space but will assist in hotel and sightseeing arrangements for the group. They will provide special handling of unusual baggage, such as band instruments and tobogganing equipment. Group rates and tour conductor passes are provided. The major drawback to booking groups is the limited routing; otherwise, groups can have more fun on the train than flying or busing. If there are enough people in the group to fill a coach car, the entire car is assigned to that group.

Tour packages, from the short, city sightseeing tours to the one- and two-week escorted tours, can be booked through Amtrak's tour department or directly with tour operators. Amtrak started consolidating its national tours in their travel planner in 1991 with MTI Vacations of Oak Brook, Illinois, administering the program. Regional tours will continue to be handled by Amtrak's regional sales offices. Colorful and informative brochures are available from Amtrak's sales offices. Amtrak can handle ticketing and reservations for all VIA Rail Canada trains, as well as the Canadian tour packages.

Amtrak and United Airlines combined to offer an exclusive air–rail transportation package in 1991 competitive with round-trip excursion fares. The plan can be a transportation-only package or combined with their Great American Vacations to include accommodations and sightseeing, a cruise or escorted tour. Amtrak's air–rail plan can be used in two ways: travel by rail one way and return by air, or travel by air to a gateway city, travel by rail around the region, and return to a gateway city for a flight home.

Gifts & Travel Accessories—another service to offer rail buffs—is a wide selection of items with the Amtrak logo. Travel agents do not earn commission on these, but most rail clients appreciate receiving the mail-order blanks.

Figure 14-3 Photo courtesy of Amtrak.

Rail transportation and tours are easy to sell and book through Amtrak's own computerized system. Automated agents who have American's SABRE system, Continental's SYSTEM ONE, United's APOLLO System, or WORLDSPAN can now check availability, reserve seats, and ticket through those systems. Amtrak has been accepted as the first non-airline participating carrier of the Airlines Reporting Corporation (ARC).

Amtrak plate-holding agents earn commission on all sales (tickets and tours), and from time to time, Amtrak announces special bonuses to travel agents who sell over an established quota. Amtrak abolished the original purchase order system in 1974 and all Amtrak-appointed agents received ticket stock. Sales were reported on a monthly basis. Now Amtrak's tickets are remitted through the airline area settlement plan. Amtrak also participates in several interline agreements with other carriers, such as VIA Rail, whose services may also be ticketed on ARC documents, identifying Amtrak as the ticketing carrier.

Each year since Amtrak was formed, sales from travel agents have doubled. They have approximately 24,000 appointed agents, who account for the majority of sales of tickets valued at $100 or more. Now that Amtrak is an ARC carrier and included in the automated airline systems, sales have increased tremendously. Agents who formerly shunned rail passengers will now accept the business that was once lost because no one knew how to write a rail ticket. Approximately 400 travel agencies have attained Amtrak's Golden Spike Award, given to Amtrak's top producers during the past 16 years. (In 1991, an agency had to gross $85,000 in rail sales to qualify.)

It is unfortunate that most younger travel consultants are unfamiliar with rail bookings, as this can be a good source of income for the agency. Today, a whole generation of people from teens to middle-agers have never set foot on a passenger train. Amtrak has stepped up its program of educational seminars for agents and is more liberal in its policy of discounted tickets to agents. Tickets are offered on a "confirmed seat basis," compared to the airlines' "space available" policy. ASTA was offering three-day seminars, School on Rails, to provide information on selling rail travel. Contact ASTA for dates and details.

When Amtrak assumed responsibility of the passenger train operations (beginning May 1, 1971), the routes were reduced to 16 basic runs. Since then, certain routes have been reinstated, a large part of the fleet has been refurbished, and new and modern equipment is in operation. Although fares have increased, the service has improved and agents have an attractive alternate to offer their clients.

As always, the first step in booking rail transportation and tours is the discussion with your clients to determine their needs and specific desires. A preliminary itinerary is then drawn up, showing the departure date, destination, length of time at each stopover, if any (one of the advantages of rail travel is that there is no extra charge for stopovers on the route unless a discounted fare is used), and date of return to the home city. Check the *Official Railway Guide*, Amtrak's schedule, or the reservation office for the number of travel hours between stopovers or between the departure city and the destination city. Some clients may prefer a night train with a bedroom so that they can arrive early in the morning rested and ready for their business or pleasure appointments. Others may prefer traveling during the day to enjoy the scenery. Although many of the schedules now offer no choice (as there is only one train operating on each route), alternate routes may be offered by checking the route map. When making a straight transportation booking, ask where and when the client may need hotel and/or car rentals. Another advantage of rail travel is that train depots are usually in the heart of town and a good hotel may be within walking distance.

Before Amtrak, rail reservations were made similar to air reservations—by calling the originating carrier to book the entire itinerary. The ticket was then issued by the originating carrier upon receipt of an RTPA (Rail Travel Promotion Agency) purchase order. Until July 1974, Amtrak continued with the purchase order system and tickets were issued by the nearest city ticket office.

The automated agency checks availability, fares, and schedules through the computer and the ticket is issued through the printer similar to airline transactions. Roughly 75 percent of agents booking Amtrak use CRSs to do so. But many will call Amtrak for the reservation and use the CRS only to print the ticket. Product knowledge is very important in making an Amtrak sale. Inexperienced agents may find that selling an Amtrak bedroom or roomette is more complicated than selling an airline seat. Amtrak's training video for travel agents, "Inside Track," can be ordered for the individual computer system used in the agency and is excellent training material. It covers all procedures from how to use the *Amtrak Travel Planner*, to selling techniques, to using the CRT displays.

Reservations can be called in to a central reservations number. A special toll-free number is used by Amtrak's appointed agents; another number is used by the public. A tariff department with its own toll-free number is used by the agents to verify fares and rules. However, the agents are advised to call this number only after they construct a fare and if they are in doubt about its accuracy or have any questions concerning the appropriate rules and validity dates for that particular situation. Official fares, rules, and schedules are found in the *Official Railway Guide*. A subscription to this guide was formerly given to each appointed Amtrak agent; they must now subscribe to it through the National Railway Publication Company.

The actual tickets are issued by each appointed agent. The tickets are now ARC-accountable documents: the two-flight passenger ticket, the four-flight passenger ticket, the miscellaneous charges order, and the tour order. The procedure is very similar to issuing documents for airline services, except for differences as explained in the *Amtrak Sales Guide*. The guide has complete illustrations and instructions on ticketing, as well as sections on equipment and accommodations, food and beverage service, special services, and most everything an agent needs to know to sell and issue a rail ticket. The guide is sent to all appointed Amtrak agents.

This manual is excellent training material. The instructions and illustrations are very clear and easy to follow. Since Amtrak's schedules and services are steadily improving, there is no reason why an agent should hesitate in selling rail travel. In 1987, Amtrak started publishing the *Travel Planner*, which contains everything a consultant or client needs to know about a train, including routes, tours, and hotel accommodations all in one brochure updated annually.

Amtrak reported a 23 percent increase in tour sales in 1987 and credited this increase to the enthusiastic agency response to its new consolidated tour book and travel planner. In the 1980s barely 20 percent of Amtrak's business was generated by travel agents; at the conclusion of 1991, that figure had jumped to 42 percent, which came to $460 million in gross sales.

RAIL TRAVEL ABROAD

A train ride abroad can be a true travel adventure, offering insights into local ways of life and opportunities to socialize with the local people who ride the trains. It offers opportunities to explore a country in depth and at leisure, without the strain of driving in unfamiliar territory. European railroads have a high regard for their passengers. They provide all the comforts and conveniences of a deluxe hotel room in their sleeper cars, hostesses, fast and efficient room service, air conditioning, private telephones, and excellent meals, as well as a speedy, smooth trip direct to the heart of each city. For those who do not want a sleeper, the reclining chairs with their own lights and air-conditioning are extremely comfortable. Coach class passengers may also purchase delicious box lunches, which include a small bottle of wine.

The best bargain in European rail travel is a *Eurailpass*. It gives clients unlimited first-class train travel throughout 17 countries in Western Europe, plus free or reduced rates on many bus lines, lake and river steamers, and ferries. (In many European countries, the railroads own certain ferry and motor coach lines.) The Eurailpass can be purchased only in the United States and Japan, and must be purchased in advance, before the client leaves the country. The passes are sold for durations of 15 days, 21 days, one month, two months, or three months. Eurailpass has six choices available besides the original Eurailpass.

In 1971, the Eurailpass committee introduced a student travel pass for North Americans for unlimited mileage in second class, which was later changed to include all persons under the age of 26. The Eurail Youthpass is sold for either one month or two months. The Eurail Youth Flexipass appeared in 1991 for use during any 15 days within three consecutive months or at an additional rate, may be used for 30 days within three consecutive months.

The Eurail Saverpass was introduced in 1985. This is good all year around. Three people or more traveling together will receive a discounted rate on this 15-day pass. During the winter months, October through March, the discount is available for two or more traveling together. The group must remain together throughout the trip.

Eurail Flexipass allows passengers to choose the number of days they want to travel by rail: They may travel any 5 days within a 15-day period, 9 days within a 21 day period, or 14 days within a month.

EurailDrive Pass for those clients who like the freedom of driving a car, but still want the comfort and convenience of riding a train, they can travel on any 7 days within a period of 21 days throughout Europe for one price. They can choose 4 days of first-class unlimited rail travel, plus any three days of travel with a Hertz rental car. Car drop-offs are free within most countries of rental. They also have the option to purchase up to 5 additional days of rail travel or 5 additional days of car rental at reasonable rates. Also available is Eurailtariff: first- and second-class point-to-point individual fares or reduced group fares for 6 or more people traveling together.

Eurailpass has been holding the line on prices for several years now. The only major change they have made is that buying the pass has been made easier. They no longer require the passport number at the time of purchase. Now the passport number is put on the ticket at the time of its first use in Europe. At this time, the pass is stamped with the beginning date and final date of use.

Eurailpass or tickets for straight rail transportation can be ordered from the U.S. offices of either of the following: Rail Europe, Inc. or GermanRail, Inc. Rhine steamer tickets for cruises operating between Cologne and Mainz/Wiesbaden can also be obtained through GermanRail, Inc. Eurailpass and rail tickets are commissionable to appointed agents at 10 percent.

FrenchRail, Inc. announced the creation of Rail Europe, Inc., an American corporation that made its debut in North America on January 1, 1991. Rail Europe, Inc. replaced FrenchRail and assumed all its operations. FrenchRail was the sole U.S. representative for the French, Swiss, Spanish, and Scandinavian rail systems and has been promoting and distributing Eurailpass products as well as point-to-point tickets for all 23 European railroad companies. Its first new product in 1991 was the introduction of the European East Pass, which provides unlimited first-class travel over the rail networks of Austria, Czechoslovakia, Hungary, and Poland. The European East Pass, distributed exclusively through Rail Europe, is available through travel agents for any 5 days over a 15-day period, or any 10 days over a one-month period.

If travelers are visiting only one country, the unlimited transportation passes of that country should be considered—the BritRail Pass for the United Kingdom, or the passes for France, Germany, Switzerland, or Italy, which offer unlimited travel within each country. Rail tickets for short trips within a country or between two adjoining countries can be ordered from one of the railroads mentioned previously.

BritRail Travel also sells passes for their local transportation system, and package tours to Scotland, Wales, and Ireland. In 1991, BritRail boosted its agency commissions to 14 percent on its three Great Britain Express luxury tours to encourage agents to promote the high-profit luxury rail tours.

Europe's national railways have discovered the business traveler and are gearing up their selling campaigns to the business world. It makes good sense to encourage the corporate traveler to try the trains in Europe. Service and speed are improving. Rail tickets are often half the cost of the equivalent air fares. Train schedules are more frequent than air, and intercity travel is sometimes faster, especially on short journeys. There are fewer time-stealers, such as waiting for airport transfers or airline check-in lines. There is also the added convenience of on-board sleeping accommodations, which eliminates hotel costs. And when a hotel is needed, it is usually next door to the train station in the heart of the city. Germany launched their high-speed InterCity Express (ICE) trains in June 1991, which are strongly geared toward businesspeople. Each train has an executive suite that can be used as a conference compartment, equipped with typewriter, fax, copier, and computer hookup. Each car has a passenger information system, displaying data such as the time, the route, speed, and next station stop.

The Orient Express, which made its first run from Paris to Constantinople (now Istanbul) in 1893, was reassembled by Venice Simplon–Orient Express Limited, a United Kingdom Company, in agreement with the national railways of Britain, France, Austria, Switzerland, Italy, and Hungary. The carriages are decorated in the original 1920s livery by permission of the Pullman Car Company Ltd. and La Compagnie Internationale des Wagons-Lits. The train was restored faithfully down to the most meticulous detail. Finally in 1982, the Venice Simplon–Orient Express was resumed.

The train travels between London and Venice twice weekly, with intermediate stops in Paris, Zurich, St. Anton, and Innsbruck. In 1991, the train's historic route to Budapest was resumed, with a departure once every two weeks via Paris, Salzburg, Munich, and Vienna. In addition to this luxury train service, the company operates a collection of luxury hotels within Europe and the MV Orient Express cruise line in the Mediterranean.

Rail services are being improved and expanded in other countries as well as North America and Europe. Australia and New Zealand installed new equipment, improved schedules, and personalized services. South African Railways has modernized its famous Blue Trains. The bullet-shaped Hikari (Light) Super Express of the Japanese National Railway's new Takaido Line attains cruising speeds of 137 miles per hour and takes you from Tokyo and Kyoto in about three hours.

Various Asian and Pacific nations are making it simple and less expensive to travel the trains via special rail passes similar in concept to the popular Eurailpass. Like their European role model, Asian and Pacific rail passes offer unlimited mileage for fixed periods of time at rates that usually are cheaper than the cumulative cost of individual tickets for a number of routes. Australia, India, Japan, Malaysia, and New Zealand are offering the rail passes in first-class or standard-class service. Passes for Malaysia and India must be purchased after arrival. New Zealand passes can be purchased either before or after arrival. The others must be purchased before departure from the United States.

Two specially fitted passenger cars are now operating in Ecuador, running along narrow-gauge routes through the Andean highlands and across the lowlands delta to the Pacific Ocean on Metropolitan Tourings's six new rail adventures. The most famous stretch of this rail trip is called the Nariz del Diable or devil's nose, a series of grand loops and switchbacks that the train follows along a ledge carved out of the almost perpendicular 1000-foot cliff.

QUESTIONS AND PROBLEMS

1. Why is rail transportation important in the travel industry?
2. List some selling points you would use to promote rail travel.
3. Where would you find Amtrak fares and schedules?
4. When would you recommend the purchase of a Eurailpass?
5. Where can you order a Eurailpass?
6. If a client wants a rail ticket from Brussels to Paris, who would you call?
7. List some of the selling points for rail travel for a business traveler who has a number of stops to make within Europe.

## chapter 15

Cruise Sales

OBJECTIVES

When you have finished this chapter you should be able to:

1. Give a brief description of the rise of the cruise industry.
2. Describe the variety of cruise offerings.
3. List some of the new ships and cruise lines.
4. Name some of the new or renovated ports.
5. Discuss transatlantic and transpacific crossings.
6. Differentiate between freighters and cargoliners.
7. Qualify a cruise customer.
8. List the advantages of a cruise vacation.
9. Book a cruise.
10. Discuss cruise-only agencies.

The major difference between selling an airline ticket and selling a steamship ticket is that when clients buy a steamship ticket, they are not just buying transportation with speed as its main characteristic, they are buying a resort-type holiday. For hundreds of years, ships plied the oceans and provided the only means of intercontinental transportation. The development of air travel along with improvements in safety and speed have admittedly hurt the steamship business. Today, steamship travel remains as today's transportation of pleasure, of relaxation—with service comparable to the best resorts and hotels. The steamship industry is now a resort activity, and that is the way it must be promoted and sold. "Cruise with the Fun Ships," "Take a Happy Ship," "Cruise Europe," "Fantasy Cruises," "Take a Bahama Break," "Choose to Cruise," "The Love Boat," and "Cruising Italian Style," are a few of the slogans used to sell steamship travel that emphasize the enjoyment found on a ship.

Many millions of dollars are spent annually by the steamship companies to promote their products and services, and the "See Your Travel Agent" phrase is standard procedure. Many clients are presold before contacting an agent. This is the plan of the steamship industry. Almost from the very beginning of the shipping industry, agents have been depended on to sell passenger space as well as freight, thus relieving the ship lines from the expense of maintaining numerous ticket offices and freeing them of the pressures involved in dealing directly with the public.

Although many of the great ocean liners have withdrawn from transatlantic service due to the decrease in passengers, the cruise ships are steadily increasing in numbers and profits. The luxury cruise is more alive today than it ever was. The cruise industry is expanding with new ships, refurbishing of older ships, and even creating new cruise lines. During the 1960s, converted ferry ships and older transatlantic ships were used for cruises. Now the new ships are designed specifically for the cruise industry and there are a variety of cruises, ranging in duration from three to more than 80 days.

Ironically, with the exception of American Hawaii Cruises, Mississippi river cruise lines, St. Lawrence Cruise Lines, and the coastal cruises, the cruise lines are all owned and operated by foreign countries. The American seamen's unions and the restrictions by intercostal transportation laws have driven American cruise lines out of the market and have caused American cities such as Seattle to lose cruise business. The law forbids the ships from picking up passengers in Seattle and taking them to Alaska. (The foreign carriers do not pay the high salaries that our seamen earn; the intercostal laws prohibit traffic between U.S. ports by a foreign-owned ship, known as *cabotage*.)

The spectacular growth of the North American cruise industry has focused attention on new legislature introduced in Congress in 1991 to make foreign-flag cruise lines subject to U.S. minimum-wage requirements and allow employees to organize unions. Another proposed bill would give the U.S. Coast Guard power to investigate accidents that occur on foreign-flag cruise ships sailing outside U.S. territorial waters on vessels that serve the United States or carry U.S. passengers. Alaska and Washington State politicians are expected to continue to work for exemptions to cabotage laws to make it easier for the cruise lines to offer Alaskan cruises out of Seattle and other west coast ports rather than having to depart from Vancouver, B.C., Canada.

In the meantime, a technical panel of the International Maritime Organization (IMO) met in London, England, to recommend that all cruise liners be required to meet the latest safety standards under a program to be phased in between 1994 and 2010. Currently, only ships built after 1980 are required to meet standards put forth at the last international safety convention, called the Safety of Life at Sea (SOLAS) 1974. Both safety and huge amounts of money are involved, hundreds of millions of dollars, which would be required to perform the extensive rebuilding of existing ships to eliminate wood bulkheads and other combustible materials.

Ship travel began to die in 1960 when the jets arrived, but it is a market that should be encouraged. Statistics show that only 5 percent of the population has taken a cruise. The majority of that 5 percent is repeat business, which means that once you sell a client on a cruise, they will be back for more. A ship represents escape from everyday worries, traffic, missed connections, unfinished hotels, transit lounges, and all the other holiday headaches. The sea today is attracting a broader interest and actual participation than ever before. More ships will mean a much greater variety of cruises at attractive prices that agents can offer their clients. Of the 161 passenger ships in the world, 123 ships, or 76.4 percent of the total, serve the North American market. During the past decade, there was an average growth rate of 7.5 percent in new berths; this rate of growth is expected to continue at least for the next five years.

The greatest inducement to taking a cruise is the *all-inclusive* feature. Bed, meals, baggage handling, recreational facilities, and all entertainment is included in the price of the cabin. A number of years ago, one of the steamship lines made an attempt to run their ships like hotels and offered cabins on the European plan (room only), with a choice of meal plans. This turned into a dismal failure. The public rejected this innovation, and the ship line returned to the standard procedure of providing all meals in the cost of the cruise.

Most people, especially the young, know little about cruises, but once they board a ship, many of them become confirmed cruise customers. The repeat passenger is also the unpaid sales force. A recommendation or reassurance from them to a first-timer will often convince a neophyte to try a cruise.

Every line, every ship, every cruise is different, but the features of all are the pleasures of a resort and the fascination of visiting new places, plus the choice of a completely relaxing, or a swinging vacation. Cruise vacations appeal to first-timers as well as veteran travelers. Keeping each passenger amused, relaxed, excited, and informed is the backbone of every successful cruise. People who take cruises are not in a hurry to get somewhere and then hurry back. They want to relax, enjoy the sun, and enter in the shipboard activities only if, and when, the mood strikes them.

Figure 15-2 The newest addition to the Princess Cruise's "Love Boat" fleet is the 70,000-ton Crown Princess, which features a streamlined exterior profile designed by renowned Italian architect Renzo Piano. Carrying 1,590 passengers, the ship offers more space per person than any other ship its size.

Introduction

New and Expanded Port Facilities

Many new and revolutionary developments have occurred in the past 10 years and more are planned. Cruises are better than ever. New ship lines have entered the cruise business; new or renovated passenger liners are in service; modern, efficient ship passenger terminals have been built at the port of Miami, Florida, and the cruise lines are continuing to enhance facilities to accommodate today's and to-morrow's increasingly large cruise vessels. The port of Miami anticipates breaking the 4 million passenger milestone by 1995.

New York is now a seasonal cruise port that hosts the bulk of its passengers from April to October. In 1991, 10 cruise lines operated 162 cruises from New York on a total of 14 ships. Bermuda is the top destination from New York, with cruises to New England and eastern Canada a close second. There has also been reemergence of 10- to 14-day cruises to the Caribbean. The caribbean cruises offer the appeal of a longer voyage and the convenience of a New York departure for passengers who either do not like to fly or want to sail from a port closer to home.

The port of Boston has expanded. A new passenger cruise terminal, formerly part of the Boston Army Base in South Boston, has undergone a $5 million ren-ovation. The Black Falcon Cruise Terminal, named to honor the seven Boston men who lost their lives in a 1953 explosion on board the cargo ship *Black Falcon* near the site of the new facility, is generating increased tourism for Massachusetts and provides a new port of call or embarkation port for the cruise lines.

While much of the travel industry experienced business reversals in 1990–1991, the port of San Diego continued to thrive as a cruise destination and is ready to embark on an expansion project. Construction on a new cruise ship terminal and additional berthing space is expected to be completed in two or three years.

The port of San Francisco and a group of Scandinavian developers are moving ahead with plans for a $176 million cruise terminal, waterfront park, and inter-national cultural complex that will induce more cruise lines to make San Francisco a base for sailings. The terminal is designed to handle two large cruise ships, or three to four small-to-medium-sized vessels, a total of up to 6000 passengers, simultaneously. They expect ground breaking in January 1993 and completion in 1995. The signing of the charger of the United Nations took place in San Francisco in 1945. A large fiftieth anniversary celebration of that event will coincide with the opening of Scandinavian Center in 1995.

The port of New Orleans provides departing cruise passengers with more than 416,000 square feet of air-conditioned check-in area and is an ideal port for the seven-day cruises as well as an ideal destination port for longer cruises. The terminal's proximity to the tourism center of New Orleans makes it an attractive port of call. At present, the port of New Orleans has Delta Queen Steamboat Co.'s two vessels, *Delta Queen* and *Mississippi Queen*, departing its terminal on a year-round basis. Also, Commodore Cruise Lines sails its *Enchanted Seas* from New Orleans during her winter season from November to March. Other vessels that visit New Orleans include Sun Line Cruises' *Stella Solaris* and the *Berlin* and P & O's *Canberra*.

The ports of the Bahamas and the Caribbean are expanding to accommodate the new megaliners of the 1990s. An estimated 1.5 million cruise passengers visit the Bahamas each year, making it the leading cruise destination in the Western Hemi-sphere. This growth, which is expected to double by the end of the decade, has encouraged the Bahamian government to spend $45 million on new port pro-jects. The ports in Nassau and Freeport will be upgraded and expanded; Eleuthra (which has no cruise docking facilities), and Andros will each have accommodations for two cruise ships, and the government will assist in developing the Abaco Cays project now being developed by Premier Cruise Lines.

The Puerto Rico Port Authority started a massive five-year improvement project in 1991. The first phase of the $90 million master plan was completed for the Columbus celebration in June 1992. In addition to a new Pier 4, plans call for creation of a shopping complex with boutiques, restaurants, and cafes, and a 150-room hotel built in restored and new buildings. Since St. Thomas, the Caribbean's second busiest port, has had a special cruise pier with shops and other facilities in operation for several years, attention has shifted to the less crowded island of St. Croix. The Frederiksted pier was expanded so that up to four ships can tie up at the same time. The island of Martinique has also begun constructing both new airport and cruise ship terminals in the capital city, Fort de France. The new port facility, an $8 million project, will be able to accommodate two ships, doubling the present capacity. Cuba is also expanding; however, it is unlikely to be a serious contender in the cruise market unless the politics change.

Jamaica, another of the region's busiest ports, is constructing a new $20 million cruise ship terminal in Montego Bay and is extending a pier at Ocho Rios. The harbor at Montego Bay has been dredged to a depth of 40 feet to accommodate the new ships. One of the most ambitious port projects is the $30 million Heritage Quay Complex at St. John's, Antigua. The 765-foot Heritage Pier accesses 40 shops, 28 condominiums, a casino, a bank, a supper club and disco, a gourmet restaurant, and a 22-room harbor-view hotel. Plans have been made for expansion of another major Caribbean port, St. Maarten. The $200 million project will include a 4290-foot breakwater pier able to accommodate up to eight ships at a time. The port will be built in three phases over a six-year period. This is the largest privately funded project of its kind in this region.

The Port of London Authority is progressing on a new deep-water mooring facility in the Thames River that for the first time will allow cruise ships to dock right in the heart of the British capital. However, the number of potential ships would be limited to those that are no more than 600 feet in length and draw 25 feet of draught or less. The width of the Thames will not allow for wider or heavier ships to turn around safely. This will increase business on the trips on British inland waterways, popular for many years with the British and more recently by American tourists. Some Americans insist that a week on the waterways is the only way to discover the real Britain.

Ports worldwide are also improving facilities for the expanding cruise market. The Italian government and private developers have teamed up to transform the port of Venice into one of Europe's major cruise ports. Venice, which can now accommodate 10 to 12 ships in scattered locations around the city, is constructing a port that will accommodate 17 ships docked in one area. A 250-room hotel, yachting marina, gambling casino, and sports center will also be part of the new port project.

Cruise Offerings

Ship lines have always been quick to use new ideas and modern marketing procedures. New markets are being reached with the new and large variety of cruises that are now offered. Cruises are arranged to *any* destination or to *no* destination. The Greek Line pioneered "Cruises to Nowhere" and "Singles" cruises. Unfortunately, the Greek Line is no longer in business, but other lines are continuing with these programs.

Air/sea combinations that include the round-trip air ticket in the price of the cruise from dozens of cities across the United States are now featured by almost every ship line. Even the international air fares are included in cruises of the Orient or the Mediterranean. If the air is not free, at least the cruise customer gets a reduced rate on the air fare.

Cruises that start in the Caribbean ports also appeal to many clients. In the past, New York City was the major embarkation port, not only for transatlantic crossings but for cruises as well. Then Florida ports started gaining in popularity. Cruise clients liked the idea of flying to a warm place to start on their winter cruise rather than wasting several days in cold weather between New York and the first port of call. Flying the cruise customer to San Juan (Puerto Rico), Jamaica, Barbados, Martinique, and Acapulco (Mexico) to board the ship is now featured by several cruise lines. Many air/sea packages to these ports allow for early arrival and stopovers in the ports for additional sightseeing. Stopovers can also be arranged at the Florida ports, and many cruise lines offer attractive, low-cost tour packages in Miami Beach, Orlando/DisneyWorld, and other Florida cities.

The west coast cities of San Francisco, Los Angeles, and San Diego are attracting more cruise lines. Their cruise offerings are beginning to rival those from Florida, from the three- and four-day cruises on Admiral's *Azure Seas* to Royal Viking's "Round the World" cruises. More Mexican and Panama Canal cruises are now leaving from west coast ports. The Alaska cruise market has grown so tremendously that many cruise lines are diverting their ships to Vancouver, Canada, in the summer months. River cruises in the United States and river/barge cruises on Europe's waterways are increasing in importance. For years the Delta Queen Steamboat Co. operated without competition on the Mississippi; now other lines are offering river cruises in that area. Floating Through Europe, Inc. owns and operates nine luxury barges in Europe. Accommodating eight to 24 passengers, the barges cruise the inland waterways of England, France, Holland, and Belgium. KD German Rhine Line cruises the Rhine and Moselle Rivers for one- and two-day cruises and three- to five-day cruises.

Cruises down the Yangtze River are now featured in many tours to China. Also offered by several lines are cruises down the Nile. International Cruise Center offers cruise–tours on the Volga River, with stops in Moscow and Lenningrad. They also offer cruises down the Danube and into the Black Sea.

Sun Line Cruises' slogan is "The Unique Fleet of the Cruise World" and they truly live up to it. Every cruise offering is unique: The Amazon River cruises in South America include a performance at the opera house in Manaus, Brazil; the "Gems of the Caribbean/Orinoco River Cruises" include visits to Angel Falls, Canaima—the jungle reserve—and many rarely visited Caribbean Islands; the "Panama Canal/Island-Hopping-and-Shopping Cruise" stops at islands known for shoppers' bargains, such as Curacao and St. Thomas; "Carnival in Rio Cruises" include reserved seats for the parade in Rio plus stops at Caribbean islands; their "Transatlantic Grand Cruises," one in the fall and one in the spring, follow the sun from Athens to Fort Lauderdale and include stops in both the eastern and western Mediterranean and the Caribbean.

A number of cruise lines now offer quite exotic itineraries to the Orient and Pacific. Clients can choose from seven-day cruises from Hong Kong or longer, more luxurious cruises on the ships of Holland America, Cunard, Royal Viking, Pearl Cruises, Ocean Cruise Lines, P & O Lines (Princess Cruises), and Royal Cruise Line. Ports include Hawaii, Tahiti, Japan, Hong Kong, China, Bombay, Singapore, India, the Philippines, Australia, and New Zealand.

Cruises for students and adventurers can be booked with World Explorer Cruises on their ship *Universe* (they hold classes on board while visiting interesting ports). Their cruises offer personal enrichment as well as relaxation. Passengers are active participants, not just cruisers. Unusual cruises for the adventure traveler are the specialty of Society Expeditions. More than providing pure adventure, Society is committed to the principles of ecotourism, also called "low impact" or "responsible" tourism. They offer shore excursions that do not pollute, respect local culture, and contribute in a positive way to the local economy. Their expeditions literally cover the globe and include air/sea from Miami to Africa and South America, and from the west coast to little-known islands in the Pacific and Indonesia.

Royal Viking Line introduced an on-board program in conjunction with the School of Foreign Service of Georgetown University that will bring at least three academic experts aboard every 1992 RVL cruise. Each day at sea will feature a minimum of two formal 45-minute lectures on topics relevant to the destinations visited. Depending on the itinerary, subjects might include foreign policy options in southeast Asia, the nature of apartheid, the problems faced by Indian democracy, or the challenges of a unified Europe. Passengers who complete the program will receive a certificate of merit with the official seal of the School of Foreign Service, Georgetown University.

Cruise Club Holidays Ltd. of Athens, Greece, specializes in student tours for travel and tourism classes. Students meet professionals in the world of travel and tourism and visit archaeological sites and cruises of the Greek islands.

The sportsminded are also accommodated—most every ship has skeet shooting. Now snorkeling and scuba diving lessons on board are offered by qualified instructors on all five of the Norwegian Caribbean Lines. Diving gear and underwater cameras are available for rent when the ship reaches their private Bahama island. Golf and tennis clinics with experienced instructors are available for groups or private classes on many ships. Quite often some of the ship lines will announce specialty cruises with famous golf and tennis pros giving demonstrations and instructions to the passengers on board; arrangements are made to visit golf courses or tennis courts on shore at port stops.

Royal Caribbean Cruise Lines (RCCL), which pioneered golf programs in 1985 as the official cruise line of the Professional Golfers Association (PGA), expanded its Golf Ahoy! programs by introducing pre- and post-cruise golf packages. By agreement with the PGA, a variety of special materials on golf were installed in the libraries of the RCCL ships. The materials include training films, videocassettes, PGA golf magazines, and other reading material. For a fixed price, golfers receive vouchers that cover greens fees for 18 holes of golf, as well as transportation from the ship to the course(s). Although there has been a limited demand for golf programs on other cruise lines, they will provide golf shore excursions for passengers upon request.

Bridge players and gamblers can take their choice of joining others in private games or visiting the casino on board for some blackjack or to try out the one-arm bandits (slot machines). Most ships that carry 300 or more passengers have casinos. The larger ships' casinos resemble those in Las Vegas or Monaco. The majority of cruise lines' casinos are operated by concessionaires who either pay a rental fee or return a share of the revenue to the cruise firms. Casino betting on cruise ships is set at minimal stakes. Players can bet as little as $2 at the table games and as low as a quarter on slot machines. Dealers are courteous and will offer to teach the players, making the ship's casino an ideal place to learn the various table games while at sea. (Casinos are not open while in port.)

Music lovers are not neglected. Big bands, classical music, rhythm and blues, jazz festivals, '50s and '60s oldies, country/western, and opera themes are a sampling of the special music theme cruises offered by a number of cruise lines. Some ships also invite passengers to jam with the ships's rhythm section, so tell clients to bring their sax or trombone.

You may have to spend more time in matching clients with a compatible theme cruise. Check the dates—does the date the client selected have a designated theme? An opera lover would feel very uncomfortable with a shipload of country/western fans. A client who just wants to get away from it all and is looking forward to a week of peace and quiet won't appreciate being told that a number of celebrities are on board the ship. Most cruise lines are very careful about notifying agents when something out of the ordinary, such as the filming of a television show, is scheduled. Special-interest and educational cruises are announced from time to time. Doctors, attorneys, and accountants can attend lectures on their specific professions and enjoy a cruise at the same time (with a tax deduction). Wine tasting with the experts and actually visiting wine-producing countries in Europe is offered by Royal Viking Line and Royal Cruise Line.

Cunard's QE2 has a computer center with 14 IBM personal computers, an instructor, and daily seminars. Marine Computer Enterprises of Tenafly, New Jersey, has installed computers for passenger use on several cruise ships, specifically the *Nieuw Amsterdam*, *Noordam*, *Rotterdam*, *Regent Sea*, and *Regent Star*. With the assistance of on-board instructors, passengers can work up business systems or mailing-list programs that are copied onto floppy disks that the passenger can take home.

The dream shared by all confirmed cruisers is to take a round-the-world cruise. (A dream shared by many travel agents is to sell these cruises.) At one time, six cruise ships, including some of the most deluxe, offered around the world cruises. Surprisingly, the ships went out at near or full capacity even though prices ranged from $310,000 for a luxury apartment on the QE2 to $17,000 for an inside cabin on a 90-day cruise from New York. The only true around-the-world cruises in 1990–1991 were Cunard's *Queen Elizabeth 2*, *Royal Viking Sun*, the *Azerbayazhan* (a Soviet ship sailing from London), and P & O's *Canberra* and the *Sea Princess*. Holland America Lines' (HAL) *Rotterdam* had made more world cruises than any other ship operating today. Unfortunately, she made the last world cruise in 1986. In 1987, the *Rotterdam's* itinerary was adjusted to a "grand circle cruise," eliminating the Mediterranean and Africa in response to passengers' fears about terrorism and political instability in both areas.

Most lines believe that a larger market can be found in extended sailings (45 to 75 days), which still provide passengers the full gala treatment typical of world cruises. All of the ships on world cruises or extended sailings also sell segments of the cruises for those who may wish to sail a particular ship but do not have the time to spend on a long cruise. Segment passengers share in the overall glamor of the cruise, and the price is comparable to shorter sailings on the same vessel. Ports of call are more exotic and because segment passengers board in one port and disembark in another, there is the additional possibility of booking pre- and posttours for them.

HAL contends that there is still a potential market for clients taking long cruises. These sailings appeal to up-scale clients who like the opportunities to dress up, to mingle with stars of stage and screen, and to visit new and exotic ports. A number of ship lines are looking with renewed interest at longer itineraries. Crystal Cruises is planning a 108-day around-the-world sailing as well as a 63-day South Pacific cruise in 1992. Cunard is sending three ships—*QE2*, *Sagafjord*, and *Vistafjord*—on special extended sailings, while Royal Viking Line has scheduled two—the *Royal Viking Sun* and the *Royal Viking Sky*. Chandris Fantasy Cruises has scheduled the *Britanis* on a 50-day sailing from Miami to South America with stops in the Caribbean. Regency Cruises is sending their *Regent Sea* on a 47-day voyage around South America from Ft. Lauderdale.

Spas at Sea

For the fitness conscious, many ships offer full spa and fitness facilities. Besides the usual jogging around the decks, passengers can join exercise and aerobics classes, sit in on nutrition seminars, or work out in the gyms. Most ships have

Figure 15-3 Seabourn Pride, Seabourn Cruise Line.

Chap. 15 / Cruise Sales

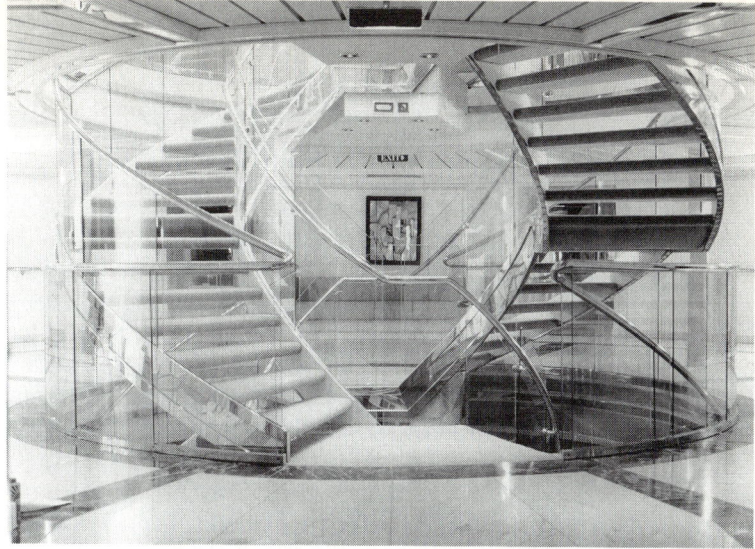

Figure 15-4 Brass and Glass Staircase, Seabourne Pride.

structured exercise classes. Five of Cunard's ships, the *Queen Elizabeth 2*, *Sagafjord*, *Vistafjord*, and *Sea Goddesses I* and *II* have what they call the Golden Door Spa at Sea, operated by the Golden Door Health Spa of Escondido, California, and it is free to their passengers. Holland America launched "Passport to Fitness" in 1990, providing its passengers with a health and fitness program with special light-cuisine menus. Guests sailing on a Royal Viking Line's ship can make use of the full spa facilities and enjoy the first croquet court afloat. The refurbished (1990) *CostaMarina* has a fully equipped fitness center with 10 exercise machines and their SpaCosta program which offers a variety of optional beauty and fitness programs.

NCL's *Norway* spent $40 million plus on construction of the most extensive spa at sea, aptly named the Roman Spa. For the first time, it is now possible to offer cruisers a complete spa vacation combined with the cruise experience. The Roman Spa has the first hydrotherapy baths on a cruise ship, with a full range of treatment and supporting programs. Five spa packages are available to passengers, but they can also purchase treatments on an individual basis. The packages are commissionable to travel agents when booked prior to embarkation.

At 12,000 square feet, the impressive Nautica Spa aboard Carnival Cruise Line's new superliner *Fantasy* is literally the biggest thing to hit the shipboard spa scene. With 35 fitness machines surrounded by glass and ocean views, passengers can work out without being shut in. A Nautica Spa Selection is presented at every meal.

The 3000-square-foot Crystal Spa and Salon aboard the new *Crystal Harmony* make this single ship a leader in ocean fitness. They offer a menu following American Heart Association guidelines and plenty of beauty and health programs. Numerous special offerings greet passengers aboard one of the seniors-oriented Royal Cruise Line ships. The company was the first to become a member of the American Heart Association's Eating Away From Home Program and provides AMA-endorsed meals. They also have "New Beginnings," a program of lectures covering health- and lifestyle-related topics.

Passengers sailing on the three ships of Regency Cruises can join "Club Physique," an on-board personalized fitness program offering everything from aerobics instruction to advice on healthy lifestyle changes. Royal Caribbean Cruises features its ShipShape program on all seven of its ships. Passengers earn redeemable ShipShape Dollars for participating in fitness activities. Seabourn Cruise Line features the program from the Thalgo Clinic of Paris aboard either the *Seabourn Pride* or the *Seabourn Spirit*, identical 212-passenger luxury ships.

New ships, new cruise lines, consolidations, and refurbished, rebuilt, or remodeled ships have been entering the cruise market so fast and furious during the expansion years from 1988 to 1992 that it is getting difficult to keep up. Fortunately, cruise seminars sponsored by *Travel Weekly*, *Travel Trade*, ARTA, and ASTA help keep the travel agent up to date. New publications, such as *Cruise Views* (sent free to qualified agents) and sales supplements from *Travel Trade*, *Travel Weekly*, and *Travel Age Publications* fill in the gaps. *OAG Cruise and Shipline Guide* is invaluable for its "Ship Profiles" and the listings "Cruise Destinations of Popular Ships" by operator names and alphabetically by ship names.

While it is debatable whether consolidations benefit the industry, some lines feel that agents will benefit with more financially stable cruise companies. Rising fuel prices may find smaller companies unable to keep afloat, but larger companies can offer sales and marketing opportunities that small ones cannot.

Niche marketing is the current buzzword in the cruise industry. Actually, the term is generally used to identify the ship lines' specialty market. With the introduction of new or refurbished ships and new programs and amenities offered to the consumer, travel agents must spend more time qualifying the clients and matching them up to the right cruise.

Admiral Cruises' two vessles *Azure Seas* and *Emerald Seas* were extensively refurbished in 1990 and 1991. While the *Emerald Seas* will continue with three- and four-night cruises from Ft. Lauderdale, the *Azure Seas* will do seven-night eastern Caribbean cruises. Admiral Cruises originated as "Eastern Cruise Lines" over 120 years ago and was the first to offer three- and four-night cruises. The line became part of the Royal Caribbean Cruises Ltd. family in 1988.

American Hawaii Cruises has little competition because it sails in Hawaii, where very few lines operate. Their ship *Constitution* was refurbished in 1990 and the *Independence* was refurbished in 1991.

Carnival Cruise Line (the "fun" ships)—now the largest cruise line in the world—with the acquisition/merger of Holland American Line and Windstar Sail Cruises can offer the entire spectrum of cruising. Their ship the *Fantasy*, a 2600-passenger superliner, was purposely built for the three- and four-day cruise market. Since its launching in 1990 it has become a leader in that market. The sister ship, the *Ecstasy*, launched in June 1991, by general acknowledgment is Carnival's most elegant and sophisticated liner. Carnival's "fun" is still there but in a more dignified atmosphere. The 2600-passenger ship will alternate seven-day eastern and western Caribbean sailings from Miami. Carnival's next ship is the superliner *Sensation*, due in 1993. In September 1991, Carnival signed a contract with Kvaernar Masa-Yards to build a sister-ship, the *Fascination*, which is slated for delivery in early fall 1994. A fifth mega-ship, the IMAGINATION, was ordered in 1992 and is scheduled for delivery in early fall 1995. The success of the first two superliners, the *Fantasy* and the *Ecstasy*, encouraged Carnival to go ahead with the new contracts.

Celebrity Cruises was designed by Chandris, Inc. to fit into the highest end of the mass market. After a year and a half, the company increased its passenger capacity by over 50 percent with the addition of a brand-new ship, the *Zenith*, which set sail in April 1992 (capacity 1374). The itinerary has alternate 7-day eastern and western Caribbean routes, or combined for a 14-day cruise. The ship is a slightly larger twin sister to the *Horizon* (capacity 1354) and larger than the completely refurbished *Meridian* (capacity 1106, formerly the *Galileo*). In 1990, Celebrity Cruises received Onboard Services' "Best Food Service" award, as well as the International Cruise Passenger Association's "Best Cruise Line of the Year" award. The ZENITH is another winner for Celebrity Cruises, reservations are breaking industry records.

Chandris Fantasy Cruises' fleet of five ships—*Amerikanis*, *Azur*, *Britanis*, *Romanza*, and the *Victoria*—sail to the Caribbean, Mediterranean, Mexico, South America, and Europe. Targeting the middle of the mass market, the line offers great diversity in itineraries and maintains its commitment to provide excellent standards at affordable prices.

The world's largest sailing ship, the 9000-ton, 386-passenger *Club Med I*, is operated by the resort company Club Med, Inc., which has over 100 vacation "clubs" all over the world. The ship is being marketed not as a floating Club Med, but as a sophisticated cruise ship which is more upscale than most Club Med resorts but still quite casual. The vessel does not cater to singles and children in the same way that the villages do. Children on board must be at least 12 years old. The ship has been alternating between sailings in the Caribbean and the Mediterranean. She is joined by *Club Med II* in December 1992. The new vessel will be based in New Caledonia and will be marketed primarily to Japanese and Australian clients.

Bermuda Star Line, formerly Bahama Cruise Lines, merged with Commodore Cruise Line by parent company Effjohn, now has three newly refurbished ships: *Enchanted Isle* (formerly the *Bermuda Star*), *Enchanted Seas* (formerly the *Queen of Bermuda*), and the *Caribe* (formerly the *Olympia*). They offer seven-day sailings to the Western Caribbean from New Orleans, the Mexican Riviera from San Diego, and selected round trips from New York to Eastern Canada; the *Caribe* continues to operate from Miami to the Caribbean.

Costa Cruise Lines, the line synonymous with "Cruising Italian Style," started an ambitious two-year project in December 1987 to completely renovate and refurbish their three Caribbean ships to reflect their concept of pleasure and elegant comfort. Miami architect and designer, Jeffrey Howard, succeeded beautifully in bringing back the Art Deco movement in the *CarlaCosta*, the *CostaRiviera*, and the *Daphne*. Activities differ from ship to ship, but the service, cuisine, and flavor of a European vacation are mainstays on every Costa vessel. The fleet started expanding with the 776-passenger *CostaMarina* in 1990, in January 1992 the 1350-passenger *CostaClassica* (one of the most expensive and elegantly designed ships ever constructed), and in November 1992 brought out the *CostaAllegra* (a modified sister-ship of the *CostaMarina*.) In September 1992 the *Daphne* joined its sister ship, the *Danae*, in Europe as part of the newly created "Prestige Cruises."

Palm Beach–based Crown Cruise Line began with one-day cruises and later added a rebuilt ferry for two- and five-day sailings. In 1990 the company entered the seven-day market with the *Crown Monarch*, the first ship built specifically for the cruise line. The 556-passenger ship is geared toward repeat cruisers looking for a yachtlike atmosphere. Crown Cruise Line will operate two new ships originally ordered for Commodore Cruise Line, which recently took a 50 percent stake in some Crown operations. The two 820-passenger vessels are being built in Spain by Commodore's parent, Effjohn International. The first vessel, *Crown Jewel*, entered service in September 1992; the sister-ship follows in 1993. Crown is aiming for the upscale end of the midmarket. Focus is on service and cuisine rather than flashy shipboard amenities. Their "Crowncierge" service offers 24-hour room service and complimentary bon voyage champagne.

Crystal Cruises is a new cruise line established by the Japanese cargo shipping giant NYK Line. With Scandinavian officers and a European hotel staff, the 960-passenger *Crystal Harmony* is Crystal's prototype and one of the most spacious ships afloat. Two more ships are expected. The ship caters to an upscale clientele and features a number of innovative firsts, including the first Caesar's Palace at Sea Casino; an elegant main dining room and two alternative dinner restaurants at no extra cost; the largest penthouses at sea; and private verandahs in more than 50 percent of its staterooms. The Coca-Cola Company chartered the *Crystal Harmony* for use as their headquarters during the 1992 Summer Olympic Games in Barcelona, Spain.

During its 151-year history, Cunard has operated more than 190 ships. Cunard today is the only cruise line to offer regular transatlantic service on its flagship *Queen Elizabeth 2*. She offers traditional ocean liner service with unlimited activities. Cunard's schedule for the next few years will feature "Festivals at Sea" on all of their ships, including voyages with classical music, opera, mystery, film, fitness, and epicurean themes.

Diamond Cruise Ltd's *Radisson Diamond* premiering in summer 1992 in the four-, five,- and seven-day market had so many advance bookings that an order was placed for a sister ship, *Radisson Ruby*. Radisson Hotels will operate and market the two ships for their owner, Diamond Cruise Ltd., a Finnish company in which Radisson holds a minority stake. The ships have their own marketing operation, Radisson Diamond Cruises, based in Miami, and will use San Juan as home port. The 354-passenger vessel will have 177 outside luxury stateroom/suites, most with balconies. The *Radisson Diamond* is noteworthy not only for its radical new twin-hull design, but also because it was designed specifically for the group and incentive market. Extensive facilities for corporate conferences include five boardrooms and one large meeting room, which can be reconfigured into six smaller meeting rooms. The vessel will also have in-house publishing facilities and secretarial services. It was hired for use in Barcelona during the 1992 Olympics.

Dolphin Cruise Line formed a new subsidiary, Majesty Cruise Line, to operate a new $200 million liner in the upscale market. The vessel *Royal Majesty*, a 1100-passenger vessel will compete in the premium market and service levels will be similar in style to the Holland America Line. Dolphin Cruise Line was launched in 1984 with the 594-passenger *Dolphin IV* in the three- and four-day Bahamian market, and two years later moved into the seven-day Caribbean market with the 800-berth *SeaBreeze*. Dolphin is widely recognized as being one of the success stories of the 1980s. They believe in relatively small ships where they can offer a high quality of ambience and service. Service on the *Royal Majesty* will be upgraded above the levels of its current ships and will feature innovations never offered before. For example they will offer a completely smoke-free dining room, and at least 132 of its 528 cabins will be set aside for nonsmokers. The owners plan to add two more ships to the Dolphin line and three more to the Majesty line.

Norwegian Cruise Line, known for its Sports Afloat Program, theme cruises, Dive-In snorkel program, and Broadway-style entertainment, keeps passengers busy and gives travel agents a whole new range of sales opportunities. Agents can now sell Bermuda and Mexican Riviera cruises upon the newly acquired and refurbished *Westward* (formerly the *Royal Viking Star*). After major refurbishments in April 1989 and again in April 1991, the 790-passenger *Westward* began service to Bermuda in the spring and summer months and seven-day cruises between Los Angeles and Acapulco in the fall and winter months. In addition, the classic liner *Norway* was also refurbished in 1991 to include a Roman spa, two new glass-enclosed decks atop the vessel, and "Le Rendezvous," an à la carte supper club.

Ocean Cruise Lines was founded in 1983 to meet the growing demand for first-class Europe cruises. In 1987, the company purchased Pearl Cruises of Scandinavia, which had been formed in 1982 to provide year-round service in the Orient. In May 1990, Ocean and Pearl were acquired by Paris-based Croisieres Paquet (Paquet French Cruises), specialists in cruising to exotic destinations since 1860. Although the three companies are owned by one corporation, each line will be kept as separate entities that will continue to function as leaders in their markets. However, the expertise gained by each line will be shared by the others. The *Mermoz*, Paquet's 530-passenger vessel, brings to the group a sterling reputation for its fine cuisine and annual theme cruises. The *Mermoz* will be the recipient of some *Ocean Princess* and *Ocean Pearl* characteristics; both ships are well known for their unique itineraries and comprehensive cruise/tours.

The building of the *Oceanic Grace* by the parent company, Showa Line Ltd., in 1989 signified a breakthrough in the Asian travel market. Carrying only 120 passengers in 60 outside cabins, the ship combines the amenities of a large cruise ship with the exclusiveness of a luxury yacht. She appeals to sophisticated, well-traveled clients who want an in-depth look at Japanese culture. Increased commissions for groups of 20 or more and volume overrides for 50 or more passengers are available to travel agents. Charters and pre- and post-cruise stays can be arranged through Oceanic's U.S. agent, Tourism Marketing Specialists.

With the addition of three new "superships," the *Regal Princess* in 1991, the *Crown Princess* in 1990, and the *Star Princess* in 1989, Princess Cruises has become a leader in the world's most popular cruise destinations—the Caribbean, Mexico, Transcanal, Europe, and Alaska—while it offers a variety of cruises to some of the most exotic destinations in the world. Princess offers a variety of ship styles, ranging from smaller, more intimate vessels to the brand-new superships. The fleet features some of the largest staterooms and has almost a 20 percent higher passenger space ratio than the industry average. Interiors throughout reflect a soft, contemporary, elegant decor. But whether it is the intimate surroundings of the *Pacific Princess*, TV's original "Love Boat," or the new five-star *Regal Princess*, all vessels feature the hallmarks of the Princess fleet; spaciousness, comfort, and casually elegant appointments.

One of the newest entrants into the all-suites passenger ship niche, Renaissance Cruises, formed in 1989 by Fearnley and Eger, the 120-year-old, Oslo-based shipping concern, offers luxurious accommodations and destination-oriented itineraries that span the globe. The company started service with the 100-passenger *Renaissance I* in 1990. By April 1992, the line completed its eight-ship fleet. The first four, *Renaissance I*, *Renaissance II*, *Renaissance III*, and *Renaissance IV*, are identical in design, while the last four are slightly larger, accommodating 114 passengers. The shallow draft of Renaissance ships will enable them to call in ports not accessible to larger vessels; nearly one-third of the line's 180 ports will be exclusive to the company. They have 13-, 20-, and 27-day packages that include deluxe hotel stays of two nights each before and after the cruise, free round-trip economy air fare from major cities in the United States, transfers, and baggage handling. The restaurant has a single, open-seating plan and guests dine when and with whom they please.

The president of Certified Tours, headquartered in Ft. Lauderdale, and Italy's Cameli Group purchased Renaissance Cruises, Inc. and its fleet of eight vessels in August 1991. Edward Rudner, president of Certified Vacations, created a holding company called Luxury Liners in order to form the joint venture with the Cameli Group. The Cameli Group, an investor in oil trading, refining, and transportation and luxury liners; each holds a 50 percent stake in Renaissance. Royal Caribbean Cruise Line (RCCL) offers a year-round medium-priced product that is geared toward the middle- and upper-class segments of the market. The *Nordic Empress*, specifically designed and built for the three- and four-day market, started service in 1990, and RCCL launched two new ships in 1991 and 1992 while the *Viking Serenade* was given a major refurbishment. The 2354-passenger vessel *Monarch of*

Figure 15-5 Princess Cruises' 63,500-ton *Star Princess* at anchor of Mayreau in the Grenadines.

the Seas made its debut from its home port of San Juan in 1991; the sister-ship, *Majesty of the Seas*, sailed out of Miami in April 1992. RCCL invested $6 million in the refurbishment of their 1390-passenger vessel *Song of America* in the fall of 1991. A conference center and boutique were added, and the casino, a bar, and a cafe were redesigned. Their ship, the 2272-passenger *Sovereign of the Seas*, launched in 1988, was the industry's first supership. Since then a number of lines are going into the supership or megaship concept.

Seabourn Cruise Line, called Signet until a lawsuit by another company using the same name forced the change, ordered a $50 million sister-ship to its *Seabourn Pride* even before the official launching in December 1988. The second ship, the *Seabourn Spirit*, was delivered in 1989. The two all-suite 212-passenger vessels are targeted for the affluent market, with per diem rates of $600 per person. Both vessels have gourmet dining rooms with long dining hours and other exclusive amenities for its discriminating clientele. Because of the Middle East crisis, Seabourne Cruise Lines redeployed the *Seabourne Pride* from Europe and the Mediterranean to New England and Canada. Originally, the move was a defensive measure, but response to the new itinerary has been very successful and plans have been made for sailings to Newfoundland and Labrador. The Canadian Maritime Provinces route could be the next Alaska for the cruise industry.

The *Song of Flower* (formerly the *Explorer Starship*, flagship of the now defunct Exploration Cruise Lines) had been promoted and sold mainly to Japanese tourists. The Japanese owners, Seven Seas Cruises, decided to shift marketing efforts to the U.S. market in 1991. The 172-passenger vessel had been cruising Alaska in the summer and the rest of the year in Asia. An impressive $7 million refurbishing was undertaken by the first buyer, businesswoman Tomoko Uenaka, and later sold to K Line of Japan, the parent company of Seven Seas. Passenger capacity was reduced from 250 to 172, which enabled Seven Seas to enlarge some of the already sizable cabins and to install amenities not found on all ships, such as a massage facility and a formal-wear rental shop. They provide one seating for meals, 24-hour room service, complimentary beverages (including all liquors), and gratuities are not accepted. Seven Seas is looking for a few hundred travel agents who have the clientele that would appreciate the affordable elegance the *Song of Flower* offers. Commissions start at 13 percent, with generous overrides on additional bookings on each sailing.

Yachtlike cruises and actual yachts are increasing in popularity and in numbers. The 1980s brought megaships and miniships into the market. In the 1990s there is a surprising variety of sizes, itineraries, and prices; and the majority are selling well. There is definitely a market for the yachtlike cruises. *Sea Goddess I* and *Sea Goddess II*, virtual private yachts with a passenger-to-crew ratio of 1.3 to 1, started the trend in 1984 for the small, luxurious ships. As noted previously, there are now a number of ships in the market that accommodate clients who prefer the smaller ships.

SAIL CRUISES

From a survey of various sail cruise companies, sail cruises are a vacation alternative that has a growing appeal for active couples over 60 or sedentary baby-boomers reaching age 40. Within this cruise niche there is a variety that distinguishes each sail ship. For example, some vessels will draw passengers who want the feeling of understated elegance, off-the-beaten-track ports of call within an intimate atmosphere; while other ships attract passengers who want the real nautical experience and can dress for dinner in their blue jeans.

Windstar is a sail cruise line that offers casual elegance aboard its 440-foot, four-masted ships, which feature 74 outside cabins. Miami-based Star Clippers is the newest entry in the sail cruise market. The line's first ship, the 3025-ton, 180-passenger *Star Flyer*, was launched in the summer of 1991 and was joined by her sister-ship in January 1992. Star Clippers' vessels are true sailing ships, with hull design derived from nineteenth-century clipper ships. Modern technology makes the ships as comfortable and luxurious as the largest cruise liner. But instead of a constant hum of engines, passengers hear flapping sails and waves lapping the hull.

Windjammer Barefoot Cruises Ltd. fills a special niche in the cruise market. Each of their "tall ships" offers the best of the old and the new, from towering masts supporting thousands of square feet of billowing sales to comfortable air-conditioned cabins with private showers and heads. And each cruise offers ship-mates the chance to live out their seagoing fantasies. The first windjammers were descendants of the American clipper ships but were built for carrying large cargos at great speed over long distances. Unfortunately, they were replaced within 60 years by the steam-driven cargo carriers and passenger liners.

Windjammer Barefoot Cruises acquired in 1988 a Scottish cargo/passenger ship to replace their *Barefoot Rogue*, bringing supplies to the cruise line's sailing ships in the Caribbean. The new ship, the *Amazing Grace*, accommodates up to 60 passengers, departs from Freeport, Bahamas, and calls on as many as 19 Caribbean islands on 21-day cruises. Windjammer now has a fleet of six ships that sail the West Indies, the Grenadines, and the British Virgin Islands. They have a club for sailing enthusiasts who are not only interested in sailing the ships but also in helping to restore these vessels.

World Yacht Enterprises Ltd. of New York, specializing in private yacht charters, can arrange for the charter of yachts in the Virgin Islands, the Windward and Leeward Islands, the Bahamas, Florida and other coastal areas of the United States, and in the Mediterranean waters of Greece, France, Italy, Spain, Turkey, and Yugoslavia. The costs vary depending on the size and type of yacht, the cruise duration, and the number of people in the party.

The Albatross Private Yacht Chartering Club of Merrick, New York, offers a wide choice of yachts for charter, not only in the Greek Islands, but in other parts of the eastern Mediterranean around the Yugoslav and Turkish coasts, as well as in the western Mediterranean from Italy to Spain. They also offer scheduled departures on sailing cruises in Greek waters in the summer.

A new entry in 1990 to the Aegean and Black Sea was Classical Cruises, whose recently redecorated, yachtlike, 140-passenger *Illiria* previously sailed under charter to university and museum groups. It sails on Mondays, round-trip, from Istanbul to the Greek Islands. Special lecturers accompany every sailing, and wine is included with meals.

OCEAN CROSSINGS

Only two lines now offer a regular schedule of transatlantic crossings: Cunard Line and the Polish Ocean Lines. They provide approximately three crossings a month from April through December in each direction. The only other transpacific crossings available are segments of round-the-world cruises or cargoliners (freighters).

Few modern travelers have the time to spend sailing round-trip to Europe, but Cunard Lines' promotion "sail one way, fly the other way, free" has been very successful. They also offer complete package tours of Europe and/or discounts at European hotels and on the Orient Express railway. Passengers have the choice of sailing one way on the *QE2* and flying one-way on the Concorde or regular British Airways flights.

The *QE2* spent six months in dry dock during the winter of 1986–1987 for a complete refurbishment. Some of the major renovations included the addition of eight new penthouse suites complete with private verandahs. First-class staterooms were outfitted with television sets, VCRs, stereo sets, and safes. Several of the ship's restaurants were refurbished. At their Tables of the World restaurant, a multimillion-dollar redesign allows passengers to stop at buffet tables throughout

Figure 15-6 *Queen Elizabeth 2*—known as the "city at sea." Cunard's *Queen Elizabeth 2* boasts a host of contemporary facilities, including an exclusive Shopping Promenade of more than a dozen international boutiques, a Golden Door Spa at Sea, four swimming pools, an indoor/outdoor Lido Magrodome Center, an executive Boardroom, an IBM Computer Center, the only seagoing American Express Foreign Exchange Service, six lounges and much more.

the room and sample food from various countries at their leisure. A shipboard tuxedo service has been added to its new shopping arcade. Tuxedos can be rented or purchased. Other special services include 24-hour room service and purser's office.

A transatlantic crossing is an ideal way for pleasure travelers to begin a tour of Europe. It gives them five days to enjoy the pleasures of ocean travel. They become accustomed to time-zone changes before they arrive in Europe—rested and ready for active sightseeing—instead of needing an extra day to adjust after flying across the ocean.

It is also a good recommendation to end a tour by ship. Travelers that have done a lot of shopping do not have to concern themselves with the overweight baggage charges; car purchasers can bring their cars back to the United States on the same ship and drive to their home city. Travelers who have been on extended

Figure 15-7 Cunard Lines.

tours throughout Europe welcome the few days' rest before returning to their homes and jobs. Businesspeople can relax and review their accomplishments before going back to the office.

FREIGHTER TRAVEL

Interest in freighter travel increased as the transatlantic and transpacific passenger ships decreased. While a voyage by freighter can be an exciting experience, with more stopovers (usually in out-of-the-way ports which are not visited by passenger liners), this type of travel is not for everyone. The appeal is to the young at heart (no matter what the age) with the time and money to adapt to the delays or sudden changes in schedules, and long layovers in ports where the only diversion is watching the ship being unloaded and loaded.

The cost of freighter travel is low on the 12-passenger vessels but equal to most cruise lines on the larger ships known as cargo liners or cargo–passenger ships. Cargo liners carry between 100 and 200 passengers. Some ships' accommodations are deluxe, while others are very spartan. Unfortunately, many cargo liners are being phased out. American President Lines is replacing the older vessels with ships without passenger accommodations. Delta Line Cruises (purchased by Prudential Lines) is also replacing their ships with nonpassenger vessels.

There are some lines, however, who are expanding their capacity. Ivaran Lines, a Norwegian passenger/freighter company, took delivery of an 88-passenger vessel in February 1988, the *Americana*. Besides the 88 passengers, the *Americana* carries up to 1120 cargo containers. Amenities on board include a swimming pool, health club, library, lounge bar, and casino. Breakfast and lunch is buffet style. Dinner is by reservation at tables of four to eight. On evenings at sea, jacket and tie are requested for the men. Fifty-four cabins divided into five categories are on three decks. They have been designed for long voyages by the Norwegian firm that designed the *Sea Goddess* interiors.

The *Americana* sails on 46- to 48-day round trips between New York–Miami and Buenos Aires, Argentina. Ivaran is targeting the *Americana* to senior citizens because they are most likely to have both the time and the money to spend on a 48-hour trip priced from $6500 to $12,600 a person, although they offer off-season discounts and a 40 percent discount on the upper berths in the single cabins. In addition, Ivaran Line operates two 12-passenger freighters, *Salvador* and *Sante Fe*, about once a month from Houston on 50- to 55-day voyages to the east coast of South America. Reservations for the Ivaran Line can be made through their New York office.

Life on a freighter is very informal. Passengers must entertain themselves. There is no cruise director and/or scheduled activities. The food is usually good and plentiful. Some ships have air-conditioned cabins. Most cabins have outside locations and are quite comfortable.

Booking a freighter voyage is not as easy or as simple as most people believe. There are many complexities, frustrations, and extra work when dealing with the insecurities of the passenger-carrying freighters. Freighters are limited to 12 passengers; otherwise, they would have to provide a ship's doctor for each voyage (for this reason, passengers aged 60 and over must present a doctor's statement that they are physically able to travel). Since there are a limited number of passengers, bookings must be made as far in advance as possible, while keeping in mind that the passenger must be prepared to sail at a moment's notice if necessary, or may require a hotel room for several nights at the port of embarkation if the sailing is delayed.

Freighter clients form a very distinct clan. They are very loyal to both their travel agent and the steamship line they prefer to sail with. They scorn the cruise liners and will repeat an itinerary rather than forgo the freighters. Travel agents who specialize in this field agree that it can be a reasonably lucrative field once the booking procedures are mastered and proper contacts with the freighter lines are established.

A special file on freighter travel can be assembled by requesting general information and sailing schedules from the passenger freighter services listed in the steamship guides. Freighter operators will usually comply with the request but will emphasize that their principal business is the transportation of cargo and that published sailing schedules and ports of call are subject to change and cancellation. *Ford's Freighter Travel Guide*, published semiannually, is a must reference book for the agent who sells freighter travel.

Travel agents who are interested in building a freighter cruise clientele can contact TravLtips cruise and freighter travel association in Flushing, New York that represents 20 freighter lines that carry passengers in addition to cargo. CAST Freighter Cruise ships, based in Belgium, one of the lines represented by TravLtips, pays 7 percent commission to travel agents and provides sailings throughout Europe (some originate in Montreal, Quebec, Canada).

Freighter World Cruises in Pasadena, Calif. represents 40 percent of passenger-carrying freighters and will work with travel agents.

SELLING CRUISES

With the wealth of cabins available, new ships, refurbished ships, new itineraries, and new features on board, selling cruises is easier and more profitable than ever. It is also the best value for the vacationer's money. With added competition, the ship lines are offering more discounts and promotions to the public. More incentives are also offered to the travel agents. Groups, in particular, are sought after by the cruise lines. The agent will receive not only the usual 10 percent commission, but also a group discount that can be passed on to the group (at the agent's discretion) and a promotional discount to offset the cost of advertising. For a large enough group, the commission scale can go up to 20 percent or more.

There is a minimum of work involved in selling cruises. Ship lines issue the tickets (most lines will also issue the airline ticket in the air/sea programs). Baggage tags, travel tips, clothing suggestions, shopping hints, and often, shore excursion brochures are furnished by the ship lines. Shore excursions that can be ordered in advance are also commissionable to travel agents (although some lines do not offer this).

Fares are easy to calculate, although the passenger must be advised that the cruise fares are determined by the location and availability of the cabins. This is the most important difference in quoting ship fares versus air fares. A specific fare cannot be quoted until the ship line is checked for availability.

Many fare inducements are offered (and they are not subject to the unexpected changes that are too frequently found in the air fares): seasonal, air/sea combinations, family plans, senior citizens' discounts, student rates, honeymooners specials, and discounts to repeat customers. Volume discounts are given for full ship charters and groups. Special itineraries can be requested for regional or convention charters, sales meetings, special events, and unusual destinations (for groups).

Successful selling of steamship cruises and transportation requires knowledge of both the client and the appropriate vessel on which he will have the most comfort, service, and enjoyment. Client's preferences may be influenced by such factors as their own standard of living, their budget, their special interests, and most important, their schedule. Cruises vary in length, price, and in the amount of time needed for booking. A long cruise takes long-range planning; a shorter cruise, such as the three- and four-day cruises out of Florida and California, can be booked on shorter notice. In addition, unless the client lives in a departure port city, transportation to the port must be considered in both time and money.

Almost everyone is a prospect for a cruise: singles, couples, families, groups. The sea voyage itself is the principal appeal. The lure of the sea is universally appealing to young or old, male or female. The second most appealing factor is the wide choice of ports of call from both the east and west coasts. Finally, there is the attraction of luxury travel, which is within the budget of almost every traveler. Nowhere else is a client more pampered and catered to than on board a cruise ship. Cruise ships are one-class ships. Passengers may be paying the minimum rate for their cabin, but they have the use of all the facilities on board and are served the same meals as passengers occupying the highest-price suite. A cruise is one of the best dollar values on the travel market. Few resort hotels can offer the luxury and service at the same price per day as the cruise ship.

The increasing number of cruises now available enable the agent to select a cruise for any age group. The elderly and retired look for comfort, excellent cuisine, and congenial companionship. They have the time and the sophistication to appreciate the longer cruises, such as round-the-world, the South Pacific and Orient, South America, and the Mediterranean cruises. The very active elderly and the middle-aged want the same, but with more shore excursions and shipboard activity. The younger crowd (20 to 30) and the younger middle-aged (40 to 55) constitute the best market for short cruises and air/sea vacations, which offer almost unlimited flexibility in length, price, and sightseeing.

Selling Groups

Group travel by ship is an expanding market that most agents have not fully exploited. Groups can be found everywhere—social clubs, religious groups, professional groups, schools, alumni clubs, special-interest groups. Business meetings, conventions, and incentive groups are using ships more and more often. The ship lines are only too happy to accommodate such groups and have actively solicited this type of business.

The advantages of using a ship are many and can be available to groups of 15 or 1500 with equal ease. The main advantage is that group members are easily and readily available for meetings and special announcements. The problem of searching for missing members is eliminated simply because they cannot stray too far on board ship.

Another important advantage is that the length of the cruise and the ports of call can be arranged for specific needs, especially for larger groups who may charter the entire ship for specific dates. There is also the advantage of having all the rooms (cabins) ready for occupancy at the same time on the same date. Except for strikes and acts of God, the ship lines are not likely to cancel or change the date for a group at the last minute as hotels might do.

Most ships provide a variety of meeting rooms as well as a theater for visual/audio presentations. Schedules for the use of these rooms are tailored to the convenience of each segment of the group. Printing facilities on board the ship are also made available to the groups. Some ships provide ship-long decks designed for display units.

Shore excursions at each port visited can be arranged for the group for general sightseeing or for visiting a special point of interest. (Many large corporations have branch offices or plants in the Caribbean, West Indies, and Europe which they would like to inspect, or they may wish to visit other companies in their own line of work.)

Last, but not least, there is the pleasure of a cruise, which the delegates and members of a group can easily enjoy (at no extra cost) between and after the business meetings. An added benefit is that spouses and children will be happily occupied with the regular shipboard activities while the business meetings are in session.

Of major importance to the travel agent is the opportunity to increase her commissions. On group sales ship lines are flexible concerning commissions, tour

Figure 15-8 *Enchanted Isle*—Commodore Cruise Line's 23,395-ton, 731-passenger *Enchanted Isle* makes 7-day Mexican Riviera cruises from San Diego in the winter/spring, 10-day Caribbean cruises from New York in the summer, and 7-day Canada cruises between New York and Montreal in the fall.

conductor tickets, promotional expenses, group discounts, and shipboard arrangements. These items are negotiable and may vary seasonally and from line to line. Naturally, the ship lines are more generous during their slow seasons. It would be rather foolish to ask or expect special favors during the two busy seasons—Christmas and Easter—even for individual bookings.

Education and Training for Cruise Sales

The main reason that more cruises are not sold is lack of product knowledge by travel consultants, the logical people to educate the public in the advantages of a cruise vacation. Travel agent education in steamship sales as well as other travel sales is best accomplished by familiarization tours/cruises. Personal experience is the best teacher. During the past few years, cruises were sold out and few cabins were available to offer to agents for fam trips or personal travel. However, with so many new ships entering the market and the pressure to sell these ships brought an increase in fam trips and seminars. *Travel Trade*, *Travel Weekly*, and *TravelAge* magazines, ARTA, and ASTA each sponsor excellent seminars which include actual inspections of ships as well as guest speakers from the cruise lines and travel agents who specialize in selling cruises. Seminars are held in Florida and at west coast ports.

CLIA (Cruise Lines International Association) started a training program in 1973 designed for beginners and a refresher course for the more experienced, which is now held in over 150 cities throughout the United States and Canada. In conjunction with ASTA, CLIA has a "school-at-sea" program which originated on the west coast and expanded to the east coast. This program consists of three to five days' intensive training in every facet of steamship services—starting with "Types of Ships," "Basic Areas of Travel," and "Deck Plans: What They Are and How to Read Them," to suggestions for tipping. The classes are held on board ship while sailing to its destination. A complete and thorough tour of the ship is included, and inspection tours of other ships that may be in the port at the time of debarkation are added. It has been noted by the ship lines that cruise sales increase markedly from each student who attends the schools at sea. The cost of the program depends on the destination. Most programs combine one way by ship and one way by air.

CLIA is launching their first cruise counselor certification program in January 1993. Two levels of certification, Accredited Cruise Counselor (ACC) and Master Cruise Counselor (MCC) are offered. Travel agents earn their degrees by accumulating points for participation in various training activities. ACCs need 100 points and MCCs need 200 points.

If participation in a seminar or school at sea is not conveniently possible, employees should be encouraged to take advantage of the reduced fares offered by the ship lines. Unlike the airlines, the reduced fares also apply to the spouses and dependent children of the agent. The reductions vary from line to line, but whatever fare is paid, the agent is usually upgraded to one of the better cabins. Reservations are made with the understanding that cabins requested are dependent on space available, and quite often the reservation is not confirmed until one or two weeks prior to sailing.

Ship inspections can also be made on your own. Cruise lines are more than willing to allow travel agents to go aboard their ships in whatever port you may be visiting. Try to give them some advance notice, as they usually limit the number of visitors who can come aboard at each port.

A subscription to one of the ship guides is also essential in selling steamship travel. The guides publish current news and sailing schedules for cruises, Atlantic crossings, passenger freighters, port-to-port and ferry schedules around the world, ship profiles (pertinent information on the individual ships), maps of all major ports of call, and maps of the passenger terminals. (Copies of these maps should be at everyone's desk.)

The travel trade publications also issue special supplements on cruises at least twice a year. Condensed cruise schedules in brochure form can be ordered with the agents' imprint to be distributed to the mailing list or issued to each member of the staff for a quick reference guide.

A good knowledge of geography, especially of the world ports and the cities they serve, is very important in selling steamship travel. For example, Piraeus is the port of Athens, while Paris is served by two Atlantic ports, LeHavre and Cherbourg. This is vital information when reading sailing schedules. The information can be found in the maps included in steamship guides.

CHECKLIST OF WHAT A CRUISE TICKET INCLUDES

Staterooms (Cabins/Rooms):   Cabins vary in size on different ships and in different price ranges. Many cruise ships have small cabins and larger public rooms, although the newer ships are going back to more spacious cabins. On all except for a few older ships, all cabins are air-conditioned and have private facilities (shower and/ or bath, wash basin, and toilet).

Food: Some of the finest restaurants in the world are found aboard ships. Although each line may specialize in the cuisine of its country, virtually every type of cooking is available for the asking. Passengers can eat around the clock if they desire. Breakfast in bed, breakfast in the dining room, midmorning bouillon, lunch in the dining room and buffet lunch at the swimming pool, midafternoon snack, dinner in the dining room, and a midnight buffet—plus fruit in the cabin upon request. Special diets can be accommodated, and baby and formula foods are provided for infants with advance notice to the ship line.

Dining Room Seating: Yachtlike cruise ships and ships with extra-large dining rooms (such as the ships in the Royal Viking Line) advertise heavily that they have

Figure 15-9 Royal Cruise Line—*The Crown Odyssey's* sumptuous Seven Continents Restaurant offers the ultimate cruise dining experience. Built on two levels with a sunken central section, it is resplendent with lacquered woods, stained-glass domes and beveled mirror panels reflecting picture-window ocean views.

only one meal seating in their dining rooms. This may seem unimportant to the novice, but experienced cruisers have been known to cancel a cruise because they could not be accommodated on the meal seating they prefer. On most ships there are two seatings: the first, or main seating, and the second seating. Some people prefer eating early in order to rush off to the daily activities; others prefer the second seating, so they can take their time over the second cup of coffee without concern over others waiting for their table. The passengers are assigned tables the first day out (advise clients to check in with the dining room purser as soon as they board ship), and unless they announce open seating for that meal, everyone is expected to sit at the same table throughout the voyage. If table mates are objectionable, a request for change should be made the first day out; it is difficult for the purser to make any changes later.

Sports: Deck tennis, shuffleboard, Ping-Pong, skeet shooting, putting greens, and other deck games provide fun and exercise and the opportunity to get acquainted with fellow passengers. Most ships also have well-equipped gymnasiums with professional attendants, as well as jacuzzis, steambaths, ultraviolet sun lamps, massage facilities, and so on.

Swimming: All the ships have either indoor or outdoor swimming pools, or both. Many now have wading pools for the children.

Movies: First-run and prerelease feature movies are shown during the voyage in the auditorium or special movie theatre. Some of the ships have closed-circuit television with programs and movies piped to the passengers' cabins. The luxury ships now also feature VCRs with a selection of cassettes.

Entertainment: Every ship tries its best to keep passengers entertained, from bingo games to big-name professional entertainers. Theme nights featuring a specific country, and talent shows for the passengers are very popular.

Social Life: Lounges, discos, cocktail bars, casinos, libraries, and other public rooms are the gathering places for the social life on a ship. Probably the most memorable occasions of most voyages are the captain's welcome aboard cocktail party and the gala farewell dinner. Dress is very casual on most ships except for these occasions, where formal or semiformal dress is expected.

For the Lazy Life: Since life aboard ship offers everything, whether you want to be vigorously active or luxurious lazy is a matter of personal choice. There is nothing

Figure 15-10 Royal Cruise Line—*The Crown Odyssey's* Penthouse Deck boasts a Penthouse Bar and Grill, a splash pool, two out-door whirlpools and twin fountains framing a stainless steel sculpture by Italian artist Carlo Mo.

anywhere more healthful and relaxing than to lounge lazily in a deck chair in the refreshing salt sea air with the warming sun above. On a ship, time is your servant, never your master.

Keeping in Touch: While getting away from the tensions of business and other shore-side activities is one of the most therapeutic parts of a cruise, the ship passenger is not isolated from the world. Important world news items, including stock market reports, are received by radio and published daily in the ship's newspaper. Also, many of the ships have ship-to-shore radio-telephone service.

The "Children's Corner": Most ships have one or more special playrooms for children, under the supervision of a nurse or stewardess. The supervisors of the playroom are also available for evening baby sitting.

Teenage Rooms: Most of the ships have set aside rooms for teenagers with video games, Ping-Pong tables, soda fountain, juke box, and so on. Evening activities are also specially arranged for them.

Shopping: Shipboard shopping centers offer a wide variety of merchandise for personal needs or gifts at low, duty-free prices. Quite often, the selection and prices are better on board the ship than they are in port. The shops are closed while the ship is in port.

Divine Services: Few ships will have services on board except during religious holidays such as Christmas and Easter. However, if a religious group is on board with their own minister, rabbi, or priest, upon advance notice the ship will provide a room for divine services.

Library: All cruise ships have extensive libraries where good books as well as a selection of the latest popular magazines are available.

Other Points to Remember

Inside/Ouside Cabins: Not much difference in size or appointments except that the outside cabins have portholes (windows) and are usually more expensive. Now that most all ships are completely air-conditioned and portholes are usually sealed shut, there is no need for a window except for the view. On some ships the outside cabins are larger.

Cruise Ships: Ships built strictly for cruises are one-class ships—everyone uses the same public rooms. Years ago the ocean liners had from two to four classes. First-class passengers were able to visit all decks, whereas the lower-class passengers were each limited to specific decks and had separate dining rooms. Some ocean liners that convert to cruises during the winter months will also convert to one class from their normal basis.

Check-Cashing Privileges: Very few ships accept personal checks on board the ship. Bar bills and other expenses should be paid by travelers' checks or one of the major credit cards. (Check with the ship line as to which credit cards are accepted.) Travelers checks can be exchanged for local currency the day before arrival at a foreign port.

Motion: Although midship is the area where the motion is said to be felt the least, there is actually not much difference in any location. All ships now install stabilizers that prevent excessive rolling in bad weather. Many experienced cruisers say that the lower decks are the most comfortable.

Bon Voyage Parties/Gifts: If the passengers or their friends and relatives want to have a bon voyage party, the canapés and drinks can be ordered in advance through the ship's catering department. There is usually a charge for this service. Wine lists may be requested from the sales office (sometimes this will be included with the deposit receipt) and gift orders should be submitted (with payment) at least one week before sailing. It has become standard procedure to order a bottle of wine for clients; otherwise, they will come back very annoyed that someone at their table received a bottle of wine from their travel agent but they did not. A good alternative to wine for a bon voyage gift would be a guidebook on the ports of call.

Deck Chairs: Very few ships charge for deck chairs on short cruises. If there is a charge, passengers can request specific locations on the deck of their choice.

Beauty Salons and Barber Shops: Advance appointments can be requested at the time that final payment is made, or arranged on the first day of sailing. Beauty shops are very busy during the days before the captain's cocktail parties or dinners.

Travel Documents: Check the cruise itinerary for the ports of call and the documentary requirements for each stopover. Advise passengers to carry their tickets and passports (or other proof of citizenship) with them whenever they leave the ship.

Port Taxes: There are fees charged to the ship lines by the individual countries or islands visited. The ship line prorates this among the passengers. Some cruise lines may add port taxes to the brochure rate; others prefer to show them as add-ons to the published rate. Make sure that port taxes are included in the final quoted rate to clients. Most people do not relish being told at the last minute that there is an additional charge.

Shore Excursions (Optional): There are sightseeing bus tours at each port stop. These are booked by cruise passengers on board the ship. A few lines will allow passengers to book them in advance with the travel agent; however, experience has shown that once on board passengers may change or cancel a tour to be with friends and cannot understand why they cannot get an immediate refund. (Arrangements paid through the travel agent must be refunded through the same office.) First-time cruisers are advised to take the shore excursions. Repeaters may prefer to go out on their own, but they must guard against unscrupulous cab drivers who are very quick to take advantage of the short-stay tourists.

Tipping: Most cruise tips average $2 to $3 per day per per person for each of the room stewards and the dining room stewards. Wine stewards and bartenders are tipped at the time of service. (Wines and alcoholic beverages are not included in the average cruise rate.) Some ships allow passengers to run a bar tab, which is paid on the last day of the voyage. Tips are handed out on the last day of the voyage on short cruises; passengers may prefer to tip the stewards every week during the longer cruises to ensure good service. The ship's purser will provide envelopes to passengers for their tips to the stewards.

SELLING AND BOOKING PROCEDURES

Determining a Client's Wishes

In general, vacation seekers who come to you may be divided into three categories. Many will be first-time travelers, some will have traveled a few times before, and a smaller number will be veterans who have sailed often. The first-time traveler requires the fullest guidance and counseling. Suggest cruises for the complete vacation experience. If time or budget does not permit, suggest short three- and four-day cruises. This will give them the opportunity to sample cruising before going on to the longer voyages.

The prospects who have traveled some before will have a good idea of what they want. They may have already decided on deck, type of cabin, and itinerary but need advice and information on which ship they would enjoy most. To these clients, sell the ship as the destination in itself. Brochures with descriptive photographs and easy-to-read deck plans are the most helpful tools to sell the ship.

The veteran traveler will ask for a specific ship and accommodations and will be reluctant to accept alternates. These clients require tactful and resourceful handling. They will accept alternative suggestions if presented properly, intelligently, and knowledgeably. If the travel consultant has done her homework and has studied ship line guides and brochures, it should not be difficult to find a similar itinerary or ship in the event that the one desired is not available.

Figure 15-11 Royal Cruise Line—*The Golden Odyssey's* comfortable staterooms are decorated in assorted inspired arrangements of cranberry, aqua, rose and lavender and sport bird's-eye maple furniture, a pull-out, freestanding occasional table, a state-of-the-art telephone system plus 24-hour room service.

In all cruise sales the following questions must be answered before proceeding with the application for space:

1. Number of people in the party (names and ages of children, if any; also the first name of the spouse).
2. Departure dates desired and number of days in the cruise.
3. Discuss alternative sailing dates, ship, or accommodations.
4. Price category preferred. (Sell up if at all possible. Minimum-rate cabins are few in number and sell out fast. These are usually upper-and-lower-berth cabins and not in the best locations. Steer clients to the moderate-rate cabins.)
5. Destination or ports of call.
6. Client's preference of ship or line.
7. Preference of dining room seating and size of table (anywhere from two to eight people). Are special diets required?
8. Decide on any pre- or post-cruise options.
9. Find out if clients will be celebrating an anniversary or birthday during the cruise. The ship lines appreciate this information, as personal celebrations contribute to the gaiety of the cruise. However, ask permission of newlyweds if they want it known that they are on their honeymoon. Some people resent being tagged as newlyweds.

Applications for Space

1. If possible, call the ship line while the clients are at your desk. Do not hang up and redial if you are put on hold; most reservation offices are very busy, but eventually someone will take your call.
2. Identify yourself and your agency.
3. Request the ship, departure date, and category desired.
4. Have the ship's deck plans open in front of you so that you can point out to clients which cabins are available.
5. If none of the choices are suitable, ask for an alternative date or ship.
6. When a decision is reached, give the reservationist all the details: names, dining room seating, table preference, and so on. Also indicate smokers or nonsmokers.
7. Make sure that you note the date and name of the reservationist to whom you spoke.
8. Make note of the option date for the deposit payment, amount of deposit, and date of final payment.

Option Date

The option date is the date the deposit is due or the reservation is cancelled automatically by the line's computer. Deposits are due seven to 10 days after the reservation is made. It is best to collect the deposit immediately. If your clients elect to return with the deposit or send it through the mail and you receive it on the option date, call the line immediately and advise that the payment is on its way (the line may ask for your agency's check number) so that the information can be entered on the computer record and cancellation avoided.

In case clients cancel, notify the line immediately to release the space. Co-operation with the lines in this release will make them more willing to cooperate with you, if or when your client wants the cruise but needs additional time to send in the deposit.

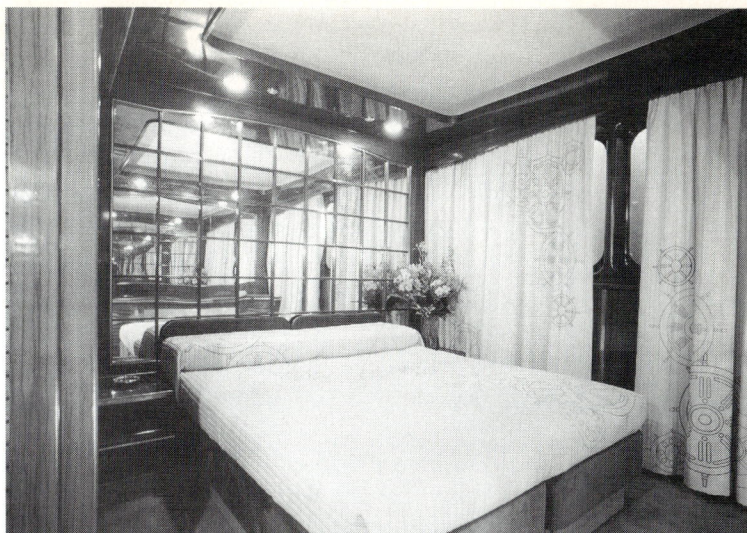

Figure 15-12 Spacious suites-only accommodations, ranging from 220 to 290 square feet, are beautifully appointed with such features as a large, modern bathroom with marble vanity and teak floors, spacious living room and seating area, color television and VCR, amenity basket and cabin bar.

Guarantees

1. At the time space is requested, the sailing may be sold out completely with every cabin under ticket or deposit, but the ship line will offer a guarantee for the category requested for a specific sailing. They know from past experience that a certain percentage of space will be cancelled due to illness or a variety of other legitimate reasons.

2. Most guarantees given are with the provision that (except for category) no specific type of room or location is specified. A guarantee may be given for the minimum rate and the client may be assigned a higher-rated cabin at the minimum fare if a cabin at the quoted fare does not become available. Make sure the client knows that an upgrade is a possibility, not a promise. On rare occasions a cabin is assigned in a lower category, in which case the passenger will then have the right to apply for a refund.

3. Remember that a guarantee is just that—a guarantee. The client is definitely booked and the agent can go ahead and complete the arrangements.

4. Guarantees are cleared through the medium of cancellations, and as the actual sailing day approaches, the percentage of cancellations cannot be transferred to a passenger who is on the waitlist. The guarantees must be taken care of first.

Ticketing

1. When a deposit is paid to the agent by the client, the agent forwards the amount to the line, which in return sends a deposit receipt.

2. Remittance of the final payment must be accompanied by the original copy of the deposit receipt issued previously, to assure proper crediting.

3. Commission is deducted from the final payment for the full amount of the cruise. (Commissions are not deducted from the deposits.) Port taxes are not commissionable.

4. Final payment is due six weeks or more prior to the sailing date, as specified in the brochure or by the reservations department.

5. The ship lines will issue the cruise ticket, and when included, the airline ticket. They are sent to the agents with baggage tags, a list of mailing addresses for each port, and other general information on the ship.

6. The baggage tags should be completed with the necessary information: date of sailing, ship line, name of ship, cabin number, pier number, and client's home address. Advise the clients to attach these tags to their baggage before leaving home even if the first part of the trip may be by air.

CRUISE COMPUTER SYSTEMS

Royal Caribbean Cruises Ltd. (RCCL), the operating company for Royal Caribbean Cruise Line and Admiral Cruises, now features the world's first computerized cruise booking system. The CruiseMatch 2000 System, which was developed over a period of seven years, was purchased in late 1989. The computerized booking system provides direct access and booking capability for RCCL or Admiral Cruises, as well as supplying information on other cruise lines through a travel agent's CRS or personal computer. RCCL has negotiated with System One and Worldspan CRSs for participation in their systems. Negotiations are under way with other CRS vendors.

CruiseMatch, operated by Cruiseship Information Systems of Coral Gables, Florida, offered an automated cruise booking system tied to airline computers. The ship lines paid them a fee for each booking made through the computer.

RCCL also became the first cruise line participant in the inaugural edition of the *Jaguar Cruise Directory*, released in December 1991 to travel agencies through American Airlines' Sabrevision. Royal Caribbean and Reed Travel Group, publisher of Jaguar directory, signed a long-term agreement that places all nine ships of the Royal Caribbean Cruise Line, the company's premium cruise product, in the directory. Each of the RCCL's ships will appear in the Jaguar directory in the form of "imaging packages." Each ship will have five screens for the display of full-color images as well as comprehensive data. Each ship will have another 10 screens for the display of ship images and data in a so-called "image brochure."

Computerized booking systems are still very controversial among ship lines and travel agents. One cruise line executive has predicted the demise of CruiseMatch and the entire concept of cruise bookings via the CRT; another predicts that such automation is the wave of the future.

Opponents say that automated systems are too slow: Agents have to go through too many screens of information to find and book a cruise—and then they have to wait for confirmation, whereas experienced cruise line reservationists can make the booking faster than travel agents can and confirm immediately. Agents lose personal touch with the cruise line. Some of the questions that clients ask cannot be answered by the computer.

CRUISE-ONLY AGENCIES

Although there have always been a number of agencies that specialized in cruises only, their numbers have been increasing in the past few years. More and more travel agents are leaving the full-service concept for the cruise-only business. The cruise market is increasing and the profitability is higher. There is also less work involved as the cruise lines issue tickets and book the pre- and postcruise tour packages. However, cruise selling involves more product knowledge and professionalism. Since it is a specialized market, it also requires more sales promotion and advertising to get the message to the traveling public.

Figure 15-13 Celebrity Cruises. The new *ZENITH*

Before the National Association of Cruise Only Agencies (NACOA) was formed in 1985, the cruise-only agencies found themselves isolated from each other and from the rest of the industry. When the group started on 1985 it had no name and no real purpose other than to establish a cohesive organization for people of like interests, to offer a system of networking.

As interest in the group increased, NACOA decided that it would have two distinct categories of membership: full-voting membership and associate membership. Full-voting membership is limited to agencies that sell only cruises, in a separate space from any other business, travel or otherwise. The voting member agencies are required to have names that allude in some way to cruising. Applying members must belong to Cruise Lines International Association or have an application pending. Associate members can be anyone with an interest in the group, such as travel agencies with a cruise desk, employees of cruise lines, or even a cruise line itself. To maintain the purity of the organization, associate members cannot vote, hold office, or sit on the board of directors.

One of the primary purposes of the organization is to develop the professional skills of its membership through education. NACOA is working on launching a Certified Cruise Counselor program, similar to the Certified Travel Consultant program. NACOA cruise specialists are required to participate in cruise industry

Figure 15-14 American Hawaii Cruises' *SS CONSTITUTION* and *SS INDEPENDENCE*, the only major ocean-going American-flagged cruise ships, depart from Honolulu every Saturday. The vessels sail for three, four, and seven days, calling at Kahului, Maui; Hilo and Kona on the Big Island of Hawaii; and Nawiliwili, Kauai.

Figure 15-15 Passengers on board American Hawaii's *SS CONSTITUTION* and *SS INDEPENDENCE* can enjoy breathtaking views of the splendors of Hawaii. Kauai's Na Pali Coast is one of the most picturesque.

education programs and cruise product familiarization programs. Appointed agency members must accrue a minimum of 10 education points with each membership year. NACOA associate locations must also earn points.

Cruise line executives are optimistic regarding the cruise industry's future and point out that the market has yet to be tapped to any large extent. Cruise analysts, however, point out several reasons for skepticism: supply coming online faster than demand, considerable discounting, spiraling operating and marketing costs, and a handful of lines increasingly dominating the industry. The good news is: that travel agents are remaining the primary channel of distribution. Within the agency framework, the industry will see little or no growth in the number of cruise-only agencies. Rather, there will be an increase in full-service agencies with cruise divisions.

QUESTIONS AND PROBLEMS

1. What is the major difference between selling an airline ticket and selling a steamship ticket?
2. Why are there fewer U.S. ships in service today than there were in the past?
3. Name some of the cruise offerings in the market today.
4. Who has the most expensive cruise?
5. How many ships offer round-the-world cruises?
6. How does freighter travel differ from the average cruise?
7. List the selling points that you could use to sell a corporation on using a cruise for a business meeting or convention.
8. How would you train a new employee in steamship sales?
9. List the information needed before you call a ship line for a reservation.
10. What are the additional charges you must collect from cruise clients? What else is not included in the cost of a cruise?
11. Are there any advantages in operating a cruise-only agency?

## chapter 16

Miscellaneous Services

OBJECTIVES

When you have completed this chapter you will be able to:

1. Advise clients on documentary requirements to go abroad.
2. Differentiate between passports and visas.
3. Assist clients with immigration procedures to bring family members to live in the United States.
4. Discuss the limits on duty-free purchases for returning citizens of the United States.
5. List other services that pay commission to agents.
6. Advise clients on medical assistance for travelers.

INTRODUCTION

The conscientious travel agent will do everything possible to make sure that his client's trip or vacation is a trouble-free and wonderfully rewarding experience. They will perform services that go beyond the call of duty; some will be commissionable, most will not. Taking a client's baby-sitter to church on a Sunday morning, pasting stamps in a trading book so that the client will have enough books to go get the luggage she needs, going to the office in the middle of the night to issue a ticket for an emergency flight, collecting posters and display material for a neighborhood luau, are a few of the noncommisionable services a travel agent may perform (not to mention the personal deliveries made to clients unable to come to the office.)

DOCUMENTARY REQUIREMENTS

Among the more important services the agent gives is the assistance with the necessary travel documents, such as passports, health certificates, visas, and so on. It is the responsibility of the agent accepting the reservation from the passenger to see that the passenger has the required travel documents. The passenger traveling abroad *must* comply with all the rules, regulations, orders, demands, or travel requirements set forth by the governments of the countries to be visited or passed through. An agent must personally check passengers' documents against the regulations of the country of departure (exit requirements), countries through which they will travel (transit visas), and the country of destination. It is especially important to check the expiration date and validity period on passports, visas, tourist cards, and health certificates. Although international carriers will try to check each passenger before they leave the country, there have been occasions when a passenger without a passport, visa, or proof of citizenship has arrived in a foreign country and either been refused entry or has created a small riot until someone was found to vouch for him or her.

It is also the agent's responsibility to keep current with regulations covering passports, visas, customs formalities and allowances, health regulations, and currency regulations. The best source of these rules and regulations is the *TIM* (*Travel Information Manual*). The *TIM* is an official joint publication of 14 airlines, members of IATA, that supplies the answers to questions about government requirements and contains information about more than 300 countries. The information contained therein is supplied by the various airlines for the country of origin and the countries serviced by the airlines. Every effort is made by the publishing airlines to maintain the most current information possible. However, the contents of the *TIM* are subject to change, and no responsibility can be accepted for inaccuracies or incomplete information. Travel agents must double-check the information with the carrier or consulate of the country before a passenger leaves the United States.

The *TIM* is published monthly and is the standard reference manual for most airlines and travel agents. For a number of years, subscriptions were limited to the airlines; travel agents can now subscribe to this on a yearly subscription basis or can purchase individual copies through the publisher in The Netherlands.

The *North American Edition OAG Business Travel Planner*, *European Travel Planner*, and *Pacific-Asia Travel Planner* also contain international travel information. The information is not as current or as detailed as that in the *TIM* but serves the purpose for most travel agents.

Other sources of international travel requirements can be found in guidebooks from individual countries, the *Pan Am World Horizon Book*, and from the sales guide supplements issued by travel trade publications and international carriers. KLM does a good job of furnishing information on the eastern Europe countries;

United Airlines and Northwest Orient Airlines issue very informative brochures on countries in the Orient and South Pacific.

PASSPORTS

A passport is an official document issued by a valid public authority to nationals of the issuing country which permits the bearer to leave and return to the country of his citizenship. Passports are required of *all* persons entering a foreign country. Besides the normal passport issued to a citizen, there are also aliens' passports, issued to alien residents of the issuing country; children's identity cards, issued to minors instead of a passport (i.e., Germany's "Kinderausweis"); diplomatic or consular passports issued to diplomatic, consular, and other government officials on missions, entitling the bearer to diplomatic or consular status under international law and custom; and other official, special, or service passports issued to government officials or other persons on government missions.

There are also other travel documents, such as certificates of identity, identification cards, travel certificates, military ID cards, seaman's book, seaman's discharge books and records, and various affidavits, but these documents may not have the same legal effect as passports and are valid only for limited countries and purposes. They should always be checked against the regulations of the countries to be visited.

Passport Requirements for U.S. Citizens

U.S. passports are issued only to U.S. citizens or nationals. Each applicant must appear in person to obtain his or her own passport. A first-time applicant must complete the application and submit (1) proof of citizenship, (2) proof of identity, (3) two photographs, and (4) fees (as explained below) to one of the following acceptance agents: a clerk of any federal or state court of record or a judge or clerk of any probate court that accepts applications, a designated postal employee at a selected post office, or an agent of a passport agency in Boston, Chicago, Honolulu, Houston, Los Angeles, Miami, New Orleans, New York, Philadelphia, San Francisco, Seattle, Stamford, or Washington, D.C.

Passports are issued immediately only in the passport agency cities listed above; outside of these cities, the acceptance agent will administer the oath and forward the application and the supporting documents to the passport agency that services the area. The passport is issued and sent to the applicant, travel agency, or address shown as the mailing address on the application. In case of an emergency, where the customer must leave the country immediately, he or she can be routed to the most convenient passport agency, with a completed application and supporting documents to pick up the passport before going overseas. If the emergency is not that great but the passport is needed in a hurry, tell the clients to request the use of overnight express mail at their expense.

1. Proof of U.S. citizenship. A native-born citizen can present an expired passport, certified birth certificate, baptismal certificate, or certified copy of the record of baptism. (Photocopies are not acceptable.) Also, birth certificates must have a first name, not just the word "male" or "female." If none of these documents are available, secondary evidence, such as census records, newspaper files, school records, or affidavits of persons having a personal knowledge of the facts of birth may be submitted. However, a statement by appropriate authorities certifying that no birth record exists must be submitted with evidence other than a birth certificate. To avoid delays, the applicant

should ask the clerk of court or the passport agent exactly what information the documents must contain to be acceptable for passport purposes.

Applicants born outside the United States must submit a previous U.S. passport, certificate of naturalization, or certificate of citizenship. If applicants claim citizenship through naturalization of their parents, they must submit the parents' certificate(s) of naturalization, the foreign birth certificate, and proof of their admission to the United States for permanent residence. If applicants claim citizenship through birth abroad to U.S. citizens, they must submit a consular report of birth or certification of birth or foreign birth certificate, parents' marriage certificate, proof of parent(s) citizenship, and affidavit of U.S. citizen parent(s) showing all periods and places of residence in the United States and abroad before the birth.

2. Proof of identity. An applicant is required to establish his or her identity to the satisfaction of a clerk of courts or passport agent through personal knowledge or the presentation of an acceptable document of identification containing the person's signature and photograph. Temporary or altered documents are not acceptable. If the applicant is unable to supply such a document, an identifying witness who has known the applicant for at least two years and is a U.S. citizen or permanent resident alien can sign an "Affidavit of Identifying Witness" before the acceptance agent. The witness must also submit proof of identity.

3. Photographs. Two identical photographs (normally taken within the past six months) 2 by 2 inches in size, front view, full face, taken in normal street attire, without a hat or dark glasses, printed on thin, white paper capable of withstanding a mounting temperature of 225°, and either black and white or color are required. Snapshot, vending machine, or Polaroid (unless it is the passport camera) prints are not acceptable.

4. Fees. In 1983 the validity period of an adult passport was increased to 10 years. Family passports were discontinued, and each child up to the age of 18 receives a passport with a five-year validity period. (The government reasons that a child's appearance will change every five years.) As of November 1, 1991, the adult charge is $55 passport fee and $10 execution fee, and the children's fee is $40. The fees are payable to the passport services and can be in check, money order, or currency. No fee is charged to applicants with U.S. government or military authorization for no-fee passports.

U.S. passports are not renewable. A completely new passport is issued at the expiration date. It is best, of course, to apply for a new passport at least eight weeks before it expires. If clients have an expired passport that had been issued within the past 12 years of the date of application and wishes to obtain a new passport without appearing in person before the clerk of court or passport agent, he may complete the form "Application for Passport by Mail." The application must be accompanied by the previous passport, two signed passport photos taken within the past six months, and a check or money order for the passport fee of $55 mailed to the passport agency in his area (addresses are on the form). The new passport will be issued in the same name as the most recent passport unless an original or certified court order or marriage certificate showing a change in name is included with the application.

Agents must also advise clients who make numerous trips to countries requiring a visa that if extra passport pages need to be inserted in their passport, there may be a delay of up to 10 working days in the U.S. passport office. The State Department, parent of the passport office, has decided to send the passport through the whole system on regular processing time, which takes about eight to 10 working days instead of the few minutes it used to take to glue extra pages in a traveler's passport. A State department spokeswoman said the new procedures were adopted to monitor the number of passports that get additional pages and to reduce the risk of fraud. Travelers must fill out a green form called Passport Amendment Form DSP-19, which may be available at local post offices.

Lost or stolen passport? Advise all traveling clients to go to the nearest U.S. consulate or embassy and report the loss or theft. A temporary document will be issued to enable them to return home. A photocopy of the center pages of the passport that shows the number, name, issuing date and issuing office, birth date, and signature should be made and stored in a separate place in your luggage. This will make it easier to get a replacement.

Passport Requirement for Canadian Citizens

Canadian passports are issued only to citizens, by birth or naturalization, of Canada. Passport applications are obtained and processed through their regional passport offices and their substations throughout Canada. Each person must have a passport, although children under 16 may be included with a parent's passport. Canadians outside Canada must apply to the nearest Canadian consulate, High Commissioner's office, legation, embassy, or if there is no such representation, to the nearest U.K. representative.

To obtain a passport, the applicant must submit the following documents:

1. Two completed passport applications.
2. Proof of citizenship: birth certificate, baptismal certificate, or expired passport; *or*
3. Certificate of Canadian citizenship or naturalization document for naturalized citizens.
4. Money order or certified check in the amount of fees required.
5. Two identical front-view photographs (approximately 2 by 2 inches). If the applicant is applying outside Canada, a third photograph is needed for the consulate or other office that is processing the application.

Note: For both U.S. and Canadian citizens, it is recommended that extra passport photographs be ordered and carried with clients, as some countries require their presentation on arrival and/or departure. They may also be needed in the event they decide to apply for an international driver's license or if they decide to visit countries that require photos for a visa or tourist card application.

VISAS

A visa is a permit to enter and leave the country to be visited (usually in the form of a stamp on a page in the passport). The visa indicates the date issued, how long it is valid for entry, and how many times the person may enter (usually indicated by notation "single" or "multiple" entries).

Visas are obtained from the foreign embassy, consulate, or legation of the country to be visited. Consulate and embassy locations may be found in the *OAG Travel Planners*, the *Travel Industry Personnel Directory*, or the *Travel Trade Personnel Directory*.

Many travel agents will use a professional visa service, especially when a client needs a number of visas and time is limited. Trans World Visa Service in San Francisco and Embassy Visa Service of Washington, D.C., are such services. They will furnish the agent with a supply of a master questionnaire, a form used for all visa applications. This form is completed, signed by the client, and sent with the passport and/or other necessary documents and passport photos (if needed). The company then proceeds to obtain all the visas. There is a fee, of course, for each visa.

Visa Advisors, Inc., a Washington-based visa service, has just created a *VisaGuide* desk reference book for travel agents. The manual has monthly updates, provides passport information, visa details around the world, travel advisories, vaccination requirements, and embassy and consulate addresses.

If travel agents have enough time to prepare and forward visa applications directly from their office to the consulates, they may charge and retain the service fees, or they may decide to pass the savings on to their clients. Some ethnic agents who do not apply for the airline appointments depend entirely on these service fees to maintain their offices.

The most commonly issued visas are:

- *Tourist visa*: issued for tourist travel for the purpose of sightseeing.
- *Temporary or business visa*: issued for an extended stay or for the purpose of doing business. If the purpose of travel is for business reasons, a business visa is required even though the stay may be as little as one day.
- *Transit visa*: issued primarily for those who are transiting a country. Usually, the passenger must prove that he or she has a visa for the country beyond before a transit visa is issued. Most countries do not require a transit visa if direct transfer is being made to an onward carrier and the passenger does not leave the airport area. A transit visa is required if the passenger is traveling across country by rail, bus, or private car.

A visa, transit visa, or a visa exemption for a country does not always guarantee admission to that country. The final decision rests with the competent authorities at the port of entry in the country concerned. Before a client leaves your office it is absolutely necessary to check carefully the visas required by the authorities of the country of destination, the country of departure (if returning to this country), and the transit stations. Passengers traveling in transit through a country must be able to prove that they will continue their journey within the prescribed period. Unless otherwise stated, they can do this by showing a ticket for the remaining portions of the trip, a ticket for the homeward journey, or a sum of money in the required currency, sufficient to buy a ticket for the onward portion or for the homeward journey.

Children must also comply with the regulations for transit in, transit through, and departure from a country. They must have their own passports and corresponding visas. Where a country permits children to be included in their parents' or guardians' passports, children are not allowed to travel on such passports unless accompanied by the holder of that passport.

Visa requirements for Russia and some of the Eastern European countries include the stipulation that passengers should have evidence of prepaid tour/hotel accommodations for the number of days the visa was requested. If no confirmed hotel accommodations were requested (for persons who wished to visit friends and/or relatives and stay with them and not at hotels), tourists had to exchange a prescribed amount of dollars per day per person. Vouchers for hotel accommodations or the prepayment or money were obtained from the official travel bureaus of the country or their designated representative in the United States. The national tourist organization in Bulgaria is Balkantourist, in Czechoslovakia it is CEDOK, in Hungary it is IBUSZ, in Poland it is ORBIS, in Rumania it is CARPATI, and in Yugoslavia it is the Yugoslav State Tourist Office.

In the new republics of Russia and Byelorussia applications for visas are sent to the Russian Embassy in Washington, D.C. Ukrania will issue visas on arrival in Kiev. Applications to visit the Baltic countries of Latvia and Lithuania are obtained from their consulates in New York City, Estonia will issue visas at their borders. Prepaid hotel vouchers are no longer required in all countries for all visitors. Business travelers and relatives need only to present written invitations from business associates or relatives to obtain a visa.

Although some of the Eastern European governments, and the new republics from the former U.S.S.R., have relaxed visa and currency exchange rules during recent years, it is still necessary to check the rules for each country before the clients leave the United States.

TOURIST AND/OR TRANSIT CARDS

Tourist cards actually are visas (permission to enter or transit a country) which are issued on separate forms rather than by a stamp on the passport. They are required for Mexico and most South American countries. Mexico will issue the tourist card upon presentation of proof of citizenship: passport, birth certificate, or baptismal certificate. The South American countries require a valid passport. Tourist cards can be issued by the consulates of the country or the carrier furnishing the transportation to the country.

Mexican tourist cards can also be issued by travel agents. Supplies are ordered from the Mexican Consulate. The card is actually a 5- by 7-inch paper (in duplicate) with instructions written in English and Spanish. The card should be typed or written legibly in capital letters.

One airline serving Mexico found so many errors on the tourist cards that they sent out a memo on how to complete the form:

1. Enter the full name, last name first. A married woman should also show her maiden name.
2. Mark appropriate X's in boxes for sex, age, marital status, and type of occupation.
3. Place of birth should be written in Spanish. For the United States, that is "Estados Unidos de America." Present nationality should be indicated as "Norte Americano" (or "Americana" for women) for U.S. citizens.
4. Permanent address in the United States can be written in English.
5. Enter the passport number if that is used for proof of citizenship. If the client plans to use another document, enter "certificado de nacimiento" for birth certificate, "certificado electoral" for voter's registration, or "certificado de naturalizacion" for naturalization certificate.
6. Indicate the principal destination city and mark the appropriate mode of transportation.

The remainder of the form will be filled out by an airline official or immigration officer.

For visits to South America, the agent must be sure to check the documentary requirements for each country to be visited or transited and forward the credentials with the signed application to the appropriate office that will issue the tourist card. They, in turn, will return the credentials with the card. Mexico and a growing number of South American countries no longer charge for the tourist card; others charge a small fee. Some countries also require two or three passport photos with the application.

REENTRY PERMITS

Reentry permits entitle the holder to return home. These permits generally are required for returning alien residents. Returning alien residents of the United States must hold one of the following documents: an alien registration card if they stay outside the United States for less than one year, or a permit to reenter the United States (a passport-like booklet with pages for visa entries), although the latter cannot be used in place of a valid passport.

A special endorsement from the Office of Immigration and Naturalization is required on the permit to reenter the United States for alien residents of the United States who travel to, in, or via a communist country. Such passengers may *not* return to the United States without the immigrant visa or a reentry permit either endorsed waiving travel restrictions or accompanied by an official government letter waiving such restrictions, or the alien registration card and such a letter.

The application for a permit to reenter the United States may be obtained from the U.S. Government Printing Office in Washington, D.C., or from the local immigration office. A separate application must be submitted by each alien, regardless of age. A parent or guardian may file an application on behalf of a child who is under the age of 14. The application (in duplicate) must be submitted to the Immigration and Naturalization Service at least 30 days before the proposed date of departure. It must be accompanied by the alien registration card, two passport photos (taken within 30 days), and the applicable fee in a check or money order. The fee is not refundable regardless of the action taken.

IMMIGRANTS

Persons wishing to take up paid employment in another country, or who wish to take up permanent residency in another country, should be referred to the consulate of the country concerned. Many colleges in the United States offer summer employment possibilities in other countries to their students. Travel agents are seldom involved in such transactions, except perhaps in chartering a plane for the school.

VISA WAIVER PROGRAM FOR VISITORS TO THE UNITED STATES

All visitors to the United States required a visa, except for nationals of the United States, Canada, Bermuda, the Bahamas, and Mexico (if they have a U.S. border crossing card), until 1988, when the U.S. State Department started a pilot program called the Nonimmigrant Visa Waiver Program (NIV), eliminating temporary visitor visas from eight countries. It started with the United Kingdom and Japan, and France, Switzerland, West Germany, Sweden, Italy and The Netherlands were added later. Under the three-year test, visitors to the United States from those countries were no longer required to apply for temporary visitor visas for stays of up to 90 days. Those countries offered reciprocal treatment to American citizens.

On October 1, 1991, the U.S. government expanded the visa waiver program to include citizens of Spain, Austria, New Zealand, Finland, Belgium, Denmark, Norway, Iceland, Luxembourg, San Marino, Andorra, Monaco, and Liechtenstein. The program now includes 21 countries, and Congress has extended the program through fiscal 1994. Although the citizens of exempted countries no longer have to apply for a visa before their trip, they must fill out a visa waiver form before their arrival. The five-page form (printed in English only) is almost as complex as the visa application and frequently causes delays when visitors reach customs and immigration counters. To make the inspection process smoother at high-volume gateways, the government wants expansion of the visa waiver program tied to preinspections. However, the requirement would stall the program because preinspection sites are expensive to set up, and many countries object to the presence of U.S. law enforcement officers in their territory. The Immigration Service hopes to eliminate the problem of processing delays by issuing new passenger information forms.

Most countries also require an exit permit that must be obtained before the U.S. Embassy or Consulate will issue the visitor's visa. The exit permit is issued upon presentation of an invitation from the prospective visitor's relatives or friends (sponsors). Unfortunately, the U.S. Immigration Service has nothing in writing as to the exact procedure to follow for each country. Because there are so many variations, each case is considered separately.

Some countries require that an official form—obtained from their consulate in Washington, D.C.—be completed, signed by the sponsor, notarized, and returned to the consulate for approval before it is forwarded to the passenger; other countries require only that the official form be completed, signed, and notarized; still others will accept a simple letter of invitation sent to the passenger.

AFFIDAVIT OF SUPPORT

An affidavit of support is essential for the approval of a visa to visit the United States for a period up to one year or for an immigrant visa. The affidavit of support assures the U.S. government that the sponsor will "receive, maintain, support and be responsible for the alien(s) mentioned above while they remain in the United States, and hereby assume such obligations, guaranteeing that none of them will at any time become a burden on the United States or on any State, County, City, Village or Municipality of the United States."

The sponsor must complete this form and be prepared to supply the supporting documents as evidence of net worth (if requested): notarized bank statements, notarized statement from employer verifying employment and salary earned, proof or real estate ownership (original or photostat copy of tax receipt), and proof of other assets shown.

The rules for bringing in a temporary visitor(s) or immigrant(s) vary for each country. In general, only members of the immediate family—spouses, children, parents, brothers, sisters, grandparents—can expect immediate approval. Others may encounter delays or refusal. The local immigration office should be contacted for current information.

PREPAID TICKET ADVICE

Most international carriers will have a prepaid ticket advice (PTA) department, which specializes in processing payment and assisting agents with clients who wish to bring relatives or friends to the United States for temporary visits or permanent residence. The ticket is prepaid; in other words, the sponsor pays for the ticket in the United States and the passenger picks it up at the most convenient ticket office or at the airport at the time of departure from the country.

Carriers can supply the agent with the invitation letter forms and the affidavits of support and will forward the completed documents to their overseas offices. The airline offices, in turn, forward them to the appropriate governmental offices to issue the visas. A PTA form is completed with the passenger's name, address, phone number, the approximate date of arrival in the United States, the length of stay, and the fare to be used. The sponsor's name, address, and phone number are also required. The PTA number is called in to the carrier and they will advise where to mail the control/reservation coupon (usually it is sent to the carrier's revenue accounting office) or it is attached to the auditor's coupon of the PTA and submitted on the next ARC airline ticket report.

The carrier will contact the passenger to notify him that the ticket is paid and to determine where it will be picked up. They will then notify the agent or the sponsor when the documents have been approved and the passenger is ready to travel.

HEALTH REQUIREMENTS

The international certificate of vaccination (commonly referred to as the health certificate) is the only acceptable document for international travel. It is valid only when the information required in each certificate is completed and signed by the tourist and by the doctor who has performed the vaccinations and has the stamp or seal of the state or local health department of the area in which the vaccinating physician practices.

To be valid in international traffic, vaccination certificates must be printed in English and French; a third language may be added. The certificate must be completed fully and correctly in English or French. Loose vaccination certificates may be accepted only if they are in conformity with those in the booklet. The booklets may be ordered directly from the U.S. Government Printing Office in Washington, D.C. for a small fee per hundred, or they may be obtained free from any international air carrier.

Since requirements change from time to time, agents must check their documentary reference books or the air carrier carefully for the latest information regarding immunization requirements. They must advise clients on the health regulations of the country of destination, the country of departure (also returning if applicable), and the transit countries. If a country requires that passengers coming via a certain area or country be vaccinated, this means that those passengers who do not leave the airport and/or continue their journey by the same aircraft in that area or country must also be vaccinated. However, as a general rule, vaccinations are not required for a passengers transiting a country who do not leave the airport and are making a connection to continue to another country.

Passengers may be put under medical surveillance or quarantine for the period of incubation reckoned from the day of departure. In case of missing or invalid certificates, quarantine expenses are charged to the passenger, not borne by the airline concerned. Although vaccination cannot be enforced, persons refusing vaccination (i.e., on religious or medical grounds) can, under certain conditions, be submitted to surveillance or to isolation.

Vaccinations should be obtained several weeks in advance of departure, as it takes time to develop immunity after vaccination; also, certain vaccinations become valid only at the end of the incubation period, which varies from six to 12 days. In the United States, immunization may be obtained from a private doctor. Many state and local health departments also give some of the shots.

The *TIM* (*Travel Information Manual*) or international air carriers provide lists of infected and/or epidemic areas and the health shots required for travel. The U.S. Health Department will also issue advisories when necessary.

CUSTOMS

Going through customs is usually considered a nuisance by most returning international travelers. But few people realize that the U.S. Customs Service is more than a collector of duties imposed on purchases abroad. A vital part of the role of Customs is to screen out items injurious to the well-being of our nation (illicit drugs, in particular). Customs maintains the integrity of our economy by protecting U.S. products, trademarks, and immigration laws; supports a healthy economy by depositing in the national treasury duties levied on foreign goods; and guards our agricultural well-being from contaminated products.

In the booklet *Know Before You Go* it is interesting to note: "From 1789 to 1914 Customs revenues were virtually the only form of federal income. Customs revenues opened the West; purchased the Louisiana Territory, Florida and Alaska; paid for the first national road and the Transcontinental Railroad; built the U.S. Military and Naval Academies, the city of Washington, D.C., and the list goes on."

Customs regulations, including information on prohibited articles, are published for import and export of tobacco products, alcoholic beverages, perfume, and eau de cologne. Personal belongings are normally not subject to restrictions. For example, the following items, if for personal use, are not restricted: clothes and toiletries, cosmetics, jewelry, cameras and films, binoculars, portable typewriter, portable radio, portable record player with records/tapes, portable musical instrument, and a small quantity of foodstuffs and travel souvenirs. However, Customs may ask for proof of prior possession, such as a receipt of purchase, bill of sale, insurance policy, or jeweler's appraisal.

Foreign-made items bearing serial numbers (cameras, watches, tape recorders) should be taken to a local Customs office for registration before leaving the United States. If personal belongings packed in the United States are mailed home, the shipping carton should be marked "AMERICAN GOODS RETURNED."

The best recommendation to give clients when going through Customs is: Tell the truth. Customs officials are trained, alert professionals. They have heard all the alibis and all the jokes. They are aware of the obvious actions or behaviors that help inspectors detect smugglers or those who might try to "sneak" articles through customs. They have the Customs Automated Data Processing Intelligence Network (CADPIN) and automatic drug detectors to assist them in preventing smuggling. CADPIN contains a record of known smugglers that can be relayed within seconds to Customs officers at ports of entry for use in identifying suspected smugglers and other criminals.

The U.S. Bureau of Customs was given the authority by the Fifth Act of Congress, on July 31, 1789, to collect tariffs or duties and the right to search vessels, conveyance, persons, and their effects. According to the Customs Service, the rules most commonly overlooked or deliberately violated by returning residents are:

- Shipped items cannot be included in the $400 duty-free exemption. Duty on those items will be assessed when received. The next $1000 worth of goods acquired abroad is dutiable at a flat 10 percent rate. The duty-free allowance is doubled to $800 if returning from American Samoa, Guam, or the U.S. Virgin Islands, and the next $1000 is dutiable at 5 percent.
- Not more than one gift under $50 can be shipped per day duty free to the same person. The packages should be marked "Unsolicited Gift" and indicate contents and retail value.
- The duty-free liquor limit is 1 liter (33.8 fluid onces), unless returning from U.S. territories (listed above), where 5 liters is the maximum.
- Articles bought but used abroad must be declared at purchase price. Customs will assess the use and duty allowance.

In an effort to reduce delays for arriving international air travelers, Customs introduced faster inspection procedures at the major airport terminals. At least 95 percent of all international passengers were processed through the so-called one-stop and red/green inspection systems. The red/green system was a voluntary lane-selection system, which allowed travelers with nothing to declare to select green lanes for fast clearance. It was a one-stop procedure for returning U.S. citizens, a two-stop procedure for foreign nationals. The one-top system allowed all travelers to clear both Customs and Immigration at one time. Citizen bypass allowed U.S. citizens with a valid passport to bypass Immigration inspection, go directly to the baggage claim area, and then to Customs for processing.

During the Persian Gulf crisis, the Immigration Service, for security reasons, terminated citizen bypass at New York (Kennedy) and Miami airports. The procedure, once widespread, was phased out at other U.S. gateways. The Air Transport Association (ATA) has asked Congress to direct the Immigration Service to reinstate the citizen bypass program. ATA has also asked Congress to require an audit to verify that a $5 immigration inspection fee paid by international air travelers arriving in the United States is used to increase the number of immigration inspectors at airports. Airlines are reporting immigration inspection delays of 90 minutes to two hours, and up to four hours during the peak summer season. The Immigration Service has indicated no plans to reinstate citizen bypass but has given its field offices discretion to use an accelerated citizen examination when severe delays build up.

Another point worth mentioning, due to the possibilities of skyjacking and other incidents that have occurred on airplanes: It is standard procedure at all major airports around the world to use x-ray machines or other scanning devices before passengers are allowed to board. Passengers should be advised to keep film (exposed or unexposed) in separate containers made for this purpose.

The Customs rules of each country to be visited should also be checked regarding travel with pets. Most countries accept cats or dogs accompanied by a veterinarian's rabies certificate issued at point of origin within 19 days before departure. Others require that the pet be placed in quarantine for a specific period.

Fresh fruits, vegetables, cut flowers or plants, meats, and other foodstuffs may also face restrictions in import or export from a country. Travelers bringing prohibited agricultural and animal products into the United States face stiffer fines under a program instituted by the Animal and Plant Health Inspection Service of the Agriculture Department. In the past, travelers could be fined up to the value of the prohibited goods, which could have amounted to only a few cents, and the inspectors confiscated the prohibited goods. The service now has set fines of $25 to $50 for such violations if paid immediately, and up to $1000 if a hearing is requested.

The Customs Service has detailed pamphlets which they send to the public and will furnish in large quantities to travel agents: "Know Before You Go" and "Pocket Hints" (hints for U.S. residents returning to the states), "Trademark Information," "Importing a Car," "Pets," "Wildlife," "U.S. Customs," and "GSP & The Traveler." Contact your local Customs office or send a postcard to the U.S. Customs Service in Washington, D.C.

Other brochures of use to the travel agent can be ordered from the U.S. Government Printing Office. There is no charge to have your name added to their mailing list for announcements of brochures, books, and other material that can be ordered from the Superintendent of Documents.

CURRENCY REGULATIONS

Years ago, giving an international traveler a currency converter was standard procedure, but with the constant currency fluctuations in effect all over the world, currency converters are useful only for the information relating to the type of currency used in the individual countries: In France it is the franc, in Denmark it is the kroner, and in Greece it is the drachma. The foreign money converter distributed by Deak-Perera is also useful for the "Tips for Travelers" section, and for information on clothing sizes, metric equivalents, and international travel signs.

International travelers should be advised to exchange currency before leaving home. Most banks now sell kits in $10 denominations containing small change in foreign currency, which are invaluable when the passenger arrives in the country and needs tipping money for porters, cabs, bellhops, and so on, until she has the time or the opportunity to exchange larger sums of money. These kits can be recommended as excellent bon voyage gifts.

Currency regulations for import and export of currency by a passenger should be checked for each country to be visited. Some countries will forbid the import or export of their own currency, others will allow a specified amount, while still others have no restrictions at all. It is not illegal to transport or cause to be transported any amount of foreign coin, currency, travelers' checks, money orders, and negotiable instruments or investment securities in bearer form into or out of the United States, but more than $5000 must be reported to Customs at all U.S. ports of entry.

TIPPING

How much and when to tip are universal questions. As a general rule, the amount of a tip should equal the amount of services rendered. No one should feel obligated to tip if service people are deliberately discourteous or careless. Omitting a tip is the only weapon that consumers have available to encourage good service. Years ago, Eleanor Roosevelt, who termed indiscriminate tipping a vulgar American habit, warned travelers: "A fair tip, or one a little on the generous side, will leave a pleasant feeling and respect for you in the one who received it. A too lavish one will create a secret disrespect and add to the reputation Americans have for trying to buy their way into everything."

The practice of adding service charges automatically to the bill is spreading even in the United States. Whether in a restaurant or in a hotel, the bill should always be checked to see if the service charge has already been included (usually from 15 to 20 percent of the total). If the service has been extra good, a small amount may be added or given directly to the waiter, chambermaid, or other service person.

If the service charge is not included in the bill, the tipper should follow the customary procedure that he would use at home. Overtipping is just as bad as undertipping. It encourages gouging and exploitation of the inexperienced traveler. The equivalent of 50 cents U.S. money is sufficient for most tipping situations— the bellhop who takes the guests to their rooms, the doorman who calls a cab, and so on. Fifty cents per bag is also the usual tip for porters at terminals or hotels (extra-large or extra-heavy bags deserve a higher tip). The housekeeping staff should receive 50 cents per night, more if special services were requested. In other words, common sense should be used regardless of the angry or sneering looks or comments from those who feel they should get more.

Clients who are booked on escorted tours will seldom need to tip, except for room services, as tipping charges are included in the cost of the tour. This is another good selling point for escorted tours.

GIFT CERTIFICATES/MONEY ORDERS SENT ABROAD

Ordering gift certificates and money orders abroad is a service performed by many ethnic agents for their clients who wish to send money or food packages to relatives in Europe. The commission earned on these orders varies between six and 10 percent, depending on the volume of orders processed by the agent.

Utsch & Associates, Inc. and Pekao Trading Corporation, both of New York City, will appoint agents as their sales representatives upon completion of a sales agency and trust agreement and application for fidelity bond. After approval, the agent is supplied with price lists and order blanks. The American Express Co. follows almost the same procedure in appointing an agent to sell their money orders. These are valid in the United States and anywhere in the world where American Express maintains an office. This can be a profitable sideline if the volume of orders is large enough to merit the additional time and work in processing the orders.

TRAVELERS' CHECKS

Travelers' checks are advised whether a trip consists of a weekend in Las Vegas or a month in Europe. A good recommendation is to suggest taking $20 to $30 dollars in one-dollar bills and about $5 in small change (for tips and small purchases); the rest of the money should be in travelers' checks. This is not only a safeguard in the event of loss or theft, but also a greater convenience, as most countries accept travelers' checks, even above the cash in U.S. dollars.

The most frequently asked question in regards to money is: How much should be taken on the trip? This depends a great deal on the length of the trip or tour, the type of tour, and the number of countries to be visited. If clients are booked on a prepaid escorted tour with all, or most, meals included, they will need only sufficient money to pay for the additional meals and as much shopping as they plan to do. On the other hand, if they are booked on a tour that provides only the minimum requirements of transportation, hotels, and some sightseeing, they will need more. As a general rule, a budget of $100 to $200 a day (per person) should be considered when visiting Mexico, South America, the Caribbean, and most of Western Europe for low- or moderate-rate accommodations. This should cover room, meals, some sightseeing, transfers, and tipping. Less is needed when visiting Spain, Portugal, or Greece; more is needed when visiting the higher-priced cities, such as New York, San Francisco, London, Paris, or Rome. Business travelers may require a larger budget if they are planning on extensive business entertaining.

The sale of travelers' checks could be another source of additional income for the travel agent. American Express and Thomas Cook will appoint the agent and pay commission on sales provided that the agent has a good financial record, a strong safe, and secures additional insurance to cover possible loss or theft. Commissions are low but sales are easy since the majority of travelers do buy them, and having them readily available at your agency will save them an extra stop at the bank. There is also the convenience of buying the checks at any time of the day or night rather than only during banking hours.

TRAVELERS' INSURANCE

Travelers' insurance is another must item which almost sells itself. Although some clients refuse to buy insurance because they feel that their personal coverage is sufficient, the majority of travelers want insurance. Visit any airport and note the crowds around the insurance counters or vending machines.

Insurance sales not only are a profitable item for agents (commissions are between 25 and 40 percent of policy premiums) but can do much to make a client's trip worry-free and relaxed. The insurance policies sold by the travel agent will protect the policyholder during the entire period that she is traveling and on any type of conveyance that she uses. The insurance sold at airports covers the policyholder only while she is on the plane.

Baggage insurance policies sold by travel agents cover all loss or damage sustained from the moment clients leave home until the moment they return, including cab driver mishaps on the way to the airport; whereas airline insurance covers only the damage that occurs after the baggage has been checked in. (*Note:* If baggage is lost or damaged en route, the claim must be filed with the responsible carrier. If satisfactory adjustment is not received from the carrier, the claim is then filed with the insurance company.)

Trip cancellation and emergency medical evacuation insurance will reimburse the insured for cancellation fees caused by illness or death of the insured or immediate family (even if they are at home) or that of a traveling companion. The insurance company will pay only up to the amount of protection purchased. However, the client does not have to buy insurance to equal the cost of the entire trip—

only the amount needed to cover the cancellation fees or the amount needed to pay for a one-way ticket home from the tour's farthest point.

An added feature in trip cancellation insurance policies is default insurance, which protects the traveler if an airline, tour operator, or cruise line defaults, that is, if the supplier fails to render services and is financially unable to reimburse travelers. Some policies also cover against unforeseen circumstances, such as traffic jams, being bumped from a flight, or being denied a visa.

The insurance firms make selling insurance easy by providing attractive brochures, policies that are very simply written and easy to understand, and assistance in obtaining state licenses (where necessary), and will train agency staff in how to sell their product. The Travelers Insurance Company of Hartford, Connecticut, has been the travel agents' supplier since 1864. A number of other companies also appoint travel agents to sell insurance.

Even if an agent does not want to take the time to talk insurance, quite often an insurance sale will be made simply by enclosing an application with each ticket or confirmation. This procedure should be a must for any sale of an APEX (advance purchase excursion fare), charter, or group fare that has a cancellation penalty. Clients should be asked to sign an insurance waiver if they decide against purchasing insurance. The insurance protects the clients, but the waiver will protect the agency from unwarranted lawsuits from returning clients with damage claims. The waiver states (courtesy Travelers Insurance Co.): "I have been offered the following travel insurance and I have declined the purchase of: (1) trip cancellation and emergency evacuation, (2) baggage, (3) travel accident, (4) all of the above. I, the undersigned will not hold this travel agency and/or its agents responsible for any expenses incurred by me resulting from cancellation of my trip, accident, sickness, stolen or damaged baggage." Travelers also states that if clients won't sign the waiver, the procedure of mentioning it helps to protect the agency's position.

BON VOYAGE GIFTS

The policy of giving bon voyage gifts to clients varies from agency to agency. In general, the decision as to what, or to whom, to give is based on the amount of commission earned on the booking and the possibility of future business from the client. As a rule, clients leaving on an extended air itinerary or tour will receive a flight bag; and cruise or ship passengers will receive a bottle of champagne, wine, or a bar credit to be used at their convenience. A growing trend is to give something more practical: a travel book, a packet of foreign currency, voltage transformer, and so on.

Luggage tags with the agent's imprint are given to every new client regardless of the length or cost of his first trip. (These are appreciated more than ever since the rule was issued that all airline baggage must have outside identification or be refused. The airlines will offer stickers or cardboard tags if passengers do not have their own.) Passport holders are usually given to every client who will require a passport for her journey. There also are many small novelty items that can be used as bon voyage gifts or promotional items in the office: sewing kits, rain bonnets, spot remover kits, laundry kits, insect repellent, suntan lotion, note pads, ball-point pens, and so on.

Corsages are also a popular item. These can be ordered from any florist and delivered to the client's home the day before departure or to the airport or pier. Lei greetings are standard procedure with all Hawaii tour operators and can be ordered for the independent traveler. There are several companies in Honolulu that will arrange for lei greetings and will also arrange delivery of bouquets, pineapples, or fruit baskets to the client's hotel room. They also provide transfers to and from the airports and hotels on the islands. Most of these services are commissionable to agents.

Travel accessories for the clients, or bon voyage gifts from his friends and relatives, may be ordered from several sources that pay a commission to the travel agent (except on liquor or wine orders), or will furnish bon voyage kits at wholesale prices. Travelers Checklist, a comany in Sharon, Connecticut, specializes in the sale of travel accessories by mail order. They furnish the agent with supplies of their booklet plus copies of a checklist for the client's use (reminders of things to do before departure, necessities for overseas travel, personal items, etc.). The booklet, or catalog, lists a wide variety of specialized items for travelers. It also contains a special section, "Electricity for Travelers," and lists transformers that convert voltage around the world and a universal adapter plug kit (an item often badly needed but difficult to find).

CLOTHING AND PACKING HINTS

Both men and women will ask about suitable clothing to pack for their destination. It is difficult to generalize about clothing. A safe rule to follow is to dress for the time and occasion, taking into consideration the weather and "social climate" of the destination. Some cities are more formal than others. Resort hotels are usually lenient in the matter of dress, but many refuse entry to their dining rooms to guests in shorts or swim suits. Although pantsuits for women are accepted generally, most European and Latin American countries frown on women in slacks or shorts in churches or on city streets.

The climate and degree of formality are usually the deciding factors in assembling a travel wardrobe. An "average temperature chart around the world" is one of the must-haves in the agent's reference files. Many of the general information or "travel tips" booklets issued by the airlines and tour operators include this chart as well as lists of comparative sizes in clothing, conversion tables on weights and measures, and customs allowances (for shoppers). Most also include a checklist on the type and amount of clothing recommended for the destination.

Suggestions for cruise wardrobes are the easiest to make, since most cruise ships emphasize casualness and informality. Plenty of sport clothes and a tuxedo or dark business suit for the men, and a few dressy cocktail dresses for the women are the usual recommendations. A transatlantic crossing or round-the-world cruise on one of the larger ocean liners may require a little more formality. The rule of no-dress on the first and last nights of a sea voyage is usually followed on most ships. This originated in the early days of shipping when there were delays in distributing the luggage to the cabins the first night out and the necessity of removing luggage from the cabins the night before landing. Although luggage handling is faster and more efficient now, the old rule still applies.

Some good travel and packing tips to pass on to to your clients are as follows:

1. Pack light. Take less clothing than you think you will need; take more money. There may be occasions when a porter is nonexistent and you have to carry your own bags. (Buy luggage with wheels, or have them added). Also, you should leave room for souvenirs and other purchases.
2. Place shoes, toilet articles, and heavy items along the bottom and toward the hinged side of the bag. Stuff socks and hosiery in the shoes and small items of clothing in between the heavy items to form the first layer. Keep a change of lingerie and night clothes on top.
3. Plan a color-coordinated wardrobe to utilize the minimum number of accessories.
4. Use plenty of tissue paper to cushion the folds of the garments and to stuff in sleeves. Use plastic bags for shoe covers and take along a few extra plastic zip bags: one for soiled clothes, one for wet swim suits.

5. Take along your own skirt or pants hangers since few hotel closets supply these.

6. Do not take completely new shoes unless they have been worn for several weeks before departure. If going on a long tour that involves lots of hours of sightseeing, take two pairs of comfortable, low-heeled shoes and rotate the wear each day. One pair of dress shoes and one pair of slippers, in addition, should be sufficient. A tip for women's dress shoes: Take metallic sandals—they go with everything and look good day or night. Take along a pair of fold-up or roll-up slippers in your carry-on bag.

7. If you wear glasses, carry an extra pair, plus a prescription if it's going to be a long trip. (Kill two birds with one stone by making the extra pair of glasses a pair of prescription sunglasses.)

8. If on medication, make sure that you carry enough medicine to last for the entire trip (in a convenient pocket, handbag, or carry-on bag; do not pack it) plus a prescription or letter from you doctor describing your condition. Ask the pharmacist, when filling your prescriptions, to label them all very clearly as to contents to avoid problems with a Customs inspector. Carry a medical identification card or bracelet.

9. For even a short trip, pack a first-aid kit, a sewing kit, a spot-remover can or tube, a small bottle of aspirin, a small flashlight, a ball-point pen, and a wind-up travel clock.

10. A large supply of cosmetics is seldom necesary since name brands are sold around the world. The cosmetics taken should be in plastic containers and only three-quarters full, to allow for expansion in the plane or in high altitudes. For additional protection, enclose each container in a plastic zip bag.

11. Unpack as soon as possible after reaching your destination. If it will be just a one-night stopover, hang up the clothes you plan to use that day and evening and the following day's travel clothes. (Steam out wrinkles by hanging the clothes in the bathroom while you run your shower or tub. Just be careful they don't fall in the water.)

12. Use the flight bag or carry-on bag for cameras, photographic equipment, cosmetics, books, and extra pairs of shoes or slippers. (Be sure to pack a bottle or tube of moisturizer—plane cabins are very dry—or try a bottle of baby oil; it is a skin cleanser, moisturizer, and bath oil all in one.)

The Samsonite Corporation/Luggage Division in Denver, Colorado, publishes an excellent booklet on packing, "Getting a Handle on Luggage." This booklet is provided in quantities to travel agents for distribution to their clients. The booklet includes not only packing hints, but also information on selecting your luggage, traveling with your luggage, and international and adventure travel.

Clients must be reminded that all but a few international airlines use the piece concept instead of a weight allowance for baggage. Passengers are allowed to check in three bags; if they want to carry-on a bag, they may check two bags, and the carry-on cannot exceed 45 inches total measurement (just large enough to fit under a seat). The bags that are checked cannot exceed 106 inches total (for two), and each bag cannot exceed 70 pounds. Measure the length, height, and width of each bag to find out if they qualify. Generally, one 24-inch bag and one 26-inch bag qualifies. Some airlines are more lenient than others and will accept larger bags; however, they are all strict on the number of pieces and will charge for the additional pieces.

Veterinarians agree that pets are better off at home when their owners travel, but there are occasions when owners are relocating and shipping a pet becomes a necessity. Trains and buses no longer accept animals except guide dogs for the blind. Some airlines allow small animals in the passenger compartment, but most are put on the plane along with the luggage and freight.

Airlines require that dogs, cats, and other animals be shipped in approved pet carriers. Each airline has its own regulations, so it is necessary to check on each individual flight. The airlines will allow one carry-on container in first class and one in coach class per flight on a first-come, first-served basis, and the container must be small enough to fit under the seat. The reservation for the pet must be made at the same time that the reservation is made for the owner. The pet carrier must be large enough to allow room for the pet to stand up and move around, be ventilated, and there must be knobs or handles on the outside to keep other baggage from blocking the air vents.

The carrier should have a label that identifies the contents as a "live animal" and provides the owner's name and address, the destination address, and the name of the person who will be picking up the animal. If the pet is traveling overseas, the information should also appear in the language of the destination country. Before shipping a pet in the baggage compartment, find out how much and what other cargo will be there; overcrowded conditions will reduce the oxygen, and fumes from dry ice may be lethal.

Airlines require proof that the animal is in good health and has been vaccinated for rabies. If the pet is going to a foreign country, immunization shots and quarantine regulations must be checked with the local veterinarian, or call or write the embassy of the country in Washington, D.C. (*Travel Planners* have these addresses and phone numbers.) Also ask if the pet should be fed before travel and whether it should be tranquilized. Unless the flight is delayed or cancelled, airline personnel will not feed or exercise a pet.

MEDICAL ASSISTANCE FOR TRAVELERS

Membership in the nonprofit organization International Association for Medical Assistance to Travelers (IAMAT) can bring peace of mind to clients with health problems while they are traveling and to those who worry that they may be left stranded in a strange country in the event of an accident or sudden illness. Although membership is free, donations are welcomed to help fill the hundreds of requests for information, brochures, and membership cards.

Vincent Marcolongo, the association founder, created IAMAT to provide a worldwide organization of responsible English-speaking physicians who meet recognized standards and who are available to administer medical assistance to North American travelers on a 24-hour basis. Under association rules, participating doctors must:

1. Be licensed to practice in their native country and belong to its national medical association.
2. Agree to medical standards established by IAMAT.
3. Speak English and have at least one year of medical training in the United States, Canada, or the United Kingdom.
4. Agree to charge the fees established by the association. IAMAT, through its general organization, offer travelers a multitude of membership benefits, including a membership card entitling the traveler to services at a fixed IAMAT rate, a world directory listing IAMAT physicians in 125

countries and territories and a traveler clinical record covering identification, immunization records, and emergency medical data. IAMAT physicians will also provide a patient with a medical report should they require it during their travels, and will send a report to their doctors at home.

Dr. Marcolongo, in an interview with *Travel Weekly*, said that at present all participating doctors are specialists in internal medicine or cardiology. He noted that the ailments most prevalent among American tourists are respiratory, circulatory, bone fractures, bowel obstructions, and appendicitis. Most of these illnesses, he said, are caused by sudden changes of climate, fatigue, and overstress during travel. "Americans don't know how to pace themselves when they travel. They don't want to miss anything, so they run, run, run. If they would keep the same pace as they have at home, and eat and sleep with regularity, they might often save themselves illness away from home."

IAMAT will send travel agents a supply of flyers to distribute to clients. The flyer directs the clients to fill in the name and address and mail it to IAMAT for free membership in the organization and a booklet listing its clinics throughout the world.

THE ARGONNE ANTI-JET-LAG DIET

Many airline travelers are learning to prevent jet lag—or at least to speed up their recovery times—by using a diet plan developed at the Department of Energy's Argonne National Laboratory operated at the University of Chicago. The diet grew out of studies of circadian rhythms, natural body cycles controlled by molecular clocks found in every cell of the body. Anyone traveling across three or more time

How to avoid jet lag:

1. **DETERMINE BREAKFAST TIME** at destination on day of arrival.

2. **FEAST-FAST-FEAST-FAST** on home time. Start three days before departure day. On day one, FEAST; eat heartily with high-protein breakfast and lunch and a high-carbohydrate dinner. No coffee except between 3 and 5 p.m. On day two, FAST on light meals of salads, light soups, fruits and juices. Again, no coffee except between 3 and 5 p.m. On day three, FEAST again. On day four, departure day, FAST; if you drink caffeinated beverages, take them in morning when traveling west, or between 6 and 11 p.m. when traveling east. Going west, you may fast only half day.

3. **BREAK FINAL FAST** at destination breakfast time. No alcohol on plane. If flight is long enough, sleep until normal breakfast time at destination, *but no later*. Wake up and FEAST on high-protein breakfast. Stay awake, active. Continue day's meals according to meal times at destination.

FEAST on high protein breakfasts and lunches to stimulate the body's active cycle. Suitable meals include steak, eggs, hamburgers, high-protein cereals, green beans.

FEAST on high-carbohydrate suppers to stimulate sleep. They include spaghetti and other pastas (but no meatballs), crepes (but no meat filling), potatoes, other starchy vegetables, and sweet desserts.

FAST days help deplete the liver's store of carbohydrates and prepare the body's clock for resetting. Suitable foods include fruit, light soups, broths, skimpy salads, unbuttered toast, half pieces of bread. Keep calories and carbohydrates to a minimum.

COUNTDOWN

	1 FEAST	2 FAST	3 FEAST	4 FAST	BREAK FINAL FAST

ON HOME TIME

B / L / S

Coffee, tea, cola, other caffeinated beverages allowed only between 3 and 5 p.m.

Westbound: if you drink caffeinated beverages, take them morning before departure. Eastbound: take them between 6 and 11 p.m. If flight is long enough, sleep until destination breakfast time. Wake up and FEAST, beginning with a high-protein breakfast. Lights on. Stay awake and active.

ARGONNE NATIONAL LABORATORY
ANTI-JET-LAG DIET

The Argonne Anti-Jet-Lag Diet is helping travelers quickly adjust their bodies' internal clocks to new time zones. It is also being used to speed the adjustment of shiftworkers, such as power plant operators, to periodically rotating work hours. The diet was developed by Dr. Charles F. Ehret of Argonne's Division of Biological and Medical Research as an application of his fundamental studies of the daily biological rhythms of animals. Argonne National Laboratory is one of the U. S. Department of Energy's major centers of research in energy and the fundamental sciences. Argonne National Laboratory, 9700 South Cass Avenue, Argonne, Illinois 60439

☆ U.S. GOVERNMENT PRINTING OFFICE: 1984—754-904

Figure 16-2 Anti-Jet-Lag Diet: (Courtesy of Argonne-National Laboratories.)

zones, such as coast to coast across the United States, can benefit from the anti-jet-lag diet, says Charles Ehret, the Argonne biologist whose research developed the diet. Normally, the body needs a full day of recovery time for every time zone crossed. But proper use of the Argonne diet can help the traveler make the change in one day. Thousands of travelers have used Ehret's diet to prevent or ease the discomfort and inconvenience of jet lag, among them President Ronald Reagan when he flew to Tokyo in 1983.

A wallet-sized card summarizing the diet is available in quantities of 15 per order to travel agents and organizations whose employees travel a lot. They also offer free camera-ready copy with Argonne's permission to make as many copies as desired, but stipulate that it must be reproduced exactly as is, with no additions or deletions. Argonne is a publicly funded research organization. They cannot give the impression of endorsing a private business. This impression might be given if, for example, such a firm were to add its name to the card. (See Figure 16-2.)

The diet requires a planned rescheduling of mealtimes, meal contents, and social cues to help reset the body's clock. It is based simply on a feast, fast, feast, fast regimen over four days, the last fast day being the travel day. Feast on high-protein breakfasts and lunches. Feast on high-carbohydrate suppers to stimulate sleep. "Fast" days—keep calories and carbohydrates to a minimum. Suitable foods include fruit, light soups, broths, skimpy salads, unbuttered toast, and half pieces of bread. There are other, more complicated steps depending on which way the traveler is going. This is all explained on the card.

It would be advisable to have a supply of these cards in the travel agent's office and make sure that every long-distance traveler receives one with her final documents.

INSTANT PASSPORT PHOTOS

An additional service that travel agents can provide their clients is instant passport photos taken right in their office. This will save their clients time and can also provide a source of additional income. Some agents use this as a promotional tool and do not charge their own clients but will charge any walk-in business.

There are agencies that have built passport photography into a lucrative enterprise while using it to gain recognition as a full-service travel agency. Clients receive passport photos free; others pay a fee. The cameras have long ago paid for themselves while making a nice profit for the agency.

In addition to providing their own clients with a needed service, the service attracts new business from two types of walk-in customers: those who seek a passport photo to complete travel preparations begun at another agency, and those who use the photo for nontravel purposes, such as college applications, immigration cards, or professional licenses.

QUESTIONS AND PROBLEMS

1. What is one of the most important services the agent gives the client preparing for a European tour?
2. Which is the most commonly used reference book where documentary requirements may be found?
3. Give the passport requirements for U.S. citizens and for Canadians.
4. What is a visa? What is a tourist card? How do they differ?
5. Who needs a reentry permit?
6. When do travelers need a health certificate?

7. Name some of the official forms that a travel agent may be called upon for assistance in preparing.

8. What is the U.S. duty-free limit on purchases abroad?

9. What are some of the commissionable services that an agent can give the clients?

10. Do you think it is worthwhile for the agent to give clients bon voyage gifts? How would you determine the value of such gifts?

11. In your own words, how would you answer the question from a cruise client: What kind of clothing will I need?

12. What is IAMAT? Who would you recommend for this?

13. When would you recommend the anti-jet-lag diet?

14. Name a service that could be profitable as well as a convenience for your clients.

chapter 17

Tourism and Travel Organizations

OBJECTIVES

When you have finished this chapter you should be able to:

1. Discuss the importance of international tourism.
2. Explain the purpose of the WTO.
3. Describe the functions of national tourist offices.
4. Discuss how to use NTOs in the travel agency.
5. Determine the importance of GATT.
6. Advise clients on safety tips while traveling abroad.

Not many people realize that international tourism today is the world's largest industry and employer. In 1991 total worldwide spending for domestic and international travel reached about $3.5 trillion. This is larger than the gross national products (GNPs) of all countries in the world except the United States, the old Soviet Union, and Japan. After considering the devastating effects of the Persian Gulf war and economic recession, 1993 expectations are for modest renewed growth, with travel and tourism growing more than 6.1 percent per year, or 23 percent faster than the world economy. By 1993 travel and tourism employment is expected to grow 50 percent faster than world employment.

These are the conclusions of the second annual report by the World Travel & Tourism Council (WTTC) in March 1992. The council, which seeks to promote the importance of tourism among government leaders, is a global coalition of 43 chief executive officers from various sectors of the travel industry. The first study in 1990 and the current report continues to put the industry at the top in capital investment, employment, and tax payments. But the chief executives who make up the WTTC are concerned that their business gets little respect from government policymakers. By publicizing the vast scope of travel and tourism, the council aims to persuade governments, their agencies, and public-policy decision makers to take such steps as removing bureaucratic barriers to travel; rebuilding and expanding airports, highways, and other travel infrastructure; encouraging environmentally friendly travel; resisting protectionism; ensuring traveler security, and developing fair fiscal policies to stimulate tourism investment.

Tourism provides employment directly or indirectly to large numbers of people. Some 127 million people worldwide, or 1 in 15 workers, are employed in travel and tourism. In the United States alone, travel and tourism maintained 9.1 million jobs in 1989. Minority workers hold 13 percent of all jobs in the industry—a higher percentage than their share of total employment. The U.S. Bureau of Labor Statistics predicts that by 1995 there will be a 27 percent increase in the leisure recreation services and a 44 percent increase in travel agents (listed among the 10 fastest-growing occupations). In 1990, international visitors to the United States numbered 38.8 million and spent $51.1 billion on tourism goods and services (per USTTA data released May 1991).

Women hold over half of all travel industry jobs (54 percent), proportionately one-quarter higher than their overall share, and the industry employs, by far, more of our nation's youth. It has been estimated that 24 percent of food service workers are teen-agers, as well as 75 percent of amusement park workers. Travel and tourism is perhaps the largest private student assistance program in the nation. The travel industry has been creating new jobs faster than the rest of the economy, even during recession periods. The increase in jobs in travel agencies, airlines, hotels, restaurants, and other service industries has been a major factor in reducing U.S. unemployment. These service jobs provide entry-level experience for millions of young people, who move up the ladder to higher-paying positions as managers, or move on to jobs in other industries that are suppliers for hotels, restaurants, and airlines.

At the 1984 Senate tourism caucus, in his request for a congressional resolution for a week of national recognition for tourism, Senator John W. Warner (Rep.-VA) said:

> But travel and tourism goes far beyond economics. In addition to its strength as both an import and export, tourism to and within the United States from abroad has an intangible, if perhaps more significant value. Experiencing America firsthand provides outstanding educational opportunities and is terrific for personal growth—there's no better way to promote international understanding and goodwill, or to explain freedom and democracy, than through travel and tourism.

Travel and tourism is an important industry. It's good business and it's great for America. It deserves a week of national recognition. And why not? It sells the best product in the world.

Tourism is a multifaceted activity that affects nearly all sectors of national life. It is not only the activity of traveling done by tourists, foreign or domestic, but includes the activity of servicing all these tourists in a great number of ways. Tourism is less an industry and more a market. It does not produce goods; it sells services. Providing these services may affect trades that have only a remote connection with travel.

The United Nations Conference on International Travel and Tourism (Rome 1963) declared that "tourism is a basic and most desirable human activity deserving the praise and encouragement of all peoples and all governments." This conference also recognized the important role played by tourism in strengthening national economies, stimulating international trade, and promoting international goodwill and understanding.

Since 1937, the travel industry has been using the following definitions of a tourist recommended by the Committee of Statistical Experts of League of Nations:

To secure the comparability of international tourist statistics, the term "tourist" shall, in principle, be interpreted to mean any person traveling for a period of 24 hours or more in a country other than that in which he usually resides. The Committee decided that the following were to be regarded as tourists:

1. Persons traveling for pleasure, for domestic reasons, for health, etc.
2. Persons traveling to meetings, or in a representative capacity of any kind (scientific, administrative, diplomatic, religious, athletic, etc.)
3. Visitors traveling for business purposes.
4. Visitors arriving in the course of a sea cruise, even when they stay less than 24 hours. The latter should be reckoned as a separate group disregarding, if necessary, their usual place of residence.

Students, travelers in transit through the country, and border visitors who spend less than 24 hours in the immediate border area of the country visited have also been included in the classification of tourists, excluding only those who arrive for gainful employment or to take up permanent residence.

Congress came up with its own definition when it passed the National Tourism Policy Act in 1981. It describes the travel industry as one that provides services to those journeying outside the same community for any purpose not related to day-to-day activity.

The travel industry of today owes much to the work of the tourism pioneers of the 1950's. Much of the market research and forecasting of the growth potential of tourism was carried out by a number of trade associations that blossomed then. The International Union of Official Travel Organizations (IUOTO), the Tourism Committee of the Organization for Economic Cooperation and Development, and the European Travel Commission (ETC) were based in Europe. In the United States there were the National Association of Travel Organizations (NATO), the Travel Research Association (TRA), the American Society of Travel Agents (ASTA), and the Pacific Asia Travel Association (PATA).

World tourism's golden years were between 1960 and 1973, when the annual rate of increase each year was 5 percent. The oil shortages and the resulting increases in fuel costs in 1974 and again in 1979 contributed to the decline in the growth rate of tourism to a 2 percent increase per year. Late in 1986, a spokesperson for the European Travel Commission predicted that international tourism is again expected to grow at an annual rate of 5 percent between now and the end of the century, when it is projected that it will be the largest single industry in the world.

The fastest rate of growth in tourist arrivals has been in the East Asia and Pacific regions. The billions of U.S. dollars pumped into Asian and Pacific countries during the Vietnam war stimulated the economies of many countries in this region along with a greater interest and awareness of these countries. Tourism, with the strong support of PATA, began to take a high-priority position in a number of countries. Even the People's Republic of China has targeted tourism as one obvious route to bolstering its economy.

A 15-year international tourism slump in Canada ended in 1986. Vancouver's Expo 86 World Fair drew a 10 percent increase in visits of Americans. Toronto reported a strong growth in convention business. Canada estimates that just a 1 percent increase in tourist traffic gives a $30 million annual boost to the Canadian economy and creates more than 800 new jobs. Previous to the Persian Gulf War, the Canadian tourism market was starting to feel the effects of a growing recession in Canada. In 1991, Canadians started to go to short-haul destinations in the United States to satisfy a pent-up demand for travel.

Ecotourism

Ecotourism is now the buzzword in the travel industry, although the concept—environmentally and culturally sensitive travel—has been around for years. Travel agents in the mid-1980s began reporting an increase in ecotourist clients, described as those for whom the environment is the most important part of the vacation picture; who prefer small locally owned lodges to big hotels and resorts; who want guided trips with an environmental–cultural orientation, or who would exchange a cruise ship for a canoe. We all need to become ecotourists by leaving destinations in better shape than they were when we arrived. When at home, we need to conserve water, electricity, and gasoline.

Changes throughout the world point to more affluent societies whose members have more time to spend and enjoy their money. Yuppies and retirees are asking for more than the standardized tour package offered in the past. Many others are also interested in travel if the travel industry can provide an attractive reason for

Figure 17-2 Horseback riders enjoy the scenery of the Grand Canyon. Photo courtesy of the Grand Canyon National Park Lodges.

traveling other than the trite "travel is broadening" and "travel is educational" themes. Travelers want to visit natural or cultural sites that are relatively unaltered by development; they want to visit areas where few have ventured before. But untouched areas are increasingly difficult to find. Exploration has developed into tourism, and tourism into crowds. Ironically, tourists are seeking something new, yet demand all the comforts of home.

A strong desire to really get to know the people (rather than places) in the countries visited has been expressed by more and more travelers. Fortunately, more and more countries are developing such programs. Bed and breakfast tours are popular throughout the United Kingdom (England, Northern Ireland, and Scotland), where tourists stay in private cottages and farms. Bed and breakfast packages are also increasing in the United States as well as in other countries. Many hotels in Japan are now featuring "Japanese" rooms. The French National Tourist Board has an excellent book on France with eight suggested itineraries to seeing France in depth: the agricultural area, wine-making centers, visits to castles and country homes, and so on. Cruise ships and private yacht charters in Greece visit the "undiscovered" islands. Tours in Italy include visits to private villas.

There are few areas remaining unspoiled after the tourists have educated inhabitants to other ways of living—involving clothing and even food and drink. For example, the Mexican's famous white teeth are deteriorating due to their love of cola drinks. And you can find a McDonald's in almost every major city around the world. In Greece, a woman wearing pants was unheard of unless she was on horseback; now, even in the smallest villages, the young girls flaunt their pantsuits because the tourists brought them in. When large numbers of tourists visit a destination, they can no longer be treated as guests. The pressure increases to make money instead of friends. Yet there are people on both sides of the tourism fence who would like to meet and understand one another.

These are the areas in which tourism will change in the future: when the needs of people and the environment take higher priority; when tourist-receiving countries develop a stronger concern among their people to satisfy the desire for individuality and participation; and when tourist boards, tour operators, and travel agents join together to promote travel with more imagination and enthusiasm. The desire for high-quality travel will increase as travelers become more knowledgeable and selective. There are steps that can be taken to protect wildlife and cultures from excessive tourism and to enhance the travel experience for those who venture to faraway places. Local tourist bureaus should adopt a code of ethics for the visitor so that tourists can be forewarned of offending or destructive behaviors and advised how best to preserve natural attractions. Local communities must be educated to the importance of tourism and encouraged to become involved in improving and maintaining existing natural resources.

Selling the ecotourism experience requires more agent time and investigation than more conventional travel options, such as motorcoach tours or cruises. According to delegates to the First World Congress on Tourism and the Environment held in May 1992, Belize City, Belize, S.A., help may be on the way in the form of rating programs meant to identify tour operators that can legitimately be called "green." To curb abuses of the term "ecotourism," the Ecotourism Society, based in Arlington, Virginia, plans also to launch a consumer-based green evaluation program. It will be developed in cooperation with tour operators and leading conservation organizations.

TEN COMMANDMENTS FOR TOURISTS*

In the coming decade, tourism is expected to be the world's largest industry, with over half a billion people traveling each year. Travelers share a responsibility to

*Courtesy of American Society of Travel Agents (ASTA).

respect other cultures and protect natural resources. Environmentally aware tourists can help themselves and the places they visit by following these rules:

1. Leave only footprints, take only photographs and memories.
2. Respect the frailty of the environment.
3. To make vacations more meaningful, take time before hand to learn the customs, manners, and culture of the area.
4. Respect and suport local cultures (religions, traditions, crafts, services and cuisines) and the privacy and dignity of residents, especially when taking photographs.
5. Never litter. Carry bags with you for trash. Leave your surroundings cleaner than when you found them.
6. Do not buy products made from endangered species, such as ivory, tortoise shell, animal skins and feathers. Read "Know Before You Go," the U.S. Customs list of products that cannot be imported.
7. Always follow designated trails. Do not disturb natural habitats of animals or plants. Keep your distance, never touch animals.
8. Make an effort to know and support conservation-oriented programs and organizations.
9. Ask travel agents, tour operators, resorts, and attractions to adopt and practice ASTA's Environmental Guidelines or other conservation codes.
10. Whenever possible, walk or use public transportation.

WORLD TOURISM ORGANIZATION

In 1908, three countries—France, Spain, and Portugal—felt the need to pool their resources in the interest of promoting tourism and founded the Franco–Hispano–Portuguese Federation of Tourist Associations. This might be considered the first international tourist organization.

In 1925, conscious of the contribution they could make in social and economic spheres, the heads of tourism of a number of countries founded the International Union of Official Tourist Publicity Organizations at The Hague. This organization functioned with considerable success until the eve of World War II.

In 1946, the representatives of the national tourist organizations met in London, and the following year, the International Union of Official Travel Organizations (IUOTO) was founded. Since that date the IUOTO has continually expanded both in number of members and in the sphere of its activities.

On November 1, 1974 the new intergovernmental World Tourist Organization (WTO) replaced the IUOTO. Fifty-one countries signed the statues ratifying the WTO, which has special links to the United Nations. It was originally headquartered in Geneva, Switzerland, the headquarters is now located in Madrid, Spain.

The formation of the WTO reflects the increased responsibilities in tourism being assumed by governments and is a response to a need for adequate machinery to deal with the industry's growing size and problems, as well as to new trends in global development strategy and the need to strengthen technical cooperation between nations. The new organization continues the technical services performed by IUOTO for member states. As an intergovernmental body, the WTO has more standing and influence.

The WTO is the only international organization that groups together the governmental or official tourist organizations of all parts of the world on the basis of one for each country and territory. The WTO cooperates with the United Nations and other international organizations in pursuing the social and economic aims of these world bodies. It is a technical and specialized organization that has been granted consultative status by the United Nations. The Madrid-based organization, which has 109 nations as full members, conducts tourism research and works to reduce international barriers to travel.

The WTO consists of full and associate dues-paying members. The category of full members is restricted to national tourist organizations or other organizations set up to promote the development of tourism that have been established or recognized by their governments (who assume full responsibility for the management of their foreign relations), or by the governments of dependent territories. The category of associate member is confined to international or national organizations, either commercial or noncommercial, representing tourist interests or interested in the promotion of tourism.

In a February 1988 news release, the WTO warned that it may not continue to operate because many developing countries have not paid their dues for years. The fallen dollar has also resulted in a loss of approximately $500,000. WTO suggests that the most practical solution is for those who can afford to pay to provide whatever extra cash they can, and they would also like to boost the annual dues of nongovernmental members.

The WTO's aims are essentially practical and based on the principle of the fifth freedom. The heads of tourism of its member states believe that their activities should not be restricted by national frontiers, but should extend beyond political and ideological barriers. They have succeeded in replacing competition by more effective methods of comprehensive international collaboration.

Among the noteworthy achievements of the original IUOTO were the simplification and standardization of the various national travel regulations, with a view to reducing or abolishing outdated or unjustified formalities, and the gradual discontinuance of visa requirements. [In September 1986 the U.S. Congress voted to exempt visa requirements for tourists from as many as eight foreign countries that provide reciprocal waiver rights. However, this was not put into effect until July 1988, when the United Kingdom and Japan were the first two countries designated for a visa wavier test. The visa waver program has now been extended to 13 countries (see Chapter 16).] No less important were the measures proposed to simplify frontier formalities, grant currency allowances to tourists, increase facilities granted to transit passengers to airports, and so on. The policies adopted by IUOTO toward taxes born directly or indirectly by tourists and the tourist industry, social tourism, and youth travel have also produced beneficial effects.

The hotel industry is one of the aspects of tourism to which the WTO pays a great deal of attention. In the field of transport, the WTO cooperates, at present through specialized study groups, with appropriate international organizations to facilitate the development of this important sector of the tourist industry.

The convention for the free circulation of tourist publicity material is another accomplishment of IUOTO, as is the standardization of sizes of tourist documents and literature. To promote the harmonious development of tourism in its member countries, WTO deals with problems posed by the training of staff and with travel research.

WTO assists in the organization and functioning of official travel organizations and their activities in the field of publicity and advertising. The WTO Tourist Documentation Centre also collects titles of technical works dealing with tourist questions, as well with tourist legislative tests and regulations. This comprehensive documentation is made available to all interested persons. WTO is the only organization that collects and publishes international travel statistics on an annual basis. A special study group publishes an international catalog of tourist publicity films and a catalog of travel organizations and their activities in the field of publicity and advertising.

Two organizations have been formed to work with governments worldwide to adopt policies to promote the growth of the travel industry. The World Travel and Tourism Council, a Brussels-based organization, was formed in 1990 by 29 airlines, hotel companies, railroads, and other travel businesses that share the goal of making governments understand the economic force of the industry. The council is not the first group to call for greater recognition of travel's standing as a major economic power or to ask governments to eliminate policies that impede the industry's growth, such as unnecessary regulation and discriminatory taxes. But the council stands out because it is the only industry group representing a broad cross section of chief executive officers of global travel and tourism companies. The council is now composed of 42 officers representing 40 major travel organizations.

In the United States, a new industry group called Go USA! ran a media and public relations campaign organized by the United States Travel and Tourism Administration (USTTA) in 1991 to rebuild domestic travel and inbound foreign tourism after the Persian Gulf war. The coalition of more than 45 travel-related organizations and companies raised $6 million for print, radio, and television advertisements.

In February 1992, after the civil strife in Yugoslavia, the World Travel and Tourism Council asked the travel industry to support a proposal to make it a war crime to destroy certain tourist attractions around the world. Specifically, the council wants the United Nations to modify the Geneva Red Cross Conventions governing war to forbid the destruction of any of the 359 sites designated by Unesco as "world cultural and natural heritage sites." Sites on the list include Persepolis in Iran, Petra in Jordan, Auschwitz in Poland, the Buda Castle in Hungary, the Great Barrier Reef in Australia and the Old City in Dubrovnik and other sites in Yugoslavia that suffered a lot of damage in 1991. The proposal would not guarantee that tourist attractions would be safe, but could give bombers pause.

NATIONAL TOURIST OFFICES AND TRAVEL AGENTS

In 1965, one hundred delegates of IUOTO (now WTO) representing 50 countries and 12 international organizations connected with the travel and tourist industry gathered together at Bordeaux, France, for the first symposium ever held to discuss the relations between national tourist offices (NTOs) and travel agents. This was the fifth of a series of international get-togethers and WTO felt that it was the most important. (A complete report was published by IUOTO and was made

Figure 17-3 Royal Cruise Line's newest luxury ship, the classic 765-passenger *Royal Odyssey*. In her 1992 inaugural year, the *Royal Odyssey* cruised in the Orient, India, Africa, Australia/New Zealand, the South Pacific, Hawaii, the Mexican Riviera, Alaska and Glacier Bay, the Panama Canal, Canada/New England and Colonial America. Pictured: the *Royal Odyssey* in Hong Kong.

available to the public.) Basil G. Atkinson, then president of WTO, who is the general manager of the Australian National Travel Association, said in his opening remarks: "Travel agents are a very important factor in modern tourism and the great responsibility they bear is not always fully appreciated. For instance, 75 percent of all air bookings throughout the world and 95 percent of all steamship bookings are done through travel agencies."

The symposium emphasized that close cooperation between all elements of the travel industry was essential. WTO was concerned with all aspects of tourism, and travel agents are one of the most important elements. Mr. Atkinson continued:

> It is they who build up sales and have the most direct contact with the customers by providing them with advice and practical assistance, while the national tourist offices are responsible mainly for publicity aimed at the encouragement of tourism generally. An exchange of ideas between these two elements of tourism would undoubtedly help to solve a great many problems. With improved transport facilities, more leisure time for most people, and increased world prosperity, the rate of business is likely to double during the next decade as it has done in the last. There are two ways to prepare for such a development and both are based on the principle of mutual help and goodwill.
>
> First, travel agents should inform national tourist offices of any difficulties, frustrations or unnecessary formalities encountered in the various countries. Then the national tourist office concerned could aproach the governmental authorities in its own country with a view to remedying the situation. A simple means should be developed to enable travel agents to provide such information easily.
>
> Secondly, travel agents should endeavor to instill in their customers a sense of respect for each country's customs, local traditions, dress, and way of life so that tourism would be a means of stimulating goodwill and mutual understanding between people instead of ill will which sometimes, unfortunately, was the case. Tourists who had not been properly briefed beforehand and who therefore, perhaps unwittingly, ruffled the feelings of people in the countries visited could, regrettably, cause harm to the industry; *a grave responsiblity, therefore, rests on the travel agents to ensure that their customers are a credit to tourism* [Italics added].

There has been, in the past, some confusion and misunderstanding between travel agents and the national tourist offices. One of the chief functions common to all national tourist organizations is the improvement of the economy of a country through tourism by increasing visitor expenditures in it. Connected to this function is the responsibility to oversee and assure that hotels, transport systems, tour operators, and tour guides maintain high standards in the care and consideration of the tourist. Some of the activities of national tourist offices are:

1. Publicizing the country. This can be quite expensive, as it must be directed at all levels of the population and a wide range of tourist markets have to be covered.
2. Assisting and advising certain types of travelers. The number of do-it-yourself travelers is increasing and it is the responsibility of the national tourist offices to look after their interests and give them help and advice.
3. Creating a demand for certain destinations.
4. Supplying information; preparing and distributing brochures and posters to travel agents.
5. Ensuring that the destination is up to expectations. The national tourist office does not merely promote the country: it is fully responsible for

ensuring the quality and availability of the destination that is being marketed by the travel agents. It is also responsible for developing resorts and places of interest in the country.

6. Preparing the market by advance advertising. The task of the national tourist offices is to encourage potential tourists to take action by going to a travel agent's office.

Using the National Tourist Offices

Most travel agents do not take full advantage of the services offered by the NTOs. Although few NTO representatives make personal sales calls on agents, NTOs are holding more and more seminars throughout the United States, either singly or in combined trade shows, in an effort to educate agents on utilizing their offices. Many NTOs now have 800 (toll-free) phone numbers, which makes it easier to contact them.

Agents that know them and use them agree that NTOs are very helpful or specialized information not usually found in normal reference material. They not only help solve problems but can also act as mediators with hotels in commission complaints or client's complaints about poor hotel accommodations.

Clients are most appreciative of all the general information agents can supply, whether they are visiting one country or a dozen countries. Informative, attractive brochures can help close the sale and encourage repeat business.

Another service offered by the European tourist offices is helping people who are searching for their roots in the "old country." While only a few of them have compiled comprehensive lists of genealogical organization and other sources, all can, at least, get the heritage-hunter headed in the right direction.

Many agents are unaware that a simple request to be placed on the mailing list of the NTO will keep them supplied with current bulletins and literature of each country. (Addresses can be found in the *Travel Industry Personnel Directory* or the *OAG Travel Planners*.) The British Tourist Authority started using American Airline's SABRE computer system in 1987 to supply detailed information to travel agents. The NTOs can supply:

- Literature about their particular destination.
- Information on hotels, airlines, car rentals, maps, transfer rates, weather, and a host of other intangibles that go into making a successful sale and repeat business.
- Representatives who will assist the agent in planning a specialized tour of their country.
- Slides, films, videotapes, and on-the-scene information for working with groups.

Tourism offices provide a vital link between motorcoach tour operators and their suppliers. The offices are often the only source of unbiased information operators have concerning suppliers in a particular city or region. Most tourism offices suggest possible itineraries for groups and many will go one step further by putting together the entire packages, complete with rates. Motorcoach tour operators also depend on tourism offices for advertising and promotion.

It must be kept in mind that the national tourist office has two objectives: to promote its own country, and to stimulate tourism worldwide.

U.S. and Canadian Tourist Offices

Every state in the United States and most provinces in Canada have their own tourist bureau (often called a travel and convention office), and major resort areas such as the Poconos, Myrtle Beach, Las Vegas, or southern California have their own offices to supply travel agents with promotional and advertising tools.

Recognizing the job-generating power of the tourism industry, the individual states and provinces are competing fiercely for an increased share of the growing domestic travel market. Many states are also increasing their advertising aimed at encouraging their residents to vacation within their own home state.

Canada is also benefiting from an advertising blitz launched in the United States to promote Canadian cities. The weak Canadian dollar continues to provide an incentive for the American market at a time when the U.S. dollar's purchasing power in Europe has fallen into decline.

Canada is the largest international travel market for the United States, annually supplying over half of all foreign visitors to the States, as well as one-fourth of total U.S. travel receipts.

GENERAL AGREEMENTS ON TARIFFS AND TRADE (GATT)

The 92 countries belonging to GATT agreed at a fall 1986 meeting in Uruguay to look, for the first time, at including service in trade agreements. Until then the 38-year-old organization's rules covered only trade in goods. The international travel market would be even larger if it were not for the large number of nontariff restrictions affecting travel and tourism services.

The U.S. representatives to GATT meetings are expected to call for talks on:

- Easing visa requirements by the United States and other nations.
- Reducing restrictive customs rules imposed on pleasure travelers.
- Eliminating or cutting entry and departure taxes and other tourist fees.
- Reviewing discriminatory practices at airports that favor national carriers over foreign airline competitors.
- Liberalizing labor regulations that now make it difficult for carriers, hotels, and tour operators to employ other-than-local workers.
- Enlarging currency allowances to enable more visits to other countries.
- Easing controls governing inflow and outflow of money in travel industry operations.
- Cutting back on restraints on foreign travel entrepreneurs imposed to protect local competitors.

A number of nations agree that tourism should be freed from many of its legal constraints. The World Tourism Organization (WTO) has long crusaded for travel freedom and is expected to play an important role in mobilizing support for any reforms urged by GATT.

TERRORISM AND TOURISM

Fear of terrorism is a problem that cannot be ignored. The public's view of travel has changed from dreams of pleasure to fears of terrorism. Although there has been a substantial tightening of security in transportation, including airports and shipping piers, at hotels, and with motorcoach tour operators, the travel agents' responsibilities have increased. They must try to calm the client's fears, yet must avoid recommendations to unsafe destinations. Even with the help of travel advisories from the U.S. government and other organizations that now issue bulletins on the current troublespots, no agent can be aware of every possible danger, and thus runs the risk of possible litigation from returning clients who may have been

Figure 17-4 Only in India is the famed Bengal tiger still found in sufficient numbers to afford it a real chance for survival. India has sanctuaries where tourists can view tigers, elephants, rhinos, wild oxen, rare birds, and, on occasion, Asiatic lions. Photo courtesy of India Tourist Office.

involved in terrorist attacks. Some agents suggest that agents protect themselves legally by having clients sign a disclaimer stating that they were advised of the possibility of unsafe conditions when they insist on traveling to a potentially dangerous country.

Terrorism takes many forms and has occurred throughout history. Gwynne Dyer, a British journalist, notes there are more than 150 countries in the world, with twice as many groups who might plausibly define themselves as nations. Among them are factions ready to lead revolts and die for ethnic and religious causes or to gain territory. The resulting violence knows no frontiers. It has become global.

Alexander Anolik (author of *The Law and the Travel Industry*) in his "Preventive Legal Care" article for the *Travel Agent*, June 19, 1986, gave some background on the law versus international criminal acts. He stated (condensed report): "Piracy has been around as long as international trade has. Since piracy was considered an international offense against humanity, any state could try the pirates under the hostis humani generi (enemy of the human race) legal concept. The state that captured the pirates could decide the fate of their cargo and of the thieves themselves. Unfortunately, the old laws did not envision modern-day terrorism.

The first reported airline hijacking took place nearly 56 years ago in Peru. But it was not until the 1960s, when planes were frequently forced to fly to Cuba, that such terrorism began to creep into the public consciousness.

According to the record, the first of two conventions dealing with the punishment of terrorism and calling for creation of an international criminal court occurred under the auspices of the old League of Nations. And just this year 1986 the request for a politically resistant international tribunal with the power to try terrorists was renewed at a meeting of the International Forum of Travel and Tourism Advocates (IFTTA) in Jerusalem. There was another brainstorm session in April 1987 in San Francisco by attorneys from all over the world on how to keep pushing for such a court."

Besides being cool toward countries soft on terrorism, what other measures might agents themselves take to help resolve the situation? They can urge their congress members and the president to take action to deter terrorists and render their acts futile. Here is what IFTTA wants done, according to the resolutions it passed at its last session. In addition to urging creation of a court to try and punish terrorists, the international forum urges:

- Additional international cooperation and research into terrorist activities and mutual sharing of information.
- Strict retribution against governments utilizing their diplomatic immunity privileges to foster terrorism.
- Strong economic sanctions, including aviation boycotts and discontinuance of bilateral agreements, with countries harboring or encouraging terroristic activities.
- Policies of "no negotiations" with hijackers. Willingness to talk only triggers more terrorism.

According to Eugene Mastrangelo, senior analyst for Risks International, 50 percent of all terrorist acts have occurred since 1980. Risks International has monitored terrorism for the business community since 1978. Awareness of the evolving terrorist threat is the first step in developing an effective response. Risks International fills this need by providing accurate, timely reporting and analysis concerning terrorist activities worldwide.

Mastrangelo's advice to international travelers:

- Don't advertise the fact that you are an American tourist.
- Don't wear religious jewelry.
- Stay in hotels not frequented by Americans or Britons.
- Don't go to restaurants and bars frequented by U.S. military personnel.
- Use eye contact with suspicious persons. Don't let them intimidate you.
- Try to use nonstop flights.
- Businesspeople should contact the U.S. embassy or consulate upon arrival.

Travel Trust International has published a small booklet containing safety tips for executives traveling overseas. Among the tips:

- Don't fly first or business class. Blend in with the passengers in the tourist section.

- Avoid routes originating in unstable areas such as the Middle East.
- Avoid conversation with fellow passengers. Never tell anyone your itinerary.
- Keep a low profile. VIP treatment singles you out. Arrange to be met by a cab instead of a limo.
- Retain your room key at all times.
- Baggage tags should have your name and business address.
- Stay clear of locker areas.
- Don't wear a business suit while traveling. This singles you out as a wealthy Westerner.

The Air Transport Association of America (ATA) reported that airline and airports responded to the Persian Gulf crisis with the tightest security in aviation history. The State Department is offering a reward of up to $4 million for information that prevents or frustrates a terrorist attack against aviation. Anyone with information should contact the nearest U.S. embassy or consulate.

The ATA is offering the following advice for airline passengers: Arrive early for flights because tightened security causes delays in processing passengers and their baggage; do not leave baggage unattended after it has been packed and closed; report anything unusual, including unattended bags and packages, to airport security personnel or to flight crews. Passengers on domestic flights may be required to show identification. Law enforcement officials and experts in terrorism continue to believe that the threat of terrorism is greatest overseas, but domestic security has been tightened substantially as an added precaution.

The Federal Aviation Administration (FAA) is upgrading hiring, training, and performance standards for workers who screen passenger and bags at airports, as required by aviation security legislation signed into law November 1990. The FAA also proposed to require each airport to designate one employee to coordinate security functions and to establish security; training programs for employees with access to secure airport areas.

The proposal would establish an entry-level requirement that applicants have earned a high school diploma or a general equivalency diploma or possess a combination of education and experience enabling them to perform screening duties effectively. Other entry-level requirements include an ability to speak, read, and write English; good powers of sight, color perception, and hearing; and physical dexterity.

Realizing the importance of educating the public to understand the problem of terrorism, the University of New Haven initiated a course called "Terrorism and Travel," taught by Caroline Dinegar, professor of political science. The class is geared toward people in law enforcement, political science, sociology, and the travel and hotel industries. The three-credit course, which runs five weeks, was offered for the first time in the summer of 1986.

Dr. Dinegar, the former head of the Peace Corps in Malaysia, where terrorism became a grisly reality, said she was prompted to offer the course because her field is international law. The course explores what terrorism is, where it is found, and hopefully, how to avoid it while overseas. According to Dr. Dinegar, terrorism is increasing at a rate of 30 percent a year. Worldwide urbanization, repressive governments, and simply "being able to get away with it," she theorized, may be the causes.

Terrorist organizations are dangerous primarily because they are unpredictable and uncontrollable. If the person who is at the center of a terrorist organization goes mad, who's going to control him? And from the terrorist's point of view, violence such as car bombings and attacks at airports are intellectual acts, although it does not appear that way when you hear that x number of people were gunned down. The terrorist is not a nut, Dr. Dinegar explained; he takes action because of his allegiance with his group.

As for advice on avoiding terrorists, Dr. Dinegar conceded that she did not have all the answers. However, with a wry bit of humor, she did share one tip she said she learned while in Europe. "If you hear any noise down the street," she said, "go the other way."

QUESTIONS AND PROBLEMS

1. How important is world tourism?
2. What is the percentage of women in the travel industry?
3. What are the four definitions of a tourist?
4. What caused a decline in tourism in 1974 and 1979?
5. What new markets are predicted in the future?
6. State some of the new trends in travel demand.
7. Put together a tour package that would satisfy some of the new demands.
8. What is the purpose of the World Tourism Organization?
9. Who would you notify if your clients returned from France and complained of discourteous treatment during their visit?
10. What are some of the activities of a national tourist office?
11. Can you give some suggestions as to how the United States could promote travel to this country?
12. What or who is GATT? How will it affect tourism?
13. List some safety tips for traveling overseas.

by air to their destination and return by ship (or vice versa). The steamship lines give passengers the round-trip discount on their fare.

Air Taxi Agreement. Agreement entered into by a scheduled airline with members of the National Air Transport Association (NATA) to handle requests for space and ticketing to points serviced by the air taxi operator.

Air Taxi Operator. A class of air carriers operating light aircraft up to a gross weight of 12,500 pounds and engaging in a wide variety of passenger and/or cargo transportation services with no necessarily fixed routes.

Air Traffic Conference of America (ATC). The ATC was a division of the ATA. Its purpose was the same as that of ATA except that its jurisdiction was solely over matters involving traffic, sales, or advertising. Two of its committees were the Reservations Committee, which dealt with interline reservations procedures, and the Ticketing and Baggage Committee, which dealt with interline ticketing and baggage procedures. The Air Traffic Enforcement Office, which insured adherence to ATC resolutions, was a branch of the ATC. An ATC committee approved and appointed new travel agencies and reviewed established agencies. The Airlines Reporting Corporation assumed these duties on January 1, 1985.

Air Transport Association of America (ATA). An association of scheduled airlines. Its purpose is to encourage the use of air transportation and to further the interests of its members through cooperative efforts to deal with their mutual problems.

A la carte. A menu from which items are chosen and paid for individually. This type of meal arrangement is seldom included in any tour.

All Expense Tour. As the term implies, one that includes in its advertised price the cost of practically all travel and tour ground arrangements. Very few tours today can rightfully be termed all-expense tours.

Aloft. Above the superstructure; in or near the mast of a ship.

American Automobile Association. *See* AAA.

American Plan (AP). Hotel accommodations that include three meals a day in the price of the room. The meals are usually *table d'hote*. Sometimes referred to as *full pension*, especially in Europe.

American Society of Travel Agents (ASTA). Large international trade organization of professional tourism and travel personnel.

Amidship (Midship). In or toward the middle of a vessel, between bow and stern.

Amtrak. National Railroad Passenger Corporation; 13 railroads merged their passenger services and created a single, centrally managed, nationwide, intercity system. Amtrak owns and operates the passenger trains but does not own the rights-of-way. These remain the property of the individual railroads.

AP. *See* American Plan.

APEX Fare (Advanced Purchase Excursion Fare). In international travel, a discounted fare that requires a 21- to 30-day advance purchase and round-trip or open-jaw travel. The international equivalent of the domestic supersaver fares.

Apollo. United Airlines' computer reservation system.

Appointments (Certificates of Appointment). Authorization granted by the various transportation conferences to travel agents who have met the proper requirements.

Approval Code. A multidigit series used on credit card sales to indicate the credit company's knowledge of the billing.

ARC (Airlines Reporting Corporation). A corporation formed by U.S. airlines to continue with the defunct Air Traffic Conference rules and regulations concerning the travel agency system.

Area Bank Settlement Plan. Under this plan, the United States and Canada are divided into geographical areas, each containing approximately the same number of travel agencies. Each travel agent, instead of reporting to the individual airlines, reports all sales to a designated bank in his or her area. The area bank forwards a separate report and remittance to each carrier, as well as one to the ARC (see above).

ARTA. *See* Association of Retail Travel Agents.

ARUNK. Arrival unknown. Term used in computer reservations systems to account for a missing segment of an itinerary; indicates that the passenger will travel to the departure site by some other means.

Association of Retail Travel Agents (ARTA). A trade association composed exclusively of retail travel agents.

ASTA. *See* American Society of Travel Agents.

Astern. Beyond the stern.

ATA. *See* Air Transport Association of America.

ATAR. Computer reservation system being considered for both airlines and travel agencies.

ATC. *See* Air Traffic Conference of America.

Athwartship. Across the ship, from side to side.

ATO. *See* Airport Ticket Office.

Authorized Agency Location. A place of business operated by an agent and included on the ARC and IATA agency lists.

Availability Charts. Space availability bulletins provided by many airlines that enable an agent to advise a client at first meeting without communicating with the carrier.

Back-to-Back. A term used to describe a series of programs of multiple air charters with arrivals and departures coordinated to eliminate aircraft deadheading and waiting. Thus when one group arrives at a destination, another is ready to depart from that point.

Baggage. Included articles, effects, and other personal property of customers necessary for their wear, use, comfort, or convenience in connection with their trip. (Also known as luggage.)

Baggage Allowance. Domestic carriers in the United States and Canada will carry free baggage of not more than three pieces per person provided that one piece is not more than 62 inches in diameter, the second is not more than 55 inches, and the third is not more than 45 inches. International first class allows 30 kg or 66 lb; economy class allows 20 kg or 44 lb. Two or more passengers traveling together to the same destination may pool the baggage allowances.

Baggage, Checked. Baggage in sole custody of the carrier to which is attached an identification tag; the claim portion is held by the customer.

Baggage Claim Check. A receipt issued by the carrier for a passenger's checked baggage. Should be kept until the passenger is certain that all the checked articles are not damaged or missing.

Baggage, Excess. Baggage in excess of combined free allowances; subject to charges for excess size or overweight. The excess baggage charge for international travel is levied at 1 percent per kilogram of applicable first-class jet fare. On U.S. and Canadian carriers, the charge for each piece of excess or oversized bag is levied according to the dollar amount of the fare paid by the passenger. The charts for these charges and general rules are shown in detail in the *OAGs* and the ARC and IATA tariffs.

B and B. *See* Bed and Breakfast.

Bank Travel Department. A special department operated by a bank exclusively for the sale of passenger transportation and general travel services, which is open to the public for such purposes.

Bareboat Charter. A boat rented without crew or provisions.

Basing Point. A master point to and from which fares are established; used to calculate and construct air fares between other points.

Beam. The breadth of a vessel at its widest part.

Bearing. Compass direction, usually given in degrees, for either steamships or aircraft.

Bed and Breakfast (B and B). A sleeping room rate, often in a private home, that includes a full breakfast. *See also* Bermuda Plan.

Bermuda Plan (BP). Hotel accommodations with a full American-style breakfast included in the price of the room.

Berth. The space allotted a passenger in a vessel for sleeping. Also the dock or pier.

Bilge. Lowest point in a ship's structure.

Binnacle. The ship's compass.

Blocked Space. Reservations that wholesalers or travel agents make with suppliers in anticipation of resale.

Boarding Pass. A document attached to an airline ticket that allows a passenger entry onto a given flight and which gives the seat assignment.

Boat Train. A service that provides two modes of travel: from boat to train, or from train to boat.

Bonding. A security purchased to ensure that if an agency or carrier declares bankruptcy, all the creditors will receive compensation.

Book (Booking). To make a reservation for the client.

Bow. The forward (front) part of a vessel.

BP. *See* Bermuda Plan.

Brochures. Also referred to as *folders*; illustrated literature with full description of a tour, hotel, resort, and so on. Tour brochures must show dates and price; hotel and resort folders often have separate inserts for their rates, which change seasonally.

Buffer Zone. Areas of Canada or Mexico within 225 miles of the nearest point of the continental United States.

Bulkhead. Partition walls used to separate various interior areas of a ship, such as rooms, holds, and so on.

CAB (Civil Aeronautics Board). Independent agency of the U.S. government that was composed of five members. Regulated both domestic and international economic aspects of U.S. air carrier operation, investigated and analyzed aircraft accidents, and was concerned with customer handling items and customer complaints. Cooperated and assisted in the establishment and development of international air transportation. Approved rates and routes for commercial airlines. Phased out on December 31, 1984.

Cabin. A room on a ship; also a separate building at a rustic hotel or lodge.

Cabotage Fares. Fares applicable to transportation between territories of the same state, sale of transportation and carriage being restricted to certain carriers.

Cargo Liners. Combination passenger–cargo liners carry between 40 and 85 passengers in one class. These vessels operate on a more leisurely schedule with generally reliable sailing timetables. Shipboard atmosphere is informal with little planned entertainment.

Carrier. A public transportation company such as air, steamship line, or railroad.

Carry-on Baggage. Any article, within acceptable limitations, that is carried on and off a flight by the customer and transported in the carry-on compartment or under the customer's seat.

CATO (Combined Airline Ticket Office). Ticket offices serving primarily government personnel. Located in Washington, D.C. at the Pentagon, Capitol, State, Navy, and Agriculture departments. They are not affiliated with any individual airline but jointly represent all airlines serving Washington, D.C.

Certificates of Appointment. See Appointments.

Certified Travel Counselor (CTC). Designation granted by the Institute of Certified Travel Agents to travel personnel with five or more years' industry experience who have completed a two-year, graduate-level program in travel management.

Charter Flight. A flight booked exclusively for the use of a specific group of people who generally belong to the same organization, or who are being treated to the flight by a single host. Charter flights are generally much cheaper than regularly scheduled line services. They may be carried out by scheduled or supplemental carriers.

Check-in. Necessary procedures, such as signing the register, when arriving for a stay at a hotel.

Check-in Time. The time a hotel is ready for occupancy after the previous check-out time.

Check-out Time. Most hotels post a specific time when guests must vacate their rooms or be charged an additional day's rate.

Circle Fare. A special round-trip fare that costs less than the total price of the point-to-point rates for a circle trip.

Circle Trip. A trip in which passengers return to their point of origin via a different routing or a different level of fare on the return than on the outward portion.

City Ticket Office (CTO). An airline ticket office, not located at an airport, where passengers may check in for a flight, check their baggage, receive their seat assignment, and secure ground transportation to the airport.

Civil Aeronautics Board. See CAB.

CLIA Cruise Lines International Association is an organization of companies (the majority are ship lines) engaged in the marketing and operations of vacations at sea. In June 1984, Pacific Cruise Conference and the International Passenger Ship Association merged with CLIA and enlarged the membership to include cruise ships that carry less than 100 passengers. Travel agents pay an annual membership fee to CLIA and benefit from CLIA's promotional efforts in selling cruises and their educational assistance in training both owners/managers and staff in selling cruises.

Client. Person who hires a travel agent.

Coach Service. Class of U.S. passenger airline service at a lower fare than first class; comparable to international economy class.

Co-host Carrier. Applies to an airline reservations system whereby another airline pays for additional information to be housed in the host company's computer.

Combined Airline Ticket Office. See CATO.

Commercial Accounts. Agency accounts with a business or commercial concern.

Commercial Rate. A fee based on an agreement between a business firm and a hotel or car rental company. Generally, the latter will provide rooms or cars of a certain quality, or higher, at a flat rate. Also referred to as a corporate discount.

Commission. An agreed-upon percentage of the rate or fare charged the customer allowed to travel agents for their services.

Common Rated. A description of two or more relatively contiguous destinations whose fare from a specific departure point is exactly the same.

Companionway. A set of steps leading from the deck to a cabin or salon below; also the space occupied by these steps.

Computer Reservations System. See CRS.

Concierge.   A person or the staff in a hotel that attends to guests' needs, including arranging for theater tickets, making dinner reservations, supplying porterage, and providing general city information.

Conducted Tour.   A prepaid, prearranged vacation in which a group of people travel together under the guidance of a tour leader who stays with them from the start to the end of the trip. *See also* Escorted Tour.

Conference.   Shortened form for, and includes coverage of, ARC, IATA, CLIA, and Amtrak.

Configuration.   The arrangement of areas, seats, rooms, and so on, inside a conveyance, especially an airplane.

Confirmed Reservation.   Confirmation by a supplier who has received a reservation.

Conjunction Ticket.   Two or more tickets issued concurrently to a passenger which together constitute a single contract of carriage.

Connecting City.   The city in which passengers must change flights in order to reach the desired destination. For example, if a passenger wants to go from Baltimore to Iron Mountain, Michigan, and the best way to get there is to take two flights, one from Baltimore to Chicago and one from Chicago to Iron Mountain, the connecting city is Chicago. *See also* Connection.

Connecting Point.   For online purposes only, any point in an itinerary at which the customer is to transfer from one flight to another. All airports through which a city or adjoining cities are served are considered a single connecting point.

Connection.   Term applied to the transfer of customers from one flight to another in order to reach their destination.

Consortium.   Coalition, or union, of incorporated companies formed expressly for marketing and service purposes.

Constructed Fares.   Fares established by combining more than one published fare for a round trip.

Continental Breakfast.   Generally consists of a beverage (coffee, tea, cocoa, or milk) plus rolls, butter, and jam. In Holland and Norway, cheese, cold cuts, or fish are generally provided also. Usually, fruit juices are not included.

Cooperative.   Business corporation acting as a joint-stock organization for establishing and maintaining a working relationship among its members.

Corporate-Owned Chain.   Fully owned group of retail chain member outlets featuring common signage and advertising and a total marketing concept, operating in a uniform manner.

Couchettes.   Sleeping accommodations provided on some European railroads (mainly French), consisting of a day compartment that may be converted into bunks for four passengers. Pillows and blankets are provided. Since the sexes are not segregated, passengers do not disrobe at night. Slight additional charge above railroad fare.

Coupons.   Documents issued by tour operators in exchange for which travelers receive prepaid accommodations, meals, sightseeing trips, and so on. Also referred to as *vouchers*.

Coupons, Flight.   An airline ticket is made up of two or four coupons; one coupon is provided for each stopover or connecting city.

Courier.   *See* Tour Conductor.

Course.   Direction in which a ship is headed.

Crow's Nest.   A partly enclosed platform high on a mast used as a lookout.

CRS (Computer Reservations System).   Generic term to describe any automated reservations system, such as American Airlines' SABRE, or United Airlines' Apollo.

Cruise Lines International Association.   *See* CLIA.

Cruise Ships. Carrying one class only, usually on a deluxe basis. Cruise ships afford passengers complete run of the vessel. Many steamers referred to under the category *luxury liners* and *one-class vessels* conduct regular sailings and convert to special cruises. While on cruise, the maximum passenger capacity is reduced by as much as 50 percent, thus offering superior comfort for the passenger. Cruise ships operate primarily for the passengers' comfort and might be likened to a "resort at sea."

CTC. *See* Certified Travel Counselor.

CTO. *See* City Ticket Office.

Currency. The current medium of exchange; the money in actual use. Currency converters are invaluable to the international traveler. Most carriers provide this information, or prepackaged money kits can be purchased from major banks containing local currency of the country to be visited.

Customer. Term used to identify a person, also called a passenger, to whom air transportation and related services are to be issued. For purposes of differentiating responsibilities in handling individuals, a "customer" becomes a "passenger" when he or she boards an airplane for a flight.

Customs. Duties or tolls imposed by law on imported, or sometimes, exported, goods. International passengers must pass through a customs inspection in each country visited upon arrival and departure. Generally, passengers will be asked to present passports and health certificates, and to declare the amount of currency carried and purchases made during their visit.

Customs Users' Fee. A service fee charged for passengers entering the United States from foreign countries. There are several exceptions based on each point of origin, when the fee does not have to be charged.

DATAS II. Delta Airlines' computer reservations system.

DATO (Discover America Travel Organization). A national nonprofit trade and promotion association working to increase travel to and within the United States.

Day Rate. A specific hotel rate charged for room use during daylight hours only.

DBC. *See* Denied Boarding Compensation.

DBLB. Double room with bath.

DBLN. Double room without bath or shower.

DBLS. Double room with shower.

Deadhead. A person who travels on a free pass. More specifically, an airline employee or crew member in transit. Also, a vehicle traveling without a payload.

Debark. Abbreviation of "disembark."

Delivering Airline. A carrier that is transporting a traveler to an interline point.

Demipension. Hotel accommodations that include continental breakfast in the price of the room either table d'hote lunch or dinner. Same as *modified American plan*.

Denied Boarding. Customers who are not accommodated on the flight and in the class of service for which they hold a valid ticket.

Denied Boarding Compensation (DBC). A payment made by the airline to an eligible denied boarding customer.

Department of Transportation (DOT). Assumed CAB's duties and responsibilities on January 1, 1985.

Destination. The final stopping place according to the contract of carriage.

Direct Access. A computer function in airlines' reservations systems that allows the subscriber to access last-seat availability on co-hosts without leaving the host reservations system.

Direct Flight. A flight that goes from origin to destination without a change of planes. For example, a flight that goes from Baltimore to Myrtle Beach with an intermediate stop in Charlotte is a direct flight, but it is not a nonstop flight. Thus a journey on which a passenger does not have to change planes, not necessarily nonstop. *See also* Through Flight.

Direct Reference System. *See* DRS.

Discover America Travel Organization. *See* DATO.

Discriminatory. As applied to fares, offering lower rates to certain classifications of persons: military personnel, young people, the elderly, and so on. Such promotional fares are constantly under attack (sometimes successfully) on the grounds that they are unfair to those ineligible for them.

Disembark. To land; to put or go ashore from a ship.

DIT. *See* Domestic Independent Tour.

Dock. In its strict nautical sense, a dock is the water space alongside a pier, wharf, or quay in which a ship floats while being loaded or unloaded. In general popular usage with the traveling public; however, the words *dock*, *pier*, *wharf*, and *quay* are used synonymously to mean the structure at which a ship stays when in port.

Domestic. Pertaining to one's own country or nation.

Domestic Air Transportation. Travel wholly within the continental United States or wholly within Alaska or Hawaii.

Domestic Fare. A fare applicable between points within the same country.

Domestic Independent Tour (DIT). A prepaid, unescorted tour within a country for an individual client or clients.

DOT. *See* Department of Transportation.

Double. A hotel room with one double bed. Sometimes refers to a hotel room meant to accommodate two guests.

Double Occupancy Rate. The price per person for a room shared by two people.

Downgrade. To move to a lower-priced or lesser-quality accommodation or class of service.

Draft. Measurement in feet from the waterline to the lowest point of a ship's keel.

DRS (Direct Reference System). A computer function in American Airlines' SABRE system that allows the user to access information related to vendors.

Duty-free. Governments sometimes permit certain goods to be sold to international travelers without paying duties or local taxes.

Efficiency. A hotel, motel, or condominium rental room that includes some type of kitchen facilities (stove, refrigerator, etc.).

Embark. To go aboard a ship to begin a journey.

Emigrant Fares. Except for a period of about six weeks during the heavy westbound season, the lines grant a special reduction of approximately 10 percent from the regular one-way fare for bona fide emigrants from Europe, Turkey, and Africa.

Encode. To identify the complete name from a two-letter code or a three-letter city/airport code.

Endorsement. The written authorization of a carrier to change the carrier specified on a passenger ticket. This is most commonly required on an international air ticket.

English Breakfast. This type of full breakfast is generally served in the British Isles, including Ireland.

En Route City. Any city, other than origin or destination, where a flight makes a stop. For example, in a flight from Baltimore to Myrtle Beach with a stop in Charlotte, Charlotte is the en route city. Also called *intermediate city*.

EP. *See* European Plan.

Escort. *See* Tour Conductor.

Escorted Tour. A prearranged, escorted program of travel, usually for a group; a guide-conducted sightseeing program. *See also* Conducted Tour.

Escrow Accounts. Funds placed for safekeeping in licensed financial institutions. Many contracts in travel require that customers' deposits and prepayments be maintained in escrow accounts.

Eurailpass. Low-cost ticket that gives unlimited first-class rail travel throughout all of Western Europe. Must be purchased in advance before arrival in Europe. Valid for 15, 21, 30, 60, or 90 days.

European Plan (EP). Hotel accommodations with no meals whatsoever included in the cost of the room.

Even Keel. A ship at true vertical position with respect to its vertical axis.

Exchange Orders. During the formative period of a new travel agency, envelopes are issued by each airline to be used for the purchase of tickets until the appointments have been received and ticket stock has been issued. These exchange orders are completed with the reservation status of the client, and a check for full payment is inserted and given to the airline in exchange for the ticket. The sale is then credited to the travel agency. A copy is kept by the travel agency, and after it has been approved by the conferences, it presents these copies for retroactive commission.

Excursion Fares. Promotional fares usually for round trip for a specified period of time.

Express Liners. *See* Luxury Liners.

FAA. *See* Federal Aviation Agency.

Familiarization Tours. Airlines, tour operators, foreign tourist bureaus, hotels, and resorts invite travel agents to visit specific areas as their guests or at a very low rate. Also known as *fam tours*.

Family Plan. Sales incentive plan used by some carriers for certain days of the week, whereby members of a family travel at a reduced fare when accompanied by one full-paying member of the family.

Fantail. The stern overhang in vessels, extending over the propeller area, that provides the rounded or elliptical endings to uppermost decks.

Fare. The amount charged by a carrier for the carriage of passengers and their baggage for the class of service to be provided.

Fare Construction. A fare other than the published fare that may be used for a specific routing by combining fares over other possible routings.

Fathom. A measure of six feet, used chiefly in measuring cordage, cable, and depth of water by soundings.

Federal Aviation Agency (FAA). Government agency that provides for the safe and efficient use of airspace by both civil and military operations, and for the regulation and promotion of civil aviation to best foster its development and safety. It assumes all safety rule-making functions of the CAB.

Fender. Anything serving as a cushion between the side of the ship and the dock or other craft.

Fictitious Construction Point. A point (other than a more distant point) not on the passenger's itinerary but used only for the construction of a fare. *See also* Hidden City.

Final Itinerary. The schedule provided for clients that spells out in great detail the exact program mapped out for them, including flight or train numbers, departure time, and so on. This is always delivered shortly before actual departure.

First Class. The costliest and highest level of service in air, rail, and sea travel.

First Refusal Rights. A government policy that permits a particular carrier or class of carrier the right to claim and operate revenue charter flights prepared by other airlines. Some governments do not allow charter airlines to operate in their territory unless certain other airlines are granted the prerogative of claiming the charter.

FIT. *See* Foreign Independent Tour.

Fly/Drive. A tour that offers air service from departure city to arrival, a rental car to the passenger's next destination, and return air travel, often from some place other than the original arrival city.

Fore/Forward. In or toward the bow (front) of a vessel.

Foreign. Not domestic or native.

Foreign Independent Tour (FIT). A prepaid travel program of many separate components, tailored to the specifications of an individual client or clients.

Franchiser. Entity that grants vested right to the use of a brand name for an extensive, contractual time frame, with the purpose of attracting consumer recognition and expectation of consistent service. This includes an entire "business format" operational plan, business package, and support services. The franchiser is regulated by the Federal Trade Commission.

Free Port. A port or place free of customs duties and most customs regulations.

Free Sale. The ability to confirm reservations without advising the principal; however, the principal must be notified within a specified time. Usually used by hotel representatives.

Freighters. Freighters usually restrict passenger capacity to 12 or fewer, depending on the ship's facilities. In most cases, every stateroom has private bath and toilet facilities, and both single- and double-occupancy rooms are offered. Since cargo governs the schedule of the ship, the ship's timetable is unreliable and constantly subject to change. Any ship carrying more than 12 passengers is required by law to have a doctor on board.

Frequent Flyer Program. Travel benefits, such as standby first-class upgrade, a free international trip, free or reduced rate travel, and so on, offered by airlines, car rental companies, and hotel chains to attract frequent customers to their product.

Full Pension. *See* American Plan.

Fully Appointed. Designation of a travel agent who has been officially recognized by the major airline/steamship companies/railroad conference.

Funnel. Smokestack of a ship.

Galley. The kitchen of a ship or airplane.

Gangway. The opening through the ship's bulwarks and the ramp by which passengers embark and disembark.

Gap. Portion of an airline itinerary that involves transportation by means other than an IATA or ATA airline (the ARUNK coupon in the ticket).

Garni. When appended to the name of a hotel, this means that the establishment does not have a restaurant or dining room.

Gateways. This term has two connotations in international travel. The physical gateway is the last city in an area out of which a flight will leave for another area. The fare construction gateway may or may not be the physical gateway, but is the city out of which fares have been established between areas. *East coast*: Bermuda, Boston, Gander, Miami, Montreal, New York, Philadelphia. *West coast*: Los Angeles, Portland, San Francisco, Seattle, Vancouver, B.C.

GIT. *See* Group Inclusive Tour.

GMT. *See* Greenwich Mean Time.

Government Travel. Discount fare available to government personnel on specific carriers that have contracted with the U.S. government for the right to carry passengers engaged in official business. Agents should be aware that government employees are eligible for this special fare only when traveling on official business. Only government-approved agencies and specified carriers may issue government fare tickets, as the sole valid forms of payment are a government-distributed Diner's Club credit card or a GTR (government travel request).

Gratuities. *See* Tips.

Greenwich Mean Time (GMT). The mean solar time at Greenwich, England, used as the reference time for all time zones throughout the world.

Gross Register Ton. A measure, not of weight, but of the cubical content of the enclosed spaces on a ship; the measurement used in giving the size of passenger vessels. One-hundred cubic feet is equal to one gross register ton.

Ground Arrangements. All services covering surface travel, including hotel accommodations, meals, transfers, sightseeing, guide services, entrance fees, gratuities, and so on. Does not include transportation. Also known as *land arrangements*.

Ground Transportation. Surface transportation operated by private limousine, bus, or cab company to provide transportation between airport and city; may include baggage transfer service.

Group Inclusive Tour (GIT). Prepaid travel package, usually round trip, that offers special air fares to the members of the tour group, all of whom must travel on the same flights.

GRT (Gross Registered Tonnage). This is a measurement of 100 cubic feet of enclosed revenue-earning space within a ship.

Guarantee. On ships, assured cabin allocation in the class paid for, or higher (sometimes lower). Based on experience, lines can calculate how many cancellations they will have as sailing day approaches. Although the vessel may be sold out when a request is made, the line is able to guarantee the availability of a certain number of berths over and above the ship's actual capacity. Most guarantees given are with the provision that (except for class) no specific type of room, location, or fare is specified.

Guarantee Share Fare. Acceptance by some lines of a single booking at the cost-saving double-occupancy fare, with the understanding that the client is willing to share the use of the cabin with a stranger of the same sex.

Guest Houses. Similar to a small hotel. *See also* Pensions.

Guide. A person licensed to take paying guests on local sightseeing excursions.

Half-Board or Half-Pension. Hotel accommodations that include full breakfast and/or lunch or dinner in the price of the room. *See also* Modified American Plan.

Half Round Trip. Half of a round-trip air charter, sold as a round trip because different seasonal pricing periods may apply to each half. Cannot be sold as one-way.

Hatch. The deck opening leading to the cargo holds.

Head Tax. A fee collected by a government from a passenger who enters or departs from that country.

Helm. The apparatus by which a ship is steered: the rudder, wheel, and so on.

Hidden City. A fictitious construction point used in determining an international air fare. A city that, though not transited by a passenger, would afford the client a lower air fare had it been on that person's route. Provided that the maximum permitted mileage is not exceeded, the fare may be broken over that location, even though it is not used, in order to save the client money. International carriers are turning against this practice.

Higher Intermediate Point (HIP). Applies to the rule stipulating that if an air fare between any two cities on an itinerary is higher, or lower, than the fare between origin and destination, the passenger must pay the higher fare.

HIP. *See* Higher Intermediate Point.

Hold. Interior of a vessel below decks where cargo is stored.

Host Carrier. An airliner that markets its computer reservations system (CRS) to agencies.

Hostels. Very inexpensive accommodations operated by the International Youth Hostel Foundation. Requires a membership card and is usually limited to guests up to age 25.

Hotelier. The owner and operator of a hotel.

Hotel Representative. A company or corporation (sometimes, an individual) appointed by a hotel to publicize the property and take reservations.

Hot File. Reservations file of cards on which requests have been sent but the answer has not been received; or where the answer has been received but has not yet been called to the passenger.

House Flag. The flag that denotes the company to which the ship belongs.

Hull. The frame or body of a ship. Does not include masts, yards, sails, or rigging.

IATA. *See* International Air Transport Association.

ICAO. *See* International Civil Aviation Organization.

ICC. *See* Interstate Commerce Commission.

ICTA. *See* Institute of Certified Travel Agents.

Immigration Guide. Reference guide that lists support documents and vaccinations necessary for travel to specific destinations.

Inaugural. First flight on a new route or with new equipment.

Inboard. Toward the centerline of a ship.

Incentive Air Tour. Same as an *advertised air tour* except that because it is offered as a prize by a specific organization and is paid for by the organization, no general promotional literature is necessary and prices do not have to be listed in the literature.

Inclusive Tour (IT). A tour whose price includes both the cost of transportation and tour ground arrangements.

Independent Tour. A tour that has been tailored to meet a person's specific desires and requirements.

Independent Tour Basing Fare. *See* ITX.

In-Plant Location. An additional authorized agency location that is on the premises of a customer. An in-plant location need not be open to the public.

Institute of Certified Travel Agents (ICTA). A nonprofit educational organization that grants accreditation to qualified travel agents.

Interchangeable Space. Many two- or three-class vessels have certain staterooms bordering on the division points of each class aboard that are decorated and equipped for use in either class. At the discretion of the line, depending on the number of passengers booked, these rooms can be used for whichever class of travel is most in demand.

Interline. Used with another word to describe anything involving two or more carriers, such as interline itinerary, interline reservation, interline stopover, and interline baggage.

Interliner. An airline employee who travels on another airline. Also an airline employee who makes reservations for passengers on other airlines.

International Air Transport Association (IATA). Association of international carriers. Governs rules of its members. The same as ATA for domestic carriers. IATA Office of Enforcement ensures adherence to IATA resolutions in the same way the ATA Enforcement Office does.

International Air Transportation.   Transportation between a point in the United States and a point outside the United States (also between two foreign countries).

International Civil Aviation Organization (ICAO).   A special United Nations agency of governments working together for the standardization of aircraft equipment, procedures, training, and the like, particularly in developing nations.

International Date Line.   An imaginary line in the Pacific Ocean at approximately 180 degrees longitude where, by international agreement, the Earth's day begins. Crossing the line eastward, one calendar day is subtracted; westward, a day is added.

International Flight.   Travel between two points, each in a different country.

International Union of Official Travel Organization.   *See* IUOTO.

Interstate Commerce Commission (ICC).   Independent U.S. government agency that regulates the finances and services of specified carriers involved in transportation between the states. Surface transportation under ICC authority includes railroads, trucking companies, bus lines, express agencies, and transportation brokers, among others.

Intraline.   *See* Online.

IT.   *See* Inclusive Tour.

Itinerary.   Sum of all portions of the customer's trip from beginning to end.

IT Number.   The code number on a tour approved by IATA that qualifies agents who sell air travel associated with such tours for an override commission.

ITX (Independent Tour Basing Fare).   To qualify for this fare, land arrangements at a designated amount must be prepaid by the client. *See also* Tour-Basing Fare.

IUOTO (International Union of Official Travel Organizations).   Now known as the World Tourism Organization.

JAMTO (Joint Airline Military Ticket Office).   A ticket office located on a military base whose primary purpose is to serve military personnel and their dependents. Each airline serving the area is represented on an impartial basis. *See also* SATO.

Jax Fax Travel Marketing Magazine.   A directory of news of the travel industry, including special features and listings of airline charters and scheduled bus tours. Published by Jet Airtransport Exchange, Inc.

Joint Airline Military Ticket Office.   *See* JAMTO.

Joint Fare.   A less than point-to-point air fare that includes travel on two or more air carriers.

Junior Suite.   Large hotel room with a partition dividing the bedroom and sitting areas.

Keel.   A plate or timber running the length of the ship along the bottom, from which all vertical frames are raised.

Knot.   A unit of speed, equivalent to one nautical mile (6080 feet) per hour.

Lanai.   A room with a balcony or patio that overlooks or is near water or a garden.

Land Arrangements.   *See* Ground Arrangements.

Land Price.   Cost quoted for tour ground arrangements only. Tour operators' brochures should specify, in detail, the services that are not included in the land price.

Layover.   A stop at a connecting point necessitated by lack of immediate connection between two services.

Lee/Leeward.   The direction away from the wind.

Leg.   Space between two consecutive scheduled stops on any given flight.

Licenser. Entity that grants the right to use national-brand identity in all marketing and operating activities; also provides access to proprietary service and marketing systems and programs.

Lido. On a ship, the swimming pool and adjacent area.

Load Seats. Seats held for accommodation of mail, fuel, or overall weight required on aircraft.

Log. A daily record of a ship's speed, progress, and so on. Also a device for measuring the speed and distance covered by a ship.

Luggage. *See* Baggage.

Luxury Liners. One-, two-, and three-class ships that provide service between two or more ports on a regular express schedule.

MAGSA. *See* Mutual Assistance Ground Service Agreement.

Manifest. The passenger, crew, and cargo list on any trip by common carrier.

MAP. *See* Modified American Plan.

Mate. A deck officer in the merchant marine ranking below the captain.

Maximum Permitted Mileage (MPM). The air miles allowed for every city pair, as designated by the IATA. Used when calculating an international air fare based on mileage.

MCO (Miscellaneous Charge Order). Used to forward deposits or payments for tours.

Member. Inclusive term meaning any airline or air carrier associated with ARC, IATA, or NATA. If the term "airline" or "member" is restricted to less than all three, it is stated.

Midship. *See* Amidship.

Mileage Surcharge. A penalty excised on a passenger's air fare when the actual mileage flown exceeds the maximum permitted mileage. These additions are based on 5, 10, 15, 20, or 25 percent charges of the original one-way or half-round-trip fare.

Minimum/Maximum Duration. Special fares, such as a tour-basing fare or an excursion fare, will have limits on the duration of the trip, such as the 22/45-day fare. Passengers cannot return before 22 days or stay longer than 45 days.

Miscellaneous Charges Order. *See* MCO.

Misconnection. En route connecting customer who does not board a flight on which he or she held reservations because of delayed arrival of the incoming flight.

Modified American Plan (MAP). Hotel accommodations that include breakfast and either lunch or dinner in the price of the room. Same as *demipension*.

MPM. *See* Maximum Permitted Mileage.

Multistop Flight. Flight that makes a number of intermediate stops between origin and destination.

Mutual Assistance Ground Service Agreement (MAGSA). A bilateral interline agreement to handle ground service at offline points.

N/A. Not available.

NATA. *See* National Air Transport Association.

National Air Transport Association (NATA). Group that represents air taxi, commuter, and small mail and cargo carriers. *See also* Air Taxi Agreements.

Nautical Mile. A nautical mile is 6080 feet, compared to a land, or statute mile, which is only 5280 feet.

Need/Need. A communication that agents with computerized reservations systems use when booking space with an offline carrier to make sure that a seat is available when there is reason to doubt the reliability of the information in the host carrier's computer. The need/need message compels the host carrier to contact the second line, which must then confirm a specific seat for the agency's client, and so advise the first airline. Generally, the host line simply confirms a second carrier's space from a small standing inventory and advises the offline carrier afterward. *See also* Sell/Sell.

Network.   Working group of independently owned travel agencies deriving benefits of lower operating costs and higher sales commissions.

No Go.   A flight that does not take off as scheduled, usually because of weather or mechanical problems.

Nonscheduled Airline.   *See* Supplemental Carrier.

Nonstop Flight.   Flight that makes no scheduled stops between origin and destination.

NOOP.   Not operating.

Normal Fare.   The fare applicable to first, tourist, economy class, or business class service with no restrictions.

No Show.   Failure to use reserved accommodations for reasons other than misconnections.

Official Airline Guide (OAG).   Any of several airline reference manuals, published by Official Airline Guides, Inc.

Offline.   Any airline other than one directly concerned.

Off Peak.   The least busy time or season; generally applies to a hotel rate or a fare applicable at that time.

Off-Route Charter.   A scheduled airline flight to or from a point that it is not authorized to serve on a regularly scheduled basis.

One Way.   Any trip where the passenger travels from origin to destination but does not return.

Online.   A term used in conjunction with other words to describe anything involving carriage over one airline only, such as online reservations, online baggage, and online connection. Also known as *intraline*.

Open Jaw.   A round trip by air in which a portion of the journey is "unknown" and the return is from a point other than the destination.

Open Rate.   A circumstance in which a carrier is free to set its own rates on certain routes when IATA airlines fail to negotiate uniform rates.

Open Ticket.   A valid ticket without a specified flight reservation, which the passenger makes at a later date.

Option.   Time limit usually given by steamship companies and tour operators to collect and forward deposit for space.

Optional.   A term used in travel literature to indicate that you have a choice of taking or not taking the service mentioned. If you take it, there is an additional charge beyond the basic tour price.

Origin.   The place of commencement of carriage according to the contract.

OSI.   Other service information.

OT.   On time.

Outward Destination.   The point farthest from the point of origin.

Overbooking.   Condition that exists when more seats or rooms have been booked on a flight or at a hotel than are available for sale.

Override.   A term used for the additional commission paid to agents when they sell over the sales quota set by the wholesaler.

Oversale.   Condition that occurs when a customer, for whom the airline or the hotel has a positive reservation, is not accommodated at flight departure or check-in time.

OW. One way.

Package Tour. The package usually consists of the minimum requirements for an advertised air tour. Accommodations, transfers, or car rental, plus a sightseeing tour or dining plan, may be included.

Parlor Car. On a train, a specific type of car with individual swivel seats, food, and bar service.

PARS. TransWorld Airlines' computer reservations system. (Merging with Datas II to become "Worldspan")

Passenger. Any person that any carrier is or will be transporting. Often used to mean "paying passenger."

Passenger Name Record (PNR). Client file, stored in a computer reservations system, that includes such information as name of passenger, flight number, travel times, dates of travel, airline to be used, and cost of tickets. Also applies to nonair bookings.

Passport. A formal document, issued to a citizen by an authorized official of a country, that permits the bearer to exit and reenter the country, and allows the person to travel in a foreign nation.

PATA (Pacific Asia Travel Association). Organization of countries and business groups to promote travel to the Pacific and Indian Ocean areas.

Peak Fare/Rate/Season. The highest level of prices charged during the year.

Pension. A French word widely used throughout Europe, meaning guest house or boarding house. Usually includes all meals in the rate, but does not offer a menu. Often located on the outskirts of a city at more reasonable prices than most hotels.

PEX Fares. Inter-European advance purchase fares. For the agent, these fares are similar to domestic supersaver fares; however, they are subject to extremely high cancellation penalties.

Pier. *See* Dock.

Pitch. Forward/backward motion of a ship at sea; or the amount of space between seats on an airplane.

Plates. Metal cards resembling credit cards, used in a validator to identify the agency and vendor issuing a document.

PNR. *See* Passenger Name Record.

Port. The left side of a ship, looking forward. *See also* Starboard, dock, or a ship's destination.

Porthole. An opening in a ship's side or a window in a cabin.

Ports-of-call. The stops made on a ship's itinerary.

Port Taxes. Passengers to or from some ports are subject to government debarkation or embarkation taxes, payable when a ticket is issued.

Prepaids. This is the method of purchasing transportation for overseas passengers by your client's payment to your office. Assigned space may be withheld until all necessary immigration and passport documents are secured, and passengers are then advised of the departure date directly by the airline's office. This is when a PTA is utilized.

Prepaid Ticket Advice (PTA). Notice sent by one airline to another, or by the travel agent, to authorize issuance of a ticket that the passenger will pick up at the airport. Generally issued when the reservation has been made within 24 hours of departure or has been paid for in another city.

Promotional Fare. A fare lower than regular rates, designed to stimulate travel, especially at those times when a carrier is not busy. These fares are almost always round trip and are always subject to certain restrictions.

Protected Commission. Guarantee by a supplier or wholesaler to pay commissions to agents, plus full refunds to clients, on prepaid, confirmed bookings, regardless of the subsequent cancellation of a tour or cruise.

Prow. Bow or stem (extreme front) of the vessel.

PTA. *See* Prepaid Ticket Advice.

Purser. Pursers and their staff are in charge of all ship's business and are directly responsible for the comfort and satisfaction of passengers. They are the representatives of the ship line ashore. They keep all passenger records and accounts, prepare all passport and visa forms (when required), and act toward passengers as a hotel front desk would. All passenger shipboard activities, such as entertainment, shore excursions, money exchange and travel checks, safety deposit boxes, dispatch of radiograms and mail, sale of postage stamps, insurance, lost and found, and informational bulletins, are arranged through this department.

Quay. Pronounced "key." The word commonly used in Europe for wharf or pier. *See also* Dock.

Quick-Reference Schedule. The flight schedule that airlines use to show their flights. These are given away to customers and are a handy reference for regular passengers. Also known as *passenger schedule*.

Rack Rate. In hotels, the official posted rate for each sleeping room.

Receiving Airline. A carrier that will be transporting passengers on their arrival at an interline point.

Reconfirm. Passengers advise the airline that they will use the reservation for their onward or return flights. Airline rules require that space must be reconfirmed within specified time limits.

Reconfirmation. Rule requiring customers, under specified circumstances, to advise the carrying airline of their intention to use their space.

Refund. Repayment to the purchaser of all or a portion of a fare, rate, or charge for unused carriage or service.

Registry. Ships are often registered in countries that offer a tax benefit. The ship may fly the flag of that country, although its owners and crew may be of a different nationality.

Representative (Rep). An individual or company representative empowered to act for a principal, generally in the area of sales or reservations.

Reservation. A request for a plane seat, hotel room, car rental, and so on, made in advance for the customer. *See also* Booking.

Reservations (Res) Agent. A person, usually connected with an airline, who takes reservations and/or sells tickets.

Resort Hotel. A hotel that provides recreational facilities and meals in addition to sleeping accommodations.

Responsibility Clause. The part of a brochure that outlines the conditions under which a tour is sold. It should give the name of the company or companies financially responsible.

Retailer. Someone (or a company) who sells directly to the public. The travel agent is actually the retailer of travel services provided to customers by the agent's principals (suppliers).

Revalidation. A change made on a ticket already issued that does not affect the fare or routing. This change is shown on a revalidation sticker, which is placed over the appropriate line of boxes on the flight coupon.

Review Dates. A periodic evaluation of the progress of the sale and promotion of a group combined with attendant cabin or room utilization.

Roll. The movement of a ship from side to side.

Round-the-World Fares. A continuous trip via both the Atlantic and the Pacific oceans, beginning at and returning to the same point. At no time may travelers on these trips reverse directions or use a surface segment that would place them geographically behind their last known airport city.

Round Trip.   A continuing journey in which travelers begin and end their trip in the same city, and use the same route in both directions.

Round-Trip Fare.   The rate for a trip to a specific destination, and a return by the same route to the point of commencement; applicable to both direct and indirect routings.

RT.   Round trip.

RTW.   Round-the-world.

Run of the House.   Accommodations guaranteed at a specific rate. The hotelier must accommodate guests in any rooms that are available, even if they are normally sold at a higher rate. Similar to the guarantee given by steamship lines.

SABRE.   American Airlines' computer reservations system.

SABRE-Assisted Instruction.   *See* SAI.

SAI (SABRE-Assisted Instruction).   Self-contained lessons on the daily operations and agent functions in SABRE.

SATO (Scheduled Airline Ticket Office).   An office at a U.S. military installation operated jointly by carriers. Formerly known as JAMTO, or Joint Airline Military Ticket Office.

Scheduled Airline.   An airline that publishes a tariff and operates flights between given points on a regular schedule. In international service, most scheduled carriers belong to the IATA. In U.S. domestic service, most are members of ATA (Air Transport Association).

Scheduled Airline Ticket Office.   *See* SATO.

Scheduled Air Taxi.   An air carrier that does not hold a certificate of public convenience and necessity or foreign air carrier permit issued by DOT, but operates pursuant to a Federal Air Taxi Operating Certificate. Usually, smaller aircraft that operate between two nearby cities.

Seat Rotation.   In motorcoach travel, the change of seating that allows all passengers the chance to see out the windows on both sides of the bus, as well as to sit in the front.

Segment.   Leg or group of legs from the customer's boarding point to a disembarking point on any given flight.

Sell/Sell.   A communication that a host airline uses to confirm a seat on an offline carrier. It tells the agent using the host line's automated reservations system that space is available on the offline carrier's flight, based on information that the offline carrier makes available to the host carrier. The host line later advises the second carrier of the seat sale without asking for specific confirmation.

Shore Excursion.   Land tours of a ship's ports-of-call, sold by cruise lines to passengers.

Shoulder Fare/Rate/Season.   Level of prices between high/peak and low/off-peak.

Shuttle.   No-reservation U.S. air service in which any passenger showing up before a scheduled departure is guaranteed a seat.

Side Round Trip.   On an international itinerary, transit by a passenger of a given city more than once during mileage-based routing, for which an additional fee is charged.

Sine.   Agent's number, name, or initials that constitute agent's signature.

Single Carrier Reservations System.   A computerized reservations package made available to travel agencies by one airline, giving the subscribing agency direct access to that carrier's computer.

Single Entity Charter.   An air charter sponsored and purchased by one person, company, or organization, on which none of the passengers is charged for any of the travel expenses.

Single Supplement. An additional fee, usually charged by hotels, groups, or charters, to a person who chooses to stay in a room for one occupant.

Space Ratio. A measurement of cubic space per passenger. This term is used by cruise lines to illustrate the spaciousness of their vessels.

Special Service Request (SSR). A request by an airline passenger for a specific service, such as a kosher meal, a wheelchair, or a special seat assignment. The request is kept in the passenger's PNR maintained by the airline.

Special Travelers Account Record System. *See* STARS.

SSR. *See* Special Service Request.

SST. *See* Supersonic Transport.

Stabilizers. Most newer vessels are equipped with stabilizing machinery, based on the principle of an airline wing, under the surface of the water that controls the rolling motion of a ship. This helps in keeping seasickness to an absolute minimum.

Stack. Funnel from which a ship's exhaust gases escape.

Standard Interline Passenger Ticket and Baggage Check. *See* Ticket.

Standard Ticket Plan. Member airlines of the ATC have adopted a standard ticket for issuance by their sales agents under the area bank settlement plan. In addition, most IATA carriers and Amtrak are now members of this plan.

Standby. A waitlisted passenger; a person with no reservation who remains at the check-in counter for space to become available.

Starboard. The right side of a ship looking forward. *See also* Port.

Star Rating System. Five-star system used by some governments and survey groups to rate hotels; five-star hotels are generally considered the best.

STARS (Special Travelers Account Record System). A STAR contains the important information pertaining to a given corporate account or to a given traveler. Often, for a large account, a primary (first level) STAR will be built into SABRE, with the company's information. A secondary (personal) STAR will be used for data on an individual traveler.

Stateroom. A private room or cabin on a ship.

Stem. The prow or bow (extreme front) of a vessel.

Stern. The rear end of a vessel.

Steward. The person in charge of all food and affiliated housekeeping services aboard ship.

Stopover. Equivalent to break of journey. A deliberate interruption of journey by a customer, agreed to in advance by the carrier, at a point between the place of departure and the place of final destination.

Stopover—International Air Transportation. A *scheduled* stop in excess of 12 hours between two segments of international air transportation.

STPC. The term used when an international traveler must stay overnight at a foreign point and the hotel accommodations are prepaid by the carrier.

Strand. To abandon a passenger during or just prior to a prepaid travel program, usually due to the business failure of tour operators or carriers.

Student Ships. Vessels that provide few small cabins and large dormitories accommodating as many as 40. These ships operate on very low fares (lower than tourist class) either as student ships during vacation periods or as immigrant carriers for the remaining season. They are prevalent in transatlantic service during the summer season.

Subject to Load. When passengers are advised that their confirmed space for a flight may be withheld due to operating load restrictions.

Suggested Itinerary. A preliminary itinerary provided by tour operators or travel agents. It generally shows routings and approximate times, as well as recommended hotels, suggested sightseeing excursions, and describes the conditions under which these services will be provided.

Superliners. Very fast ships of about 50,000 to 80,000 gross register tons, and speeds of about 28 to 35 knots. The *Queen Elizabeth 2 (QE2)* is now the only ship in this category.

Supersonic Transport (SST). Type of aircraft that flies faster than the speed of sound.

Supplemental Carrier. An airline certificated by the U.S. government to carry out charter flights, but not permitted to engage in regularly scheduled services.

Supporting Documents. Supplementary papers required to validate a transaction, such as driver's license, birth certificate, health card, visa, and passport.

System One. Computer reservations system owned by Continental Airlines and run as a separate entity.

Table d'hote. A complete menu from which deviation may not be made without incurring additional charges. The type of meal that is generally provided when included in the price of the tour. In Europe, table d'hote menus rarely include coffee or tea after the meal. These are considered extras.

TALAC. Travel Agents Legal Action Committee.

Tariffs. Publications that indicate the rules, regulations, fares, and charges of all participating carriers. An airline tariff is the only official reference when quoting fares to a passenger. Various types of tariff publications are used; however, the two most used for airlines are the ARC Tariff, published by C. C. Squire, and the IATT (International Air Travel Tariff), published on behalf of international carriers.

Taxable Amount. The amount on which the tax is computed is the total amount paid for taxable transportation.

Technical Stop. A stop en route to a destination, planned or unplanned, to refuel, change crews, and so on, but not to discharge passengers or take on new revenue traffic.

TEE (Trans European Express). A high-speed train traveling in certain parts of Europe.

Tender. A vessel used to carry passengers from ship to shore and back when the ship cannot dock.

Terminal. The office where a bus/limousine service to and from the airport originates and/or terminates.

TGV. A very high speed French train.

Through Flight. A flight on which the passenger does not have to change planes between point of origin and destination, even though the airplane may have to stop at other cities along the route to pick up passengers.

Through Passenger. Customer originating prior to, and destined beyond, the station concerned, on the same flight.

Thwart Berth. Berth placed crosswise on a ship.

Ticket. Officially referred to as the standard interline passenger ticket and baggage check. Form issued by member airline, or its authorized representative, to cover the customer's complete itinerary and indicate the actual status (at time of issuance) of each segment. The ticket is a contract between the customer and the airline.

Ticket Agent. Person employed by a carrier to take reservations and sell tickets. The federal government applies this term to anyone who sells an airline ticket: for example, travel agents and tour operators.

Ticket Exchange Notice. A nonaccountable document used by travel agents and airline personnel to show that an accountable document has been exchanged for another at either an additional collection, even exchange, or exchange with a refund due the client.

Ticket Stock.   Airline ticket blanks, used by carrier employees and travel agents, that become contracts when filled out and validated.

Time Limit.   Mutually agreed upon time by which customers must purchase a ticket to avoid cancellation of space.

Tips.   Gratuities to hotel employees, porters, guides, drivers, and so on. Be sure to check which tips are and are not included in your itinerary. They can make quite a difference in the cost of a tour.

Tour.   A journey involving visits or stopovers in more than one city.

Tour-Basing Fare.   A reduced, round-trip fare available on specified dates, and between specified times, only to those passengers who purchased preplanned, prepaid tour arrangements prior to their departure.

Tour Conductor.   A professional travel escort; a person qualified by experience to assume the responsibilities of accompanying a group and of relieving tour members of the bothersome details of checking reservations, looking after baggage, tipping porters, and handling hotel check-in and check-out details. The person is in charge and is the tour operator's or travel agent's representative. With tours visiting foreign countries the tour conductor must also, of course, be fluent in several languages.

Tour Escort.   *See* Tour Conductor.

Tourist Board.   An office maintained by a government (city, state, or country) to promote tourism in its area.

Tourist/Transit Cards.   Issued mostly by Mexico and South American countries giving permission to tourists to visit their countries for a specified time. Valid from 15 days to six months.

Tour Leader.   *See* Tour Conductor.

Tour Manager.   *See* Tour Conductor.

Tour Operator.   A company that specializes in the planning and operation of prepaid, preplanned vacations, and makes these available to the general public through travel agents. Most U.S. leading tour operators belong to the United States Tour Operators Association, which seeks to maintain the highest ethical standards.

Tour Organizer.   A person, usually not professionally connected with the travel industry, who organizes tours for special groups of people.

Tour Package.   A travel plan that includes most elements of a vacation, such as transportation, accommodations, and sightseeing.

Tour Program.   Usually, a series of tours or packages.

Tour Wholesaler.   Similar to a tour operator, but the traveler can purchase the wholesaler's tour only from the carrier, organizer, or travel agent. The wholesaler does not deal directly with the passenger.

Trans European Express.   *See* TEE.

Transfer.   The service provided travelers when they arrive and leave a given city, which takes them from the airport, air terminal, pier, or railway station to their hotel, and vice versa; generally accompanied by a local representative of the U.S. tour operator who planned the tour. There is a tremendous variation in cost, depending on whether transfers are carried out by private, chauffeur-driven car or by taxi, and whether the transfer is provided between airports and downtown air terminals, or between the airport and the hotel directly.

Transit Without Visa (TWOV).   Term applied to non-U.S. citizens who, by agreement with the U.S. Immigration Service, when originating in a country outside of, and destined to, a country beyond the United States, are permitted to travel through the United States without U.S. transit visas.

Transportation Tax. A tax levied by the government of a country on services rendered to the public by a common carrier. At the present time, the U.S. government has a 10 percent tax on all air transportation sold in the 50 states and an area extending 225 miles beyond U.S. borders. This tax is not collected on tickets issued for international travel unless a stopover is made before or after leaving the country.

Travel Agent. An individual authorized by one or more principals to effect the sale of travel and related services.

Tug. A vessel, equipped with heavy-duty engines and machinery, used for towing another vessel.

Turnaround Point. Point in a round-trip journey where the outward journey ends and the inward journey begins.

Twin. A hotel room with twin beds, designed for two people.

Twin Double. A hotel room with two double beds, to accommodate two, three, or four people.

TWOV. See Transit Without Visa.

UATP. See Universal Air Travel Plan.

Uninterrupted International Air Transportation. Transportation entirely by air which does not begin and end in the United States, or a 225-mile buffer zone, provided that the scheduled stopover at any U.S. city is 12 hours or less.

United States Travel Service (USTS). Government bureau formed to promote travel in the United States.

Universal Air Travel Plan (UATP). Standard credit plan used by most business firms issued by the airlines. Requires a permanent deposit.

Upgrade. To change to a better class of service or accommodation.

USTS. See United States Travel Service.

Validation Plates. Airline identification plate; under the Standard Ticket Plan, each individual airline issues a plate to the travel agent, showing the airline name and code. The travel agent's name, address, and ARC/IATA number are on the validation plate issued by ARC when the agent's appointment is approved.

Validators. Ticket writers, authorized by IATA and ARC to validate the tickets issued. Tickets will not be honored by the airlines unless they have been validated.

Validity of Fare. A rule whereby normal one-way, round-trip, or circle-trip fares may be used to complete the transportation for one year after the commencement of the journey.

Visa. Government authorization by a country to permit entry to and travel within that country. Appended to a passport.

Vouchers. See Coupons.

Wagon-Lits. Railroad sleeping cars in Europe, consisting of a private bedroom with accommodations for one or two people. Pillow, blankets, and a sink are included.

Waitlist. Listing of customers waiting for a travel service that has been sold out. As space becomes available, waitlisted passengers are confirmed in the order in which reservations were received.

Wharf. See Dock.

Wholesaler. See Tour Operator.

Worldspan. Delta's DATAS II and TWA's PARS airline reservations services are now consolidated under the name of Worldspan.

Youth Hostels. See Hostels.

Appendix

AIRLINE TARIFF PUBLISHING CO. (ATPCO), Washington–Dulles International Airport, P.O. Box 17415, Washington, DC 20041.

Publications:

United States Passenger Fares Tariff	Every 4 weeks
Canadian Passenger Fares Tariff	Every 2 weeks
North American Routing Guide	Quarterly
Domestic General Rules	Every 2 weeks
Canadian General Rules	Every 2 weeks
Joint Passenger Fares Tariff-EJ (Canada)	Every 8 weeks
Visit Another Country Tariff	Every 4 weeks (included in NAPT)
Canadian Domestic General Rules	Every 2 weeks

AIR TARIFF. For travel agents in Western Hemisphere (and colleges/schools in Western Hemisphere except Canada): Air Tariff, P.O. Box 649, Rockville Centre, NY 11571; fax: (516) 764-5629. For colleges/schools in Canada: Air Tariff, 86 Hartford Avenue, Pointe Claire, Quebec H9R 3E1.

Publications:

Book 1: Worldwide Fares Book
Book 1: Worldwide Rules, Routings and Ticketed Point Mileages
Book 1: Worldwide Maximum Permitted Mileages
(Includes selected European normal fares/rules, selected Western Hemisphere fares/rules, and also selected domestic fares.)
Book 2: Western Hemisphere Fares
Book 2: Western Hemisphere Rules, Routings and Ticketed Point Mileages
Book 2: Western Hemisphere Maximum Permitted Mileages
[Contains much broader range of Western Hemisphere fares/rules (but not within or between United States–Canada) than those shown in Book 1.]
Book 3: Europe Fares, Rules, Routings and Mileages
(Contains much broader range of European fares/rules, including U.K. domestics, than shown in Book 1.)

AMERICAN HOTEL & MOTEL ASSOCIATION (AH&MA), Communications Department, 1201 New York Avenue N.W., Washington, DC 20005. Their *Hotel & Motel Redbook* is now merged with the OAG *Travel Planners*; however, they also publish *The Directory of Hotel & Motel Systems*, *Who's Who in the Lodging Industry*, and the "Tips for Travelers" brochure.

BUSINESS TRAVEL NEWS, CMP Publications, Inc., 111 East Shore Road, Manhasset, NY 11030. Distributed free of charge to corporate travel arrangers, travel agents, travel schools, and business travel suppliers in the United States and Canada.

CRUISE VIEWS, 60 E 42 Suite 905, New York, N.Y. 10165. MONTHLY.

DIRECTORY OF TRAVEL AGENCIES FOR THE DISABLED. Disability Bookshop, Box 129, Vancouver, WA 98666. Lists more than 350 agencies worldwide.

EUROPEAN TRAVEL PLANNER, European Travel, Box 1754, Rockefeller Center Station, New York, NY 10185. Published by AT&T and the European Travel Commission (ETC). Includes basic facts on all 23 member ETC countries.

HOTEL & TRAVEL INDEX, Reed Travel Group, 500 Plaza Drive, Secaucus, NJ 07096. Quarterly.

JAX FAX Travel Marketing Magazine, Airtransport Exchange, 397 Post Road, Darien, CT 06820-1413. Will send back issues to travel training schools for the shipping costs.

THE LAW AND THE TRAVEL INDUSTRY, Anolik Law Corp., 693 Sutter Street, San Francisco, CA 94102. Travel law attorney Alexander Anolik also has a seven-hour seminar on tape cassette album and book of forms, contracts, and disclaimers entitled "Preventive Legal Care for Travel Agents," designed to aid both agents and their attorneys. In addition, the book *The Law & The Travel Industry*, Third Edition, and also *A Personnel & Operations Manual for Travel Agencies*, are of great value to, and widely used by U.S. travel agents.

M&C Meetings and Conventions magazine published monthly (2 in March) by the Reed Travel Group, 500 Plaza Drive, Secaucus, N.J. 07096.

MEETING PLANNERS HANDBOOK, MPI, 3719 Roosevelt Boulevard, Middletown, OH 45044.

OFFICIAL AIRLINE GUIDES, INC., 2000 Clearwater Drive, Oak Brook, IL 60521.

Publications:
   OAG Pocket Flight Guides (monthly)
      North American Edition
      Europe/Middle East/Africa Edition
      Pacific/Asia Edition
      Latin American/Caribbean Edition
   OAG Travel Planners (quarterly)
      Business Travel Planner (North American Edition)
      European Edition
      Pacific Asia Edition
   OAG Desktop Flight Guide North American Edition (twice monthly, with or without fare section, or monthly with or without fare section.)
   OAG Desktop Flight Guide Worldwide Edition (monthly)
   OAG Cruise and Shipline Guide (bimonthly)
   OAG Electronic Edition

OFFICIAL CRUISE GUIDE, Reed Travel Group, 500 Plaza Drive, Secaucus, N.J. 07096. Published annually with periodic updates. (New publication—the 1993 edition debuts December 1992.)

OFFICIAL HOTEL AND RESORT GUIDE (OHRG), Reed Travel Group, 500 Plaza Drive, Secaucus, NJ. 07096. Yearly, with revision service.

OFFICIAL MEETING FACILITIES GUIDE, Reed Travel Group, 500 Plaza Drive, Secaucus, NJ. 07096. Semiannually.

OFFICIAL RAILWAY GUIDE, K-III Press, Inc., 424 West 33rd Street, New York, NY 10117. North American travel edition for United States, Canada, and Mexico. Four issues per year.

OFFICIAL STEAMSHIP GUIDE, Transportation Guides, Inc., 111 Cherry Street, Suite 205, New Canaan, CT 06840. Bimonthly.

REED TRAVEL GROUP, 131 Clarendon Street, Boston, MA 02116.

Publications:
    ABC World Airways Guide Monthly
    ABC Air Cargo Guide Monthly
    ABC Guide to International Travel Quarterly
    ABC Airways Guide World Map
    ABC Shipping Guide Monthly
    ABC Rail Guide Monthly
    Star Service Quarterly
    Executive Flight Planner Monthly

RUSSELL'S OFFICIAL NATIONAL MOTOR COACH GUIDE, 834 Third Avenue, S.E., Cedar Rapids, IA 52403. Monthly.

THOMAS COOK EUROPEAN TIMETABLE (Formerly called "Cook's Continental Timetable"), P.O. Box 227, Peterborough PE3 8SB, England. Monthly. A simple guide to the principal rail services of Europe, with shipping services in the North Sea, the Baltic, and the Mediterranean. Single copies can be purchased from the Forsyth Travel Library.

TOUR & TRAVEL NEWS, CMP Publications, Inc., 600 Community Drive, Manhasset, NY 11030. Distributed free of charge to qualified travel agents, tour operators/wholesalers, incentive travel companies, travel suppliers, and travel schools in the United States and Canada.

TRAVEL AGENT, P.O. Box 1456, Riverton, NJ 08077. Twice weekly.

TRAVEL AND TOURISM LAW BIBLIOGRAPHY. Quarterly. For single copies or a subscription, contact the International Forum of Travel and Tourism Advocates (IFTTA), 693 Sutter Street, San Francisco, CA 94102.

TRAVEL COUNSELOR MAGAZINE, Published by the Institute of Certified Travel Agents (ICTA) for CTCs. Quarterly.

TRAVEL INDUSTRY PERSONNEL DIRECTORY, Fairchild Books, 7 West 34th Street, New York, NY 10001. Revised annually.

TRAVEL INFORMATION MANUAL (TIM), P.O. Box 7627, 1117 zj Schiphol Airport, The Netherlands. Monthly. A joint publication of 14 member IATA airlines and provides documentary requirements on passports, visas, health, tax and customs regulations.

TRAVEL MAGAZINES DIVISION (TravelAge MidAmerica and others), Division of Official Airline Guides, Inc., 320 North Michigan, Suite 701, Chicago, IL 60601. Weekly; free to travel agents and their staff.

TRAVEL MARKETING MAGAZINE (Jaxfax), Airtransport Exchange, 280 Tokeneke Road, Darien, CT 06829-4899. Monthly.

TRAVEL TRADE, 15 West 46th Street, New York, NY 10036. Weekly.

TRAVEL WEEKLY, Reed Travel Group, 500 Plaza Drive, Secaucus, NJ. 07096. Weekly.

VISA GUIDE, Visa Advisors, Inc., 1900 18th Street, N.W., Washington, DC 20009. Revised as needed.

WATA MASTER-KEY, World Association for Travel Agencies, Secretariat General, 37 Quai Wilsons, Case postale 2317, 1211 Geneve 1, Switzerland. Carries the tariffs of WATA members offering incoming services. Also furnishes a country description sheet provided by the respective national tourist offices, containing a wealth of background information. Free to all travel agents upon request. Revised annually.

WEISSMANN TRAVEL REPORTS, Cowles Business Media, P.O. Box 49279, Austin, TX 78765. A highly recommended source of unbiased reliable information on every country in the world. Subscribing members receive 100 country profiles in a three-ring binder and 60 more in the first year. Renewals receive additional countries as well as quarterly updates. Also offers a *Travel Geography and Destinations* textbook.

WORLD TRAVEL DIRECTORY, Reed Travel Group, 44 Cook Street, Denver, CO 80206. Annual—lists all travel agents, tour operators, etc. Also sells mailing lists.

TRADE SUPPLIERS AND SERVICES

AMSTERDAM PRINTING & LITHO CORP., Wallins Corner Road, Amsterdam, NY 12010. Travel document cases and other promotional items.

ARGONNE ANTI-JET-LAG DIET. Cards and other information may be obtained from the Argonne National Laboratory, 9700 South Cass Avenue, Argonne, IL 60439.

ARIS ISOTONER INC. 417 5th Avenue, New York, NY 10016, Will send travel agents and travel schools a supply of brochures "Tips for Travelers' Feet" to distribute to their clients or students.

BON VOYAGE, THE EXOTIC GARDENS, 4800 Biscayne Boulevard, Miami, FL 33137. Can deliver fresh flowers, wine, gourmet gift baskets, candy, or fresh-fruit baskets to any cruise ships leaving such ports as Port Everglades, Miami, Los Angeles, or San Francisco, or anywhere in the United States or around the world.

CRUISE CLUB HOLIDAYS LTD., 181 Doiranis Street, 176 73 Athens, Greece. Specializes in student tours and cruises.

CULTURGRAM. Provide information on "customs and courtesies, the people, lifestyle, the nation, economy, education, transportation and communication, health, and travel for more than 100 countries." May be ordered in complete sets of single copies on the country of your choice. For a sample copy and catalog send $1.00 to Brigham Young University, David M. Kennedy Center for International Studies, Publication Services, 280 HRCB, Provo, UT 84602.

DEAK–PERERA U.S., INC., 29 Broadway, New York, NY 10006. Foreign drafts, money orders, currencies, travelers checks in foreign currencies, pre-packed currencies.

DEPARTMENT OF HEALTH & HUMAN SERVICES, Public Health Service Centers for Disease Control, Atlanta, GA 30333. Request sanitation inspections of international cruise ships.

EUROPEAN TRAVEL STUDY PROGRAM, Travel to Europe, P.O. Box 439, Lexington, MA 02173. A self-study program on Europe in four sections. The course was created by Travel to Europe in cooperation with the national tourist offices. Many major tour operators are offering exclusive bonus commission coupons to participants in the program.

EVERGREEN TRAVEL SERVICE, INC., 4114-198th Street S.W., Suite 13, Lynnwood, WA 98036. Specialize in group tours for the wheelchair disabled, and white-cane tours for the blind. Commissionable to travel agents.

FARE AUDIT INC., 85-159 Air Exchange Building, Windsor Locks, CT 06096-1030. A new service for automated agents. Audit PNRs (passenger name records) on a daily basis for the lowest fare available.

FORSYTH TRAVEL LIBRARY, P.O. Box 2975, 9154 West 57th Street, Shawnee Mission, KS 68201-1375. (Travel books, maps, guides, and other publications. Catalog available upon request.)

GRANDTRAVEL, 6900 Wisconsin Avenue, Suite 706, Chevy Chase, MD 20815. 1-800-247-7651. Specializes in group tours for grandparents and grandchildren.

GREETERS OF HAWAII, P.O. Box 29638, Honolulu, HI 96820, or toll-free fax: 1-800-736-5665. Provides airport arrival or departure fresh flower or novelty lei greetings; delivery of fruit baskets, flower bouquets, or combination gifts to hotel rooms and cruise ship cabins; optional sightseeing reservations; airport transfers, limousine service; mailing service of cut tropical flowers; incentive gifts; and wedding arrangements. All major islands.

IAMAT (The International Association for Medical Assistance to Travelers), 417 Center Street, Lewiston, NY 14092. Publishes a worldwide directory of English-speaking doctors who were trained in the United States, Canada, or Great Britain. Membership is free. Provides detailed information on immunization requirements, malaria and tropical disease risks, and climatic and sanitary information worldwide. This nonprofit organization depends on donations.

INTERNATIONAL FEDERATION OF WOMEN'S TRAVEL ORGANIZATION (IFWTO) 4545 North 36th St., Suite 126, Phoenix, AZ 85018-3473. Membership consists of 62 clubs for women in the travel industry throughout the United States, the Phillippines, Japan, Australia, New Zealand and Europe, over 5,000 travel professionals worldwide. Some 51% are travel agents; the rest include airlines, tour operators, hotels, meeting planners and corporate travel managers.

INTERNATIONAL GAY TRAVEL ASSOCIATION (IGTA), Box 4974, Key West, FL 33041.

KAMPGROUNDS OF AMERICA (KOA), P.O. Box 30558D, Billings, MT 59114. $3 charge for postage and handling for a list of more than 600 KOA campgrounds in the United States and Canada.

"KNOW BEFORE YOU GO," Customs information and various brochures can be ordered in bulk quantities from the U.S. Customs Service, National Distribution Center, P.O. Box 68912, Indianapolis, IN 46268.

MINES PRESS, 342 West 14th Street, New York, NY 10014. A variety of short, snap-out form letters for travel agents.

SAMSONITE CORPORATION, P.O. Box 39609, Dept. 80, Denver, CO 80239. Upon request and in limited quantities, will supply agents and travel schools with the brochure "Lightening The Travel Load," which contains tips on how to pack, travel documents, customs, and so on.

SANITATION INSPECTIONS—CRUISE SHIPS. For a copy of the biweekly inspections summary: Special Programs Group, Centers for Disease Control, C27 MS F-29, 1600 Clifton Road, Atlanta, GA 30333. For a copy of the most recent inspection report on a specific ship: Chief, Vessel Sanitation Activity, Center for Environmental Health and Injury Control, 1015 North America Way, Room 107, Miami, FL 33132.

SIEGEL DISPLAY PRODUCTS, P.O. Box 95, Minneapolis, MN 55440. 1-800-626-0322. Large selection of literature display equipment and pegboard brochure brackets.

SUPERINTENDENT OF DOCUMENTS, Government Printing Office, Washington, DC 20402. Order supplies of passport applications, international certificates of vaccination, and other travel pamphlets. Ask to be placed on the mailing list of publications.

THAYER, P.O. Box 500, Westville, NJ 08093. Document cases and imprinted greeting cards "Welcome Home," "Have a Wonderful Trip," "We Miss You," "Congratulations," and so on.

TRAVELER'S CHECKLIST, 335 Cornwall Bridge Road, Sharon, CT 06069. A national mail-order and merchandising company specializing in travel products of all kinds. Offers travel agents and travel schools a catalog of hard-to-find travel accessories and appliances. Also publishes a "Fam Trip Book," which is purchased by airlines, hotels, and destinations for distribution to travel agents, so they can record their evaluations of hotels, attractions, shops, and restaurants. Agents and travel schools can order bulk supplies at low cost.

U.S. CHAMBER OF COMMERCE, ADA Guide, Resources Policy Department, 1615 H Street NW, Washington, DC 20062. They issue the publication "What Businesses Must Know About The Americans With Disabilities".

U.S. TRAVEL DATA CENTER (an affiliate of the Travel Industry Association of America), Two Lafayette Centre, 1133 21st Street, N.W., Washington, DC 20036-3390. Fax: (202) 293-3155. Subscribers receive the published data on consumers' travel patterns and overall national and regional travel trends. Educators are able to join the data center at the lowest dues category.

VACATIONS ON VIDEO, 1309 East Northern, Phoenix, AZ 85020. A wide selection of travel videos at very reasonable prices.

WESTERN FOLDER DISTRIBUTING COMPANY, 1549 West Glenlake Avenue, Itasca, IL 60143. Distributor of tour brochures, promotional materials, and travel kits for consumers and agents. No charge to travel agents or travel schools for the service.

WILLOW PRESS, 75 Oser Avenue, Hauppauge, NY 11788 (Travel agency printer since 1946). Because of their high volume, they offer the lowest rates for invoices, checks, letterheads, envelopes, and a large variety of forms for the office, including computer forms, maps, and goodwill gifts. Catalogs are free. They will also furnish sample kits to travel schools for a fee of $3 per kit. 1-800-444-FORM.

TRAVEL TRADE APPOINTMENTS/ENDORSEMENTS

AIRLINES REPORTING CORP. (ARC)—replaced ATC (Air Traffic Conference), 1530 Wilson Blvd., Suite 800, Arlington, VA 22209-2448. Phone (703) 816-8000, FAX (703) 816-8104.

CRUISE LINES INTERNATIONAL ASSOCIATION (CLIA), 500 Fifth Avenue, Suite 1407, NY 10110.

INTERNATIONAL AIRLINES TRAVEL AGENT NETWORK (IATAN), 300 Garden City Plaza, Suite 400, Garden City, NY 11530. Mailing address: P.O. Box 93, Essex Junction, VT 05452. (For applications and due payments.)

INTERNATIONAL AIR TRANSPORT ASSOCIATION (IATA), 2000 Peel Street, Montreal, Quebec H3A 2R4, Canada. Mailing address: P.O. Box 2988, Plattsburgh, NY 12901-0269.

NATIONAL PASSENGER RAILROAD CORPORATION (AMTRAK), 60 Massachusetts Avenue, N.E., Washington, DC 20002.

TRADE ASSOCIATIONS

ALLIANCE OF CANADIAN TRAVEL ASSOCIATIONS (ACTA), 75 rue Albert Street, Suite 1106, Ottawa, Ontario K1P 5E7 Canada.

AMERICAN AUTOMOBILE ASSOCIATION (AAA), 1000 AAA Drive, Heathrow, FL 32746-5063.

AMERICAN SIGHTSEEING INTERNATIONAL (ASI), 309 Fifth Avenue, New York, NY 10016.

AMERICAN SOCIETY OF TRAVEL AGENTS (ASTA), 1101 King Street, Alexandria, VA 22314. Mailing address: P.O. Box 23992, Washington, DC 20026-3992.

ASSOCIATION OF RETAIL TRAVEL AGENTS (ARTA), 1745 Jefferson Davis Highway, Suite 300, Airlington, VA 22202.

CANADIAN INSTITUTE OF TRAVEL COUNSELLORS (CITC), Shipp Centre, Suite 2880, 3300 Bloor Street West, Etobicoke, Ontario M8X 2X3 Canada.

CARIBBEAN TOURISM ASSOCIATION (CTA), 20 East 46th Street, New York, NY 10017.

COUNCIL ON HOTEL, RESTAURANT AND INSTITUTIONAL EDUCATION (CHRIE), 1200 17th Street, N.W., Washington, DC 20036.

EUROPEAN TRAVEL COMMISSION (ETC), c/o Donald N. Martin Co., 630 Fifth Avenue, New York, NY 10111.

GRAY LINE WORLDWIDE, 13760 Noel Road, Suite 1000, Dallas, TX 75240. Phone: (214) 934-8700; FAX: (214) 934-1910

INSTITUTE OF CERTIFIED TRAVEL AGENTS (ICTA), 148 Linden Street, Box 56, Wellesley, MA 02181.

INTERNATIONAL FORUM OF TRAVEL AND TOURISM ADVOCATES (IFTTA), Alexander Anolik, U.S. Delegate, 693 Sutter Street, Sixth Floor, San Francisco, CA 94102. The fundamental objective of IFTTA is to provide a forum for cooperation and exchange of information on the legal aspects of travel and tourism throughout the world. Member attorneys will provide information on relevant legislation, regulations, agreements, and case law from members' jurisdictions in order to create and keep an updated record of the current legal standards of law in travel and tourism.

INTERNATIONAL GAY TRAVEL ASSOCIATION (IGTA), P.O. Box 18247, Denver, CO 80218.

NATIONAL ASSOCIATION OF CRUISE ONLY AGENCIES (NACOA), P.O. Box 7209, Freeport, NY 11520.

NATIONAL TOUR ASSOCIATION (NTA), 546 East Main Street, P.O. Box 3071, Lexington, KY 40596. NTA is the premier association of 3800 tour operators, suppliers, and destination marketing organizations in North America.

PACIFIC ASIA TRAVEL ASSOCIATION (PATA), Secretariat, 1 Montgomery Street, Telesis Tower, Suite 1750, San Francisco, CA 94104. (Chapters are also formed in individual states and countries.)

PROFESSIONAL ASSOCIATION OF COMMISSIONED TRAVEL AGENTS (PACTA), P.O. Box 70, Gillette, NJ 07933.

SOCIETY FOR THE ADVANCEMENT OF TRAVEL FOR THE HANDICAPPED (SATH), 26 Court Street, Brooklyn, NY 11242.

SOCIETY OF TRAVEL AND TOURISM EDUCATORS, INC. (STTE). Official mailing address: 19364 Woodcrest, Harper Woods, MI 48225. Phone: (313) 526-0710. Membership info: Marilyn Kern-Ladner, Miami-Dade Community College, Aviation Dept., 11011 S.W. 104th Street, Miami, FL 33176, Phone: (305) 237-2978.

SPA FINDERS, 91 Fifth Avenue, Suite 301, New York, NY 10003-3039.

TRAVEL INDUSTRY ASSOCIATION OF CANADA (TIAC), Suite 1016-130 Albert Street, Ottawa, ON K1P 5G4 Canada.

TRAVEL INDUSTRY AND DISABLED EXCHANGE (TIDE), 5435 Donna Avenue, Tarzana, CA 91356.

TRAVEL AND TOURISM RESEARCH ASSOCIATION (TTRA), P.O. Box 8066, Foothill Station, Salt Lake City, UT 84108.

UNITED STATES TOUR OPERATORS ASSOCIATION (USTOA), 211 East 51st Street, New York, NY 10022.

UNITED STATES TRAVEL DATA CENTER, Two Lafayette Center, 1133 21st Street, N.W., Washington, DC 20036.

UNIVERSAL FEDERATION OF TRAVEL AGENTS ASSOCIATIONS (UFTAA), 89-93 Rue Froissart, 1040 Brussels, Belgium.

WORLD TOURISM ORGANIZATION (WTO), Captain Haya, 42; Madrid, Spain 28020. Phone: 5710628.

RESERVATIONS SYSTEMS

AIR CANADA CENTRE, (Reservec II) P.O. Box 14000, Saint Laurent, Quebec H4 Y1 H4.

AMERICAN AIRLINES (SABRE), Subscriber Automation, P.O. Box 619616, Mail Drop 3424, DFW Airport, TX 75261-9616.

CANADIAN AIRLINES INTERNATIONAL (Formerly Canadian Pacific) (PEGUSUS), Scotia Centre, 700-2nd Street S.W., Calgary, Alberta 2800 Canada.

SYSTEM ONE CORP., 1301 Fannin, Suite 1800, Houston, TX 77002.

UNITED AIRLINES (APOLLO), P.O. Box 66100, Chicago, IL 60666.

WORLDSPAN TRAVEL AGENCY, Information Services, 2405 Grand, Suite 400, Kansas City, MO 64108. (800) 346-6269. Sells the DATAS II and PARS automated reservations system for airline and other supplier bookings. DATAS II products include a dial-up option that agents install at corporate sites; agency accounting dial-up system for agents and a dial-up option that agents install on corporate sites; a PAR version that is available for use by the general public; retailer accounting; PC software to subscribers who use Altos hardware, and satellite ticket printers.

DIRECTORY OF CO-OPS AND CONSORTIUMS

ACTION 6, 237 Church Street, Lowell, MA 01852. National joint marketing organization with nationwide membership. Started in 1976.

AMERICAN EXPRESS TRAVEL RELATED SERVICES CO., INC. 100 Church St., 10th Floor, New York, N.Y. 10007. Travel department started in 1915. The more than 1700 representative offices of American Express are located in 50 states and worldwide. American Express travel agencies are owned by American Express Travel Related Services, but representative agencies are independently owned.

AURA, INC., 255 East Roselawn Street, Suite 48, St. Paul, MN 55117. National travel agent network with membership concentration in Central and Western U.S. Started in 1980.

CARLSON TRAVEL NETWORK RETAIL-ASSOCIATES, Carlson Parkway, P.O. Box 59159, Minneapolis, MN 55459-8206. National franchiser and corporate-owned chain started in 1984. Number of associates 949. Number of associate locations: More than 2100 worldwide.

CORP-NET INTERNATIONAL, 3040 Riverside Drive, Suite 208, Columbus, OH 43221. National joint marketing organization/consortium with nationwide member concentration. Started in 1981.

CRUISE CONSORTIUM, 254 South Main St., New York, N.Y. 10956. National consortium started in 1991 specifically for increasing cruise business and developing cruise specialists.

CRUISE HOLIDAYS INTERNATIONAL, P.O. Box 23559, 9089 Clairmont Mesa Blvd. #306, San Diego, CA 92123. National franchiser started in 1984.

CRUISELINK PLUS, P.O. Box 1897, Massapequa, NY 11758. FAX: (516) 799-3220. National consortium started in 1990.

GEM, INC., 917 N. Broadway, N. Massapequa, N.Y. 11758. National consortium started in 1984.

GIANTS, 915 Broadway, New York, NY 10010. International, U.S. and Canada. Member-owned consortium started in 1968.

HICKORY TRAVEL SYSTEMS, Park 80 Plaza East, Saddle Brook, NJ 07662. Fax: (201) 843-4764. Global travel management company. Started in 1977.

INTERNATIONAL TOURS, 5810 E. Skelly Drive, Tulsa, OK 74135. National franchiser started in 1968.

MAST (Midwest Agents Selling Travel Co-op), P.O. Box 3453, Oak Brook, IL 60521. (Regional nonprofit association with membership concentration in Illinois, Michigan, Indiana, Iowa, and Wisconsin. Started in 1970.)

RIVERSIDE TRAVEL GROUP, INC., Airport Business Center, 6645 N.E. 78th Ct., Suite C9, Portland, OR 97218. Regional co-op started in 1981.

SPACE, 1900 Glades Road, Boca Raton, FL 33431. National consortium started in 1969.

T.I.M.E. (Travel Industry Marketing Enterprises, Inc.), 200 West Main Street, Babylon, NY 11702-3413. National joint marketing organization started in 1982.

TRAVEL AGENTS INTERNATIONAL, INC., 111 Second Avenue N.E., 15th Floor, P.O. Box 31005, St. Petersburg, FL 33731. National franchiser started in 1980.

THE TRAVEL AUTHORITY, 1872 Pleasantville Road, Briarcliff Manor, NY 10510. National joint marketing organization with members in 42 states and the U.K. Started in 1984.

TRAVEL NETWORK, 560 Sylvan Ave., Englewood Cliffs, N.J. 07632. National franchiser started in 1982.

TRAVELSAVERS, 290 Community Drive, Great Neck, NY 11021. Some of their subsidiaries: Travel Helpline, Travelsavers Incentives and Meetings, Cruise Express, Sports Express, Air Express, Travelsavers Trip Protection Plan, Heartland Publishing. National individually-owned chain. Started in 1972.

UNIGLOBE TRAVEL, 1199 W. Pender St., Suite 900, Vancouver, B.C. V6E 2R1. National and international franchiser started in 1980.

WOODSIDE TRAVEL TRUST, 4350 East-West Highway, Suite 603, Bethesda, MD 20814. (Merged with Travel Trust International July 1992.) Woodside was founded in 1973, Travel Trust in 1978, both as international consortiums with emphasis on business travel management.

INDEX